SOUL OF CHAOS
Critical Perspectives on Gao Xingjian

Soul of Chaos

Critical Perspectives on Gao Xingjian

Edited by

Kwok-kan Tam

The Chinese University Press

Soul of Chaos: Critical Perspectives on Gao Xingjian
  Edited by Kwok-kan Tam

© **The Chinese University of Hong Kong,** 2001

ISBN 962–201–993–5

THE CHINESE UNIVERSITY PRESS
The Chinese University of Hong Kong
SHA TIN, N.T., HONG KONG
Fax: +852 2603 6692
    +852 2603 7355
E-mail: cup@cuhk.edu.hk
Web-site: www.chineseupress.com

Printed in Hong Kong

Front cover illustration: Gao Xingjian, *Rêve*, 1994, 89 × 90 cm.
© Gao Xingjian. Courtesy of Mabel Lee.

Contents

Preface

Gao Xingjian 高行健 (b. 1940), the Nobel Laureate in Literature 2000, is a dramatist, novelist, stage director and painter. Gao's achievements in both fiction and the theatre undoubtedly place him in the forefront of world literature. In the press release on the Nobel Prize, the Swedish Academy states that Gao is a French citizen and the media in Europe generally regard him as such. It is also true to say that Gao is a Chinese writer, especially in the cultural sense of the Chinese language. Gao's career as a writer, first in China and now in Europe, is typical of a globalized/dislocated cultural identity that poses as a challenge to people who still cling to the idea of national identity at the end of the twentieth century. In his Nobel lecture delivered on 7 December 2000, Gao emphasizes that literature has no national boundaries. As a writer, he is an individualist, in whose heart Chinese culture naturally resides.

Gao is known to the diverse world of Chinese literary writings as a highly innovative writer, whose creative use of language "opens new paths for the Chinese novel and drama." To the theatre circles both in Europe and Asia, Gao is an avant-garde dramatist, whose art goes beyond the narrow confines of any single tradition. As testified by the studies collected in this book, Gao's achievements are due much to his artistic vision, which transcends the cultural limitation of an either/or identity between China and the West. Not just his identity, Gao as a writer culturally and linguistically situated in between China and the West is itself a subject that has attracted critical attention from both sides. Though many articles and essays, in Chinese and European languages, have been published on Gao, there is so far no book in English entirely devoted to the study of his achievements. Hence, one of the purposes of this collection is to provide a critical introduction to Gao as a writer and a theatre practitioner. Most of the articles that appear in this book were written before Gao was awarded the Nobel Prize in October 2000. In a sense, they serve as a historical record of the critical reception of Gao in the

English language. About half of them deal with Gao's achievements in his early experimentation with the theatre in the mid-1980s before he left China. The other half focus on Gao's further development in the 1990s after he settled in France, particularly on his vision of a postmodernist theatre that integrates traditional Chinese aesthetics and on his latest experimentation with a self-transcendent theory of subjectivity in narrative.

In the preparation of this book, I had been assisted by many individuals and friends, in particular Mabel Lee, William Tay and Terry Yip, who all have researched on Gao Xingjian and closely followed the latest developments of world literature in an age when cultural and national boundaries no longer hold as fixed parameters for the definition of an individual. I would also like to thank all the other contributors of this volume, Xiaomei Chen, Gilbert Fong, Michael Gissenwehrer, Amy Lai, Torbjörn Lodén, Ma Sen, Quah Sy Ren, and Jo Riley, whose work I always read with admiration. Olivia Wong, Project Editor of The Chinese University Press, gave me much help in editing the manuscripts.

The following publishers generously gave me permission to republish the articles that previously appeared in their journals or books: *China Studies* (Hong Kong); *Comparative Literature Studies* (Penn State University Press); *Journal of Asian Pacific Communication* (Ablex); *Issues and Studies, A Journal of China Studies and International Affairs* (National Chengchi University, Taiwan); *The Stockholm Journal of East Asian Studies* (University of Stockholm); Peter Lang; Engelhard-Ng Verlag and M. E. Sharpe.

Kwok-kan Tam
December 2000

Introduction

Gao Xingjian, the Nobel Prize and the Politics of Recognition

To professionals in the theatre as well as scholars in Chinese and comparative literary studies, Gao Xingjian is no stranger. But to the general Chinese reading public, he remained little known until he received the Nobel Prize. As Gao himself admits, his works never enjoyed good sales records. Such a phenomenon is perhaps partly due to the fact that he is a Chinese writer in exile and his works have been banned in mainland China since the late 1980s. Thus when the Swedish Academy announced to the world on 12 October 2000 that Gao Xingjian was awarded the Nobel Prize in Literature 2000, the news came as a surprise not only to Gao himself, but also to many readers in the Chinese speaking communities.

Born in 1940, Gao is typical of many Chinese who suffered from the hardships of the Sino-Japanese war (1937–1945) and the disastrous Cultural Revolution in China (1966–1976). As the son of a bank employee, Gao had a family education that allowed him the opportunity to read and write early in his life. He owes his knowledge of Western literature to the French education he received at the Beijing Institute of Foreign Languages in 1957–1962 and to the various jobs as translator for the magazine, *China Reconstructs*, and the Foreign Languages Press. Unfortunately, he had to destroy all his diaries and writings during the Cultural Revolution for fear of being labelled an anti-revolutionary. His creative energy, however, did not subside despite all the hardships. His literary career made its formal debut with the publication of a dozen short stories and theoretical essays on literature in the late 1970s after the Cultural Revolution ended. In the early 1980s, when he was assigned to work as a playwright for the Beijing People's Art Theatre, he began to come into contact with the theatre and experiment with various forms of performance.

It was in playwriting that he had the first chance to put into practice his vision to integrate literature with other forms of art and aesthetics of the East and the West, which is an experiment he later extended to fiction writing.

The articles in this book provide critical readings of Gao's major works in the context of his contribution to the rejuvenation of Chinese tradition and his significance in world literature. Gao's literary talent lies in his successful synthesis of Chinese heritage with Western cultural and literary traditions. In his Nobel lecture delivered on 7 December 2000, Gao once again affirms that Chinese culture resides in him, though he lives in exile in the West. For Gao, exile is relevant to his experience in two senses. He is now physically in exile, but he also has long been spiritually in exile since his journey among the mountains in Sichuan, China in an effort to flee from the political persecution of a collectivist culture in the early 1980s. The sense of fleeing, being in exile and in cultural dislocation, is not exclusive to the Chinese, but is a human condition of the twentieth century, which has been vividly described in Gao's *Lingshan* 靈山 [Soul mountain, 1989] and *Yige ren de shengjing* 一個人的聖經 [One man's bible, 1998].

The Nobel citation included the following comment on Gao: "for an *œuvre* of universal validity, bitter insights and linguistic ingenuity, which has opened new paths for the Chinese novel and drama." It is apparent from this comment that the award was given to Gao on the basis of his Chinese writing, which have been considered as both innovative in the use of language and transcultural in their validity beyond the limit of national boundaries. The award of the Nobel Prize to Gao is more a form of recognition of Gao's personal achievements than an attempt to assess the achievements of contemporary Chinese writings from the perspective of national literature. Such a recognition, more importantly, not only places Gao in the forefront of world literature, but also sees in him the success in experimenting with new dramatic and narrative forms that provide transition from tradition to modernity.

CRITICAL RECEPTION IN CHINA, TAIWAN AND HONG KONG

Over the past two decades many scholars, in particular the Chinese, have reacted strongly to the lack of representation of Chinese writers for the Nobel Prize since its inception in 1901. To quote Liu Zaifu 劉再復, a critic from mainland China who now lives in the United States, the phenomenon that "Chinese writers had been absent from the family of Nobel Laureates" was due partly to the lack of adequate translations of Chinese literary works in major Western languages, but largely to the non-recognition of non-Western languages.[1] What made the case more complex was that this absence was taken as "absence of due recognition," which characterized the Chinese complex of non-recognition and exclusion. Many Chinese scholars and writers had taken it as a gross denial of the achievements of contemporary Chinese literature. Denial is more than non-recognition, because hidden in it is a politics of exclusion, which injures the pride of a nation that strives to establish its own voice and place in global politics.

When Gao was awarded the Nobel Prize, many Chinese scholars and writers who live outside China rejoiced at the news. The same news, however, was received quite differently by the Chinese government and the official literary organizations on the mainland, such as the Chinese Writers' Association. They dismissed Gao as an unknown writer in China and denounced the Swedish Academy for awarding the Prize to Gao with a political intent.

To the older generation of readers and theatre audience, Gao is still remembered for his controversial plays that are innovative in the indigenization of Western elements for a contemporary Chinese theatre. Gao was deeply involved in the debate over modernism in China in the early 1980s and he was a highly acclaimed playwright in the experimental theatre. He showed his talent as a writer and critic in his early works that include two theoretical treatises, *Xiandai xiaoshuo jiqiao chutan* 現代小說技巧初探 [A preliminary exploration of the techniques of modern fiction, 1981] and *Dui yizhong xiandai xiju de zhuiqiu* 對一種現代戲劇的追求 [In search of a modern form of drama, 1987], and six plays, *Juedui xinhao* 絕對信號 [Alarm signal, 1982], *Chezhan* 車站 [The bus-stop, 1983], *xiandai zhezixi* 現代折子戲 [Highlights from modern Chinese opera, 1984], *Dubai* 獨白 [Monologue, 1985], *Yeren* 野人 [Wild man, 1985], and *Bi'an* 彼岸 [The other shore, 1986]. Mainland Chinese response to Gao's pre-exile plays was in general favourable toward his experimentation with new techniques.[2] However, with his departure in 1987, he has become an unfamiliar name in China today.

The official Chinese literary organizations regard Gao as a dissident and the award of the Nobel Prize to him certainly denotes a political implication. Thus Gao's recognition by the Swedish Academy was taken as non-recognition of the Chinese government. As a writer who was criticized for "spiritual pollution" and had denounced the Chinese government for the Tiananmen massacre, Gao has had severe tensions with China. The award, however, challenges China's non-recognition of Gao. The Chinese poet Yang Lian 楊煉, an exile in Australia, responded to the selection of Gao for the Nobel Prize by saying that it signifies the victory of exiled writers. The Nobel Prize is much more than a literary award; it is a form of international recognition, which hits hard on the complex of Chinese nationalism, in that recognition of the non-recognized implies non-recognition of the recognized. In the Chinese tradition as well as in contemporary Chinese politics, identity is not just a choice of how one defines oneself, but also a politics of dialogical constitution in relation to recognition. As Charles Taylor observes in his essay, "The Politics of Recognition," embedded in nationalism is a strong desire for recognition (Taylor, 1994). The award of the Nobel Prize to Gao has thus caught the Chinese nationalists in the politics of "double absence of recognition." In the politics of identity, non-recognition is non-acceptance and exclusion.

In Taiwan and Hong Kong, the news of Gao's being awarded the Nobel Prize was received enthusiastically with wide coverage by the media. Soon after the news reached the two places, all the major literary journals and magazines in Hong Kong, such as *Asiaweek*, *Yazhou zhoukan* 亞洲周刊 [International Chinese newsweekly], *Ming bao yuekan* 明報月刊 [Ming Pao monthly], *Zheng ming* 爭鳴 [Cheng ming magazine] and *Kaifang zazhi* 開放雜誌 [Open magazine], published special issues in celebration of the event. The news also made the headlines of many newspapers, such as *South China Morning Post*, *Xin bao* 信報 [Hong Kong economic journal] and *Xingdao ribao* 星島日報 [Sing tao daily]. The same occured in Taiwan, with the news reported in *Zhongguo shibao* 中國時報 [The China times] and *Lianhe bao* 聯合報 [United daily news]. As a newspaper stated in its headline news, the award of the Nobel Prize to Gao was "unexpected, but reasonable." The sudden burst of enthusiasm over Gao since mid-October 2000 reflects an interest not only in the Nobel Prize, but also in the Laureate's ethnic and linguistic background in relation to Chinese speakers all over the world.

Despite his non-recognition in mainland China and low popularity among general readers, Gao has been a frequent subject of study in

Taiwan and Hong Kong. As early as 1984, the Hong Kong-based English translation journal, *Renditions*, published a special issue on contemporary Chinese literature, in which Gao Xingjian's play, *Chezhan* 車站 [The bus-stop, 1983], was excerpted and translated.[3] This represents the earliest interest in Gao Xingjian outside China and in the English language, in which the playwright was highly esteemed for "breaking away from the staid fifty-year old conventions of the Chinese theatre" (Barmé, 1983, p. 373). In subsequent years in the 1980s prior to his exile, Gao's experimentation with European avant-garde drama and a postmodernist style of performance continued to arouse the interest of critics. He was the centre of interest in conferences held in Taiwan and Hong Kong (Tam, 1990, 1995; Ma, 1989).[4]

Since the mid-1980s, Gao's plays have been favourite choices for stage production and adaptations for dance performance in both Taiwan and Hong Kong. Stage productions of his plays in Hong Kong include *The Bus-Stop* by Horizonte in 1986, *Mingcheng* 冥城 [The nether city] by Hong Kong Dance Company in 1989, *Yeren* 野人 [Wild man] by Seals Theatre Company in 1990, and *Bi'an* 彼岸 [The other shore] by the Hong Kong Academy for Performing Arts in 1995. In Taiwan, the National Arts College, Taipei, also staged Gao's *The Other Shore* in 1990. All of these performances sparked heated discussion in Taiwan and Hong Kong,[6] with Gao being hailed as a leading dramatist in the experimental theatre in Chinese speaking communities.

Since his exile from China, Gao has further developed his view regarding the integration of Chinese aesthetics into modern performance, which has culminated in a number of new plays and theoretical essays published in Taiwan and Hong Kong. Critical analyses of his works have often appeared in Chinese newspapers. In 1995, his major plays were published in *Gao Xingian xiju liuzhong* 高行健戲劇六種 [Six volumes of plays by Gao Xingjian],[5] and in 1999 one of Taiwan's leading literary journals, *Lianhe wenxue* 聯合文學 [Unitas: a literary monthly], published a special issue on Gao. In that same year, five of his plays, including *The Other Shore*, *Shengsijie* 生死界 [Between life and death, 1991], *Duihua yu fanjie* 對話與反詰 [Dialogue and rebuttal, 1992], *Yeyoushen* 夜遊神 [The nocturnal wanderer, 1993] and *Zhoumo sichongzou* 周末四重奏 [Weekend quartet, 1995], were translated into English.[6] A notable development in Gao's recent experimentation is the use of Zen Buddhist concepts in the theatre, which has been discussed by many scholars (Zhao, 1999; Huang,

2000). Besides dramatic writings, Gao's remarkable experimentation with multiple perspectives of the split selves can be found in his two novels, *Soul Mountain* and *One Man's Bible*, published in Taiwan, respectively in 1989 and 1998.

Today bookstores in Taiwan and Hong Kong are flooded with reprints of Gao's books, both in Chinese and in English translation, and this only confirms the fact that due recognition had not been given to Gao and that he remained little known to many readers until he received the Nobel Prize. Many readers in Taiwan and Hong Kong are now eager to learn more about Gao as a writer and stage director in particular, as well as his artistic achievements in general.[7]

GAO XINGJIAN IN THE WEST

Gao enjoys quite a different "fortune" in Europe and North America. When Gao was awarded the Nobel Prize, all the major newspapers in Europe reported the news with enthusiasm. In French newspapers such as *Le Monde, L'Humanité, Le Figaro* and *Libération*, there were special sections devoted to reports and discussions on Gao's unique identity as a French citizen who writes in Chinese. In the United States, the reports in *The New York Times* and *Times Literary Supplement* focused on Gao's being a dissident writer banned in China.

In the academic world, Gao has long been recognized in Europe and North America as an avant-garde dramatist and hailed as the first Chinese dramatist to enter the world theatre. As early as 1986, at a conference on "the Commonwealth of Chinese Literature" held in Günzburg, Germany, Gao's *The Bus-Stop* was acclaimed in the context of avant-garde experiments in China (Tay, 1990).[8] His achievements, as shown in *The Bus-Stop, Wild Man* and *The Other Shore*, caught the German attention and were considered not just simple adaptations of Western ideas and techniques, but innovative fusions of Chinese and Western elements in a new form (Riley and Gissenwehrer, 1989). His *Wild Man* and *Taowang* 逃亡 [Fugitives, 1989] were also translated into English and discussed in American academic journals. Besides scholarly studies in journals, Gao is also the topic of postgraduate studies in the US, UK and Canada (Li, 1991; Quah, 1997, 1999; Zou, 1994). A common feature underlying the academic reception is the general view of Gao as a playwright whose achievements are not limited to experimentation with Western conceptions of literature and the theatre, but also to a successful integration of Chinese elements to develop a new form for theatrical performance.

Gao is a multi-talented artist. In Europe, he is better known as a painter, dramatist and novelist. Since he took up residence in France in 1988, his paintings have been collected by museums and he has held numerous exhibitions throughout Europe.[9] Besides being a painter, Gao is also known to speakers of major European languages as an innovative stage director. His later plays, such as *Fugitives* and *Between Life and Death*, have been well received in Europe. Though in exile, he continues his writing. Of his eighteen plays, half were written during his residence in France. Some of his post-exile plays, for example, *Between Life and Death*, *Nocturnal Wanderer* and *Weekend Quartet*, were first written in French, and then in Chinese. His achievements in literature and painting have long been recognized in Europe; in 1992 he was awarded *Chevalier de l'Ordre des Arts et des Lettres* in France.

Gao's works have been well received in the West and many of them are available in the major European languages of French, German, English and Swedish.[10] In Australia, Gao's plays, such as *Fugitives* and *Between Life and Death*, are among the favourites of stage production. He has also been much studied in Australian journals.[11]

Besides being a creative writer and painter, Gao also devotes himself to writing about his experience in directing stage productions and thought in the theory of drama. For the thirteen years since he left China and settled in France, Gao has been actively engaged in a dialogue with scholars and writers, especially on his views of literary language and subjectivity. He is an active participant in academic conferences. He presented more than thirty essays on playwriting, performance theory, the art of fiction, Chinese aesthetics and politics. Many of these essays are now collected in the book, *Meiyou zhuyi* 沒有主義 [Without isms],[12] which may be regarded as a record of his recent orientation in theoretical and critical thinking. Among all the Chinese writers living in exile, Gao is the most open in expressing his views on fiction and playwriting. Apart from being a creative writer, Gao shows on such occasions that he is well versed in the philosophy of art and in literary and performance theory. Representing a Chinese voice in theoretical discussions, he has written essays and critiques on European art from a Chinese perspective.

WRITING IN-BETWEEN CHINA AND THE WEST

As a dramatist, Gao is aware that performance as an art form needs experimentation and innovation. He is familiar with the Western movements in art and philosophy that have contributed to the development of contemporary drama since the end of the nineteenth century. In his early plays, he experimented with the techniques of different theoretical orientations that include the Brechtian theatre, the Theatre of the Absurd, Theatre of Cruelty and Poor Theatre. In the West, all these different orientations represent modern efforts to break away from the Aristotelian tradition, which is based on a positivistic philosophy that sees the world as constructed on logical and rational principles. Hence, the starting point of Gao's experiments is a "re-visioning" of the world and seeing it basically as non-logical and non-rational. Such a "re-visioning" entails a process that calls into question the nature of the cognitive subject. Brecht puts the question squarely in the face of the audience, whose critical participation in a theatrical performance breaks down the division between the performing subject and the receiving subject by repeatedly reversing their positions. The use of narrative in Brechtian theatre not only interrupts identification in the cognitive process, but also reinforces the idea of agency in the receiving subject. From an Existentialist perspective, Beckett views the subject in both his drama and fiction as lost in the linear and rational schemata of the mind, which seeks meaning in the non-linear and non-rational dimensions of time and space. Beckett succeeds in presenting the subject caught in an irresolvable paradox.

As informed by the discovery of the unconscious in psychoanalysis, the subject is subjected not only to ideological construction as a relation between self and culture, but also to the hidden drives and conflicts within the self, such as those between consciousness and unconscious, desire and repression, and body and mind. For Freud as well as for Lacan, language reflects these hidden drives and conflicts within the self and thereby serves as a means to analyzing the self. On the contrary, both Brechtian theatre and the Theatre of the Absurd rely heavily on language as the theatrical form and also as a means of perception, through which the (de/)construction of the subject hinges on an externalized process of "re-visioning" the world. Artaud's advocacy of a performance style based more on the body than on language is not just meant as a new theatrical form, but also theoretically founded on the conception of body as subjecthood, which at the same time becomes contradictorily the object of gaze. In the same vein, Grotowski's idea of Poor Theatre takes on a deconstructionist approach aiming at restoring the stage for performance. As Gao states in the "Notes for Performance" appended to his plays, all the Western experiments with theatrical representation of the subject become useful sources of inspiration.

As a writer historically situated at the end of the twentieth century, Gao is no less under the "anxiety of influence." In his essay, "Meiyou zhuyi" [沒有主義 Without isms], he expresses his wish to be freed from the influence of previous experiments:

> Although I have my own ideas on literature, I also attach importance to artistic form and technique. Western literature, particularly the ideas and methods of modern Western literature, has given me great inspiration, but I do not think that borrowing them indiscriminately will lead to any great work. I therefore attach more importance to the work itself, and I do not want to put the label of any "ism" on myself....
>
> I should perhaps reaffirm that I do not belong to any school, whether in politics or in literature, and also not to any ism, which includes nationalism and patriotism. I of course have my own ideas about politics and my own views of literature, but I don't think it is necessary to nail myself down to any political or aesthetic framework.   (Gao, 1996b, pp. 8–9)

The problems that Gao as a playwright and director has to address are no less complex than those faced by his Western counterparts, for he has to work within the intercultural context of theatrical performance. As discussed in the articles by Xiaomei Chen, Jo Riley and Michael Gissenwehrer collected in this volume, Gao's pre-exile plays show a strong desire to go beyond the limits of Western experiments by "re-visioning" the theatrical space from a Chinese perspective. William Tay's article, also included in this volume, has succinctly argued that the innovations in Gao's play *The Bus-Stop* are technical borrowings which succeed in transcending their Western cultural contexts. In a similar vein, Ma Sen argues in his article that Gao's early experimentation with the theatre of the absurd has brought in a new paradigm for the Chinese stage that demands new rules of criticism, as well as new modes of appreciation. The use of performance elements from the Chinese tradition, such as the *xiqu* techniques, are evident in the plays, *Wild Man* and *The Other Shore*, which allow Gao to synthesize Western style with the Chinese aesthetics of performance. Quah Sy Ren, in his article, gives numerous examples to demonstrate how Gao uses Western techniques for a reconceptualization of the theatrical space according to the Chinese concept of "suppositionality."

In the play, *Dubai* 獨白 [Monolgue], as Amy Lai observes in her article, Gao for the first time experiments with the changing positions of the actor, which eventually matures in his later works into an exploration of the linguistic constitution of subjectivity. In his post-exile plays written in France, Gao continues this experimentation with the flexible and interchangeable subject positions in the Chinese language and gradually develops, as Gilbert Fong points out in his article, his theory of Zen Buddhist contemplation [靜觀 Jingguan] as a language for theatrical performance. In Gao's later plays, such as *Between Life and Death* and *Dialogue and Rebuttal*, he shows how dialogue can be used to demonstrate changing subject positions and changing points of view. In *Nocturnal Wanderer*, for example, he examines how language and subjectivity work in the unconscious by presenting the protagonist as a sleepwalker caught in the conflicting, yet complementary, states between dream and reality. All such attempts are part of an ongoing process in Gao's experimentation toward a new theory of subjectivity in language.

LANGUAGE AND THE SELF-TRANSCENDENT SUBJECT

Out of the need for theatrical practice, Gao has developed a unique view of performance, which is Chinese in its aesthetic origin and postmodernist in its representation of the subject. This notion of subjectivity, which leads to new modes of expression in both Gao's drama and fiction, is more than just experiments with literary and theatrical techniques. To understand its theoretical significance, one must place Gao's works in the history of the subject as a critical inquiry. The notions of the subject, both Chinese and Western, and its threatened fragmentation in the face of cultural disintegration since the end of the nineteenth century have come under critical examination by philosophers, psychoanalysts, anthropologists and feminists. In this context, Gao's experimentation with the Chinese Zen Buddhist concepts of subjectivity offers a new perspective in understanding the self which goes beyond linguistic and psychical analysis.

Gao's experimentation with the new narrative language succeeds in finding sources from traditional Chinese aesthetics. The inter-changeable use of pronouns in the Chinese language signifies a flowing subjectivity in the transcendental and distanced self that has its roots in Zen Buddhism. The Tang poet Li Bai 李白 also experimented with tran-scendental objectifications of the self when the speaking subject invited the moon and his shadow, both of which are his other selves, to drink with him. Gao said in his Nobel lecture, "In my fiction I use pronouns instead of the usual characters and also use the pronouns I, you and he to tell about or focus on the protagonist. The portrayal of one character by using different pronouns creates a sense of distance. As this also pro-vides actors on the stage with a broader psychological space I have also introduced the changing of pronouns into my drama" (Gao, 2000, p. 12).

In his search for new modes of expression, which is much indebted to the Chinese language, Gao has the following observation:

> I search for new modes of expression simply because I feel restricted by the conventions of language and I cannot express my true feelings. When I was struggling to find a more reliable way of expressing my personal experiences, I was greatly enlightened by Western writers such as Proust and Joyce, and the *nouveau roman* writers. Their interest in the conscious and the subconscious, as well as their use of narrative points of view, com-pels me to look at the differences between the Chinese and Western languages.... The technique of writing which I call "stream of language" has grown out of my experimentation with the Chinese language.

> The Chinese language is not as restricted by subject or tense inflections as many analytical languages of the West. There is enormous flexibility for expressing the mental activities of people, at times so much so that short-cuts in thinking and ambiguity in meaning often occur.... In Chinese, reality, recollection and imagination all manifest themselves as an eternal present transcending grammatical concepts, thus constituting a stream of language which also transcends concepts of time. Thinking and feeling, the conscious and the subconscious, narrative and dialogue, as well as soliloquy, and even the alienation of self-consciousness, can all be sub-jected to examination in the method of Zen Buddhist contemplation. In-stead of adopting the method of psychical and semantic analysis that can

be found in Western fiction, I bring them together in the linear stream of
language.   (Gao, 1996b, p. 11)

It is clear that Gao's experimentation with the changing and interchangeable subject positions in narrative has its origin in the Chinese
language, which allows flexibility in tense and subject inflexions. This
characteristic of the Chinese language has much to do with Chinese Daoist
philosophy, which sees language as a barrier in communication and also
in limiting the human capacity of perception. Through the use of
language, the speaker assumes the position of a speaking subject and is
thus separated from the knowable object. Generally speaking, language
entails the adoption of a perspective in an interpretive framework and
thus sets boundaries for perception. To go beyond the limit of language,
the ancient philosophers, Laozi 老子 and Zhuangzi 莊子, advocate an
intuitive mode of perception, the first principle of which is to transcend
the self (Tam, 1988, pp. 108–116). That is to say, the Chinese flexibility
in using interchangeably the pronouns "you" and "he" for "I" is a way to
go beyond the limit of the self, so that the subject can be objectified.
Gao has the following view with regard to freeing the speaking subject
from the "prison-house of language":

> In the Chinese language, the subject of a sentence is often omitted. Verbs
> do not need to inflect according to the change of subject. All these char-
> acteristics give flexibility to the shift of narrative points of view. When the
> self which assumes the subject of a sentence is absent in expression, the
> self becomes a transcendental self, and ultimately a no-self. When the self
> is shifted to you, and then to he, the you-me is an objectification of me,
> and the he-me can be considered as a detached me who observes me. This
> is a process which I call "self-detached self-contemplation" [抽身靜觀
> choushen jingguan], or observation-contemplation [觀想 Guan xiang].
> In this process, the self reaches a state of unlimited freedom in self-
> detachment.   (Gao, 1996, pp. 174–175)

In this way of shifting the points of view and detaching from the self,
the protagonists in Gao's novels and plays are objectifications of their
selves. The various articles by Mabel Lee and Torbjörn Lodén collected
in this volume show how, by transcending the self, the protagonists in
Gao's novels have created many selves.[13] Gao's play with language in
the interchangeable use of pronouns demonstrates the self's incessant

yearning for complete detachment and thus freedom, even from the self. The play with language, in Gao's works, can thus be viewed as playing with the different facets of the self, which offer a new space not only for the representation of the subject, but also for breaking away from the positivistic mode of logical narrative. As Gao said in his Nobel lecture, "Literature is simply man focusing his gaze on his self and while he does a thread of consciousness which sheds light on his self begins to grow" (Gao, 2000, p. 9). It is in this sense that Gao has indeed opened new paths of language for the representation of subjectivity in the Chinese novel. Gao's talent as a novelist is seen in his two novels, *Soul Mountain* and *One Man's Bible*. Generally speaking, Gao takes novel writing as a means of self-exploration and self-affirmation. In his usual unassuming manner, he uses the fictional form to develop his personal voice, to sort out his problems and to explore the ultimate meaning of life, of human existence.

SOLILOQUIES OF THE SOUL

Soul Mountain is organized on the principle of a dual structure, with a spiritual journey alongside a physical one. While the physical journey takes the protagonist to different places in the hope of finding Soul Mountain, a physical and a spiritual site, his displacement also denotes a journey of the self, trying to seek the meaning of life through an encounter with nature, to come to an understanding of his true selves through various relationships, and ultimately to transcend them. The journey thus brings the protagonist to his discoursing with his selves, for all other characters in his encounters are projections or reflections of these true selves: "I am on a journey — life. Life, good or bad, is a journey and wallowing in my imagination I travel into the inner mind with you who are my reflection.... You who are my creation, created her and her face naturally would have to be imagined, ... She is a hazy image of associations induced by memories and is therefore indefinite,... For you and me, the women who constitute they are simply a composite image of her." (Gao, 2000, pp. 298–299; Lee, trans., 2000, pp. 312–313). Hence, the novel is a soul-searching journey made up of imagined encounters and dialogues between the protagonist's selves.

Gao Xingjian has repeatedly emphasized the importance of fleeing for the revelation of one's true selves. Only by fleeing from culture, politics, history, society and even the limitations of one's own selves, can a person be totally free to examine his true, natural selves in a detached and transcendent manner. In *Soul Mountain* the protagonist, through his trip of fleeing into the mountains, comes to see how human nature has been distorted in the process of civilization and subsequently calls for a return to nature: "Man follows earth, earth follows sky, sky follows the way, the way follows nature" (Gao, 2000, p. 45; Lee, trans., 2000, p. 48).[13] With such an awakening, the protagonist cries out in the wilderness: "Don't commit actions which go against the basic character of nature, don't commit acts which should not be committed" (Gao, 2000, p. 45; Lee, trans., 2000, p. 48). The journey allows the protagonist to come to a fuller understanding of his true selves, and yet it also leads him to see the difficulties in freeing his selves from themselves, as he remarks at the end: "I have not reached a state of utter despair, I am still seduced by the human world, I still haven't lived enough" (Gao, 2000, p. 456; Lee, trans., 2000, p. 477).

The interchangeable pronouns denoting the transcendent subject positions are various means to objectify the selves, which Gao has earlier experimented with in his short story, "Yu, xue ji qita" [Rain, snow and others] published in 1982. In *Soul Mountain* Gao allows the protagonist to move and flow between nature and culture so as to reveal the psycho-cultural dimensions of the selves as subjects. By retreating from the city to the mountains, the protagonist flees from the bonds of politics and civilization. Confronted by his true selves, the protagonist finds himself caught in his psychical desire of sex — a desire that the selves struggle hard to free but fail. The female characters are extensions of the protagonist's carnal desire. In one of his encounters with women, the protagonist says, "She wraps herself around you, kisses you wildly, wet kisses on your face, your body, and rolls around with you. She has won, you can't resist and again sink into carnal lust, unable to free yourself" (Gao, 2000, p. 263; Lee, trans., 2000, p. 274).

While Gao's *Soul Mountain* consists of memories and fantasies presented in a long soliloquy that are meant to be an exposition of the protagonist's selves, *One Man's Bible* is a story built upon the dialogical constitution of the protagonist's self disguised in the "he" and the "you." In *One Man's Bible*, Gao places his speaking subject in new temporal and spatial dimensions. The "he" represents the protagonist in the past, his memories of his experience in China, while the "you" denotes the protagonist in the present, his experience as a writer in exile outside China. In this "he-you" dialogical framework, the selves of the protagonist are explored in the spatiality of exile, with the past fusing with the present, and the dislocated existence in confrontation with national identities. Gao's non-traditional mode of narrative enables him to represent spatial relationships that are heavily loaded with psychological meanings. In the novel, Gao uses a cinematic mode, which he borrows from the *nouveau roman*, to fuse the temporal with the spatial to create a narrative of subjectivity interspersed with scenes of memories of persecution and anxiety of dislocated existence. The opening episode, which relates the Chinese male "you's" encounter with the German lady Marguerite, whose mother is a Jew, reminds the reader of the spatial narrative in Marguerite Duras's novel, *Hirsohima mon amour*. In a comparable cinematic style, Gao brings two characters together in a sharing of experience of dislocated existence, which thematically serves as an introduction to the stories of exile and diaspora experienced by the "you" in China and the "she" in Europe.

The sense of exile as a conscious attempt of fleeing presented in *Soul Mountain* is further developed into a quest for meaning in a life of diasporic existence in *One Man's Bible*. The "he" and "you" are no longer mere pronouns used to describe the protagonist. They are used as psychological representations of the temporal and spatial dimensions of experience in the split selves of the protagonist. In *One Man's Bible*, Gao successfully creates an alternative mode of narrative for fiction writing. His success in experimenting with a new mode of narrative in the two novels gives rise to a reconsideration of the language of literature, the narrative structure of fiction, as well as the representations of self. Gao's experimentation with the mode of narrative originates in his conscious break from convention in an attempt to develop a new theory of subjectivity in literary representation.

However different it may be in people's views on the Nobel Prize in Literature 2000, Gao's achievements have long been recognized by scholars, literary critics, and theatre professionals. His works have been performed on the stage and taught at universities. Gao's shadow self, that self of a writer projected in the image of the "Silent Passer-by" in persistent search in *The Bus-Stop*, has now embarked on his journey. His voice, that voice of a lonely individual speaking in a non-Western language, is now being heard, as Gao concludes in his Nobel lecture:

I thank you for awarding this Nobel Prize to literature, to literature that is unwavering in its independence, that avoids neither human suffering nor political oppression and that furthermore does not serve politics. I thank all of you for awarding this most prestigious prize for works that are far removed from the writings of the market, works that have aroused little attention but are actually worth reading. At the same time, I also thank the Swedish Academy for allowing me to ascend this dais to speak before the eyes of the world. A frail individual's weak voice that is hardly worth listening to and that normally would not be heard in the public media has been allowed to address the world.   (Gao, 2000, p. 14)

NOTES

1. Liu Zaifu's article bears the Chinese title which means "A Hundred Years of Nobel Prize in Literature and the Absence of Chinese Writers." For details of this article, see Liu Zaifu 劉再復 (1999).

2. See for example Xu Guorang 許國榮 (2000).

3. The special issue was later republished in book form, entitled *Trees on the Mountain: An Anthology of New Chinese Writing*, by The Chinese University Press in 1984.

4. In 1986, there was a conference on comparative drama held at The Chinese University of Hong Kong, in which a paper was read on Gao's *The Bus-Stop* (Tam, 1990). In Taiwan there was a conference on "Literature of Mainland China" held at the National Zhengzhi (Chengchi) University in 1989. In this conference, Ma Sen presented a paper on the role Gao played in experimenting with the Theatre of the Absurd in China. In a conference on "Asian/Western Theatre" organized jointly by the International Association of Theatre Critics (Hong Kong) and the Urban Council of Hong Kong in 1994, there was a paper, in which Gao's theatrical experimentation was discussed in the light of Asian experience in postmodernist performance (Tam, 1995).

5. Appended to this collection is a lengthy article by Hu Yaoheng 胡耀恆 (John Yaw-herng Hu), "Bainian gengyun de fengshou" 百年耕耘的豐收 [The harvest of one hundred years' ploughing], in which Gao's major achievements in drama are evaluated against the historical development of modern Chinese drama.

6. See for example the Chinese essays published in Taiwan and Hong Kong: Chen Ganquan 陳敢權 (Anthony Chan Kam Kuen), "Cong *Shengsijie* kan Gao Xingjian de xiju lilun" 從《生死界》看高行健的戲劇理論 [Gao Xingjian's theory of drama as expressed in *Between Life and Death*], *Xiju yishu* 戲劇藝術 [Dramatic arts], No. 9 (1995); Chen Fangzheng 陳方正 (Chen Fong Ching),

"*Lingshan* zhiwai de shengsijie — juzuojia Gao Xingjian yinxiangji"《靈山》之外的生死界 —— 劇作家高行健印象記 [Life and death beyond *Soul Mountain* the dramatist Gao Xingjian], *Xin bao* 信報 [Hong Kong economic journal], 26 October 1993; Zhou Fanfu 周凡夫, "Sanchongxing guanzhong — kan Gao Xingjian de *Bi'an*" 三重性觀眾 —— 看高行健的《彼岸》 [Tripartite audience — seeing Gao Xingjian's *The Other Shore*], *Lianhe bao* 聯合報 [United daily news] (Hong Kong), 23 April 1995; Hu Yaoheng 胡耀恆 (John Yawherng Hu), "Yi yangyuan wei zhuzhou de xiju — lun Gao Xingjian de xiju yishu" 以演員為主軸的戲劇 —— 論高行健的戲劇藝術 [Actor-centred theatre — on Gao Xingjian's dramaturgy], *Zhongyang ribao* 中央日報 [Central daily], 23 December 1995.

6. Translated by Gilbert Fong and published in *The Other Shore: Plays by Gao Xingjian* by The Chinese University Press. In the book, Gilbert Fong, the translator, has provided readers with a detailed introduction to Gao's career as a dramatist.

7. For example, the Commercial Press in Hong Kong and The Chinese University Press specially organized a seminar, "Understanding Gao Xingjian; the Writer, the Dramatist and his Works," on 29 October 2000 to give readers an opportunity to learn more about the Laureate.

8. Tay's paper shows that the individual talent of a writer may transcend the limit of social conditions. In this paper, detailed information and analysis are given on how the Theatre of the Absurd has been transformed in Gao's play to incorporate other elements of the avant-garde in Western theatre.

9. The most recent exhibition of Gao's paintings was held in Louvre, Paris from 19 October 2000.

10. Gao's most well-known play, *The Bus-Stop*, was translated into German and published in *Drama Today* in 1987. His other play, *Wild Man*, was translated into English and appeared in *Asian Theater Journal* in 1990, while *Fugitives* was translated into French in 1992. His major novel, *Soul Mountain*, has been translated into Swedish by Göran Malmqvist in 1992, into French by Noël and Liliane Dutrait in 1995, and into English by Mabel Lee in 2000, while his latest novel, *One Man's Bible*, is being translated by Mabel Lee and expected to appear soon.

11. Geremie Barmé is one of the Australian scholars who translated excerpts of Gao's play, *The Bus-Stop*, and has written on his other contributions to the theatre. For ten years since 1990, Mabel Lee has been translating Gao's works and introduced him to the English-speaking world. Over the years 1995–99 she has written seven articles (Lee, 1995, 1996, 1997a, 1997b, 1998, 1999a, 1999b) dealing with different aspects of Gao's views of literature. Her numerous essays on the novel *Soul Mountain* have shed light on Gao's theoretical contributions to a new Chinese aesthetics.

12. For details of Gao's essays and their titles, see Terry Yip's "A Chronology of Gao Xingjian" included in this book.

13. Selected articles, some previously published and some new, by Xiaomei Chen, Gilbert Fong, Amy Lai, Mabel Lee, Torbjörn Lodén, Quah Sy Ren, Jo Riley and Michael Gissenwehrer, Kwok-kan Tam, and William Tay are included in this volume.

REFERENCES

Barmé, Geremie (1983). "A Touch of the Absurd — Introducing Gao Xingjian and His Play *The Bus-stop*." *Renditions*, Nos. 19 & 20 (Spring & Autumn), pp. 373–377.

Chen, Xiaomei (1992). "A *Wildman* Between Two Cultures: Some Paradigmatic Remarks on 'Influence Studies.'" *Comparative Literature Studies*, Vol. 29, No. 4, pp. 397–416.

Dissanayake, Wimal, ed. (1988). *Communication Theory: The Asian Perspective.* Singapore: Asian Mass Communication Research and Information Centre.

Fang Zixun (Gilbert C. F. Fong) 方梓勳, ed. (2000). *Xinjiyuan de huawen xiju* 新紀元的華文戲劇 [Chinese drama in the new millennium]. Hong Kong: Xianggang xiju xiehui 香港戲劇協會 and Xianggang zhongwen daxue xiju gongcheng 香港中文大學戲劇工程.

Findeisen, Raoul D., and Robert H. Gassmann, eds. (1998). *Autumn Floods: Essays in Honour of Marián Gálik.* Bern: Peter Lang.

Fong, Gilbert C. F., trans. (1999). *The Other Shore: Plays By Gao Xingjian.* Hong Kong: The Chinese University Press.

Gao Xingjian 高行健 (1995). *Gao Xingjian xiju liuzhong* 高行健戲劇六種 [Six volumes of plays by Gao Xingjian]. Taipei: Dijiao chubanshe 帝教出版社.

—— (1996a). *Meiyou zhuyi* 沒有主義 [Without isms]. Hong Kong: Tiandi tushu youxian gongsi 天地圖書有限公司.

—— (1996b). "Meiyou zhuyi" 沒有主義 [Without isms]. In Gao (1996a), pp. 8–17.

—— (1996c). "Wenxue yu xuanxue: guanyu *Lingshan*" 文學與玄學 • 關於《靈山》 [Literature and metaphysics: On *Soul Mountain*]. In Gao (1996a), pp. 167–182.

—— (2000a). *Nobel Lecture: The Case of Literature.* Trans. Mabel Lee. Stockholm: Nobel Foundation.

—— (2000b). *Yige ren de shengjing* 一個人的聖經 [One man's bible]. Hong Kong: Tiandi tushu youxian gongsi 天地圖書有限公司. Original work published in 1998.

Goldblatt, Howard, ed. (1990). *Worlds Apart: Recent Chinese Writing and Its Audiences.* New York: M. E. Sharpe.

Gutmann, Amy, ed. (1994). *Multiculturalism: Examining the Politics of Recognition.* Princeton, NJ: Princeton University Press.

Hu Yaoheng 胡耀恆 (John Yaw-herng Hu) (1995). "Bainian gengyun de fengshou" 百年耕耘的豐收 [The harvest of one hundred years' ploughing]. In Gao (1995), Appendix.

Huang Meixu 黃美序 (2000). "Shitan Gao Xingjian xiju zhong de sengdao renwu" 試探高行健戲劇中的僧道人物 [A preliminary discussion of the Buddhist and Daoist figures in Gao Xingjian's plays]. In Fang Zixun 方梓勳, ed. (2000), pp. 296–309.

Lee, A. Robert, and Vicki Ooi, eds. (1995). *Old Worlds, New Worlds.* Hong Kong: International Association of Theatre Critics.

Lee, Mabel (1995). "Without Politics: Gao Xingjian on Literary Creation." *The Stockholm Journal of East Asian Studies*, Vol. 6, pp. 82–101.

—— (1996). "Walking Out of Other People's Prisons: Liu Zaifu and Gao Xingjian on Chinese Literature in the 1990s." *Asian and African Studies*, Vol. 5, No. 1, pp. 98–112.

—— (1997a) "Personal Freedom in Twentieth Century China: Reclaiming the Self in Yang Lian's *Yi* and Gao Xingjian's *Lingshan*." In Lee and Wilding, eds. (1997), pp. 133–155.

—— (1997b). "Gao Xingjian's *Lingshan/Soul Mountain*: Modernism and the Chinese Writer." *Heat*, No. 4, pp. 128–157.

—— (1998). "Gao Xingjian's Dialogue with Two Dead Poets from Shaoxing: Xu Wei and Lu Xun." In Findeisen and Gassmann, eds. (1998), pp. 401–414.

—— (1999a). "Gao Xingjian on the Issue of Literary Creation for the Modern Writer." *Journal of Asian Pacific Communication*, Vol. 9, Nos. 1 & 2, pp. 83–96.

—— (1999b). "Pronouns as Protagonists: Gao Xingjian's *Lingshan* as Autobiography." *China Studies*, No. 5, pp. 165–183.

——, trans. (2000). Gao Xingjian. *Soul Mountain.* Sydney: Harper Collins.

Lee, Mabel, and Michael Wilding, eds. (1997). *History, Literature and Society: Essays in Honour of S. N. Mukherjee.* Sydney: Sydney Association for Studies in Culture and Society.

Li Jianyi (1991). "Gao Xingjian's *The Bus-Stop*: Chinese Traditional Theatre and Western Avant-garde." M. A. thesis, University of Alberta.

Liu Zaifu 劉再復 (1999). "Bai nian Nuobei'er wenxuejiang he Zhongguo zuojia de quexi" 百年諾貝爾文學獎和中國作家的缺席 [A hundred years of Nobel prize in literature and the absence of Chinese writers]. *Lianhe wenxue* 聯合文學 [Unitas: A literary monthly], No. 171, pp. 44–77.

Lodén, Torbjörn (1993). "World Literature with Chinese Characteristics: On a Novel by Gao Xingjian." *The Stockholm Journal of East Asian Studies*, Vol. 4, pp. 17–39.

Luk, Yun-tong, ed. (1990). *Studies in Chinese-Western Comparative Drama.* Hong Kong: The Chinese University Press.

Ma Sen (1989). "The Theatre of the Absurd in China: Kao Hsing-chien's *The Bus Stop.*" *Issues and Studies, A Journal of China Studies and International Affairs,* Vol. 25, No. 8 (August), pp. 138–148.

Quah, Sy Ren (1997). "Gao Xingjian and China's Alternative Theatre of the 1980s." M. Phil. Thesis, University of Cambridge.

—— (1999). "The Theatre of Gao Xingjian: Experimentation Within the Chinese Context and Towards New Modes of Representation." Ph. D. thesis, University of Cambridge.

Riggins, Stephen Harold, ed. (1997). *The Language and Politics of Exclusion: Others in Discourse.* London: Sage.

Riley, Jo, and Michael Gissenwehrer (1989). "The Myth of Gao Xingjian." In Riley and Gissenwehrer, eds. (1989), pp. 129–151.

——, eds. (1989). *Hai Shi Zhou Hao: Chinese Poetry, Drama and Literature of the 1980s.* Bonn: Engelhard-Ng Verlag.

Soong, Stephen C., and John Minford, eds. (1984). *Trees on the Mountain: An Anthology of New Chinese Writing.* Hong Kong: The Chinese University Press.

Tam, Kwok-kan (1988). "Taoism and the Chinese View of Literary Communication." In Dissanayake, ed. (1988), pp. 105–125.

—— (1990). "Drama of Dilemma: Waiting as Form and Motif in *The Bus-Stop* and *Waiting for Godot.*" In Yun-tong Luk, ed. (1990), pp. 23–45.

—— (1995). "Postmodernist Performance in Contemporary Chinese and Japanese Theatre." In Lee and Ooi, eds. (1995), pp. 43–49. Republished with the same title in *Performing Arts International,* Vol. 1, Part 3 (1999), pp. 65–73.

Tay, William. (1990). "Avant-garde Theatre in Post-Mao China: *The Bus-Stop* by Gao Xingjian." In Goldblatt, ed. (1990), pp. 111–118.

Taylor, Charles (1994). "The Politics of Recognition." In Gutmann (1994), pp. 25–73.

Xu Guorong 許國榮 (2000). *Gao Xingjian xiju yanjiu* 高行健戲劇研究 [Studies on Gao Xingjian's plays]. Beijing: Zhongguo xiju chubanshe 中國戲劇出版社.

Yang Lian 楊煉 (2000). "Liuwang de shengli" 流亡的勝利 [The victory of exile]. *Zhongguo shibao* 中國時報 [China times], 14 October, p. 37.

Yeung, Jessica W. Y. (1996). "From China to Nowhere: the Writings of Gao Xingjian in the 1980s and Early 90s." M. Phil. Thesis, University of Hong Kong.

Zhao Yiheng 趙毅恆 [Henry Y. H. Zhao] (1999). *Jianli yizhong xiandai chanju — Gao Xingjian yu Zhongguo shiyan xiju* 建立一種現代禪劇 —— 高行健與中國實驗戲劇 [Toward a modern Zen drama — Gao Xingjian and the Chinese theatre experimentalism]. Taipei: Erya chubanshe 爾雅出版社.

Zou Jiping (1994). "Gao Xingjian and Chinese Experimental Theatre." Ph.D. thesis, University of Illinois at Urbana-Champaign.

1 MABEL LEE

Gao Xingjian on the Issue of Literary Creation for the Modern Writer[1]

Notions of a self and an other are born in the same instant: one cannot exist without the other, and furthermore the existence of a self and an other inevitably is a political situation. In endeavours of academic enquiry, aggressive one-way applications of the self/other paradigm can create blind spots which lead to ignoring, obscuring, or distorting substantive differences and similarities within both what is denoted as self and what is denoted as other.

RECONTEXTUALIZING THE SELF/OTHER
(ASIA VS. WEST) PARADIGM

During the first two decades of this century, Carl Gustav Jung, Peter Kropotkin, Hermann Hesse, D. H. Lawrence, Franz Kafka, and Isadora Duncan were amongst a group of young intellectuals who frequented the small Swiss village of Ascona to ponder the implications of industrialization on human existence. They, like Nietzsche who died in 1900, despaired of the direction European civilization was taking and were engaged in discussions on how to solve the spiritual malaise and the general sense of unhappiness afflicting Europe despite its material wealth (Green, 1986, pp. 1–3).

The lakeside village of Ascona near the Italian border, with its rarefied air and tranquil setting, constituted an "other" to the industrialism of the big urban areas — particularly of Germany, which in the years immediately preceding the outbreak of World War I had eclipsed the rest of Europe as an industrial power. By conveniently removing themselves from the scene of aggressive industrial growth typifying the rest of Europe and relocating themselves within this "other" environment, the

frequenters of Ascona were provided with an exaggerated sense of distance which allowed them to critique with great clarity human existence,
particularly that of Western civilization. These critiques, manifested in
their widely acclaimed writings, subsequently influenced later generations throughout the Western world. Emphasized here is that for strong
intellects and enquiring minds, knowledge of "other" intellectual systems challenges conventional habits of thought, providing actual or perceived space for creative reflection on the self's own culture. Even as
these young minds addressed the problems of Europe, industrial capitalism was already probing other parts of the world in search of raw
materials to feed its voracious machines and new markets to sell its
manufactures.

Ascona has been invoked to recontextualize the self/other paradigm
which has dominated much of postcolonial discourse with increasingly
ghettoistic (or myopic) regional tendencies. It is maintained that the
self/other (Asia vs. West) paradigm imposes the false assumption that
some sort of cultural homogeneity exists in Asia. Geographical proximity does not guarantee cultural homogeneity, and the suggestion that
some form of monolithic culture exists in Asia works against extending
knowledge and understanding of the region. The proposal for re-
contextualization is simply to return applications of the self/other paradigm to the broader global stage.

The application of the self/other (Asia vs. West) paradigm is prob-
lematical for the investigation of literature premised on a fundamental
belief in the universality of literature as a form of artistic creation, the
central concern of the present study. The notion of the universal nature
of art (including literature) posits the elimination of differences between
the self and others. In the specific case of Chinese literature, the problem of the self/other paradigm is further compounded for three important reasons: (1) The notion of universality in literary creation lies at the
core of Chinese aesthetics — although not systematically articulated, this
is intimated in many, and may be intuited in even more, writings over
the ages right up to present times. Generations of Chinese writers and
artists have drawn inspiration from Daoist texts which are permeated
with the unifying notion of the essential equality of all beings (see
Murakami, 1987, p. 118; Metzger, 1977).[2] (2) The great philosophical
traditions of Buddhism and Daoism have significantly influenced the
formulation of European (particularly German) philosophical systems

of thought. (3) In the establishment of China's modern literature in the May Fourth period, Chinese writers appropriated both Nietzsche and Lu Xun (1881–1936) as icons. Nietzsche authenticated and legitimized the modernity (= Western origins) of the new literature and Lu Xun's writings with their identifiably Zhuangzean-Nietzschean texture exemplified modernity in Chinese literature (Lee, 1998b).

Striking similarities in Daoist texts and Nietzsche's thinking have intrigued scholars (Chen 1991; Ames, 1991; Figl, 1991). An indirect influence of Daoist thinking may be assumed from Nietzsche's contacts with Schopenhauer, although to date no corroborating archival evidence has been found (Figl, 1991). Nevertheless, it can be assumed that living in the intellectual matrix of nineteenth century Europe with its interest and enthusiasm for Daoist texts it is highly improbable that Nietzsche would not have been familiar with the available French and German translations (Lee, 1998b). The example of Nietzsche has been introduced here to emphasize that Chinese intellectuals, and writers in particular, were drawn to Nietzsche's work because of its affinity with their own philosophical traditions and because of its "otherness" in order to critique their own culture.

The extensive direct and indirect borrowings from Daoism and Buddhism by Western philosophers from Leibniz, Schopenhauer, and Nietzsche, and to Heidegger, mean therefore that these Chinese and Indian philosophies have inspired the formulation of systems of thought which underpin much of Western philosophy and literature in modern times. Modern mainstream Western academic research has until recent times tended to dismiss such borrowings, but the research by Reinhard May, which established a solid case of plagiarism against Martin Heidegger, will perhaps signal change. Heidegger is charged with "clandestine textual appropriation of non-Western spirituality" and appropriation in some instances "wholesale and almost verbatim of major ideas from the German translations of Daoist and Zen Buddhist classics" (May, 1996, p. xviii).

The above demonstrates how international power politics of the twentieth century have valorized the Asia vs. West paradigm, virtually obliterating from mainstream academic investigations the West's appropriation of ideas from the philosophical traditions of Asia, even if this may not have been the intention of the individual Western thinkers concerned, and hence insinuating that these are the West's own unique creations.

Interestingly, this valorized paradigm came to be generally accepted by intellectuals and writers of less industrialized nations — such has been the impact of equating modernity with Western, as in the case of Chinese literature, as writers go through various stages of adapting literary traditions to suit modern needs in the post-Mao era.

The Nobel Laureate of 1990, Mexican writer Octavio Paz (1914–1998), who acknowledges extensive learning from his cultural others, in particular India and China, provides some enlightening insights on the intercrossings of ideas. For example, noting that the greatest creative periods of Western poetry have been preceded or accompanied by intercrossings that have taken place in the form of imitation or translation, he suggests that European poetry should be viewed as "a chronicle of the convergences of the various traditions that compose what is known as Western tradition." He acknowledges in modern Western poetry the presence of Japanese *haiku* and Chinese poetic traditions (Paz, 1992, p. 160). Paz sees Western literature as "an integral whole in which the central protagonists are not national traditions but styles or trends, as no style or trend has ever been national. Styles have invariably been translinguistic.... Styles are coalescent and pass from one language to another; the works, each rooted in its own verbal soil are unique ..., unique, but not isolated" (Paz, 1992, p. 160).

As a writer of stature from the developing world, Paz's understanding of world literary history is helpful for understanding the situation confronting Chinese writers in present times. A staunch believer of the universality of literature (Paz, 1992, p. 155), he salutes in his poetry the classical poets of China, Japan, and India who have inspired him (Lee, 1996). Paz, as well as other significant writers of the Western tradition, is well known to Chinese writers such as Gao Xingjian, just as Paz was familiar with significant writers of India, China, and Japan. In the understanding of these writers, literature is universal and intercrossings between cultures are a continuing and dynamic process.

In summary, the above paragraphs have sought to establish the following:

(1) A recontextualized globalized self/other literary paradigm (which as shown above constitutes a vast interactive network of innumerable self/other paradigms) in which the writer Gao Xingjian may be meaningfully located.

(2) How centuries of intellectual intercrossings between Asia and the West underpin the modern literary traditions of the West and how intellectual and literary intercrossings are continuing into the present. In the case of China, it should be noted that such intercrossings were severely disrupted by the Japanese invasion of China and later the rigid implementation of Mao Zedong's policies on literature and the arts until the late 1970s. The relative freedom of the 1980s allowed Chinese writers such as Gao Xingjian to gradually reformulate their ideas on literature as well as to engage in significant experimentations in their creative writings.

(3) That the notion of the universality of literature underpins Chinese aesthetic thinking, and that this notion was transmitted with considerable force to the Western world via Daoism, particularly from the early nineteenth century after the establishment of Sinology as a discipline in Europe (Schipper, 1995).

I propose now to return to Carl Jung who is listed first amongst the frequenters of Ascona at the beginning of this paper. Jung's analyses of the human mind and literature are informed by his readings of Daoist texts, and his comments will be used to bring into focus essential elements of literary creation sought by Chinese writers, such as Gao Xingjian. In a sense, my strategy is to elucidate by using the perspective of the other to describe the self.

JUNG'S PRIMORDIAL UNCONSCIOUS, DAOSIM AND LITERATURE

The notion of the universality of literature is clearly endorsed by Jung whose psychoanalytical theories were formulated with the help of Eastern philosophies. Jung's intellectual foundations are grounded in German idealism, in which many aspects of Daoism were internalized and transformed. He clearly acknowledges his indebtedness to Daoism, Yoga, and Buddhism (Clarke, 1994, p. 7). This, however, has been dismissed by many Jungian scholars, and not subjected to systematic enquiry until recent years, notably by Clarke (1992, 1994). Jung's own writings on the East have also been edited by Clarke and published with an introduction (Clarke, 1995). In the latter work Clarke writes:

The philosophical and religious traditions of China and India in fact played an important role in his [Jung's] intellectual development. Right from the early days when he was distancing himself from Freud and fashioning his own distinctive approach to psychology, up to the 1930s when his ideas were reaching full expression and maturity, Eastern ideas and concepts wove their way in and out of his writings, and were used to clarify and substantiate his own controversial views. Concepts such as "self," "individuation," "archetypes," and "active imagination," which are central to the theory and practice of Jungian psychology, were all shaped to some extent by his investigations into texts and ideas from the ancient traditions of China and India.   (Clarke, 1995, p. 1)

It is Jung's notion of the primordial psyche and his definition of the visionary poet that provides a key to understanding why much of modern Chinese literature is reminiscent of Western writings. Jung ruminates on psychology and literature in *Modern Man in Search of a Soul* (Jung, 1944, p. 190). His explication of the primordial unconscious as the source of the visionary mode of creation, which has distinctly Daoist overtones, distinguishes between two modes of artistic creation: the psychological and the visionary. The psychological mode deals with materials drawn from the realm of human consciousness, that is, man's "conscious life." With this mode, the experience and the expression remain within the bounds of psychological intelligibility. It is the visionary mode, which is of interest to Jung's analysis of the human psyche. In the visionary mode the experience derives its existence from the hinterland of man's mind, and although this primordial experience is beyond man's understanding, Jung claims for it psychic reality and therefore physical reality (Jung, 1944, pp. 180–187). The primordial experience is the source of visionary creation:

It is merely a deep presentiment that strives to find expression.... It is like a whirlwind that seizes everything within its reach and, by carrying it aloft, assumes a visible shape. Since the expression can never exhaust the possibilities of the vision, but falls short of it in richness of content, the poet must have at his disposal a huge store of materials if he is to communicate even a few of his intimations. What is more, he must resort to an imagery that is difficult to handle and full of contradictions in order to express the weird paradoxicality of his vision. Dante's presentiments are clothed in images that run the gamut of Heaven and Hell; Goethe must bring in the Blacksburg and the infernal regions of Greek antiquity; Wagner needs the whole body of Nordic myth; Nietzsche returns to the heiratic style and recreates the legendary seer of prehistoric times....

(Jung, 1944, pp. 189–190)

In Jung's analysis what appears in the vision is "the collective unconscious," that is, a certain psychic disposition shaped by inherited forces from which consciousness develops. He asserts that the manifestations of the collective unconscious is compensatory to the conscious attitude, and this compensation is effected through the visionary poet being "guided by the unexpressed desire of his times." The creative being is both a human being with a personal life and at the same time an impersonal creative process:

> ... the specifically artistic disposition involves an overweight of collective psychic life as against the personal. Art is a kind of innate drive that seizes a human being and makes him an instrument. The artist is not a person endowed with free will who seeks his own ends, but allows art to realize its purposes through him. As a human being he may have moods and a will and personal aims, but as an artist he is "man" in a higher sense — he is "collective man" — one who carries and shapes the unconscious, psychic life of mankind. To perform this difficult office it is sometimes necessary for him to sacrifice happiness and everything that makes life worth living for the ordinary human being.   (Jung, 1944, pp. 192–194)

This being so, the artist is interesting for Jung's psychoanalysis. The artist's life is necessarily full of conflicts: on the one hand, he will have ordinary human longings for happiness, satisfaction and security in life, and on the other, a ruthless passion for creation which may go so far as to override every personal desire. As a general rule, the artist "must pay dearly for the divine gift of creative fire" for the individual is born with a certain capital of energy and it is the strongest force that will monopolize this energy:

> Whenever the creative force predominates, human life is ruled and moulded by the unconscious as against the active will, and the conscious ego is swept along on a subterranean current, being nothing more than a helpless observer of events. The work in process becomes the poet's fate and determines his psychic development. It is not Goethe who creates Faust, but *Faust*, which creates Goethe. And what is Faust but a symbol? ... Could we conceive of anyone but a German writing *Faust* or *Also sprach Zarathustra?*

... The archetypal image of the wise man, the saviour or redeemer, lies buried and dormant in man's unconscious since the dawn of culture; it is awakened whenever the times are out of joint and a human society is committed to a serious error.... These primordial images are numerous, but do not appear in the dreams of individuals or in works of art until they are called into being by the waywardness of the general outlook. When conscious life is characterized by one-sidedness and by a false attitude, then they are activated — one might say "instinctively" — and come to light in the dreams of individuals and the visions of artists and seers, thus restoring the psychic equilibrium of the epoch.   (Jung, 1944, pp. 196–198)

It is in this way that the work of the poet meets the spiritual needs of the society in which he lives and it is for this reason that his work means more to him than his personal fate, for he is subordinate to the work. In his work he penetrates to "that matrix in which all men are embedded, which imparts a common rhythm to all human existence, and allows the individual to communicate his feeling and his striving to mankind as a whole" (Jung, 1944, p. 198).

GAO XINGJIAN AND CHINESE LITERATURE

It is against the above lengthy comments that the Chinese playwright, novelist, and artist Gao Xingjian will be scrutinized as an example of a Chinese writer who in the past decade has been articulating definitions of modern Chinese literature in numerous creative and critical writings. He is informed by an incisive mind and a high level of artistic sensitivity as well as sustained extensive reading in both Chinese and Western literature. His access to Western literature is mainly via French and to a limited extent, English. At the beginning of the 1980s, Gao Xingjian was at the centre of a controversy in literary and political circles for his writings on the techniques of modern fiction. Then, when he heard that he would be sent to Qinghai to be re-educated for writing the experimental play *Chezhan* 車站 [The Bus-stop] which was closed by the authorities in 1983, he quietly fled Beijing, returning five months later after tensions had relaxed. However, he continued to despair over restrictions on freedom of artistic expression, despite the increasing liberalization of government policies. When he left China in 1987 to travel to Germany, he had already decided not to return, for he had with him his most precious belonging, the manuscript of his novel *Lingshan* 靈山 [Soul mountain; Gao, 1990] which he had started writing in Beijing in the summer of 1982 and completed in Paris in September of 1989. In Germany he applied for residence in France (Lodén, 1993; Lee, 1995, 1998a).

Gao Xingjian's self-identification is unambiguously stated: he is an artist. For him the challenge is how he as an artist working in various media can employ his knowledge, aesthetic sensitivity, talent, and power of critical observation to achieve in his work a universality which transcends the apparent boundaries existing between human beings. He acknowledges that he has his roots in Chinese culture and while he writes mostly in Chinese, he critiques with confidence and conviction literature by both Chinese and French writers. This is demonstrated for example in his lengthy recorded dialogue with the journalist and writer Denis Bourgeois (Gao and Bourgeois, 1997). Gao Xingjian's literary achievements have been recognized by the French literary world and in 1992 he received the award *Chevalier de l'Ordre des Arts et des Lettres*. Plays constitute his largest output, and he is writing innovative and highly experimental works at a steady rate, most of which have been staged throughout Europe and in other parts of the world.[3] He also enjoys a significant reputation for his large black ink paintings which sustain his literary endeavours and are being collected by private and public galleries.[4] The publication of his long novel *Soul Mountain* has established his credentials in the writing of fiction.

As Gao Xingjian's writings are being published in French as well as Chinese and, moreover, receiving significant reviews in the French media,[5] it would seem that the self/other (Chinese vs. Western) problematics of readership and reception do not exist. Living in a modest apartment in suburban Paris, Gao Xingjian has achieved the freedom he demands for his obsessive drive to express his artistic reality in various media. His continuing challenge to conventional thinking in each of his works is unique as he pits his capabilities as an artist and writer to extend the expressive limits of the artistic medium he has chosen for a particular work. He queries the notion that literary and artistic genres such as fiction, drama, poetry, prose essay, and even dance, music, and cinema are fixed and unchangeable. "In other words, can genre boundaries be crossed, can established forms be smashed to seek new forms?" (Gao & Bourgeois, 1997, p. 1). Here he enunciates an artistic attitude that permeates all of his works, even the early works from when he was in China and writing under considerable restrictions.

The events of June 1989 in China galvanized Gao Xingjian's thinking on literature, and one of the results has been a conscious and clear separation in his mind of the personae of the individual as writer and social person, as described in the quoted passages above from Jung's *Modern Man in Search of a Soul*. He had been invited to write a play about Tiananmen and the resulting work was *Taowang* 逃亡 [Fugitives; Gao, 1996d], which made no specific references to the events in the square and contained no heroes. It was a politico-philosophical play and he pleased no one: "The Americans wanted me to change it, so I withdrew the manuscript and paid the translation fee myself. When I write I have to write what I want to say, I do not write in order to please others." (Gao, 1996c, p. 15). It was the search for total freedom of artistic expression that had led him to leave China and, treasuring this artistic freedom, he rejects any compromise of the artistic self in literature.

Born in January 1940 during the Japanese invasion of China, Gao Xingjian's childhood, youth, and adult life roughly parallel the life of the Chinese Communist Party. He engages in a Bakhtinian dialogue with readers, not just in China but in a global context, as he reflects on the traumatic events of China's recent past, its present bid to achieve fast-track modernity on all fronts in order to catch up with the Western industrialized world, and the implications of these for literary creation. In his novel *Soul Mountain*, Gao Xingjian recalls that as a student he used to recite a line of one of Lu Xun's early classical poems: "I offer my blood to the Yellow Emperor" (Lu Xun, 1903/1980). This line and others by Lu Xun were appropriated by party ideologues to encourage patriotic sentiments and a spirit of self-sacrifice for the nation (and by extension for the Communist Party). But now, fully committed to literature, Gao Xingjian expresses strong reservations: "Why must one glorify one's ancestors with blood? Is spilling one's own blood glorious? A person's head is one's own, why must it be chopped off for the Yellow Emperor?" (Gao, 1996d, pp. 497–498).[6] For Lu Xun, his poem turned out to be a prophecy: after establishing his reputation as a writer of powerful fiction, he was to sacrifice his creative self for the sake of the nation. His series of 23 prose-poems written between 24 April 1924 and 10 April 1926 and later published as the collection *Yecao* 野草 [Wild grass, 1981] graphically portrays the agonizing process which leaves him like a copse with its heart gouged out.[7]

Gao Xingjian sees Lu Xun's commitment to literary creation as similar to his own and he laments the choice made by Lu Xun to abandon creative writing in favour of political involvement. Lu Xun was a writer by instinct and inclination but his times and personal experiences as well as the revolutionary times in which he lived had inculcated a deep sense of social responsibility which demanded social action. For many decades, Lu Xun's *Wild Grass* collection was dismissed by critics as having been written while he was under the influence of Nietzsche, and misconstrued as Lu Xun's farewell to the baneful influences of the German philosopher who promoted individualism and despised the collective will (Lee, 1998b, pp. 408–409). Like Gao Xingjian more than half a century later, Lu Xun's readings in European literature and philosophy had enriched his creative writings but his choice was to sacrifice the creative life which he loved rather than to have it sullied by his choice to devote himself to political life (Lee, 1982).

Despite his admiration for Nietzsche, it would seem that Lu Xun did not heed, or indeed probably had not read, Zarathustra's warning: "Beware lest a statue slay you" (Nietzsche, 1969, p. 220). In Gao Xingjian's analysis, patriotism had distorted China's modern literary development. From the May Fourth period, Chinese intellectuals had regarded themselves as the spokespersons for the masses. In so doing they abnegated their rights as individuals. Chinese intellectuals had the courage to attack the traditional ethical and political systems, as well as the bureaucracy, but had been impotent in opposing the modern myth of the nation. Gao Xingjian is cognizant of how the threat to China's territorial sovereignty by the industrialized West (and later Japan) had coerced intellectuals into willing submissiveness to the collective will. He attributes this thinking and behaviour to a national collective unconscious, which is more deeply embedded than ethical thinking and practices: its strength is derived from the primitive instinct for survival. After the collapse of the imperial system, feudal ethics based on loyalty to the ruler transformed into a patriotic nationalism which possessed moral and ethical powers (Gao, 1993). It is Gao Xingjian's opinion that Lu Xun was a victim of the myth of the nation, and as a result Lu Xun the writer was crushed to death by Lu Xun the politician, a tragedy for literature. He concedes that Lu Xun may not have considered this a tragedy, but suggests that it was probably a cause for regret (Gao, 1996a).

Historical circumstances had forced Lu Xun to choose, as an intellectual, to shoulder the yoke of responsibility for the nation and to devote himself to writing polemical essays to bestir his compatriots. Lu Xun and other writers of his time had sacrificed literature of the individual self in order to create the new strong socialist state in which Gao Xingjian grew up. The external threat was removed and China isolated itself from the rest of the world. All but a trickle of politically sanctioned literary and cultural intercrossings occurred, and the intellectual space opened for Chinese intellectuals at the beginning of the twentieth century by significant one-way global intercrossings (via Japan particularly of German thinkers such as Schopenhauer and Nietzsche, as well as waves of anarchist and socialist thinkers) was closed by the Maoist regime: all forms of individualism were bitterly opposed and an intricate psychology was developed to inculcate a new tradition of self sacrifice which would empower the party-led collective against the individual.

It would seem that a psychological reprieve from the brink of death instilled in Gao Xingjian considerable spiritual strength and a strong determination to live his life for himself and no other. He had spent weeks waiting for a final X-ray to determine the extent of his lung cancer. Two X-rays on two separate days at two separate hospitals had confirmed that he had lung cancer. His father who died a couple of years earlier of the disease also had the final X-ray. However, it turned out that the final X-ray indicated a wrong diagnosis had been made. In this period of waiting, Gao Xingjian found himself reading the *Yijing* 易經 [The book of changes], and finally at the hospital silently invoking Buddha and hoping for a miracle, acting quite out of character from his former self (Gao, 1990, pp. 73–78). It would seem that the psychological experience of what seemed to be an interminable period of confrontation with death caused him to review the whole of his life. In his novel *Soul Mountain*, dislodged fragments of memories are woven into his reflections on his personal history, the history of the people who constitute his cultural matrix, and the history of human society and its impact on the environment. The novel also constitutes an unarticulated commitment to literary creation of which he is the sole author. This may be discerned from his unique use of pronouns as protagonists and his avoidance of the pluralized "we" which is sustained throughout the entire 560-page novel. Superimposed on his confrontation with death was the reality of political interventions in literary creation, for following soon after the wrong diagnosis of lung cancer was the necessity for him to flee Beijing where he had been singled out for criticism as the author of the play *The Bus-Stop.*

There is no doubt in Gao Xingjian's mind that he lacks the required talent for politics; Lu Xun's choice was not an option for him in China, even in the 1980s, even if he had been so inclined. He chooses instead to stand as an observer at the margins or in the cracks of society (Gao, 1993), just as an uncle had advised him. This uncle was someone dear to him and many of the stories related in *Soul Mountain* are reconstructions of stories he heard as a child when this uncle came and engaged in all-night chats with Gao Xingjian's father. It was during the chaos of the Cultural Revolution that the uncle was given a wrong injection and died within two hours of being admitted to hospital for pneumonia. The uncle's comprador-capitalist father had offered him money to go to America to study so that he would not get further involved in under-ground communist activities, but he had run off to join the New Fourth Route Army to fight the Japanese. When Gao Xingjian last saw the uncle in Shanghai, he asked if he had written the novel he said he wanted to write. The uncle's response was that "luckily he hadn't, otherwise he probably wouldn't be alive.... He told me that it was not the time for literature. He also warned me not to get involved in politics. If you do you'll become disoriented and will lose your head without even noticing" (Gao, 1990, pp. 526–527). Gao Xingjian is determined to keep his head.

Gao Xingjian's thoughts on literature in the modern age can be gleaned from the collection of essays, *Meiyou zhuyi* 沒有主義 [Without isms, 1996]. "Bali suibi" 巴黎隨筆 [Jottings from Paris, 1996], "Meiyou zhuyi" 沒有主義 [Without isms, 1996], and his "Author's Preface" (Gao, 1996e) are concise but comprehensive summaries. Some salient points from "Jottings in Paris" are outlined below. Arguing against Lu Xun's spirit of self-sacrifice and what became the May Fourth literary tradition, as well as the Maoist literary traditions which continued into the recent past, Gao Xingjian declares: "The writer is not the conscience of society nor is literature the mirror of society. The writer flees to the margins of society: he is a non-participant, an observer who looks on dispassionately. There is no need for the writer to be the conscience of society for there has long been a surplus of social conscience. The writer simply uses his own conscience and knowledge to write his own works. He has responsibility only to himself" (Gao, 1996a, p. 23).

But how does Gao Xingjian view the self and the intellectual under-pinnings of literature in this modern age of the present? Squashed be-tween totalitarian regimes of the East and the materialist, commodity-oriented societies of the West, modern man struggles desperately to af-firm his self, only to find that his self has disintegrated; his environment, opportunities, and conditions only permit him to constitute a part of the social machinery. The value of man's person is commodified as merchandise, his person is replaced by his status, actions replace the heart, even sexuality is turned into some sort of expenditure and the mystery of humankind is virtually lost. Man now confronts an anti-ideol-ogy age — superstitious belief in ideologies has been replaced by ever proliferating methodologies and procedures (Gao, 1996a, p. 24). While noting that at the end of the nineteenth century Nietzsche had declared rebellion against society, it is Gao Xingjian's opinion that in the materi-alistic age of the present the reemergence of the will to life is futile, as is the use of philosophy to affirm the value of humanity. Ludwig Wittgenstein (1889–1951) had sought to apply mathematical logic to phi-losophy but in the end announced the end of philosophy premised on logic. Gao Xingjian attributes the absurdity of all theories to the absur-dity of human rationality and concludes that philosophy is nothing more than mankind's clever but futile intellectual strivings. And literature is nothing more than a description of these futile strivings. In his analysis, modern man's reliance on rationality derives from a need for self expression, but much more attention is given to the mode of descrip-tion than to the conclusion, and the quest for philosophical methodolo-gies has gradually replaced philosophy itself: "This is a philosophical age of prescriptions and not cures." When people realize that philosophy has become intellectual games they see there is no need to be too seri-ous about the various "isms" in literature. The proliferation of dry tri-fling theories constitutes the death of thinking: freedom of thought is not restricted by logic nor does it answer to what is called a system. The delimiting of the self according to some system can only strangle free thought. It is contradictions, chaos and different interpretations of meanings, which constitute the source of thinking (Gao, 1996a, pp. 24–25). Gao Xingjian's "Jottings from Paris" adopts the precept-style found in traditional Chinese philosophy. It is terse and concise and is intended to provide space to encourage the reader to reflect and form his own conclusions.

No. 27: When weapons of murder are deployed by politicians in their contest for power the writer simply confronts language, there is no need for him to fight with anyone, he talks to himself, torments himself and absolves himself. In this world rampant with material lust, he endorses himself as an intellectual aristocrat or else wanders alone in the irrelevant world of language. (Gao, 1996a, p. 26)

No. 28: It is only when literature receives no public attention and pays no heed to society, and yet still exists that it can be considered to have found a rationale for existence, is no longer merchandise or a means to a livelihood, and can be said to have intrinsic worth and is worth reading.... (Gao, 1996a, p. 26)

No. 30: Responsibility is a strange word, a tight fitting band forcibly clamped around the writer's head so that he can be easily led here and there like a sheep. There is no need for the writer to stupidly put it around his own head. Having responsibility to one's self is to allow the self to feel inner satisfaction. It is enough if the self finds his writing interesting. (Gao, 1996a, p. 27)

No. 31: Literature itself generally has no mission, no group, no movement, no ideology; the writer is solitary, unique. The placards of various ideologies have been attached to him by others so that he can be easily identified and put into archives or else put up for sale. (Gao, 1996a, p. 27)

WITHOUT ISMS

Gao Xingjian's precept-like thoughts in "Jottings from Paris" are developed into his essay, "Without Isms." In the essay, he formulates his notion of "without isms," which could arguably constitute yet another "ism." In the "Author's Preface" to the collection, the precept-style is again adopted to elucidate the notion of "without isms" and again to suggest that the reader reflect, rather than accept, what is written as dogma. The excerpts below require little comment but anticipate the possibility of being labelled as some sort of "ism." Gao Xingjian sees "without isms" as restoring the self to modern man, allowing him to live as the initiator and arbiter of his own thinking and actions, instead of having these dictated by any other.

Without isms has choice.... If one wants to do something one does it and if one does not want to do it everything is not thereby totally negated. If one wants to do something then go ahead and do it, to whatever extent one can. This does not mean that one absolutely must do it to the point of self-sacrifice in the fight for justice, either by being executed or by suicide.

Therefore, to be without ideology is not nihilism, nor is it eclecticism, egoism or authoritarianism. It both opposes totalitarian rule and opposes the inflation of the self to God or Superman, and it detests other people being trampled on like dog shit.

Without isms is not political and is not involved with politics but does not oppose people participating in politics, whoever wants to participate in politics should go ahead. Only it opposes any type of politics being forced upon the individual in the name of abstract collectives such as the people, the race or the nation.

Without isms does not create illusions of some abstract society or ideal society. Furthermore, such utopias have already been smashed one by one by reality. There is no need to create another lie about tomorrow.

Without isms does not require the mobilization of cliques and factions, the organization of a collective or becoming a force. It is neither a standard bearer nor a foot soldier. It does not make use of others and is not made use of by others.

Without isms does not promote political ideas and moreover is incapable of doing so. However this is not because it does not have a political stance.

Without isms is not the equivalent of anarchism, it does not unequivocally reject government. Moreover present societies must have effective governments otherwise they would become havens for gangsters, terrorists and secret sects. There would be no guarantee for one's home and life and so how could there be talk of being with or without isms?

To gain the freedom of being without isms one must oppose totalitarianism whatever the brand: fascism, communism, nationalism, racism or religious fundamentalism.

Without isms is the most basic right for being a person. Without talk of any greater freedom, at least one must have the freedom not to be the slave of an ism.

To achieve without isms requires opposition to compulsion, opposition to hectoring and opposition to indoctrination ...

Without isms is the minimum requirement today for individual freedom. If even this bit of freedom does not exist, is one still able to be a person? Before discussing this or that ism, people must first be allowed to be without isms.

Without isms is a means for protecting a person's self. Without this prerequisite, to rave on about some ism is empty talk.

... At birth a person is without isms but after birth all sorts of isms are forced upon him and to discard these later is not a simple matter. People are permitted to convert from one ism to another but they are not permitted to be without isms....

Without isms is a great liberation, and as spiritual freedom is not restricted by any isms the Heavenly Horse traverses the Heavens, coming and going freely. If one says there are rules there are rules, if one says there are none there are none. If one says there are rules they are rules established by oneself, and if one says there are none one is free from them.

Without isms brings one closer to truth, because it is better to search directly for it rather than to follow the winding paths established by others. Furthermore, as no one has yet found that irrefutable truth, it is surely a waste of effort to go on following behind other people. Also, as everyone can be said to embrace the truth, it is obvious there is a multitude of truths. In the end whose truth is more authentic remains an issue, so best look for it oneself....

Without isms is not pragmatism. This unredeemable self, however, is not necessarily without value. The commodification and commercialization of a person is the end of a person. If a person cannot say no to commodification and preserve this last bit of dignity, can he still be a person?

For the individual to be able to say no to force, custom, superstition, reality, other persons and the thinking of other persons and to commodification probably is the final meaning of being a person. If existence still retains some meaning it is without isms.

Without isms does not waste effort in vainly constructing consistent systems, because speculation and dialectics, logic and paradox, and even language which is used for the actualization of thought, are all very dubious, for human life is an inexplicable mystery.

Without isms is simply a form of resistance, of life's ebullience against death. Although futile, it is at least a stance. Artistic creation is a trace left by this stance. Of course there are all sorts of other traces but they all derive from the choice of the individual.

Without isms is not to be without reverence but what is revered is not divinities, authorities or death, but the profound and vast unknowable on the other side of death.... (Gao, 1996e, pp. 3–6)

While "without isms" is possible for Gao Xingjian, it may not yet be an option for all Chinese writers. The extent of freedom of artistic expression alluded to in the discussion of literature above does not exist in

China, yet it must be acknowledged that two-way literary intercrossings are occurring on a large scale between China and the West via translations and the acquisition of linguistic skills. However, as Gao Xingjian notes, the commodification of literature is endemic in the West. It would seem that this aspect of Western culture has been transplanted successfully and is undergoing phenomenal growth in China. Gao Xingjian's notion of "without isms" does not specifically address a Chinese audience, it is his reflection on the life of modern human existence and its implications for literature of the self. His notion of "without isms" permeates the whole of his artistic creations as he continues in his quest to express the totality of his multi-faceted artistic self. The result has been his unique and sustained experimentations in dramaturgy and narrative, which often simultaneously break through the conventional boundaries of literary, performance, and visual arts.

NOTES

1. This is a revised version of an article with the same title published in *Journal of Asian Pacific Communication*, Vol. 9, No. 1 & 2 (1999), pp. 83–96.
2. Murakami (1987, p. 117) maintains that German idealism is represented by Kant. In Kant's philosophy the concept of human dignity is emphasized and man's inner world achieves realization "by denying all restrictions except his own reason"; reason is defined as the essence of human existence and in an ideal society "each individual aims at the perfection of his self, and in so doing the true equality of society is realized." Murakami observes that a modern democratic society reflects this Kantian view but cannot claim to "attain Kant's ideal society" for it is more likely that while personal rights are claimed, the human dignity of others is easily ignored.
3. Zhao (1999) is a comprehensive and definitive study of Gao Xingjian's achievements as a playwright; and Fong (1999) contains translations of five of Gao's recent plays.
4. Recent exhibitions include a major solo exhibition *Ink Paintings by Gao Xingjian* (Taipei Municipal Gallery, December, 1995), and two exhibitions by Michael Goedhuis, *XIXe Biennale Internationale des Antiquaires* (Carrousel du Louvre, Paris, September–October, 1998) and "Asian Art in London" (London, November, 1998).
5. For example, the publication of Noël and Liliane Dutrait's French version of Gao Xingjian's *Lingshan* received up to full-page reviews in most major newspapers in France.

6.   See also Lee (1998a), pp. 402–404.
7.   See also the discussions in Lee (1982, 1998a).

REFERENCES

Ames, Roger T. (1991). "Nietzsche's 'Will to Power' and Chinese 'Virtuality' (De): A Comparative Study." In Parkes, ed. (1991), pp. 130–150.

Chen, G. (1991). "Zhuang Zi and Nietzsche" Trans. I. Sellman. In Parkes, ed. (1991), pp. 115–129.

Clarke, J. I. (1992). *In Search of Jung: Historical and Philosophical Enquiries.* London: Routledge.

—— (1994). *Jung and Eastern Thought: A Dialogue with the Orient.* London: Routledge.

——, ed. (1995). *Jung on the East.* London: Routledge.

Davis, A. R., and A. D. Stefanowska, eds. (1982). *Austrina: Essays in Commemoration of the 25th Anniversary of the Founding of the Oriental Society of Australia.* Sydney: Oriental Society of Australia.

Figl, J. (1991). "Nietzsche's Early Encounters With Asian Thought." Trans. G. Parkes. In Parkes, ed. (1991), pp. 51–63.

Findeisen, Raoul D., and Robert H. Gassmann, eds. (1998). *Autumn Floods: Essays in Honour of Marián Gálik.* Bern: Peter Lang.

Fong, Gilbert C. F., trans. (1999). *The Other Shore: Plays by Gao Xingjian.* Hong Kong: The Chinese University Press.

Gao Xingjian 高行健 (1990). *Lingshan* 靈山 [Soul mountain]. Taipei: Lianjing chuban shiye gongsi 聯經出版事業公司.

—— (1993). "Guojia shenhua yu geren diankuang" 國家神話與個人癲狂 [The myth of nation and insanity for the individual]. *Mingbao yuekan* 明報月刊 [Ming Pao monthly], No. 8, pp. 114–121.

—— (1995). *Gao Xingjian xiju liuzhong* 高行健戲劇六種 [Six volumes of plays by Gao Xingjian]. Taipei: Dijiao chubanshe 帝教出版社.

—— (1996a). "Bali suibi" 巴黎隨筆 [Jottings from Paris]. In Gao (1996b), pp. 21–28. Original work published in 1990.

—— (1996b). *Meiyou zhuyi* 沒有主義 [Without isms]. Hong Kong: Tiandi tushu youxian gongsi 天地圖書有限公司.

—— (1996c). "Meiyou zhuyi" 沒有主義 [Without isms]. In Gao (1996b), pp. 8–17. Original work published in 1993.

—— (1996d). *Taowang* 逃亡 [Fugitives]. In Gao (1995), pp. 1–68. Original work published in 1990.

—— (1996e). "Zixu" 自序 [Author's preface]. In Gao (1996b), pp. 1–6. Original work published in 1996.

Gao Xingjian and D. Bourgeois (1997). *Au plus prés du réel: Dialogues sur l'écriture (1994–1997)*. Paris: Éditions de l'Aube.

Green, M. (1986). *Mountain of Truth: The Counterculture Begins. Ascona, 1900–1920.* London: University Press of New England.

Jung, Carl G. (1944). *Modern Man in Search of a Soul.* W. S. Dell & C. F. Baynes, trans. London: Kegan Paul, Trench, Trubner.

Lee, Mabel (1982). "Suicide of the Creative Self: The Case of Lu Hsun." In Davis and Stefanowska, eds. (1982), pp. 140–167.

—— (1995). "Without Politics: Gao Xingjian on Literary Creation." *The Stockholm Journal of East Asian Studies*, Vol. 6, pp. 82–101.

—— (1996). "Octavio Paz on Literary Translation and Yang Lian's Poems on Poetry." *Canadian Review of Comparative Literature*, Vol. 23, No. 4, pp. 943–959.

—— (1998a). "Gao Xingjian in Conversation with Two Dead Poets from Shaoxing: Xu Wei and Lu Xun." In Findeisen and Gassmann, eds. (1998), pp. 401–414.

—— (1998b). "Nietzsche Appropriated: Towards Establishing a New Literary Tradition in the May Fourth Period." Paper presented at the International Symposium on Nietzsche and East Asia, 26–29 September 1998, at Sils-Maria (Switzerland), organized by Ostasiatisches Seminar der Unversität Zürich.

Lodén, Torbjörn (1993). "World Literature with Chinese Characteristics: On a novel by Gao Xingjian." *The Stockholm Journal of East Asian Studies*, Vol. 4, pp. 17–39.

Lu Xun 鲁迅 (1980). "Ziti xiaoxiang" 自題小像 [Self portrait]. In Zhou, ed. (1980), p. 24. Original work published in 1903.

—— (1981a). *Lu Xun quanji* 鲁迅全集 [Complete works of Lu Xun]. Beijing: Renmin wenxue chubanshe 人民文學出版社.

—— (1981b). *Yecao* 野草 [Wild grass]. In Lu Xun (1981a), Vol. 2, pp. 159–225.

May, R. (1996). *Heidegger's Hidden Sources: East Asian Influences on His Work.* Trans. G. Parkes. London: Routledge.

Metzger, T. A. (1977). *Escape From Predicament: Neo-Confucianism and China's Evolving Political Culture.* New York: Columbia University Press.

Murakami, Y. (1987). "Conceptions of Equality and Human Nature in Daoism." In Siriwardena, ed. (1987), pp. 114–134.

Nietzsche, F. (1969). *On the Genealogy of Morals* and *Ecce Homo.* Trans. and ed. W. Kaufmann. Toronto: Random House.

Parkes, G., ed. (1991). *Nietzsche and Asian Thought.* Chicago: University of Chicago Press.

Paz, Octavio (1992). "Translation: Literature and Letters." Trans. Irene del Corral.

In Schulte and Biguenet, eds. (1992), pp. 152–162. Original work published in 1971.

Schipper, K. (1995). "The History of Daoist Studies in Europe." In Wilson and Cayley, eds. (1995), pp. 467–491.

Schulte, Rainer, and John Biguenet, eds. (1992). *Theories of Translation: An Anthology of Essays from Dryden to Derrida.* Chicago: University of Chicago Press.

Siriwardena, Reggie, ed. (1987). *Equality and the Religious Traditions of Asia.* London: Frances Pinter.

Wilson, M., and J. Cayley, eds. (1995). *Europe Studies China.* London: Han-Shan Tang Books.

Zhao Yiheng 趙毅恆 (1999). *Jianli yizhong xiandai chanju: Gao Xingjian yu Zhongguo shiyan xiju* 建立一種現代禪劇：高行健與中國實驗戲劇 [Towards a modern Zen theatre: Gao Xingjian and Chinese theatre experimentalism]. Taipei: Erya chubanshe 爾雅出版社.

Zhou Zhenfu 周振甫, ed. (1980). *Lu Xun shige zhu* 魯迅詩歌注 [Lu Xun's poetry with annotations]. Hangzhou: Zhejiang renmin chubanshe 浙江人民出版社.

Drama of Paradox: Waiting as Form and Motif in *The Bus-Stop* and *Waiting for Godot*[1]

The search for a new theatre beyond that represented by the trinity of socialist realism, Ibsenism and Stanislavsky's system, which dominated the contemporary Chinese stage for almost thirty years since the founding of the People's Republic, became the major concern of the new generation of playwrights in China in the 1980s.[2] The experimentation with other forms of expression than the conventional Western realistic theatre has brought about the large-scale introduction of Brechtian and absurdist drama to the Chinese stage since 1979.

Although Brechtian drama was first introduced to the Chinese audiences in the late 1950s for the reason, firstly, that it is a Marxist theatre and, secondly, that it has its source in traditional Chinese theatre, it has never been so consciously considered by both the Chinese playwrights and audiences as an alternative to the Ibsenian theatre in China. When Bertolt Brecht's *Galileo* was staged in Beijing by the Chinese Youth Art Theatre [中國青年藝術劇院 Zhongguo qingnian yishu juyuan] in 1979, it aroused a stir and was hailed as a breakthrough from the stagnant Chinese stage. The performance was originally construed as a debate on the pursuit of truth against blind doctrinism and valued for its political implication, but the real effect of the play lies in its offering a new perspective on the nature of theatre.

INNOVATIONS IN THE NEW THEATRE

From 1979–1981 there were a considerable number of Chinese plays written under the influence of Brechtian drama, the most successful of which is undoubtedly Sha Yexin's 沙葉新 *Jiaru wo shi zhende* 假如我是真的 [The imposter], published in the summer of 1979. The introduction and subsequent imitation of the Brechtian style was not so much the result of a programmed effort in replacing Ibsen by Brecht as a desire to look forward to something new in the theatre. Thus Arthur Miller's *Death of a Salesman* was also staged in Beijing in 1984, while Shakespeare was sinicized on the Shanghai stage several times since 1980. The general trend in Chinese theatre of the 1980s was to break away from doctrines and formulae in playwriting and performance. This breakaway has as much artistic significance as political implication for the playwrights.

Accompanying this breakthrough was the introduction of the Theatre of the Absurd to China. As early as 1978, the Chinese journal *Shijie wenxue* 世界文學 [World literature] published a translation of Harold Pinter's *The Birthday Party* along with Zhu Hong's 朱虹 "Huangdanpai xijü shuping" 荒誕派戲劇述評 [A critical introduction to the Theatre of the Absurd]. Chinese playwrights and readers were thus given an opportunity to know the more recent developments of Western theatre and drama. Two years later, a collection of drama, in Chinese translation, from the contemporary Western avant-garde theatre came out in Shanghai, included in which were such typical plays as *Waiting for Godot*, *Amedee or How to Get Rid of It*, *The Zoo Story*, and *The Dumb Waiter*. Although the process of introducing Chinese readers to the most avant-garde works of the Western theatre was rather slow, it allowed Chinese readers and playwrights time to adjust their way of appreciation which is necessary for a culture in which the prevalent interpretive code remained to be that of nineteenth-century Western realism. In early years of the 1980s, essays introducing Western absurdist dramatists could be found in Chinese journals from time to time.[3]

The first Chinese attempt at an absurdist play was made by Gao Xingjian, a playwright who has a great interest in French literature, in 1983 when his play, *Chezhan* 車站 [The bus-stop], appeared in the literary magazine *Shiyue* 十月. In many respects, Gao Xingjian's *The Bus-Stop* can be considered a Chinese response to Beckett's *Waiting for Godot*. In his book *Xiandai xiaoshuo jiqiao chutan* 現代小説技巧初探 [A preliminary exploration of the techniques of modern fiction], Gao openly shows his admiration of Beckett, especially Beckett's contribution to the contemporary theatre (Gao, 1981, p. 50). It is, however, the absurd social conditions in contemporary China that form the basis of Gao's play, which was an immediate stir to both the Chinese audience and critics for its shocking effect and apparent violation of the traditional style of stage presentation. When the Beijing People's Art Theatre [北京人民藝術劇院 Beijing renmin yishu juyuan] performed it in a small theatre-in-the-round studio to a limited audience, it was obvious that the play was considered mainly as an experiment to be conducted with control to test the theatre-goers' response. The controversy this play aroused, however, was chiefly on its ideological inclination and challenge to the socialist doctrines of literature and art rather than on its artistic achievements and innovations, which are unique among contemporary Chinese plays. The critic He Wen 何聞 blames Gao Xingjian for being pessimistic about Socialism, as well as for his "blind worship" of Beckett (He, 1984, pp. 21– 25). But the more senior theatre historian and critic Qu Liuyi 曲六乙 defended the play for its originality and optimistic views about social reality (Qu, 1984, pp. 29–33). The debate over the social implication of Gao's play has made it one of the most controversial Chinese plays of the 1980s.

VISIONS OF THE ABSURD

Like *Waiting for Godot*, *The Bus-Stop* can be interpreted as a piece of pessimistic writing as well as an optimistic treatment of the belief that there is always hope in waiting. Godot may be allegorized as "little God" or taken as a combined form of the names of the two tramps, Gogo and Didi, thus representing their false hope and imagination in salvation. It is true that in Beckett's play there are a number of philosophical and religious references, which all tend to point to the basic absurdity of the human situation. Yet it is not simply a morality play; nor is it merely an Existentialist play in the vein of Sartre or Camus. It is an absurdist play with its mode of expression characteristic of the abandonment of the rational approach. In this respect, the sociopolitical references in *The Bus-Stop* are not as important as the act of waiting, for what matters is not so much in where and for what the passengers are waiting as in the fact that they are waiting. If in *Waiting for Godot* what counts is not Godot but the subject of waiting and the hope, frustration and anxiety thus caused, then in *The Bus-Stop* the bus or the bus company is only of secondary importance. Actually, the uniqueness of both plays lie in their treatment of the subject of waiting, that is, how the devices in structure, characterization and language are used to present the motif of waiting. A major and easily noticed technique employed in *Waiting for Godot* is the device of contrast and paradox, which is also successfully used in the Gao's play, *The Bus-Stop*. The technique of contrast and theme of paradox fully used and developed in the two plays include the freedom of choice but with no alternative, expectation for change and unchangeability, the waiting and the drifting, and the absurdly rapid flight of time and the sense of indivision of time. These technical as well as thematic devices have all become the basis for presenting the absurdist motifs of waiting, boredom, time passing, anxiety, and anguish in the two plays.

The playwright Gao Xingjian calls *The Bus-Stop* "a lyrical comedy of life with no division of acts and scenes." Although there is no physical division of scenes in the play, there are actually six repetitive episodes with the coming and going of the bus or the sound of the bus as division, in which nothing happens. It makes more sense to say that it is the situation of waiting and hope deferred in *Waiting for Godot*, as well as in *The Bus-Stop*, that give both plays a circular structure with the end repeating the beginning. At the end of both Act I and Act II, the two tramps Estragon and Vladimir in Beckett's play say that they will go, but in fact they stay and continue to wait. In the Chinese play, all the seven characters also remain at the bus-stop though they say that they will go. Besides the contradiction between what the characters say and what they do, which is a comic and absurdist device, there is also the suggestion that the characters have no choice except for staying on.

Nothing is more frustrating to the characters in both plays than the fact that they are presented without any alternative except continuing to wait. Estragon and Vladimir say that they are tied to the situation and the only alternative they have is to attempt suicide. Thus Estragon and Vladimir have to think of some way to end their lives as an alternative to the Existentialist frustration of waiting:

> Vladimir: ... What do we do now?
> Estragon: Wait.
> Vladimir: Yes, but while waiting.
> Estragon: What about hanging ourselves?
> Estragon: Let's hang ourselves immediately!
> Vladimir: From a bough? (*They go towards the tree.*) I wouldn't trust it.
> Estragon: We can always try.
> Vladimir: Go ahead.

Estragon: After you.

Vladimir: No, no, you first.

Estragon: Why me?

Vladimir: You're lighter than I am.

Estragon: Just so!

Vladimir: I don't understand.

Estragon: Use your intelligence, can't you?

Vladimir uses his intelligence.

Vladimir: (*finally*). I remain in the dark.

Estragon: This is how it is. (*He reflects.*) The bough ... the bough ... (*Angrily*).
　　Use your head, can't you?

Vladimir: You're my only hope.

Estragon:(*with effort*). Gogo light — bough not break — Gogo dead. Didi
　　heavy — bough break — Didi alone. Whereas —

Vladimir: I hadn't thought of that.

Estragon: If it hangs you it'll hang anything.

Vladimir: But am I heavier than you?

Estragon: So you tell me. I don't know. There's an even chance. Or nearly.

Vladimir: Well? What do we do?

Estragon: Don't let's do anything. It's safer.

Vladimir: Let's wait and see what he says.

Estragon: Who?

Vladimir: Godot.

Estragon: Good idea.　　　　　　　　　　　(Beckett, 1975, pp. 17–18)

The only hope the two tramps have in life is to wait for Godot and
see what he will say about their situation. Hence, at the beginning of
the play the two tramps are full of the hope that they will be saved
and do not expect to do anything themselves. When they talk about
suicide, they take it as a funny thing. On the one hand, they want Godot
to come and change their situation. On the other hand, they fear that
if they try to make the change themselves, the worse may happen to
them. Estragon therefore says that it is safer not to do anything. But
in Act II, after so much distress and anxiety, they begin to consider
suicide seriously and decide to hang themselves again. This time they
also fail as they have not even got a rope strong enough to hang either
one of them. But how about the next day? Vladimir says, "We'll hang
ourselves tomorrow. (*Pause.*) Unless Godot comes" (Beckett, 1975,
p. 94). This remark serves as a conclusion to their situation: either they
keep on waiting for Godot or they keep on trying to hang themselves.

But what has happened previously in the play suggests that neither will come true. What is more despairing is the fact that they cannot even kill themselves and in this way they have lost the only alternative to waiting.

Actually all the while the two tramps are waiting for Godot, they try to do something constructive or meaningful, which they expect will change their situation while they are waiting. Only that whatever they do will amount to nothing:

> Vladimir: Nothing you can do about it.
> Estragon: No use struggling.
> Vladimir: One is what one is.
> Estragon: No use wriggling.
> Vladimir: The essential doesn't change.
> Estragon: Nothing to be done.   (Beckett, 1975, p. 21)

The most distressing thing for the two tramps is fully expressed here that whatever they do will not change the essence of their situation. Since they cannot change their situation by their own effort, they expect and have to rely on something from the external to save them.

As in *Waiting for Godot*, the characters in *The Bus-Stop* are tormented between the proper wish of achieving something through waiting and the Existentialist frustration of having nothing done. The play begins with an allegorical stage direction:

> In the middle of the stage is a bus-stop sign. The words on the sign have become illegible due to long exposure to the natural erosion of weather. Next to the bus-stop sign are two rows of iron railings for people to line up. The railings are arranged in such a way that they form the shape of a cross of different lengths, which is symbolic of a crossroads, an intersection, or a stop in the lives of various people.   (Gao, 1983, p. 119)

Like the barren willow tree, which is a sign of the place of appointment, in *Waiting for Godot*, the bus-stop sign in Gao's *The Bus-Stop* serves as a link between the characters and the bus, as well as a device linking up all of them in a situation that will not lead to anywhere. But the implication of both plays does not lie in the tree or in the bus-stop sign. Neither does it lie in Godot, nor in the bus. The message is in the characters themselves and in their very act of waiting.

SOCIAL ABSURDITIES IN CHINA

Right at the beginning of *The Bus-Stop*, the Old Man complains about the absurdity of life:

> Do you smoke? (*The Silent Man shakes his head.*) It is a good thing not to smoke. Actually it is impossible to get good cigarettes anyway, not to mention that smoking is a money-causing way to get bronchitis. When people hear that the "Great Front Gate" is available, they will all flock to buy it and the line will be so long that it winds round the street corner several times. One person is allowed to buy only two packs. When your turn comes, the sales person may leave the counter without even glancing at you. If you ask why, there will not be any answer. Is this what is called "Serve the People?" It is only lip-service. The "Great Front Gate" has already silently slipped away through the back door! This is like waiting for a bus. Are you not waiting for the bus in an orderly way? But someone may just have to run a little bit further ahead and wave to the driver, then the front door will open for him. He must be a "man of connections," gee, always this trick. When you reach the front door, it will close with a bang. If this is called "Serve the Passengers," won't you open your eyes wide? Everybody knows this, but none can change it.   (Gao, 1983, p. 120)

The Old Man's complaint sets the play against the backdrop of a society, which is so chaotic and unreasonable that whatever happens in it has gone far beyond rational human thinking. The cigarette brand "Great Front Gate" provides an ironic image to contrast with such an absurd social phenomenon as "Backdoorism" in China in the 1980s. Similar to the "Great Front Gate" in its effect of irony and absurdity is the slogan "Serve the People," which has turned to its opposite and is totally beyond the Old Man's comprehension. The failure of the Socialist ideal, which bears a moral and politically "religious" message and has had an impact in China no less strong than that of Christianity in the West, can be seen in the light of the human condition in an absurd world described by Ionesco: "Absurd is that which is devoid of purpose.... Cut off from his religious, metaphysical, and transcendental roots, man is lost; all his actions become senseless, absurd, and useless" (Ionesco, 1957). The Old Man's feeling of being lost in a strange world is actually a result of this *crisis of belief* and his alienation from a world which is within his comprehension, as Camus puts it:

A world that can be explained by reasoning, however faulty, is a familiar
world. But in a universe that is suddenly deprived of illusions and of light,
man feels a stranger. His is an irremediable exile, because he is deprived
of memories of a lost homeland as much as he lacks the hope of a promised land to come. This divorce between man and his life, the actor and
his setting, truly constitutes the feeling of Absurdity.

                                                          (Camus, 1942, p. 18)

At the metaphorical level, both *Waiting for Godot* and *The Bus-Stop* can
be considered modern morality plays, referring subtly to social and religious absurdities. G. S. Fraser considers the message of *Waiting for Godot*
as something nearer a message of religious consolation (Fraser, 1975,
p. 62). References to the Christian faith are obvious in the play, but the
play does not simply pose a question of the validity of religion, for it has
generalized the situation of waiting to cover all aspects of the human
condition of hope and hope deferred in waiting. Similarly, *The Bus-Stop*
is not merely about the chaotic and absurd social conditions in China in
the 1980s. It brings forth to the audience the question of waiting and its
senselessness, for as in *Waiting for Godot* the image of waiting is given a
generalized and philosophical significance. Hence, in *The Bus-Stop* the
actor, who plays the double role as Director Ma and later as a detached
observer, gives a "meta-comment" on the situation of waiting:

> Sometimes we really need to wait. Haven't you had the experience of queu-
> ing in a line to buy fish? Oh, suppose you don't cook! How about waiting
> in a line for a bus? Queuing is waiting. Even if you have queued for half a
> day, what is for sale is not hairtail, but washing boards — fine washing
> boards which do not damage clothes, and you've already got a washing
> machine, then you have wasted half a day queuing for nothing. There is
> no way you don't get angry. Hence, what matters is not waiting, but that
> you must make sure what you've been waiting for is what you want. Other-
> wise you're just making a fool of yourself if you waste half or even the
> whole of your life waiting for nothing.   (Gao, 1983, p. 137)

The Existentialist dimension of the theme of waiting in *The Bus-Stop*
is explicitly stated in the comment made by the actor, who plays the
carpenter, in response to the above comment: "... I don't mind waiting.
When someone is waiting, it means that he has a hope. It will be really
bad if one doesn't even have a hope.... To borrow the words of the

bespectacled young man [Glasses], this is called hopelessness" (Gao, 1983, p. 137). This is reminiscent of the remark made by Vladimir: "Hope deferred maketh the something sick" (Beckett, 1975, p. 10).

To the characters in the play, the purpose of waiting sheds much light on the meaning of life, which is metaphorically presented as a process of waiting. They ask such questions as those in the following:

> Mother: What chaos.
> Glasses: Ah, life.
> Girl: Do you call this living?
> Glasses: Sure it is. Despite everything we are still alive.
> Girl: We might as well be dead.
> Glasses: Why don't you end it all, then?
> Girl: Because it seems like such a waste to come to this world and then get nothing out of life.
> Glasses: There should be some meaning to life.
> Girl:To live on like this, not really alive and not dead either — it's so boring!
> (Gao, 1983, p. 133)

It is exactly the same kind of boredom as that experienced by the two tramps in *Waiting for Godot* or Rosancrantz and Guildenstern in *Rosancrantz and Guildenstern Are Dead*. In *The Bus-Stop*, Glasses says, "We can't wait any longer; it's useless to keep on waiting. This is meaningless torture" (Gao, 1983, p. 129). While the two tramps in *Waiting for Godot* look upon suicide as an alternative to waiting and try but fail to commit suicide, the passengers in *The Bus-Stop* think that it is a waste not to get anything out of life. However, the characters in both plays recognize the fact that it is boring to live on, waiting for something that will change their situation or fate to happen.

Like what Rosancrantz and Guildenstern do in the play *Rosancrantz and Guildenstern Are Dead*, the characters in *The Bus-Stop* also think that life is as absurd as flicking a coin and there is no logical and sensible way to predict the result. They, however, believe that since life or fate is absurd, it should be dealt with in an absurd way when they finally resort to the flicking of a coin to determine whether they should continue to wait or to go:

> Glasses: You can think of life as a coin. (*Takes a coin out of his pocket.*) Do you believe in this? (*He flicks the coin in the air and then catches it.*) Head

or tail? *Pig, book, desk, dog,* that's decided! *Are you teachers? No, Are you pigs?* No, I'm none of those. *Am I?* I am who I am. You don't believe in yourself, but you do believe in this? (*Self-mockingly he flicks the coin again and catches it.*)

Girl: What do you think we should do? I don't even have the strength to make a decision.

Glasses: Let's gamble with Fate: heads we wait, tails we go. It all depends on the *coin* — (*He flicks the coin into the air. It falls to the ground and Glasses covers it over with the palm of his hand.*) Do we stay or do we go? Stay or go? Let's see what Fate has decreed.

(Gao, 1983, pp. 129–30)

The resolution to flicking a coin in order to determine whether or not to stay stands for not only the characters' loss of confidence in approaching problems in life in a rational way, but also their submission to Fate and the absurdity of life. In this sense, the Existentialist theme of waiting is explored in *The Bus-Stop*, as well as in *Waiting for Godot*, though treated in different situations.

Martin Esslin defines the Theatre of the Absurd as an expression of the "sense of the senselessness of the human condition and the inadequacy of the rational approach by the open abandonment of rational devices and discursive thought.... The Theatre of the Absurd has renounced arguing *about* the absurdity of the human condition; it merely *presents* it in being — that is, in terms of concrete stage images" (Esslin, 1977, p. 24). In this respect, *The Bus-Stop* is in line with the main tradition of the Theatre of the Absurd, although in the play there are arguments here and there about the absurdities of life and the passengers try many times to seek a rational explanation for such absurdities, as the purpose of using "rational devices and discursive thought" in the play is to show the inadequacy of them and the impossibility of reaching a conclusion by the rational approach. That is why the Old Man says, "What logic is this? (*Coughs*) Making passengers stand around waiting till their hair turns grey? ... (*Suddenly becoming decrepit.*) Absurd ... too absurd ..." (Gao, 1983, p. 131).

The act of waiting in *The Bus-Stop* is only a metaphor of life in China. There is nothing absurdist or Existentialist in the act of waiting itself, but once the act of waiting is turned into a metaphor of life and the question of the meaning of life is asked but not answered, then the act of waiting is no longer simply a matter of waiting for the bus, for it has become life itself, in which there is hope which is never realized but always promised. It is absurd to waste one's life waiting for something that has posed itself as a promise of change to the passengers, but at the same time there is always the promise, which is symbolically represented by the sound of the bus approaching from all directions at the end of the play. It is the same situation of dealing with the effects of hope in waiting and hope deferred upon the characters as in *Waiting for Godot* that is explored in *The Bus-Stop*.

TIME AS PSYCHOLOGICAL DIMENSION

Related to the theme of waiting is the flight of time, which is used both as a theme and as a dramatic device to intensify the anxiety of waiting in the two plays. Time is one of the most significant elements in the two plays as it links the act of waiting with the value of life and how the time during the waiting should be spent. In *A Preliminary Exploration of the Techniques of Modern Fiction*, Gao Xingjian calls for a representation of time as a psychological dimension in characterization. The characters' lamentation upon the absurd flight of time not only shows their metaphysical anguish, but also provides one of the major comparative aspects of *Waiting for Godot* and *The Bus-Stop*. The rapid passage of time is contrasted with the age-old lamentation of the short span of human life. The paradox of how significance can be achieved in a seemingly insignificant life becomes one of the central questions in both plays, in which the flight of time serves not only as a technique of contrast, but also to provide a thematic dilemma. As Martin Esslin says,

> The subject of the play [*Waiting for Godot*] is not Godot but waiting, the act of waiting as an essential and characteristic aspect of the human condition. Throughout our lives we always wait for something, and Godot simply represents the objective of our waiting — an event, a thing, a person, death. Moreover, it is in the act of waiting that we experience the flow of *time* in its purest, most evident form. If we are active, we tend to forget the passage of time, we *pass* the time, but if we are merely passively waiting, we are confronted with the action of time itself. (Esslin, 1977, p. 49)

While the two tramps in *Waiting for Godot* are not sure how long they have been waiting for Godot and how much longer they still have to wait for him to come, the passengers in *The Bus-Stop* are becoming more and more confused about the passage of time and less and less sure how long they have been waiting. Yet, to the characters in both plays, the most contradictory thing is that, on the one hand, they want the time to pass rapidly so that they do not have to invent ways to kill time, but on the other, they lament over the fact that time passes so rapidly that they grow old and also that they have wasted their time in waiting. Estragon says that the visit of Pozzo helps pass the time (Beckett, 1973, p. 49), but Vladimir thinks that the passage of time makes them grow old (Beckett, 1973, p. 91). The passengers in *The Bus-Stop* are tormented by the absurdly rapid flight of time, which is even more unbearable when it is given the "illusion of value" (Robinson, 1969, p. 246):

> Glasses: (*Looks at his watch. Shocked.*) I don't believe it.
> (*The Girl goes over to look at his watch. They count the numbers indicated on the
>   face of the watch in time with music.*)
> Glasses: (*Continuously pressing the indicator button on his digital watch*) Five,
>   six, seven, eight, nine, ten, eleven, twelve, thirteen months ....
> Girl: ... One month, two months, three months, four months.
> Glasses: ... Five months, six months, seven months, eight months.
> Girl: ... One year and eight months altogether.
> Glasses: Another year has just gone by.
> Girl: That makes it two years and eight months.
> Glasses: Two years and eight months, ... No, it's three years and eight
>   months. No, I'm wrong — five years and six months.... Seven, eight,
>   nine, ten months.
> (*They all look at each other in amazement.*)
> Lout: This is crazy.
> Glasses: I am sane!
> Lout: Wasn't talkin' about you. I said this watch's had a nervous breakdown!
> Glasses: Mechanical devices don't have nerves. A watch is a device for
>   measuring time, which is not affected by the psychological state of
>   man.   (Gao, 1983, p. 131)

Although Glasses affirms that time is not affected by the psychological state of man, the audience will wonder whether it is time that passes so rapidly or it is the anxiety of waiting that gives the passengers the feeling. Both are possible. The absurdly rapid passage of time in *The Bus-Stop* is reminiscent of the sudden growing of leaves on the previously barren tree in *Waiting for Godot*. In this respect, *The Bus-Stop* is even more explicit in its absurdist treatment of time than *Waiting for Godot*, in which the two tramps only feel the confusing indivision of time and circular repetition of events but do not take the fast growth of leaves on the tree as a sign of time passing, which is objective and indifferent to their anguish. In *Waiting for Godot*, time passes but is at first not consciously noticed and seriously taken by the two tramps. The waiting thus seems an endlessly long process, in which what counts is boredom. Yet, in *The Bus-Stop* the rapid passage of time is contrasted with the passengers' sudden awakening that they have already grown old, thus producing a strong sense of anxiety and futility of action.

Actually the anxiety, boredom, and the absurd flight of time in both plays are presented in a framework, which is based on a dramatic structure of circular repetition. Commenting on the structure of *Waiting for Godot*, Michael Robinson says:

> Nothing ends in this infinity which is composed of an infinite number of periods of finite time for ever repeating themselves. This is demonstrated by the principle of renewal in the conventions of drama, and in the structure and dialogue of *Godot* itself. The second act repeats the first: both open with the tramps coming together again after the night, end with their motionless withdrawal, and are punctuated, in the middle, by Pozzo and Lucky on their journey.   (Robinson, 1969, p. 247)

The Bus-Stop is structured on the same principle with six episodes, each being a repetition of the previous one, with the bus coming and going but not stopping for the passengers. As Martin Esslin points out: "What passes in these plays are not *events* with a definite beginning and a definite end, but types of *situations* that will forever repeat themselves" (Esslin, 1977, p. 75). In each of these episodes, the passengers' patience is stretched to its limit until finally all of them feel frustrated and angry. Like the two tramps in *Waiting for Godot*, the passengers in *The Bus-Stop* do not move, though they have said several times that they will go. This pattern of circular repetition provides the dramatic foundation for the belief that life is cyclical and essentially unchanging, as Vladimir remarks, "The essential doesn't change" (Beckett, 1975, p. 21). The essential here refers, of course, to the essence of the characters' predicament rather than to the objective passage of time and the growth of the tree in *Waiting for Godot*, which signifies that "something is still taking its course in time" (Robinson, 1969, p. 247). The effect of time passing is noted by Vladimir:

All I know is that the hours are long, under these conditions, and constrain us to beguile them with proceedings which — how shall I say — which may at first sight seem reasonable, until they become a habit. You may say it is to prevent our reason from foundering. No doubt. But has it not long been straying in the night without end of the abyssal depths?

(Beckett, 1975, p. 80)

The most awful thing for the more philosophical Vladimir is that time passes without bringing about any change in their life or predicament but making life a habit, which is "a great deadener" (Beckett, 1975, p. 91). At the intellectual level, there is of course change in the two tramps, for they finally understand that there is no way to rationalize the world they live in. This kind of change can never be found in the wandering pair, Pozzo and Lucky, as they change only in appearance. However, to Pozzo and Lucky, who wander and change in their appearance, time passing is equally awful, as Pozzo remarks,

Have you not done tormenting me with your accursed time! It's abominable! When! When! One day, is that not enough for you, one day like any other day, one day he went dumb, one day I went blind, one day we'll go deaf, one day we were born, one day we shall die, the same day, the same second, is that not enough for you? (*Calmer.*) They give birth astride of a grave, the light gleams in an instant, then it's night once more.

(Beckett, 1975, p. 89)

In contrast to the two tramps, who note that it is safer not to do anything at the beginning of the play (Beckett, 1975, p. 18), Pozzo and Lucky are changing, though superficially, from bad to worse. And to the latter pair, time passing only signifies the worsening of their situation.

The change in the outside world as well as in other people technically provides a contrast to the stagnant situation of the two tramps in *Waiting for Godot* and the passengers in *The Bus-Stop*. This contrast reminds them of two things: time passing and change in the outside world; and time passing but no change in themselves. It is the Hegelian concept that time is measured by the change in the objective world that confuses the characters in both plays as they do not see any change in themselves. Thus Estragon says in *Waiting for Godot*, "Very likely. They all change. Only we can't" (Beckett, 1975, p. 48). And Glasses notes in *The Bus-Stop*, "You don't know what pain is — that's why you're so indifferent. We've been cast aside by life, forgotten. The world is fleeting by in front of you and you don't even notice it. Do you understand? You don't" (Gao, 1983, p. 136). Martin Esslin's comment on *Waiting for Godot* is also applicable to *The Bus-Stop:* "Waiting is to experience the action of time, which is constant change. And yet, as nothing really ever happens, that change is in itself an illusion. The ceaseless activity of time is self-defeating, purposeless, and therefore null and void" (Esslin, 1977, p. 51). But the longer they keep on waiting, the less they feel about the change of time and the more they are confused about the passage of time. In *Waiting for Godot,* the two tramps finally have lost the sense of time and date:

> Estragon: (*Very insidious*). But what Saturday? And is it Saturday? Is it not rather Sunday? (*Pause.*) Or Monday? (*Pause.*) Or Friday?
> Vladimir: (*Looking wildly about him, as though the date was inscribed in the landscape*). It's not possible!
> Estragon: Or Thursday?   (Beckett, 1975, p. 15)

In *The Bus-stop,* however, the characters are too much confused by the long time they have been waiting for the bus that they do not know exactly when they began waiting there. When they talk about whether the bus-stop has been cancelled, they argue about the date as the two tramps do in *Waiting for Godot:*

> Mother: What? This bus-stop has been cancelled? But last Saturday I was still....
> Girl: Which last Saturday?
> Mother: That Saturday before the last, or that before ... before ... before ....
> Glasses: The Saturday of which month and which year are you talking about? (*Looking very closely at his watch.*)   (Gao, 1983, pp. 136–37)

In this respect, both plays can be viewed as a portrayal of the effects of waiting on human psychology and the causes of frustrations, anxiety, confusion, and anguish. The sense of nothingness and forever-repetition is so strong in both plays and that this sense of timelessness is reinforced by the loss of the consciousness of time and date in the characters. To the characters in both plays, what can be sure of are the events in the present. The endlessness of waiting "reduces everything in time to the same level of significance — insignificance" (Robinson, 1969, p. 249).

HOPE AS A TRAP

While the characters' expectation for change is contrasted with the unchangeability of their situation, the waiting is juxtaposed with the drifting. In *Waiting for Godot*, the intrusion of the drifting pair Pozzo and Lucky, unfortunately, does not bring about any change to the two tramps, but serves technically as a contrast to them. This contrast is skillfully used by Beckett as a device to intensify the effect of monotony in waiting. While Estragon and Vladimir wait, Pozzo and Lucky wander and seek for change, but Pozzo and Lucky are no better than Estragon and Vladimir. For Estragon and Vladimir, nothing changes; for Pozzo and Lucky, their change is from bad to worse. But this change is already an envy to Estragon and Vladimir, who are like audiences of a drama performed by Pozzo and Lucky but expect to participate in the performance:

> Vladimir: How they've changed!
> Estragon: Who?
> Vladimir: Those two.
> Estragon: That's the idea, let's make a little conversation.
> Vladimir: Haven't they?
> Estragon: What?
> Vladimir: Changed.
> Estragon: Very likely. They all change. Only we can't.
>
> (Beckett, 1975, p 48)

In Act II when Pozzo and Lucky return, Estragon and Vladimir also hope for change. They begin to ask for something "tangible" (Beckett, 1975, p.79) and think that what they did in the past was just to kill time in the expectation that Godot would come soon. Now the change in Pozzo and Lucky is so tempting that they do not want to waste their time any more:

> Vladimir: Let us not waste our time in idle discourse! (*Pause. Vehemently.*) Let us do something, while we have the chance! It is not everyday that we are needed. Not indeed that we personally are needed. Others would meet the case equally well, if not better. To all mankind they were addressed, those cries for help still ringing in our ears! But at this place, at this moment of time, all mankind is us, whether we like it or not. Let us make the most of it, before it is too late! Let us represent worthily for once the foul brood to which a cruel fate consigned us! What do you say? (*Estragon says nothing.*) It is true that when with

folded arms we weigh the pros and cons we are no less a credit to our species. The tiger bounds to the help of his congeners without the least reflection, or else he slinks away into the depths of the thickets. But that is not the question. And we are blessed in this, that we happen to know the answer. Yes, in this immense confusion one thing alone is clear. We are waiting for Godot to come —

(Beckett, 1975, pp. 79–80)

It is obvious that the two tramps are confused and are full of contradictory thoughts in their mind. The most fearful thing in their waiting, however, is the sense of boredom and lack of direction, as Vladimir laments:

We wait. We are bored. (*He throws up his hand.*) No, don't protest, we are bored to death, there's no denying it. Good. A diversion comes along and what do we do? We let it go to waste. Come, let's get to work! (*He advances towards the heap, stops in his stride.*) In an instant all will vanish and we'll be alone once more, in the midst of nothingness.   (Beckett, 1975, p. 81)

Almost at the end of the play after the two tramps have tried every possible means to change their situation and done something to remind themselves of their existence and value, Vladimir comes to an understanding of their situation and the ineffectuality of individual struggle:

All I know is that the hours are long, under these conditions, and constrain us to beguile them with proceedings which — how shall I say — which may at first sight seem reasonable, until they become a habit. You may say it is to prevent our reason from foundering. No doubt. But has it not long been straying in the night without end of the abyssal depths? That's what I sometimes wonder.   (Beckett, 1975, p. 80)

This understanding of their situation is not necessarily a good thing to Vladimir as he says, "What is terrible is to *have* thought" (Beckett, 1975, p. 64). What can the two tramps do if they even cannot end their boredom by killing themselves? The act of waiting is an absurd combination of doing something and doing nothing. For the more contemplative Vladimir, this is even more distressing as he cannot find any rational explanation in the combination. At any rate, they have to do something in order to pass the time. It does not matter whether what they do is meaningful or meaningless, for it will finally amount to nothing. Vladimir's final comments on the horror of having thought and the contrast between the change in Pozzo and Lucky and their unchangeability, as well as their idling away the time, technically serve to intensify the dramatic irony that whatever change in the objective external world may not necessarily cause any change in them and that Godot may only be a false hope for change.

DILEMMA AND AMBIGUITIES

The technique of ironic contrast by using a foil is also employed in the Chinese play *The Bus-Stop,* in which the Silent Man, who wanders and has the same function of contrast as that of Pozzo and Lucky, at first stands with the group waiting for the bus but later departs and continues his own journey without the notice of any of the passengers. Portrayed as a mysterious figure of wanderlust and quest, the Silent Man is a character-type based on the lonely traveller in Lu Xun's one-scene play, *The Passer-by,* written in 1925, whose reappearance in a play in 1983 symbolizes the motif that the quest is an endless process, which can be allegorically equated with "the journey and struggle of the Chinese people for a more hopeful albeit uncertain future" (Barmé, 1983b, p. 374). Although the Silent Man's departure can be interpreted as a constructive and positive action as some critics do, the endlessness of his quest also gives the audience a strong sense of uncertainty. Thematically the Silent Man is an ambiguous figure whose quest, like the drifting of Pozzo and Lucky, may not necessarily be a better alternative than waiting and not doing anything, as Glasses remarks:

> What if the bus comes after we leave? (*Faces the audience and continues as if thinking out aloud.*) And if it comes but fails to stop again? Looking at the problem rationally, I know I should start walking; it's just that I'm not one hundred percent sure. What's stopping me is the nagging suspicion that it'll come. I must make a plan! *Desk, dog, pig, book,* should I stay or go? It's the enigma of our existence. Perhaps Fate has decreed that we must wait here forever, till we grow old and die. But why do people accept the capricious rulings of Fate? Then again, what exactly is Fate? (*Addressing the Girl.*) Do you believe in Fate?   (Gao, 1983, p. 129)

This speech by Glasses is so far the most illuminating of the paradoxical situation in which the characters are involved and very Existentialist in perspective, which renders invalid all interpretations of the passengers' waiting as negative and of the Silent Man's quest as positive, particularly when it is taken into consideration that the Silent Man has already travelled a long way and for many years, but this time he also tries to wait before he makes up his mind "to go in great strides without looking back, with the accompaniment of light music to express his pain but stubbornness in the quest" (Gao, 1983, p. 125). Actually, most of the drama at the bus-stop occurs after the Silent Man has departed and, therefore, the contrast between the Silent Man and the other passengers is not so much a difference between the "positive" and the "negative" ways to go to the city as one between questing and waiting, either one of which may not be less painful and frustrating than the other. In the dramatic context of *The Bus-Stop*, the Silent Man is presented mainly as a foil to the group of passengers and thus has as much technical as its thematic significance.[4] In contrast to the mysterious Silent Man, the babbling Director Ma is also a foil who serves the technical purpose of intensifying the failure of the rational approach to their problems, social and metaphysical. In this sense, his effort to explain rationally the absurdity of Socialism provides an ironic contrast to the long speech of complaint made by the Old Man at the beginning of the play.

As is true in *Waiting for Godot*, what is conveyed in Gao's *The Bus-Stop* is not its social reference but its dramatic form (Williams, 1978, p. 345). The play can be allegorized at many levels, thus yielding various, even contradictory, interpretations. As a drama, what is more important is not its reference to the social reality in China, but its use of dramatic devices that deviate from the main current of modern Chinese drama. If *Waiting for Godot* can be considered as a play with an Existentialist situation presented in an absurdist dramatic form, then *The Bus-Stop* is a Chinese experiment with an allegorical social situation, which on the surface seems to be presented in a realistic mode of the commonly-seen scene of a group of passengers waiting for the bus, but is actually presented in a symbolic way, signifying the whole drama of the socialist promise of a utopian society, and in a dramatic form which questions the validity of rational thinking and defies the tradition of realism. Like *Waiting for Godot*, *The Bus-Stop* is undramatic, but theatrical.

The Bus-Stop is purposely written to question the validity of rational thinking and the tradition of dramatic realism by beginning with a realistic scene and rational dialogue and moving gradually toward a greater degree of philosophical absurdity in its mode of presentation. In terms of form, the play has a mixture of both realistic and absurdist elements, which are juxtaposed against each other, but its ending emphasizes the absurdity of the realistic and rational approach to life. Hence, in the play absurdism presents itself only gradually as a replacement of realism. Perhaps, this is the reason why some Western readers consider the play mainly as a realistic one, while the Chinese critics who are used to the realistic tradition regard it as an absurdist play.

LANGUAGE AS EXISTENCE

The sense of absurdity is also expressed in the peculiar form of dialogue employed in the two plays. Martin Esslin points out that most plays of the Theatre of the Absurd present the authors' "intuition of the human condition by a method that is essentially polyphonic; they confront their audience with an organized structure of statements and images that interpenetrate each other and that must be apprehended in their totality, rather like the different themes in a symphony, which gain meaning by their simultaneous interaction" (Esslin, 1977, p. 51). This can be seen in the language of the two plays. The sense of absurdity and insignificance of life can be found in the tramps' invention of various kinds of games with words and engaging themselves in artificial conversation:

> Vladimir: Ceremonious ape!
> Estragon: Punctilious pig!
> Vladimir: Finish your phrase, I tell you!
> Estragon: Finish your own
> *Silence. They draw closer, halt.*
> Vladimir: Moron!
> Estragon: That's the idea, let's abuse each other.
> *They turn, move apart, turn again and face each other.*
> Vladimir: Moron!
> Estragon: Vermin!
> Vladimir: Abortion!
> Estragon: Morpion!
> Vladimir: Sewer-rat!
> Estragon: Curate!
> Vladimir: Cretin!

Estragon: (*With finality*). Crritic!
Vladimir: Oh!
He wilts, vanguished, and turns away.
Estragon: Now let's make it up.
Vladimir: Gogo!
Estragon: Didi!
Vladimir: Your hand!
Estragon: Take it!
Vladimir: Come to my arms!
Estragon: Your arms?
Vladimir: My breast!
Estragon: Off we go!
They embrace. They separate. Silence.
Vladimir: How time flies when one has fun!   (Beckett, 1975, pp. 75–76)

The purpose of this artificial conversation is twofold. First, it gives them fun. Second, it gives them the impression that they exist: "They speak, therefore they are." Director Ma and the Old Man in *The Bus-Stop* also make similar comments on what they do in life:

Dir. Ma: (*Turns to the Old Man balefully.*) I'm telling you it's not worth it, old man. Why not grow old in the peace and calm of your home. All this playing of the lute, chess, calligraphy and painting is for whiling away the hours at home. Why do you have to go into the city to find yourself a partner anyway? Is it worth throwing your last years away here on the road?

Old Man: What would you know about it? All you can think of is your infernal wheeling and dealing. The whole point of chess is the feeling of exhilaration you get from it; it's all a matter of the spirit of the thing. The spirit of the thing, that's what life's all about.

(Gao, 1983, pp. 131–132)

For the Old Man, the meaning of his life is equivalent to the significance of a game of chess in that both are as meaningful as they are trivial. Yet, no matter how insignificant the game of chess is, it gives the Old Man a point of reference in life as well as a sense of his own existence. The Old Man's going to the city for a game of chess is thus no less important than the Girl's going to the city to meet her boyfriend, for the game of chess has been inflated to signify the purpose of his life. On the other hand, it is no more important than Vladimir's and Estragon's game with words for they have the same purpose of giving significance to an insignificant life. Though the characters in *The Bus-Stop* accuse each other of going to the city for nothing great and significant, they all think in their own ways that their purposes of going to the city are great and significant enough for them to spend years and years waiting on the road. In this way the two tramps' imitating a manikin, squirming like an aesthete, playing at Lucky and Pozzo, permuting their hats, doing exercises, examining their boots, or trying to kill themselves can be considered equivalents of the different life pursuits of the characters in *The Bus-Stop*. Besides showing that there is no absolute standard to measure the significance of things, the play is also an allegory of the meaninglessness of life, in which all the seven characters as a whole serve to symbolize different stages of man's life rendered meaningless, irrespective of their difference in sex. It is in this allegorical nature of the seven characters that the greatest metaphysical anguish of life lies.

Absurdism is further reinforced by the incongruity and contradiction between dialogue and action in *The Bus-Stop*. Toward the end of the play, the characters all talk together at the same time in a disjointed way. The scene is reminiscent of that in a mental hospital with all the lunatics speaking together, each talking about his or her own things. Yet, what they say and the style in which they speak are related to the theme of the play. In his "Playwright's Suggestions for the Performance of *The Bus-Stop*," Gao points out that "the speech of the characters is at times clear and direct, while at other times it is vague and purposely inept, or uttered merely for the sake of speaking, just as the act of endlessly waiting for the bus gradually makes the characters forget the reasons and meaning for doing so" (Gao, 1983, p. 138). This technique of babbling, multiple soliloquy and mismatched conversation is for the first time used in a contemporary Chinese play. In his book, *A Preliminary Exploration of the Techniques of Modern Fiction,* Gao Xingjian points out that a common technique in modern literature is the use of a fool or a mentally sick person to tell a profound truth. It is probably the inspiration of Lu Xun's story, "Kuangren riji" 狂人日記 [Diary of a madman] in which the author conveys his message of social criticism through the seemingly insane words of a madman, that Gao Xingjian has learned to use this technique in his play.

The device of multiple soliloquy, polyphonic dialogue and mismatched conversation resembling that of lunatics reinforces the sense of absurdism and loneliness in the play *The Bus-Stop,* for although the passengers gather together at a bus-stop and can be seen as a group sharing a common goal of expecting the bus, they are in fact separate. Each of them is a loner in the world, entertaining his or her own hope and pursuing his or her own goal in life, the nature of which is so insignificant in its seeming significance. What counts in the play is the fact that they all participate in the waiting. This is equally true in *Waiting for Godot,* in which the two tramps are different in all aspects, and it is their common goal of waiting that brings them together as figures reflecting the predicament of modern man. In short, nothing is particularly significant or bears any great meaning in both plays except that all the major characters are waiting for something to change their situation, but nothing happens. In view of its technical innovations and philosophical treatment of the theme of waiting in relation to the crisis of belief and loss of roots, *The Bus-Stop* signifies the most important milestone in the endeavour of con-temporary Chinese playwrights to break away from the tradition of Ibsenian drama and to introduce the Chinese audiences to the Theatre of the Absurd.

NOTES

1. This is a revised version of a paper presented at the conference, "Chinese-Western Comparative Drama," held at The Chinese University of Hong Kong, 1986. The paper was published in Tam (1990). Quotations from *The Bus-Stop* follow the translation in Barmé (1983a).

2. For more details of the changes in contemporary Chinese theatre, refer to Tam (1986).

3. An example of the Chinese reception of absurd drama can be found in Guo Jide 郭繼德 (1986).

4. The simplistic interpretation of the Silent Man as a positive hero is perhaps a reflection of the mentality of mechanically dividing the characters in the play according to the traditional standard of distinguishing between the good [忠 zhong] and the evil [奸 jian] and also the morality of blaming a person who waits for gains without pains as what the stupid farmer in a famous traditional Chinese story does by waiting behind a tree for a hare to break its neck by running into the tree. It is precisely with this mentality that some critics interpret the Silent Man as the embodiment of a positive message in the play and subsequently regard Gao's work as a didactic play with a "moral undertone."

REFERENCES

Barmé, Geremie (1983a). *The Bus-Stop. Renditions*, Nos. 19 & 20 (Spring & Autumn), pp. 379–386.

———, trans. (1983b). "A Touch of the Absurd — Introducing Gao Xingjian and His Play *The Bus-stop.*" *Renditions*, Nos. 19 & 20 (Spring & Autumn), pp. 373–377.

Beckett, Samuel (1975). *Waiting for Godot.* London: Faber and Faber.

Camus, Albert (1942). *Le Mythe de Sisyphe.* Paris: Gallimard.

Esslin, Martin (1977). *The Theatre of the Absurd.* Revised and enlarged edition. London: Penguin.

Fraser, G. S. (1975). *The Modern Writer and His World.* Westport: Greenwood Press.

Gao Xingjian 高行健 (1981). *Xiandai xiaoshuo jiqiao chutan* 現代小說技巧初探 [A preliminary exploration of the techniques of modern fiction]. Guangzhou: Huacheng chubanshe 花城出版社.

——— (1983). *Chezhan* 車站 [The bus-stop]. *Shiyue* 十月 No. 3, pp. 119–138.

Guo Jide 郭繼德 (1986). "A'erbi yu huangdan pai xiju" 阿爾比與荒誕派戲劇 [Albee and absurd drama]. *Waguo wenxue yanjiu* 外國文學研究 [Studies in foreign literature], No. 3, pp. 32–38.

He Wen 何聞 (1984). "Huaju *Chezhan* guan hou" 話劇《車站》觀後 [On seeing the play *The Bus-Stop*]. *Wenyi bao* 文藝報, No. 3, pp. 21–25.

Ionesco, Eugène (1957). "Dans les armes de la ville." *Cahiers de la Compagnie Madeleine Renaud-Jean-Louis Barrault* (Paris), No. 20, October.

Luk, Yun-tong, ed. (1990). *Studies in Chinese-Western Comparative Drama.* Hong Kong: The Chinese University Press.

Qu Liuyi 曲六乙 (1984). "Ping huaju *Chezhan* ji qi piping" 評話劇《車站》及其批評 [On the play *The Bus-Stop* and the criticism of it]. *Wenyi bao* 文藝報, No. 7, pp. 29–33.

Robinson, Michael (1969). *The Long Sonata of the Dead: A Study of Samuel Beckett.* London: Rupert Hart-Davis.

Tam, Kwok-kan (1986). "From Social Problem Play to Socialist Problem Play: Ibsen and Contemporary Chinese Dramaturgy." *The Journal of the Institute of Chinese Studies of The Chinese University of Hong Kong*, Vol. 17, pp. 387–402.

——— (1990). "Drama of Dilemma: Waiting as Form and Motif in *Waiting for Godot* and *The Bus-stop.*" In Yun-tong Luk, ed. (1990), pp. 23–45.

Williams, Raymond (1978). *Drama from Ibsen to Brecht.* London: Penguin.

Avant-Garde Theatre in Post-Mao China:
The Bus-Stop by Gao Xingjian[1]

Always historicize!

— Fredric Jameson, *The Political Unconscious* (1981)

ABSURD THEATRE IN CHINA

In 1977, Zhu Hong 朱虹, a specialist in Anglo-American literature, wrote
a lengthy critical survey of the Theatre of the Absurd (Zhu, 1997, pp.
147-193). This piece, a pioneering effort in the PRC, was published in
the prominent journal *Shijie wenxue* 世界文學 [World literature] in 1978
along with a Chinese translation of Harold Pinter's *The Birthday Party*. In
March 1979, Bertolt Brecht's *Life of Galileo* was publicly performed by
the Chinese Youth Art Theater in Beijing (Xue, 1982, p. 72). The thematic implications of the play inevitably made the performance at that
particular historical juncture controversial and full of political innuendo
(Chen, 1982, p. 50); a discussion of "illusionism" was also evoked by the
performance. In the summer of 1979, the satirical play *Jiaru wo shi zhende*
假如我是真的 [If I were real, or The imposter] by Sha Yexin 沙葉新 and
others was staged "internally" in Shanghai.[2] The play clearly bears certain affinities with Gogol's *The Inspector-General* (Gálik, 1984, pp. 49–50),
but the prologue, which takes place partly among the audience, is a departure from traditional dramatic illusionism.

The first anthology of Western Absurd Theatre was brought out in
Shanghai in 1980 and contained plays by Samuel Beckett (*Waiting for
Godot*), Eugene Ionesco (*Amédée or How to Get Rid of It*), Edward Albee
(*The Zoo Story*), and Harold Pinter (*The Dumb Waiter*) (Shi, 1980). The
first anthology of Western modernist works also came out in the same
year and contained plays by Strindberg (*The Ghost Sonata*), Georg Kaiser

(*From Mom to Midnight*), Ernst Toller (*Masses and Man*), and Eugene
O'Neill (*The Hairy Ape*), which are loosely grouped together under
Expressionism (Yuan, 1980). In the second volume of this anthology,
which appeared a year later, Jean-Paul Sartre's *Morts sans sépulture* [The
victors] was included (Yuan, 1980).

In February 1982, the Taipei playwright Yao Yiwei's 姚一葦 *Hong bizi*
紅鼻子 [Red nose, 1969], which deals with modernist themes such as
alienation in modern society and the dilemma of human existence, was
staged by the Chinese Youth Art Theatre to the enthusiastic reception of
the audience (Lin, 1984). In late 1982 and early 1983, Gao Xingjian's
Juedui xinhao 絕對信號 [Alarm signal] had more than one hundred performances at Beijing People's Art Theatre. Widely acclaimed and highly
controversial, the play is a psychological portrait of an unemployed youth.
The heated discussion was evoked not by the contents, but by the formal
experiment with stage design, lighting, and the abandonment of
illusionism.

AVANT-GARDISM AND *THE BUS-STOP*

Despite the controversy, Gao's second play, *Chezhan* 車站 [The bus-stop],
was staged in the small studio of the same theatre in June 1983.[3] The play is
truly a "great leap forward," for it tries to break away from the realist and
socialist-realist traditions of modern and contemporary Chinese drama by
employing, for the first time in the PRC, certain elements of the Western
avant-garde drama, including that of the Theatre of the Absurd.

The characters of *The Bus-Stop* range from a nineteen-year-old hood-
lum to an old man in his sixties — clearly meant as a representative
cross-section of Chinese urban society. The group gathers at a suburban
bus-stop waiting for a bus to take them into the city. Buses (suggested by
sounds) come and go, and none has stopped for them, but the group
just keeps waiting. Like many plays of the Theatre of the Absurd, the
structure of *The Bus-Stop* is circular; it ends as it begins, in waiting. There
is no resolution as there is no traditional dramatic complication. As with
many Absurdist plays, *The Bus-Stop* has no linear plot development; in
fact, it is nearly plotless. The play has no conventional "dramatic" development and is mainly interested in the exploration of a "static" situation.
As there is no plot to speak of, there are no characters in conflict and no
genuine action, although physical activities seem to abound.

In Western Theatre of the Absurd, the dialogues sometimes contradict or are out of sync with the immediate actions. The repetition, cliché, nonsense, and jibberish of the dialogues are supposed to suggest the futility or impossibility of human communication. Gao's dialogues are far more comprehensible and referential than those of his Western counterparts, but communicative disintegration is still implied by mismatched conversations and polyphonic dialogues, the latter culminating with seven actors speaking all at the same time. As the playwright has observed in his "Suggestions for the Performance of *The Bus-Stop*" (Gao, 1983, p. 138), the aspects of inarticulation, incomprehensibility, and non sequitur make the characters comical; as a result, the play is essentially comical.

In a published conversation with Lin Zhaohua 林兆華, the director of *Alarm Signal* and *The Bus-Stop*, Gao observes that modern Chinese drama, literally known as "spoken drama," is excessively dominated by the tradition represented by Ibsen and has unfortunately forsaken the brilliant performing convention of classical Chinese drama, which includes singing, stylized and formulaic acting, chanting, and even acrobatics. Gao believes that the impact of drama cannot depend solely on the actors' dialogues. One Western example that he cites to illustrate the point is Antonin Artaud's Theatre of Cruelty, which elevates pure theatricality — stylized gestures and movements, lights, sounds, and colours — above the meaning of the literary text and compels the spectator to participate not just intellectually but emotionally and through the senses. Like Artaud, Gao also stresses the need to overwhelm the spectator completely and profoundly (Beijing renmin yishu juyuan *Juedui xinhao* juzu, 1985, pp. 104–108). In his "Suggestions for the Performance of *The Bus-Stop*," he urges the actors to look for "spiritual verisimilitude," such as Mei Lanfang's 梅蘭芳 performance of *The Drunken Lady*, rather than external, detailed truthfulness. He also states that the sound of the play, which includes music, should not be explanatory — the sound should be granted an independent role and should enter into some kind of dialogue with the characters as well as the spectators. These suggestions share certain affinities with Artaud's theory and practice, but Gao's appropriation of Artaud is clearly selective, for his works do not share the mystic, primitive rituality of Artaudian theatre, and Gao's published discussion of acting, dramatic effect, and sound is always grounded in the context of classical Chinese dramaturgy.

Equally selective is Gao's appropriation from Jerzy Grotowski, who believes that the essence of the theatre lies solely in the interaction of and live communion between actor and spectator. Grotowski believes that the theatre should not try to compete with film and television by using sets, costume, make-up, and technology, but should instead become a "poor theater," stripped of all these traditional theatrical elements, providing an experience that is the opposite of the supposedly "rich" synthesis of the total theatre (Grotowski, 1968). Echoing Grotowski, Gao also thinks that "facing the two new strong opponents of television and film, drama can still exist as an independent art form because the actors, through their roles, can communicate directly with the audience" (Beijing renmin yishu juyuan *Juedui xinhao* juzu, 1985, p. 105). Specifically mentioning Grotowski's emphasis on actor-spectator interaction, both Gao and Lin seem to share the belief that there is stronger and freer communion in classical Chinese theatre, and their experiment is a revival of an indigenous tradition (Beijing renmin yishu juyuan *Juedui xinhao* juzu, 1985, pp. 106–107). In this sense, the minimalism of the stage design; the theatre-in-the-round stage, which abandons illusionism; the continuous performance with no scenic division; the direct address to the audience; and the conscious reflection on acting in *The Bus-Stop* are only contemporary resurrections of native conventions.

An admirer of Artaud, Grotowski often talks about the molding of the actor into a sign, a representation of an impulse. For him, "impulse and action are concurrent: the body vanishes, burns, and the spectator sees only a series of visible impulses" (Grotowski, 1968, p. 16). Devoid of such ritualistic mysticism, Gao explains *The Bus-Stop* as "an attempt to unify mobile and immobile performances." Far less radical than Grotowski, Gao only wants the immobility of the actors to be "static forms and shapes" (Gao, 1983, p. 138), stilled images in a larger pattern and design. Gao's work does not contain the grotesque gesture, the vocal incantation, and the ritualistic atmosphere of Grotowski's experiments. In this sense, Gao's indebtedness to Grotowski is at most limited and selective.

The appropriation of Artaud and Grotowski and the revival of classical Chinese theatrical conventions by Gao and Lin are, as their conversations indicate, reactions against the pre-1949 Ibsenian tradition and the post-1949 Stanislavsky System. The psychological realism of the System, because of its Soviet origin, has become so dominant in the PRC that even the performance of the Beijing opera has been subjected to its interpretation. Both Gao and Lin believe that this approach is wrong, and that the two acting methods are incompatible. They also cite the authority of Meyerhold — who, for some years, was a "non-person" in the PRC — in their condemnation of enshrining the System as the acting orthodoxy. Specifically, Lin quotes Meyerhold's reprobation of the naturalistic theatre and his admiration for Mei Lanfang's performance in Moscow (Beijing renmin yishu juyuan *Juedui xinhao juzu*, 1985, p. 101). It is worth noting that Meyerhold once advocated a stylized theatre as a substitute for naturalism and wanted to make the spectator a "fourth *creator*, in addition to the author, the director, and the actor" (Meyerhold, 1969, p. 60), by employing "his imagination *creatively* in order to fill in those details *suggested* by the stage actions" (Meyerhold, 1969, p. 63).[4]

CONTROVERSIES OVER *THE BUS-STOP*

Although Gao's appropriation of the Western avant-garde is highly selective, his experimentation immediately aroused a heated debate. Comparing *The Bus-Stop* with *Waiting for Godot,* He Wen 何聞 assails Gao for his "enormous veneration for Beckett" and for blindly following the latter's "bourgeois idealism" and "nihilism." Arguing that the play has abandoned "the progressive function of socialist art and literature," He Wen views the appearance of the play as a demonstration of how some writers seize upon political liberalization to produce "deviant works which distort history, twist the facts, spread all kinds of negative, pessimistic, corrupt, and vulgar ideas, and propagate all manner of bourgeois, idealistic, egoistic world views, creating harmful effects on readers and the theatre-going public."[5] Far more seriously, He Wen suggests that the play is not just an exposé of the "darker aspects" of "socialist reality" but is implicitly anti-socialist: "Both [*Waiting for Godot* and *The Bus-Stop*] deal with the 'futility of waiting': waiting in a capitalist society, where the future offers no solution to those wishing to free themselves from poverty and hardship; and waiting in socialist society" (He, 1983, p. 391). Though He Wen stops short of an explicit denunciation, the verdict is obvious.

Coming to the defence of Gao, Qu Liuyi 曲六乙, a senior drama critic, tries to argue that not all modernist drama techniques are inherently "bad," and that the play actually encourages people to overcome pessimism and to be the masters of their time (Qu, 1984, pp. 29–33). Indeed, comparing *The Bus-Stop* with *Waiting for Godot,* it should be obvious to anyone familiar with Western avant-garde theatre, in particular the Theatre of the Absurd, that *The Bus-Stop* remains fairly realistic and touches upon a host of current social problems: traffic chaos, the erosion of basic manners, shortages of certain commodities, networks of connections, the corruption of cadres, and the prevalent "backdoorism." Although the form may manifest certain resemblances to Western avant-garde theatre, the content can actually be described as a kind of revived "critical realism." But clearly this is not the way the orthodox critics chose to view the play, and a rebuttal of Qu Liuyi's strained but sympathetic article appeared immediately. The rejoinder by Xi Yan 溪煙 not only reinforced He Wen's thesis, but further charged the play with reflecting a "crisis of faith," an "erroneous trend of thought" that is "a distortion of our reality and of life" (Xi Yan, 1984, pp. 14–19).

BASE AND SUPERSTRUCTURE REVISITED

The problem with the critiques of He Wen and Xi Yan is simply that they once again adopt the mechanical reflectionist view toward the base-superstructure relationship. It is true that even a great Marxist critic like Georg Lukács had condemned Western modernism unsparingly and unreservedly by employing a reflectionist model (Lukács, 1971). Less rigid and more dialectical than Lukács, Theodor Adorno sees a mediated and even organic relationship between avant-garde formalism and capitalist society by arguing that the formal experiment, either subtly or vociferously, is a condemnation and negation of bourgeois society and its dominant consumptive practice (Adorno, 1973). Like Adorno, Lucien Goldman also argues for an indirect homology between the capitalist infrastructure and the cultural products (Goldmann, 1976, pp. 76–88). These discussions, from the reflectionist to the more dialectical, are all situated in the Western base-superstructure relations. The PRC, although far more relaxed in its current control of the economy, simply does not have the same infrastructure; and, as Gao's play has shown, the socialist economy of the PRC has a different set of problems. In this sense, the critiques of He Wen and Xi Yan turn out to be quite ironical, for they have borrowed a "vulgar" or "orthodox" model that was originally grounded in a Western context. The Chinese situation fundamentally repudiates that model, and Gao's indebtedness to Western avant-gardists can only be seen as technical borrowings, which come without the ideological trappings. From the perspective of comparative literature, Gao's case is clearly one of influence and affinity, a case of intersubjectivity that lies in the realm of consciousness rather than economics. Even in the Western context, there is Bertolt Brecht's view of technique as inherently neutral, an argument first put forward in his famous debates with Lukács, which contends that the same devices can be used by different authors for different effects and purposes (Brecht, 1977, pp. 73–75). It is in this perspective that Gao's innovations should be analyzed and understood.

IDEOLOGY OF AMBIGUITIES

When *The Bus-Stop* was staged, Lu Xun's "The Passer-by," a one-scene skit from the prose-poem collection *Yecao* 野草 [Wild grass, 1925], was performed as a prelude. The actor who played the passer-by also played the Silent Man in *The Bus-Stop*, who is described by the playwright in this way: "He impatiently waits for the bus and, as if responding to some inaudible call, starts out for the city by himself without a word to any of the others. His silhouetted form appears from time to time along with the music of his 'signature tune'" (Gao, 1983, p. 379). Lu Xun's passer-by is a solitary traveller who, undeterred from difficulty and urged forward by a voice, plods on without hesitation. Clearly an allegorical figure, Lu Xun's passer-by can be interpreted as a representation of his flickering hope and vague aspiration for the future. Besides these similar implications, the resurfacing of the lonely passer-by may also suggest that the struggle and the journey are not yet over, although nearly sixty years have elapsed between his two appearances.

Some critics have assailed the Silent Man as an "individualist who has abandoned the masses" and "has refrained from promoting the people's constructive and positive spirits" (Jing Da, 1984, p. 69). He Wen is quite indignant about the parallels between the two appearances of the Silent Man. Following the Zhdanovist line that the establishment of the new society also ushers in the new man, the new ideals, and new spiritual conditions, He Wen argues that since the society and time of "The Passer-by" are long past, to stage the two plays simultaneously and to describe in the programme notes that one is the descendant of the other is a "deliberate confusion." To him, Gao's play is no continuation of the Lu Xun tradition, but simply "a product of the blind worship and mechanical copying of the social viewpoints and creative theories of modernist drama in the West" (He, 1983, p. 390). Even Gao's defender, Qu Liuyi, while observing that the Silent Man is a positive character, concedes that he is "abstract" and "pale."

There is no doubt that a "new" society, with its new institutions and relationships, usually creates new ideals and consciousness and also tries to transform what Louis Althusser has called the "ideological state apparatuses"; but unless one relapses into a "vulgar" model of economic determinism, it should be equally clear that while the older dominant ideologies, no longer enjoying a material basis, may be completely shattered in their hegemony (in the Gramscian and not the Maoist sense), their residue may continue to linger, playing a certain role in the constitution of the individuals as subjects, overdetermining to a certain degree the perception and acceptance of their positions within the system of production relations. Many instances from the history of the PRC can be cited to illustrate this theoretical argument. Furthermore, the new system of production relations inevitably creates new problems, which Gao's play has briefly touched upon. The allegorical recycling of the Silent Man, a politically "safe" figure, is undoubtedly a social critique, which presupposes a hermeneutical understanding on the part of the audience for the critique to function. To some orthodox critics, the intertextual appropriation of Lu Xun may appear to be quite "negative" and even "pessimistic"; but one must not forget that the Silent Man is ultimately an allegorical representation of determination and hope.

In *Das Prinzip Hoffnung*, Ernst Bloch contends that even music, the most abstract of the art forms, may have a "connection with this world" in such a way that the artistic expression is "nothing less than a seismograph of society. For it reflects any cracks beneath the social surface, expresses desires for change, and is synonymous with hoping" (Bloch, 1985, p. 227). Bloch's emphasis on music as the embodiment of hope reflects the utopian vision that dominates all his writings; this view of the transcendent power of hope is certainly applicable to the play under discussion, for the opposite of hope is nihilism, which is precisely what the play attempts to negate by resurrecting a familiar, unmistakable, and sanctioned figure of this utopian wish.

NOTES

1.   This article was originally presented at a conference on contemporary

Chinese literature held in Germany in 1986 and was later published with the same title in Howard Goldblatt, ed., *Worlds Apart: Contemporary Chinese Writing and Its Audience* (New York: M. E. Sharpe, 1990), pp. 111–118.

2. For a discussion of this play and its controversy, see Barmé (1983). Daniel Kane's English translation of the play is in the double issue of *Renditions* (1983), pp. 333–369. The Chinese text can be found in *Xiju yishu* 戲劇藝術, special supplement (September 1979).

3. Gao's *Chezhan* 車站 was first published in *Shiyue* 十月, No. 3 (1983), pp. 119–138. It can also be found in Gao (1985), pp. 84–135. Since *Shiyue* is more readily available, all subsequent references to this work are to this edition. An excerpt has been translated into English by Geremie Barmé and published in *Renditions*. See Barmé, trans. (1983).

4. Original italics.

5. He Wen 何聞 (1983), pp. 387–392. This double issue of *Renditions*, in which He Wen's essay appeared, was not published until the end of 1984. The Chinese version first appeared in *Wenyi bao* 文藝報, No. 3 (1984), pp. 21–25.

REFERENCES

Adorno, Theodor (1973). *Philosophy of Modem Music.* Anne Mitchell and Wesley Blomster, trans. New York: Seabury.

Barmé, Geremie (1983). "A Word for the Imposter? Introducing the Drama of Sha Yexin." *Renditions,* Nos. 19 & 20 (Spring & Autumn), pp. 319–332.

———, trans. (1983). *The Bus-stop. Renditions,* Nos. 19 & 20 (Spring & Autumn), pp. 379–386.

Beijing renmin yishu juyuan *Juedui xinhao* juzu 北京人民藝術劇院《絕對信號》劇組, ed. (1985). *Juedui xinhao de yishu tansuo* 《絕對信號》的藝術探索 [The art of *Alarm Signal*]. Beijing: Zhongguo xiju chubanshe 中國戲劇出版社.

Bloch, Ernst (1985). *Essays on the Philosophy of Music.* Trans. Peter Palmer. Cambridge: Cambridge University Press. The last part of this book is from *Das Prinzip Hoffnung.*

Brecht, Bertolt (1977). "On the Formalistic Character of the Theory of Realism." In Taylor, ed. (1977), pp. 73–75.

Chen Yong (1982). "The Beijing Production of *Life of Galileo*." In Tatlow and Wong, eds. (1982), pp. 88–95.

Gálik, Marián (1984). "In the Footsteps of the Inspector-General: Two Contemporary Chinese Plays." *Asian and African Studies,* No. 20, pp. 49–80.

Gao Xingjian 高行健 (1983). *Chezhan* 車站 [The bus-stop]. *Shiyue* 十月, No. 3, pp. 119–138.

——— (1985). *Gao Xingjian xiju ji* 高行健戲劇集 [Plays by Gao Xingjian]. Beijing: Qunzhong chubanshe 群眾出版社.

Goldmann, Lucien (1976). *Cultural Creation.* Bart Grahl, trans. St. Louis: Telos.

Grotowski, Jerzy (1968). *Towards a Poor Theatre.* New York: Simon & Schuster.

He Wen 何聞 (1983). "On Seeing the Play *The Bus-Stop.*" Trans. Chan Sin-wai. *Renditions,* Nos. 19 & 20 (Spring & Autumn), pp. 387–392.

—— (1984). "Huaju *Chezhan* guan hou" 話劇《車站》觀後 [On seeing the play *The Bus-Stop*]. *Wenyi bao* 文藝報, No. 3, pp. 21–25.

Jing Da 敬達 (1984). "Huaju *Chezhan* zai lunbian zhong" 話劇《車站》在論辯中 [Controversies over the play *The Bus-Stop*]. *Zuopin yu zhengming* 作品與爭鳴, No. 10, p. 69.

Kane, Daniel, trans. (1983). *The Imposter. Renditions,* Nos. 19 & 20 (Spring & Autumn), pp. 333–369.

Lin Kekuan 林克歡, ed. (1984) Hong bizi *de wutai yishu* 《紅鼻子》的舞台藝術 [The theatrical art of *Red Nose*]. Beijing: Zhongguo xiju chubanshe 中國戲劇出版社.

Lukács, Georg (1971). *Realism in Our Time.* John and Necke Mander, trans. New York: Harper.

Meyerhold, V. E. (1969). *Meyerhold on Theatre.* Trans. and ed. Edward Braun. New York: Hill & Wang.

Qu Liuyi 曲六乙 (1984). "Ping huaju *Chezhan* ji qi piping" 評話劇《車站》及其批評 [On the play *The Bus-Stop* and its criticism]. *Wenyi bao* 文藝報, No. 7, pp. 29–33.

Shi Xianrong 施咸榮 et al., trans. (1980). *Huangdanpai xiju ji* 荒誕派戲劇集 [A collection of absurd drama]. Shanghai: Shanghai yiwen chubanshe 上海譯文出版社.

Tatlow, Antony, and Tak-wai Wong, eds. (1982). *Brecht and East Asian Theatre.* Hong Kong: Hong Kong University Press.

Taylor, Ronald, ed. (1977). *Aesthetics and Politics.* London: New Left Books.

Xi Yan 溪煙 (1984). "Pingjia zuopin de yiju shi shenme?" 評價作品的依據是甚麼？ [What are the criteria for assessing literary works?]. *Wenyi bao* 文藝報, No. 8, pp. 14–19.

Xue Dianjie (1982). "Stage Design for Brecht's *Life of Galileo.*" In Tatlow and Wong, eds. (1982), pp. 72–87.

Yuan Kejia 袁可嘉 et al., eds. (1980). *Waiguo xiandaipai zuopin xuan* 外國現代派作品選 [Selected works from foreign modernist literature]. Vol. 1, Parts 1 and 2. Shanghai: Shanghai wenyi chubanshe 上海文藝出版社.

Zhu Hong 朱虹 (1984). *Ying-Mei wenxue sanlun* 英美文學散論 [Essays on British and American literature]. Beijing: Sanlian shudian 三聯書店.

The Theatre of the Absurd in China: Gao Xingjian's *The Bus-Stop*[1]

The Theatre of the Absurd is unquestionably a product of Western society. This is not to imply that Western society is absurd. As a matter of fact, many highly "absurd" societies could not produce such a literary genre. For example, there have been countless instances of "absurdity" in mainland China, particularly during the ten-year-long "Great Proletarian Cultural Revolution." But, this has not encouraged the creation of a Theatre of the Absurd. Therefore, it is reasonable to say that the Theatre of the Absurd which has emerged in mainland China is imported from the West, just as naturally as hi-tech products, nuclear power plants, and computers. Since I have played something of an active part in introducing the Theatre of the Absurd to mainland China, a personal sense of involvement has motivated me to write this paper.

Although it is not difficult to find materials which explain why the Theatre of the Absurd is a product of Western but not Chinese society, this article will not attempt to ascertain the reasons why societies do or do not give birth to a Theatre of the Absurd. It is generally accepted that the Theatre of the Absurd first appeared in Paris in the 1950s, although one may easily associate it with *Ubu Roi* by Alfred Jarry (1873–1907),[2] or *Le Grotesque Polonais* in Poland in 1920-30.[3] Indeed, no school of literature can be called unprecedented. Careful research may uncover analogies, similarities, or striking resemblances between entirely different things. The Theatre of the Absurd is no exception. Therefore, one cannot deny that certain playwrights prior to the 1950s paved the way. Nonetheless, the emergence of such talented playwrights as Eugène Ionesco (1912–), Samuel Beckett (1906–1989), Arthur Adamov (1908–70), and Jean Genet (1910–86), formed a tide of the absurd which swept across the world of theatre in less than ten years.

THE THEATRE OF THE ABSURD IN THE WEST

The audience reaction to the first performance of Ionesco's *La Cantatrice Chauve* [The bald soprano] in Paris in May 1950 was very cold because they saw neither a bald head nor a soprano. The audience felt cheated and reacted with a mixture of anger and bewilderment. Those cherishing tradition rejected this type of play off hand, whereas those seeking something new became curious. After repeated evaluations by literary and dramatic critics, the conclusion was that the Theatre of the Absurd is not entirely unreasonable, resulting in the play's continued performance for more than thirty-five years.[4] Samuel Beckett's *En Attendant Godot* [Waiting for Godot][5] was even more successful. Coming out two years after *La Cantatrice Chauve*, it earned almost immediate approval.

The term "Theatre of the Absurd" was not coined during the 1950s. In the preface to the first collection of Ionesco's plays, it was called "théâtre d'aventure."[6] Meanwhile, Ionesco himself named it "anti-théâtre" or "anti-pièce." Ironically, Beckett's *En Attendant Godot* was called by some people a parody of circus clowning. The general term for it was "Le Théâtre de dérision."[7] It was not until the publication of Martin Esslin's *The Theatre of the Absurd* in 1961 that the name became formalized.

Of course, Esslin was not the first to use the word "absurd" in literature, but borrowed it from the philosophy of Existentialism. Albert Camus (1913–1960) placed particular emphasis on the concept of "absurdity" in his *Le Mythe de Sisyphe* [The myth of Sisyphus], saying:

> A world that can be explained through reason, however faulty, is a familiar world. But in a universe that is suddenly deprived of illusions and of light, man feels a stranger. His is an irremediable exile, because he is deprived of memories of a lost homeland and also the hope of a promised land. This divorce between man and his life, the actor and his setting, truly constitutes the feeling of Absurdity.   (Camus, 1942, p. 18)

The post-World War II generation in the West not only felt pangs for a lost homeland, but, more seriously, lost faith in God. In seeking the meaning of life, they saw nothing but "nothingness." When a man loses direction, "absurdity" becomes the best word to describe and explain everything. When Ionesco visited Taipei in 1982, I interviewed him concerning the absurdity in life. In addition to affirming his belief that life is absurd, he emphasized that human life appears quite unreal, and that existence is something very strained and unnatural (Ma, 1985, p. 74). Stemming from his life as an existentialist, he sees life itself as a Theatre of the Absurd. Since World War II, there have been few literary and dramatic works in the Western Hemisphere which have not been influenced by Existentialism.

In the Existentialist theatre, there are at least two ways to convey absurdity. One is by using the traditional form of drama, as in the plays of Jean-Paul Sartre and Albert Camus. The other is by using the form of the Theatre of the Absurd, as in the works of Eugène Ionesco and Samuel Beckett. During the 1960s, I saw Sartre's *Huis-clos* [No exit] and Ionesco's *Les Chaises* [The chairs] performed in a double billing. *Huis-clos* seemed excessively conventional, philosophical, and didactic. It lacked the unity and harmony found in *Les Chaises* (Ma, 1985, p. 259). Martin Esslin has rendered a more precise definition of the Theatre of the Absurd:

> They [Sartre and others] present their sense of the irrationality of the human condition in the form of highly lucid and logically constructed reasoning, while the Theatre of the Absurd strives to express its sense of the senselessness of the human condition and the inadequacy of the rational approach through the open abandonment of rational devices and discursive thought. While Sartre or Camus express the new content in the old convention, the Theatre of the Absurd goes a step further in trying to achieve unity between its basic assumptions and the form in which these are expressed. In some sense, the theatre of Sartre and Camus is less adequate as an expression of the *philosophy* of Sartre and Camus — in artistic, as distinct from philosophic, terms — than the Theatre of the Absurd.
>
> (Esslin, 1987, p. 24)

What then is the difference between the form adopted by Ionesco, Beckett, and others, and the form used by those before them? First, the Theatre of the Absurd departs from the Aristotelian tradition of using plot to present theme. Contrary to the "well-made play," it has almost no plot at all. Secondly, traditional plays always attempt to present to the audience a convincing theme, whereas the Theatre of the Absurd claims to be non-polemical. Thirdly, the Theatre of the Absurd ignores Aristotle's teaching which regards personality and thought of the characters as the essence of a play. Thus, characters in the Theatre of the Absurd resemble puppets and symbols devoid of distinctive personalities. Fourthly, while traditional drama uses clear and logical language, the Theatre of the

Absurd uses intentionally muddled language. Because it is obviously different from the traditional theatre, Ionesco chose to call his plays "anti-théâtre" which caused an uproar in Paris when his *La Cantatrice Chauve* was first staged.

THE THEATRE OF THE ABSURD IN CHINA

During the 1960s, the Theatre of the Absurd had a firm foothold in several large cities in the West, its influence nearly worldwide. However, there was no response from mainland China.[8] Upholding realism, the literary and dramatic circles in mainland China rejected anything that was incompatible with the official line. Mao Zedong's literary theories developed on his "Talks at the Yan'an Forum on Literature and Art" hold that Western modernism was heresy, and the postmodernist "Theatre of the Absurd" could be nothing but a further embodiment of the decadence of capitalism. It was not until August 1980, long after the downfall of the "Gang of Four," that the Shanghai yiwen chubanshe 上海譯文出版社 [Shanghai translation press] published the *Collected Plays of the Theatre of the Absurd* in its Series of Foreign Literary Works as an introduction to the major playwrights and works. Although supposedly an "introduction," the tone was critical. The book's preface states:

> In current capitalist literature, man has further degenerated into a "non-person." We can see this from the *huangdan ju* 荒誕劇 [plays of the absurd]. We see that man's image is reduced to the lowest degree, with virtually no characteristics of the human. He has no origin, no development, no social existence, and no personality. He is a man of "no roots," "jettisoned into existence" as shown in the concept of Existentialism. From the God who commands the wind and clouds down to a worm of "non-personality," the process vividly suggests that the bourgeoisie has completely lost its initiative in history and is destined to decline and perish. The fantastic and absurd images reflect this historical trend, betraying in all respects a sense of decadence — shattered ideals, broken faith, helplessness, hysteria.... [These] are typical ideological manifestations of a class doomed to destruction.   (Shi, 1985, p. 29)

Labelling the Theatre of the Absurd a "typical ideological manifestation of a class doomed to destruction" signified that the playwrights in mainland China should not "learn" from it. At that time, I was teaching at the University of London and was invited to lecture at Nankai and other universities in mainland China. One of the subjects I chose to lecture on was the Theatre of the Absurd.[9] The main reason for choosing such a "reactionary" subject was that mainland China had begun to open its doors. After more than thirty years of self-imposed isolation from the outside world, the people became tired of monotonous preaching, and even the Chinese Communists wished to see new things and to hear other voices. I thought that the Theatre of the Absurd could counterbalance mainland China's political style of "What I say goes," as well as that of the "single flower blossoming."

I talked about the Theatre of the Absurd at Nankai and several other universities, and was once even invited by the Association of Chinese Dramatists to deliver a speech. The audience understood the purposes and techniques of the Theatre of the Absurd, especially with their bitter experience during the "Cultural Revolution." They were fully aware of the fact that what happened in their society was even more absurd than what they were seeing on stage. When my plays were circulating in mainland China, critics classified them as "plays of the absurd." In March 1985, *Ju ben* 劇本 [Dramatic script] magazine published Lin Kehuan's 林克歡 article entitled "Ma Sen de huangdan ju" 馬森的荒誕劇 [Ma Sen's plays of the absurd]. Lin concludes:

> Rationality has been the foundation of the recent bourgeois revolutions; nonetheless, Ma Sen sees the crisis of rationality as the crisis of Western society in modern times. He believes that rationalization in society has become increasingly removed from the control of the people and has turned into an objective force to control them. The rational world of appearance is in fact full of absurd disorder. This is undoubtedly a kind of advancement. In negating the existing social order, the author manifests his irrepressible anger, which implies a certain undefined expectation for the normal development for humanity.   (Lin, 1985, p. 91)

Lin's article was the first one that took a positive attitude toward "plays of the absurd." In the same issue, *Dramatic Script* also reprinted one of my plays, entitled *Ruozhe* 弱者 [The weakling], which was staged by the Nanjing Theatre Company in early 1985.

During the same period, some playwrights in mainland China also began to experiment with "plays of the absurd." The first and most popular was Gao Xingjian, playwright of the Beijing People's Art Theatre.

Gao's play *Chezhan* 車站 [The bus-stop] was published in issue no. 5 of *Shiyue* 十月 [October] in 1983. A note at the end of the script printed in *Gao Xingjian xiju ji* 高行健戲劇集 [Plays by Gao Xingjian], published in 1985, indicates that the first draft was completed in July 1981 and the second in November 1982 (Gao, 1985, p. 113). Therefore, the first appearance of a "theatre of the absurd" in mainland China was in the early 1980s.

GAO XINGJIAN'S EXPERIMENT

Gao Xingjian, a native of Taizhou, Jiangsu Province, was born at Ganzhou, Jiangxi province in 1940. In 1957, he graduated from the Nanjing No. Ten Municipal Middle School. In 1962, he graduated from the Beijing Institute of Foreign Languages with a major in French. He then became a translator, but was sent down to the countryside for more than five years during the Cultural Revolution.

In 1979, Gao began to publish. In 1981 he became a professional writer, taking on the job of playwright at the Beijing People's Art Theatre. In the same year, he published *Xiandai xiaoshuo jiqiao chutan* 現代小說技巧初探 [A preliminary exploration of the techniques of modern fiction] which led to debates on "realism or modernism?" in literary circles. In 1982, his first play, *Juedui xinhao* 絕對信號 [Alarm signal], was staged by the Beijing People's Art Theatre. The play earned both praise and censure for its deviation from the orthodoxy of realism.

In 1983, *The Bus-Stop* was staged by the Beijing People's Art Theatre. The play touched off another round of debate, and Gao was criticized. As a result, the play was suspended after thirteen performances. Gao then took a long journey, going into the mountainous areas along the Yangtze River to investigate primitive ecological conditions and folk cultures. He then wrote another play, *Yeren* 野人 [Wild man, 1985], which was staged in 1985 by the Beijing People's Art Theatre under the direction of Lin Zhaohua, his longtime collaborator. Once again, his work stirred up controversy. In 1986, he completed *Bi'an* 彼岸 [The other shore], and in 1987, he wrote a song-and-dance drama *Mingcheng* 冥城 [The nether city] for the dancer Jiang Qing 江青.[10] In the same year, he was invited to visit Europe and then took up residence in Paris.

Two of Gao Xingjian's dramatic works, *The Bus-Stop* and *The Other Shore*, can be considered plays of the absurd. As the title of this chapter suggests,

The Bus-Stop is singled out for analysis. The cast of *The Bus-Stop* consists of eight characters: Silent Man (middle-aged), Old Man (over sixty), Girl (26 years old), Lout (19 years old), "Glasses" (30 years old), Mother (40), Carpenter (45), and Director Ma (50). The inclusion of figures of different ages, genders, occupations, and personalities in the cast appears to be an attempt to symbolize a miniature society.

The "bus-stop" is located in a suburb of Beijing. The characters come one by one to wait for the bus to go to town, but all the buses whiz past in front of the stop, completely ignoring the waiting masses. The Silent Man walks away silently when he sees that nothing is going to happen, the others keep waiting.

From the dialogue, the audience learns that these people have been waiting for a year. "Glasses" takes a look at his watch and finds out that a year and eight months have passed. Immediately, he states that five years and ten months have slipped by. Then, we find out that ten whole years have gone by, coinciding with the duration of the ten-year-long Cultural Revolution. The Girl becomes grey-haired while the Mother has a head of white hair. "Glasses" has passed the official age limit for entrance examinations. In short, invaluable time has been squandered for nothing. At this point, all of them suddenly see that there is no name for the stop on the sign and that possibly it has long ago ceased being a bus stop.

Gao was probably inspired by Beckett's *En Attendant Godot*. In the latter, two vagabonds wait for Godot, who does not show up. The main characters Gogo and Didi let time slip by without accomplishing anything. The difference between Gao and Beckett's works is that the latter is comparatively ambiguous in that Godot could be a number of things. The process of waiting is portrayed as not necessarily a waste of time. One may perceive from *En Attendant Godot* that the ends of life matter less than the means. Thus, life is a kind of anticipation while what one is anticipating is not as important.

Connotations of *The Bus-Stop* are quite concrete. The people expect a "promised" society, but the vehicle that is supposed to carry them there passes by without stopping. It appears that Gao Xingjian does not think that the aim of a more prosperous society is an illusion but that the means to attain that goal are deceptive. For further elucidation of his point, Gao turns characters in *The Bus-Stop* into narrators. For instance, Director Ma says: "Waiting itself doesn't matter. What matters is that you must have a clear idea in the first place about what you are waiting for in the queue. If you just stand in the queue and keep waiting in vain for half a lifetime, aren't you making a big joke of yourself?" Socialist critics have commented on the theatre of the absurd as "unmistakably very direct political criticism of realistic society" (Tang et al., 1984, p. 3).

IDEOLOGICAL CRITICISM IN CHINA

Debates concerning *The Bus-Stop* mostly centred on the political stand that "literature and art should serve society and the people." In its third issue of 1984, *Xiju bao* 戲劇報 [The drama journal] published an article entitled "*Chezhan* sanren tan" 《車站》三人談 [A three-man discussion on *The Bus-Stop*]. Participants Tang Yin 唐因, Du Gao 杜高 and Zheng Bonong 鄭伯農 all believed that the play was excessively tendentious. Tang said: "This play is an expression of the strong doubts in our life," Du criticized: "In fact, it is nothing but an imitation of the Western Theatre of the Absurd in content and form, following in the footsteps of the decadent literature and art of the West." And Zheng commented: "In this work, *The Bus-Stop*, we do not see a single gleam of light or a single ray of hope for reform. All the depictions are a kind of untrue and twisted reflection of our reality and our future."

It is clear that what they criticize is the playwright's ideology and not the Theatre of the Absurd. It seems that these commentators have no interest in knowing what this new type of theatre really is. In July of 1984, the seventh issue of *Wenyi bao* 文藝報 published an article in defence of Gao Xingjian, which ironically is even less to the point. The article states: "Through the methods of contrast and comparison, *The Bus-Stop* satirizes the futile squandering of time, youth, and life, by foolishly waiting at a deserted stop. At the same time, it eulogizes the no-nonsense Silent Man who has the spirit of conscientiously seeking advancement" (Qu, 1984). The article has shifted the target of criticism from the deceptive buses to the waiting passengers. One may wonder whether Gao would appreciate such a well-intended defence.

From the above discussion, it becomes clear that literary criticism in mainland China in the 1980s followed an established procedure, no matter what the subject material was. In the first place, orthodox critics sifted through the work according to the materialist theory of mimesis and reflection, and then by the orthodoxy of instrumentalism. It is no wonder that the Theatre of the Absurd was crushed into nothingness.

The Theatre of the Absurd occupies a place in the development of Western drama that is comparable to the replacement of paradigms in scientific development. Thomas S. Kuhn asserts that the replacement of paradigms in science (such as from Newtonian physics to Einstein physics) is a readjustment, of cosmological epistemologies (Kuhn, 1962). Playwrights of the Theatre of the Absurd view life differently from that of their counterparts in the theatre of realism of the late nineteenth century. There are two obvious differences: first, the Theatre of the Absurd does not abide by the norms of mimesis and reflection; and secondly, it is not intended to reform society or to convey any ideology. Using the norms of the theatre of realism to judge the Theatre of the Absurd is equal to employing concepts of Newtonian physics to criticize the world described by Einstein.

Furthermore, mainland Chinese critics have failed to see that Gao's works are not an "imitation of the Western Theatre of the Absurd in content and form." Gao only borrowed certain techniques of the Theatre of the Absurd, such as the confusion of time. The characters in his plays talk logically and their characterization is realistic. Most important is that he does not have the pessimistic ideology of Ionesco or Beckett which completely negates the meaning of life. Gao still tries to make a point and to criticize. Therefore, under the cloak of "absurdity" there throbs a heart of realism. Other mainland playwrights allegedly of the Theatre of the Absurd are similar in nature. For instance, Wei Minglun's 魏明倫 "absurd" Sichuan opera *Pan Jinlian* 潘金蓮 includes in its dramatis personae well-known figures in Chinese and Western literature such as Jia Baoyu 賈寶玉 and Anna Karenina, as well as famous historical personalities such as Shi Nai'an 施耐庵 and Wu Zetian 武則天. Indeed, Wei has adopted the technique of confusing the characters, but the point is to reverse the judgement passed on Pan Jinlian for the purpose of promoting women's rights.

The defiant attitude of totally negating the meaning of human life, and the creative spirit which disregards criticism, as demonstrated by Western playwrights of the Theatre of the Absurd, can only emerge when societies respect individual thought and uphold the freedom of speech. Catholic France tolerates anti-Christian atheism and Existentialism. This fact indicates that the Catholic Church in France is no longer an oppressive institution, so that French writers can enjoy an environment of free expression. Socialist China tolerates nothing that is anti-socialist.

The freedom of creative writing is still rather a luxury. The postmodernist Theatre of the Absurd was purported to oppose conventionalism which audiences accustomed to conventionalities could not readily accept.

Therefore, the emergence of "plays of the absurd" in mainland China may be no more than an ornamental episode, one which earns no praise from the critics and lacks a supportive audience. Some may think that the Chinese audience does not appreciate the tragic. If so, this may be because there have been so many serious tragedies in China's long history. In the same way, the mainland Chinese audience's lack of appreciation for "play of the absurd" is perhaps attributable to the numerous absurdities that have been occurring around them in the past fifty years. Under the existing ruling system, the development of theatre in mainland China will probably be determined by two major factors: the limits of tolerance of the cultural authorities who give the orders, and tastes of the audience.

NOTES

1. This is a revised version of an article with the same title published in *Issues and Studies, A Journal of China Studies and International Affairs*, Vol. 25, No. 8 (August 1989), pp. 138–148

2. Alfred Jarry's comedy imitates the *Oedipus Rex*, which earned unexpected success. Later on, Jarry authored a series of scripts about the character Ubu.

3. This refers to works of Witkacy and others. See Mignon (1978), pp. 225–229.

4. *La Cantatrice Chauve* was first staged at the Théâtre des Noctambules in Paris on 11. May 1950. It was moved on 20 February 1952 to the Théâtre de Poche for simultaneous performance with *La Leçon*. This production was still running when I revisited Paris in 1986.

5. The play is written in French. The name Godot has many Chinese transliterations.

6. For details, see Jacques Lemarchand's preface to Ionesco's *Théâtre I* in Ionesco (1954).

7. For instance, the plays of Ionesco and Beckett are called "Le théâtre de dérision" in Michel Corvin's *Le Théâtre Nouveau en France*, which was published by the Presses Universitaires de France in 1966. Moreover, the works of Jean Genet, R. Weingarten, B. Vian, Fernando Arrabal, and R. Pinget are classified under the same category.

8. Chen Shouzhu has pointed out in his article entitled "Tan haungdan xiju shuailuo ji qi zai woguo de yingxiang" 談荒誕戲劇的衰落及其在我國的影響 [The decline of the theatre of the absurd and its influence in our country]

(Chen, 1988) that as early as 1965, Beckett's *Waiting for Godot* and Ionesco's *The Chairs* were translated into Chinese and published, then the Cultural Revolution came, and the play of the absurd did not exert much influence on our theatre. However, Chen did not give specific information about publication of the two translated plays.

9. From October 28, 1981 to March 5, 1982, I lectured at the universities of Nankai, Beijing, Shandong, and Shanghai. In addition to the Theatre of the Absurd, I also lectured on the subjects of "The Stream of Consciousness in Modern Western Fiction" and "Modern Fiction in Taiwan."

10. The information was provided by Gao Xingjian.

REFERENCES

Camus, Albert (1942). *Le Mythe de Sisyphe*. Paris: Gallimard.

Chen Shouzhu 陳瘦竹 (1988). "Tan haungdan xiju shuailuo ji qi zai woguo de yingxiang" 談荒誕戲劇的衰落及其在我國的影響 [The decline of the theatre of the absurd and its influence in our country]. In Chen (1988), pp. 252–261. Original work published in *Shehui kexue pinglun* 社會科學評論 [Review of social science], No. 11 (1985).

—— (1988). *Xiju lilun wenji* 戲劇理論文集 [Essays on dramatic theories]. Beijing: Zhongguo xiju chubanshe 中國戲劇出版社.

Corvin, Michel (1966). *Le Théâtre Nouveau en France*. Paris: Presses Universitaires.

Esslin, Martin (1987). *The Theatre of the Absurd*. London: Penguin Books.

Gao Xingjian 高行健 (1985). *Gao Xingjian xiju ji* 高行健戲劇集 [Plays by Gao Xingjian]. Beijing: Qunzhong chubanshe 群眾出版社.

Ionesco, Eugène (1954). *Théâtre I*. Paris: Gallimard.

Kuln, Thomas S. (1962). *The Structure of Scientific Revolution*. Chicago: University of Chicago Press.

Lin Kehuan 林克歡 (1985). "Ma Sen de huangdan ju" 馬森的荒誕劇 [Ma Sen's plays of the absurd]. *Ju ben* 劇本 [Dramatic script], No. 3, pp. 90–92.

Ma Sen 馬森 (1985a). "Huangmiao de rensheng, Huangmiao de xiju — yu Younaisike zuotan" 荒謬的人生、荒謬的戲劇 —— 與尤乃斯柯座談 [Absurd Life, absurd drama — A talk with Ionesco]. In Ma Sen (1985b), p. 71–75.

—— (1985b). *Ma Sen xiju lun ji* 馬森戲劇論集 [Collected dramatic criticism by Ma Sen]. Taipei: Erya chubanshe 爾雅出版社.

—— (1985c). "*Yizi* de wutai xingxiang" 《椅子》的舞台形象 [Stage image of *The Chairs*.]. In Ma (1985b), pp. 249–261.

Mignon, Paul-Louis (1978). *Panorama du Théâtre au XXe Siècles*. Paris: Gallimard.

Qu Liuyi 曲六乙 (1984). "Ping huaju *Chezhan* ji qi piping" 評話劇《車站》及其批評 [On the play *The Bus-Stop* and the criticism on it]. *Wenyi bao* 文藝報, No. 7, pp. 29–33.

Shi Xianrong 施咸榮 et al., trans. (1980). *Huangdanpai xiju ji* 荒誕派戲劇集 [A collection of absurd drama]. Shanghai: Shanghai yiwen chubanshe 上海譯文出版社.

Tang Yin 唐因, Du Gao 杜高 and Zheng Bonong 鄭伯農 (1984). "*Chezhan* sanren tan"《車站》三人談 [A three-man discussion on *The Bus-Stop*]. *Xiju bao* 戲劇報 [The drama journal], No. 3, pp. 3–7.

Wild Man Between Two Cultures[1]

In May 1985, when Gao Xingjian premiered his third play, *Yeren* 野人 [Wild man], in Beijing, its critical reception was quite different from his first two plays, *Juedui xinhao* 絕對信號 [Alarm signal] staged in 1982 and *Chezhan* 車站 [The bus-stop] in 1983.[2] Both of his earlier plays have been immediately recognized as being strongly "influenced" by the Western modern theatre — by such people as "the formidable French dramatist," Antonin Artaud, and "a host of writers and theorists of the Theatre of the Absurd."[3] The Western critics were unanimous in reviewing *The Bus-Stop* as "the first play to introduce elements of the Theatre of the Absurd to a Chinese audience" (Barmé, 1983, pp. 373–376). Their Chinese counterparts, likewise, expressed a similar view. One of the striking features of *The Bus-Stop*, as Wang Xining argued in a review in *China Daily*, is that it successfully "dissected modern Chinese urban society in a manner reminiscent of Beckett's *Waiting for Godot*" (Wang, 1985, p. 5).

A NEW TURN IN GAO'S EXPERIMENTATION

Wild Man, the third of Gao Xingjian's plays to be performed, however, elicited a quite different critical response. On the one hand, some Chinese and Western critics were still enthusiastic about its Western style and technique. Others, however, pointed to a new turn in Gao's interest, one which drew on the rich resources of Chinese theatrical traditions. Those who celebrated the return of Chinese tradition in Gao's latest play insisted that it owed its success mainly to its endeavor to enrich "the range of expression open to artists in all performing arts in China" (Wang, 1985, p. 5). What is perhaps most interesting in this critical

disagreement is the way that it heightens our awareness of the complexity of cultural relations which underlie the play, and leads to what has
already become a central question about it — is the play primarily
founded on a Chinese or Western model? This disagreement about *Wild
Man* has been further complicated by Gao's own declaration of intention,
which stresses his allegiance to the classical Chinese traditions in theatre.
In the "Postscript" to the published form of the play, Gao explains that
Wild Man is an attempt to realize his ideal of establishing a "modern
theatre" by drawing on traditional Chinese operas characterized by its
artistic techniques of *chang* 唱 [singing], *nian* 念 [speech], *zuo* 做 [acting],
and *da* 打 [acrobatics].[4] Interestingly enough, in characterizing this native Chinese tradition Gao uses the term "Total Theatre" — a term which
cannot fail to suggest to the Western consciousness the work of Antonin
Artaud, and indeed the whole *Gesamtkunstwerk* tradition since Wagner
— to designate his "ideal" theatre in which artists would easily "recover
many Chinese artistic techniques already lost in the last century" (Gao,
1985a, p. 169).

Gao explicitly claims in his "Postscript" that this play does not attempt
to win over its audience by the art of dialogue, a feature which he associ-
ates with the Western drama; instead, he claims, *Wild Man* seeks a full
employment of the traditional Chinese operatic, and above all, non-
verbal techniques of dance, music, images, costumes, and make-up to
compose a "dramatic symphony" which consists of several different
themes, themes which overlap harmonies and disharmonies in order to
fashion a "polyphony." In *Wild Man*, therefore, both language and music are used in such a way that they create a kind of "multi-voicedness."
Just as a symphony seeks to create "a total musical image," Gao asserts,
Wild Man "tends to realize a total effect of action through multi-
voicedness, counter-points, contrasts and repetitions" (Gao, 1985a,
p. 169). For the visual aspect of the play, Gao symphonizes a "multi-layer-
visual-image" through the use of dance, flash-back scenes, shadows, and
movements. Each actor in *Wild Man*, therefore, must possess the "skills
required by the traditional Chinese theatre": he must perform at once
as a dancer, a singer, an acrobat as well as a speaking character.
Costuming, our playwright demands, should not only be strikingly bright
in colour, as is required by the traditional theatre to enhance the visual
and physical effect on the senses of the audience, but it should also "truth-
fully reflect the local colour of the mountain area along the Yellow River"

which provides the play with its geographical background. A faithful portrayal of the primitive and natural lifestyle of the mountain folks, Gao Xingjian insists, is crucial for a successful production of the play. Fortunately, Lin Zhaohua 林兆華, the Beijing director of *Wild Man*, fundamentally preserved the "Chineseness" that Gao Xingjian so painstakingly spelled out. *Wild Man* was for the most part performed in the local dialect of Sichuan Province, with episodic scenes which remind one of the traditional "opera-drama sketches," mixed up with local folk songs, national minority dances, and Han epic singing.

INDIGENOUS THEMES IN *WILD MAN*

In addition to the traditional Chinese theatrical conventions consciously explored both by the playwright and the director, *Wild Man's* dramatic structure and theme are also indigenously Chinese. Unlike Western drama, which usually has an Aristotelian plot with a beginning, a middle, and an end, *Wild Man* carries no obvious story-line. Instead, the play consists of a series of diverse episodes peopled by nameless characters who move in a more or less definite and identifiable place. The play is set in contemporary China in the rapidly-vanishing virgin forest of Sichuan province where some scientists and local people believe in the existence of wild men, a sort of man-like monkey which is believed to offer the much sought "missing link" of traditional evolutionary theory. A nameless scientist, designated in the script only by the character name "ecologist," goes into the forest to undertake research on wildmen, hoping to learn not only something about these strange "living fossils," but also about the preservation of a living and natural environment which he believes is ultimately linked to the continuation of the human species.

In his travels the ecologist encounters lumber men, wood-cutters, and local "cadres" — bureaucrats who make their fame and living by destroying the forests. By virtue of their occupations, all of these people threaten the living environment of wild men and thus come into conflict with the ecologist. In the course of the play he also sets himself in opposition to other city-dwellers who, like him, have ventured into the forests for the sake of tracing the whereabouts of the wild men, though motivated by purposes quite different from his own. A newspaper man — again the character has no name and is designated only by his profession — for instance, is merely interested in hunting for "hot" or "exotic" news to please his readers in the city. Similarly, scientists representing opposing sides in a scholarly debate are at work collecting data only to prove or disprove the existence of the wild men. Unlike the ecologist, they have no interest in investigating living creatures and their environmental conditions in order to protect them. They bribe innocent local people, especially children who cannot even understand the issues at stake, in order to prove the existence or non-existence of wild men, thus bringing about quarrels, disputes, and disharmony in the mountain village in which peace, unity, and harmony once prevailed.

Another episodic strain of the play concerns a school teacher who devotes all his time and energy attempting to rescue an epic of the Han nationality — the only one of its kind — by writing down the performance of an old and dying epic rhapsodist. This epic, *The Song of Darkness,* recounts the history and development of the Han nationality from the time of its childhood — when it first began to separate itself from the wild men — up to the present time. Because of its nature and scope, the ecologist and teacher believe that the epic should be regarded as a "national treasure" which is "as precious as panda and wild man" for the Chinese nation. Integrated into this episode are other overlapping themes and "subplots" which deal with problematic and still unanswered questions in contemporary China about love, marriage, ethics, custom, tradition, corruption, and even ideological issues left unresolved from the Cultural Revolution.

Wild Man is infinitely more complex than what I have just indicated here, but enough has been said, I think, to indicate the ways in which the play offers a view of an exceedingly problematic world that is full of contradictions and disharmonies. Yet unexpectedly at the end of the play we are offered an episode which is connected with many of the play's diverse concerns. Here a wild man appears to a little boy in a dream. The wild man imitates the boy's language and gesture, dancing with him happily, running with him into the depth of the forest. While these actions are taking place, the audience becomes increasingly aware of the epic singing and folk music which grows louder and more prominent in order to furnish an accompaniment to the scene. Central to this moment in the play's economy is a silent but nonetheless real "dialogue" between this child of modern man and his predecessor, between "mankind and Nature."[5] The image created by this last scene, one so strongly suggestive of harmony and cosmic totality, is clearly related to the spectacular ending of the traditional Chinese theatre that overwhelms its audience with a *Gesamtkunstwerk*-like effect of singing, dancing and acting. Such an ending thematically embraces the Daoist vision of a harmony between nature and culture. It provides its audience with a catharsis that supposedly enabled them to come to grips with the cosmic and mythological forces in the universe. As the director of the play, Lin Zhaohua, points out: ultimately *Wild Man* is about harmony, "a harmony between people and their nation, a harmony among people themselves. It urges the audience to think about its relationship to nature and to culture, especially ancient culture" (Baum, 1985, p. 9). It seems clear, then, that both in form and content *Wild Man* can be viewed as a contemporary restoration of the theatrical, cultural, and philosophical traditions of China.

ARTAUDIAN ELEMENTS IN *WILD MAN*

It, nevertheless, would be a serious mistake to see in Gao Xingjian's play only a recuperation of indigenous Chinese traditions. As the terminology in which Gao describes his play suggests, anyone at all acquainted with the modern Western theatre will not fail to be immediately impressed by the way it seems to exploit conceptions of the theatre strikingly similar to those advocated by Antonin Artaud's notion of "the total theatre" and Brecht's theory of "epic theatre." Artaud, of course, spent much of his life longing for a theatre of "a pure action," a theatre of a latent force beyond rational speech or language, beyond "a written text" and "a literary tradition." He therefore sought to create a theatre wholly unlike the Western theatre of his time, one which would present an "archetypal and dangerous reality, a reality of which the Principles ... hurry to dive back into the obscurity of the deep" (Artaud, 1958, p. 48). Artaud believed that fixed text, language, reason, order, even civilization itself with its attendant traditions, were barriers to the human spirit. He therefore called for a theatre of physicality that was to create "a metaphysics of speech, gesture, and expression" which would be capable of throwing its spectators back to real life, not by imitation or illusion, but by a mystical, ritual, primitive, or archetypal spectacle of signs and gestures which spoke for the anti-rational element in human experience. Artaud therefore proposed to resort to mass spectacle, providing his audience with a "pure experience" which would create a sensation of totality, awakening in them an intuitive force, which was expressed in a theatre of the body. If language is used at all, Artaud observed, it must be a language beyond words and senses capable of evoking that which cannot be spoken. He therefore called his ideal theatre "a sacred theatre" because it was to have "the solemnity of a sacred rite" (Artaud, 1958, p. 58). Thus the Artaudian theatre aims at a more universal, primordial force deeper than any psychological or social reality, a force that touches on "an idea of Chaos, an idea of the Marvelous, an idea of Equilibrium" (Artaud, 1958, p. 36).

All of these Artaudian elements of the theatre can easily be identified in *Wild Man*. By means of non-verbal elements, *Wild Man* provides for its audiences the kind of total and physical experience that Artaud so painstakingly emphasized. The time span of 8,000 years in *Wild Man*'s action and its invocation to *Pangu* 盤古, the Chinese God of creation in the primordial times, suggest to its spectators a cosmic view of the universe. The sharp contrast between the non-verbal, primitive wild man and the verbal but confused, problematic modern man shocks the spectators and thus attempts to throw them into a mystical and ritual experience which is "deeper than any psychological or social realities." The world of *Wild Man* extends far beyond the boundaries of anything uniquely Chinese and modern; indeed, the play seems finally concerned with issues that belong to a world much larger than that which is codified in the details of its dialogue, language, and setting. Much of the effect of the play is achieved by its spectacular physicality which seeks to create the sensation that Artaud said would simultaneously "touch on Creation, Becoming, and Chaos" (Artaud, 1958, p. 90).

To a large extent, then, *Wild Man* participates in the traditions of the Artaudian theatre with its "passionate equation between Man, Society, Nature and Objects" (Artaud, 1958, p. 90). All of these concerns are crystallized in the last scene where, as we have already seen, amidst a mixture of pantomime, mimicry, and musical harmonies and rhythms, a wild man, the image of the primitive and the natural, dances with a little boy, a symbol of the childhood of civilization. At the end of the play, we are provided with the following stage directions:

> They [the wild man and Xi Mao, the little boy] run onto an elevation at the back of the stage. XI MAO does a forward roll. He turns expectantly to the WILD MAN, who clumsily does the same. XI MAO runs, calling to the WILD MAN, who runs after him. They play hide and seek. XI MAO

looks out from behind a stone. The WILD MAN sees him and runs toward him. XI MAO runs toward the elevation, and the WILD MAN follows. Gently, music starts and their movements slow down until they look as though they are in a slow-motion film. Then they perform a dance. XI MAO is nimble, the WILD MAN clumsy. When XI MAO and the WILD MAN play together, the WILD MAN tends to copy XI MAO's movements, even when in slow motion. The WILD MAN should always have his back to the audience. XI MAO draws back into an area of light at the rear of the stage, in front of a backdrop depicting the forest. All performers enter wearing masks, each mask expressing a different shade of emotion. The "happier" masks should be in the centre of the stage. All move slowly toward the WILD MAN, to the rhythm of the LUMBERJACKS' dance and the melody from the song of the TEAM OF SISTERS. The sad cries of the OLD SINGER are heard, gradually fading out. XI MAO is seen and faintly heard saying, "Xia, xia, a shame, xia, xia, xia, xia. A shame, a ... shame." (*Curtain*).[6]

All these and other theatrical conventions seek to put the audience into a state prior to language and therefore help them to break away from the intellectual subjugation of the language, thus conveying to them a sense of "a new and a deeper intellectuality which hides itself beneath the gestures and signs, raised to the dignity of particular exorcisms" (Artaud, 1958, p. 91). With this world of "the Absolutes" and "the invisible" cosmic forces, *Wild Man* also meets the demands of the Artaudian theatre for a "a religious ritual," and therefore moves towards what Leonard Pronko has characterized as "that meeting point where human and nonhuman, meaning and chaos, finite and infinite, come together" (Pronko, 1967, p. 15).

Yet, as soon as we have identified the similarities between *Wild Man* and its Western counterparts, we are also tempted to "decentre" this claim by arguing for the opposite "truth." Artaud emphasizes the dynamics of action and the higher forces of violent physical images that "crush and hypnotize the sensibility of the spectator." He even went so far as to exclude from the theatre any "copy of life," or any concern with aspect of social and psychological realities (Artaud, 1958, p. 83). Within his limited concern of trying to restore theatre to its original direction, to "reinstate it in its religious and metaphysical aspect," Artaud makes explicit that his theatre must "break with actuality," and that its object must not be to "resolve social or psychological conflicts" or "to serve as battlefield for moral passions." The function of theatre, he insists, is to express objectively certain secret truths that "have been buried under forms in their encounters with Becoming" (Artaud, 1958, p. 70). For him, language, tradition, and the theatrical masterpieces of the past are responsible for the decline of the Western theatre. If a contemporary public does not understand *Oedipus Rex*, he argues, it is the fault of this ancient Greek play, not of the public, since the latter has learned too well that the theatre frequently deals with the themes of incest, morality, falsehood, and illusion. A concentration on social realities and their attendant problems is regarded in the Artaudian model as being outside of the legitimate concern or the proper domain of theatre.

A TOTAL THEATRE BEYOND ARTAUD

In recognizing this claim of Artaud's "total theatre," we are immediately brought face-to-face with the way that *Wild Man* rejects some of Artaud's demands. There can be no denying that *Wild Man* is firmly foregrounded in contemporary Chinese society; its concerns, as we have noted earlier, are occasional in the best sense of that term. Though its episodic structure forecloses the possibility of its offering a "solution" at the end of the play, *Wild Man* nonetheless raises in a striking and even direct way unanswered and perhaps unanswerable questions about love, marriage, tradition, bureaucracy, science, morality, and even the current national preoccupation with ecology and environmental protection. It is true that *Wild Man* can be categorized as a traditional dance and music drama, and that in this sense it seems to meet Artaud's demand for a form of theatre that is closely related to ritual and religious ceremony. But it is also true that its basic thematic matter is concerned with a conflict between nature and culture that is specific to a moment in late twentieth-century Chinese history. In fact, precisely because these thematic concerns are historically so far removed from the primitive and the ritual experience in which they are theatrically mediated to us, the play is able to go beyond Artaud by combining that sense of primitive "magic culture," which Artaud's theatre seeks, with much that is not Artaudian — an entirely modern world with its own social and psychological dimensions.

The same dichotomy between that which belongs to the "total theatre" and that which does not becomes apparent when we attempt to locate the kinds of theatrical gestures and movements which *Wild Man* employs. From one perspective the play's actions seem to look back to that moment when religious ceremony emerged from its purely ritualistic origins and was transformed into the beginnings of what we know as theatre.[7] On the other hand, the play's action definitely goes beyond the first beginnings of the theatre. It includes elements which we associate with a "mature" theatre, with its combination of the verbal with the nonverbal, the actual with the imaginative, the social with the psychological, and above all, the sensational with the individual. *Wild Man* is at once descriptive and narrative, spectacular and physical. The opposing claims for the traditional and the modern, the intellectual and the physical — seen by Artaud as irreconcilable or as hurled against each other — are here coupled together. It is perhaps in this sense that *Wild Man* realizes the ideal of a theatre of "totality" which goes well beyond Artaud's demands and in which the basic disparity between self and others, subject and object, reason and sensations, language and signs are finally engulfed and united.

But Artaud is not the only Western theoretician of the drama whose work is relevant to *Wild Man*. Gao Xingjian observes in his "Postscript" that *Wild Man's* emphasis on the *mise en scène* and spectacle does not aim at creating verisimilitude. It is intended, on the contrary, for reminding "its audience that it is acting," not real life. Gao therefore expressly requires that masks be used in the production of *Wild Man* in order to emphasize the dichotomies, contradictions or multi-voicedness within the characters. At the outset of the play, the actor who plays the part of the ecologist steps out of his character and exhorts his audience to enjoy the play fully without worrying about the whereabouts of the actors, who may sometimes appear sitting in the audience. There need not be, he implies, any barriers between the world of the audience and the world of the play. In the middle of the play, for instance, the ecologist takes off his mask more than once in order to assume his identity as an actor. In this guise he recites poems and provides background information. Earlier, at the outset of the play, he even "narrates" what would normally be regarded as stage directions and theatrical comments. In this way, the actor openly disowns his character. He calls attention to his many different roles — the ecologist, the actor who plays the ecologist, and a stage director. He is, he reminds us, at different times all of these figures, and yet he is "really" none of them. Such a discourse seems intended to prevent us from establishing an emotional identification with the ecologist or any other character. All of these devices are suggestive of the Brechtian theatre, of course. In his article "*Yeren* yu wo" 《野人》與我 [*Wild Man* and I], Gao Xingjian openly admits such a Brechtian influence, especially as concerns the now classic theory of the "alienation effect" (Gao, 1985c, p. 2). For him, Brechtian distancing devices help break down the conventional notion of the theatre as representation of real life.[8]

But just as our observation of the Artaudian elements in *Wild Man* led us also to see the presence of the opposite, so here too the Brechtian nature of the drama is undercut in our very act of recognizing its presence. Brecht's "alienation effect" aims basically and fundamentally at keeping the spectators from being emotionally involved so that they can intellectually contemplate the possible meanings of the play. In the "Postscript" to *Wild Man*, however, Gao Xingjian paradoxically specifies that the director should create in the play a kind of "cordial atmosphere" in which the actors directly communicate with the audience (a Brechtian technique as well as one that recalls the works of Thornton Wilder) so that the audience can feel free and happy to participate in the total experience of the theatre, as if they were enjoying an entertainment during a festival (a notion which is decidedly un-Brechtian). The production, our playwright specifies, should also leave enough time between each act so that the audience is able to think intellectually, reflect, and ponder over what they have just experienced. *Wild Man*, therefore, offers its audiences a multiple, polyvalent, and even contradictory experience in which the body and mind, the primitive and the contemporary, the universal and the local, the sensational and the intellectual, the subjective and the objective, the illusionary and the actual are all joyfully united and combined. It is at once Brechtian and anti-Brechtian, Artaudian and anti-Artaudian. It is at once both and yet neither.

RE-VISIONING "INFLUENCE"

Gao Xingjian's *Wild Man*, therefore, presents to us a strange and yet stimulating dramatic phenomenon which raises in a radical way a number of theoretical issues that are not restricted to "the dramatic" in the narrower sense of that term, but which reach into the theory of literature in general, and, as the rest of this study will suggest, into the theory and practice of comparative literature in particular. Gao's play raises questions of the first order about the "canonical" practice of "influence studies," and it is to this concern, both relevant for the comparative study of dramatic texts and non-dramatic texts, to which I shall now turn.

Ulrich Weisstein has said: "the notion of influence must be regarded as virtually the key concept in Comparative Literature studies, since it posits the presence of two distinct and therefore comparable entities: the work from which the influence proceeds and that [to] which it is directed" (Weisstein, 1968, p. 29). That is to say, cross-cultural literary studies, as a comparative discipline, have depended largely on the "key notion of influence studies" which are characterized as one-to-one relationships between "emitter" and "receiver" texts. At first sight, the general concerns of this essay — the relationship between one national theatre and that of the other — seem to be the proper subject for these kinds of "influence studies."[9] On further consideration, however, these concerns can be seen to raise, perhaps in a radical way, theoretical questions on the validity and legitimacy of such traditionally conceived "influence studies." It will be the burden of the rest of this essay to set the discussion on *Wild Man,* and the Western dramatic theories on which it seems to draw, within a broader context of some critical theories of canon formation in the West and the East alike.[10]

As our discussion of *Wild Man* has already suggested, it is exceedingly difficult if not impossible, to determine which cultural tradition evoked in *Wild Man* is the "emitter" and which is the "receiver." Did the Chinese traditional theatre influence the West by means of Brecht's theories, which, as Brecht himself admitted, were derived in some sense from Chinese sources? In that case, Chinese theories of drama made a detour through Western cultural traditions only to come back to China to exert an influence on the modern Chinese theatre. Or did Artaud and Brecht influence Gao Xingjian, who, in turn, found in the West that which had been lost in the contemporary Chinese theatre? Or is it, more simply, the case that Gao reached back into his own national traditions to create his play?[11] To raise these questions is to see that it is impossible simply to posit the "presence of two distinct and therefore comparable entities."

The question of whether *Wild Man* is indigenously "Chinese" or characteristically "Western" can here be seen as deeply puzzling. *Wild Man* appears to be both, and yet, it can never be "proven" to be one or the other. As we have seen earlier, *Wild Man* has been received as the most

"Chinese" play Gao has ever written, and this very "Chineseness" in the play has even been declared as part of his own attempt to rescue modern Chinese theatre from being too much influenced by its Western counterparts. However, as soon as we have discovered everything that can be identified as "Chinese," these characteristics can immediately be "decentred" in order to prove just the opposite claim. We might, then, be tempted to say that the play is the product of Western influence. But clearly the matter cannot be solved so facilely. Furthermore, talking about the play's "Westerness" invites yet another confusion: one perceives at the same moment the Artaudian as well as the anti-Artaudian elements, the Brechtian as well as the anti-Brechtian characteristics. It seems pertinent, therefore, to first of all attempt to "decide," if ever possible, the nature of "Chineseness" and of "Westerness" in the context of our discussion before one can even begin to discuss, and therefore to challenge, the concept of the relationship between an "emitter" and a "receiver" in the traditional mode of "influence studies."

But our difficulties are not due solely to the complications and contradictions embedded in the term "Western dramatic tradition." The words "Chineseness" and "the Chinese theatre" have a similar long and seemingly "confusing" history, and this history is further complicated, in the West at least, by generations of Western critical acts of "misreading" and "misunderstanding."[12] As Leonard C. Pronko has rightly pointed out in his *Theater East and West*, the traditional Chinese theatre "has had a history of singular mis-comprehension and mis-interpretation in the West" (Pronko, 1967, p. 35). When one considers the sheer difficulty of communicating across cultural boundaries, it is easy to agree with Pronko's claim. But Pronko's implied evaluation of misunderstanding and misreading, common as they are, constitutes at best only a partially valid view of these activities. Pronko assumes that "mis-comprehension" and "mis-interpretation" are undesirable activities, and that it is the task of cross-cultural studies to remove them. But as a good deal of recent literary theory has insisted, "misreading" and "misunderstanding" are not wholly negative actions. On the contrary, for critics like T. S. Eliot and Harold Bloom, these once-thought "negative" activities are the means by which literary history is made and — I would add — cross-cultural influence takes place.

For Eliot, Bloom, and a number of other theorists, Western literary production is motivated by an intense quest for the novel, or the apparently new. "Strong" writers and critics seek ways of escaping — or apparently escaping — the "father" tradition in which they have been formed, and the process of "misunderstanding" and "misreading" provided a convenient means for their accomplishing this goal. In an attempt to say what apparently had not been said before, some Western writers turned, and continue to turn, to the novelty of exotic literature. But the exotic literature was not studied or appropriated for its own sake. Rather it was appropriated and reworked for the apparent strangeness, which it offered to audiences. Yet paradoxically, the otherness could not be allowed to remain as otherness, for in order for Western audiences to appropriate it in some way, the strange had to be made familiar; the exotic had to be domesticated, even if in the process it ceased to be exotic. To take a specific example, eighteenth-century European writers, motivated by an "anxiety of influence," turned to classical Chinese drama as a source of novelty. Yet in order to make these strange texts comprehensible, they "misread" them by making them conform to traditions of Western drama. Let us first of all consider briefly the process by which this paradoxical transformation took place.

Fan Xiheng, in his essay "From *The Orphan of Chao to Orphelin de la Chine*," describes for us a brief history of the transformation of a Chinese drama from the Yuan dynasty (1279–1368) into Western dramatic repertory. This Yuan drama, known as *Zhaoshi gu'er dabaochou* 趙氏孤兒大報仇 [The great revenge of the orphan of Zhao], is attributed to Ji Junxiang and was first performed in China around the thirteenth century. The same play was later re-written by another anonymous author under the title of *Zhaoshi gu'er ji* 趙氏孤兒記 [The story of the orphan of Zhao]. According to Fan Xiheng, Ji Junxiang's Yuan drama was first translated into French in the 1730s, which brought about other translations into English, German, Italian, and Russian.[13] This Chinese Yuan play has thus over the centuries inspired several generations of Western dramatists such as the Englishman William Hatchett, who adopted Ji's Chinese story into his *The Chinese Orphan,* and the Italian playwright Pietro Metastasio, who wrote his own version of *Eroe Cinese*, to name only a few. A better-known case, of course, is Voltaire's *Orphelin de La Chine*, which was so successful in its Paris premier that it was immediately translated into Italian and English. Yet, this process of transformation was by no means a one-way street. Not only did the original Chinese text inspire Western readers, but Chinese readers, upon reading their Western peers' re-creation of the Chinese text, did not hesitate to translate these Western texts back into Chinese language again. During the Second World War, for instance, a Chinese writer by the name of Zhang Ruogu translated Voltaire's French play, which was originally based on Ji's Chinese orphan story, into an abridged *prose* version "in order to raise the morale of the Chinese people in their struggle against Japanese invaders" (Fan, 1987, pp. 159–195).

Among several Western transformations mentioned above, one of the earliest "creative misreadings" was William Hatchett's well-known adaptation of the Chinese Yuan drama, published in England in 1741. He attracted his audience and gained a certain amount of notoriety for himself by his "new" work with a borrowed "exotic" story and a foreign "parentage." Having to cope with the burden of his own Western tradition in order to find for himself a place in his own cultural tradition, Hatchett "creatively" distorted the Chinese Yuan play and actually presented it as "an English neo-classic play, observing the unity of time," though in fact his Chinese "father" story takes place over some twenty-five years (Pronko, 1967, p. 37). It is clear that the so-called "Chinese influence" at this early stage of cultural exchange amounts to nothing more than an expression of the European taste for the exotic, the different, the dissimilar which must be garbed in Western clothing to make it attractive. The image of the "Chinese theatre" that Hatchett's work suggests is only a Westerner's own arbitrary interpretation — or, better, "misinterpretation" and "misunderstanding" — of it. It is a product of a Western search for things "anew" — foreign manners, interesting events, plots or characters of curiosity. Yet in Hatchett's play these elements end up pathetically conforming to the older taste and tradition for which they were intended as an antidote, in this case, the neo-classical theatre.

"CHINESENESS" IN WORLD THEATRE

The above account, however, is not complete in itself. It does not represent a naive moment in Chinese-Western cultural relationships. Attempts like Hatchett's to offer to the West such distorted and "creative" introductions of the Chinese theatre decisively shape the literary and theatrical expectations of the Chinese theatre. The word "Chineseness," therefore, inescapably means for the eighteenth century English audience something drastically different from what it meant in its original Chinese setting. Such audiences found in the Oriental theatre what on first consideration seemed not available in their own. And these "exotic" elements "found" there and "introduced" to the West were always strikingly different from their Chinese "sources" in terms of stylization, symbolizing, movement, makeup, and music. Even in the twentieth century, despite increasing knowledge of contacts with China and Chinese scholars, the reception of the Chinese theatrical tradition by figures like Bertolt Brecht was still to some extent inspired by a "creative" misunderstanding of the ingenious works of his foreign "critical" fathers and appropriated in such a way as to enrich his own limited space of "imagination." Since Brecht appeared on the historical scene much later than his "fathers" like Hatchett and Voltaire, he explored with much more vigour than his predecessors what had been left unsaid in the Western reception of the Chinese theatre. In order to outwit his Western predecessors, Brecht's "creative misreading" of the Chinese dramatic tradition was, to employ again the mechanism described in T. S. Eliot's "Tradition and the Individual Talent," a conforming and a surrendering to the two cultural traditions. At the same time, of course, it was an oedipal rebellion against both.

Brecht's concept of "*Verfremdungseffekt*" first occurred in his essay entitled "Alienation Effects in Chinese Acting," written in 1936, occasioned by Brecht's seeing Mei Lanfang's performance in Moscow. As his article reveals, Brecht was deeply impressed by the Chinese actor "who constantly keeps a distance between himself, his character, and the spectator.... Consequently he never loses control of himself; his performance is constantly on a conscious, artistic level with all emotion transposed" (Pronko, 1967, p. 56). As Pronko rightly points out, however, Brecht's "alienation effect" was a product of nothing more than his "misunderstanding" of the Chinese stage conventions. Chinese spectators were expected to react emotionally to the sad or happy scenes in Chinese opera. Pronko has also observed that Chinese music, originally used to appeal to deep emotions, was interpreted by Brecht as a means to break illusion and to establish a distance.[14] In terms of the present argument, Brecht rebelled against his Western "father critics," who first introduced the Chinese theatre to the West, by pointing out those elements of "Chineseness" in the Chinese theatre which they failed to perceive. He was therefore no longer interested in the exotic foreign manners and curious plots, as were his predecessors. Above all, he was not interested in seeing the Chinese tradition as "classical" and hence Aristotelian. His notion of "alienation effect" which he believed to be "Chinese," however, as Pronko has rightly pointed out, "inspired" only his own version of reading the Chinese performing arts. His "unfamiliarity" with the Chinese theatre, however, paradoxically makes him conform to the earlier tradition of the Western "critical fathers," who revised Chinese theatre in order to make it palatable to the West.

Seen from this perspective, Brecht is no "genius," nor is he a "strong" poet. For all of his attempts to do otherwise, he only repeats what his Western "father critics" had done in the past. His "misreading" and "misunderstanding" of the Chinese theatre, and as the result of it, his creative notion of "alienation effect" are no more "ingenious" than his "critical" fathers' creation of a Chinese neoclassical drama. At the same time his "misreading," or the deliberate use, of the Chinese theatre also betrays Brecht as an unfaithful "critical son" to his Chinese ancestors. By an act of "creative" treason, however, he paradoxically fits himself into the foreign tradition as well as his own. He is therefore making a place for himself only by standing on the shoulders of ancient "giants" in two traditions.

Like Brecht, Gao Xingjian proved himself as no exception in following this law of the formation of a literary history. Coming quite late on the scene of the Chinese dramatic imagination, Gao Xingjian tried to create things "new" for his Chinese audience by introducing "exotic" and foreign theatrical traditions in his first two plays — *The Bus-Stop* and *Alarm Signal*. As we have already mentioned, his first two plays were heavily influenced by such Western dramatists as Artaud, Beckett, and Brecht. Later on, however, when the Chinese audience was overwhelmed by a flood of Western-style theatre on the Chinese stage after the "open-door" policy was instituted, Gao Xingjian abandoned his Western critical fathers and returned to his own Chinese "parentage" in the traditional theatre. In this way he was able to meet the changing literary expectations of his Chinese audience. Yet for reasons already suggested, his return to his own cultural father figures was in fact a return to the "Chineseness" of a theatre which had earlier appealed to his foreign "fathers," and appropriated by them through acts of creative "misreading." Once again, then, we have an example of "belatedness" in which a son poet, in this case Gao Xingjian, felt compelled to find things "new" in a foreign culture, a culture which in fact is "originally" his own.

In this case Gao was fortunate enough to live in a time and place which enabled him to embrace simultaneously his own literary tradition — "to recover many artistic techniques already lost in the last century" — at the same time he could use something newly "created" by his Western "parental critics" out of his [Gao's] own tradition (Gao, 1985a, p. 169). As a belated critical son owing his debts to numerous "parental" critics from more than one culture, Gao benefits from both cultures, the East and the West, and from both historical heritages, the ancient and the modern, but he does so in a way that depends on misreadings and misunderstanding on every hand and in every direction. Because of this he ends up belonging exclusively to neither East nor West, but inclusively to both.

These remarks help us to understand the strange reception history of *Wild Man* in which the play has been claimed by more than two national "parentages" in the critical reviews. On the one hand, *Wild Man* can be perceived as a Chinese play only by those whose dramatic expectations are confined to a knowledge of the traditional Chinese theatre. On the other hand, however, it can be regarded as being influenced by the Western theatre only by those who take the concepts of Artaud and Brecht as purely Western, thus disregarding their debts to their Oriental "critical fathers." In both cases, however, readers from different cultural backgrounds, with different dramatic and cultural expectations, inevitably receive *Wild Man* differently. It could not be otherwise, even for those Chinese readers knowledgeable in Western theatre or for Westerners who are acquainted with Chinese dramatic traditions. Just as producers of texts can only write from within their own historical and cultural space — and in Gao's case, that space was both Chinese and Western in paradoxical ways — so readers can only read on the basis of their own place in history. There are no ontologically grounded "truths" by which we can distinguish "Chineseness" from "Westerness." The implications of this observation seem clear: what is important for us to pursue in our critical inquiry is the dynamics of interreactions and inter-relationships between tradition and individual talents, between literary production and literary reception. Needless to say, we cannot define or even separate one "comparative entity" from the other. Neither can we fruitfully determine such things as "emitter," "receiver," "origin," "beginning," "causality," and "continuity." Each term is inextricably tied to its opposite. There is no final reference, only shared properties of *différance*. Within that *différance* all that is Chinese appears as Western, all that is Western as Chinese. For sinology, then, world literature and world culture can no longer be ignored or assigned a secondary status as mere source or influence. Rather all that is "other" and "alien" to it — which is finally to say, all that is Western — must now be recognized and inscribed within its proper interests. All future studies of "comparative" drama, therefore, and perhaps in a more general sense, all future studies of any "national literature" situated in the context of world literature, need to take their departure from this observation.

NOTES

1. This piece first appeared as an article entitled, "A *Wildman* Between Two Cultures: Some Paradigmatic Remarks on 'Influence Studies,'" *Comparative Literature Studies*, Vol. 29, No. 4 (1992), pp. 397–416. Copyright 1992 by The Pennsylvania State University. Reproduced by permission of The Pennsylvania State University Press. I wish to thank Marvin Carlson, Eugene Eoyang, Clifford C. Flanigan, Iriving Lo, and Brian Caraher for reading an earlier draft of this article. A revised version was later included in my book, *Occidentalism: A Theory of Counter-discourse in Post-Mao China*, pp. 99–117. New York: Oxford University Press, 1995.
2. For an English translation, see Boubicek (1990).
3. For a brief survey of the Western influence in Gao Xingjian and his plays, see Geremie Barmé (1983). For an account of Gao Xingjian's indebtedness to Antonin Artaud, Jerzy Grotowski, V E. Meyerhold, and Mei Lanfang, see William Tay (1990).
4. For an informative study of the main features of traditional Chinese theatre available in English, see Hsu Tao-Ching (1985). Hsu's work is especially helpful in the context of this essay for its comparative perspective, which treats as well other theatrical conventions such as the Greek, the Elizabethan, and the Japanese.
5. The quotations of the Chinese text in this essay are from Gao (1985b). The translations are mine unless indicated otherwise.
6. This quotation is cited from Roubicek (1990), p. 245.
7. For a study in English in the primitive Chinese theatre as religious ritual, see Yu Qiuyu (1989). Drawing examples from various types of exorcistic performance [nuoxi], which are still more popular than film and TV programs in the Guangxi Zhuang Autonomous Region, Yu argues that in primitive Chinese performance, the aesthetic and ritual experience are very difficult to separate and that "ancient Chinese ritual performance to a great

degree reflected the principal aspects of ancient Chinese society — ritual performance actually had become a rich social ceremony" (p. 15).

8. For an early account of Brecht and China, see Tatlow (1973). For a study of Brecht's reception in China, see Hsia (1982).

9. A number of important earlier essays on the notion of literary influence have been collected in Primeau (1977). For some polemical observations that seek to defend the traditional claims of "influence study," see Balakian (1990), in which Balakian observes that "the word 'influence' has become a bad word, been confused with 'imitation,' and has even been viewed as a threat to ethnocentrism. It has been replaced by the theoreticians with the concept of 'intertextuality,' which is random, idiosyncratic, resulting in a free play of inter-referentiality which displays the virtuosity of the critic-manipulator rather than the fruits of scholarly research in the form of deep-sea plunging into literary works. The current theoretical version of influence study has become a major feature of what could be called 'aleatory criticism' "(p. 18).

10. For an informative survey of the scholarship in Chinese-Western comparative literature, see Sun (1986). For Sun, there are two common types of Chinese-Western comparative literature writings in the past twenty years which failed to recognize "1) what comparative literature is about and 2) the unique role of Chinese-Western comparative literature in the field" (p. 533). The "*myopic*" school of comparison, for example, is "characterized by an over-emphasis on surface and random aspects of the works compared. The cultural contexts and literary conventions are seldom taken into account, in order to render the similarities tenable. The main purpose of this type of comparison is to claim that, after all, Chinese literature is not all that different from Western literatures" (p. 533). The "*hypermetropic*" school, according to Sun, primarily applies Western theories to Chinese literature, "often in a wholesale fashion" (p. 533). Sun believes that the "danger of this kind of approach lies in its undue confidence about the universal applicability of Western theory at the expense of the distinctive (and frequently intractable) features of Chinese literature" (p. 542). Insightful and well-documented, Sun's article focuses on the lyric, and to a much lesser degree, the narrative, without touching on the issues of Chinese-Western dramatic studies, which in many ways remain the step-child of comparative studies of Chinese and Western culture.

11. In his essay "Lun xijuguan" 論戲劇觀 [On dramatic theories] (Gao, 1983), Gao Xingjian surveyed the major dramatic traditions in the West, including those of Brecht and Artaud. Exploring the reasons why in recent years Chinese audiences have increasingly lost their interest in modern Chinese drama, Gao pointed out that the predominant Ibsenian tradition of social

plays on the present Chinese stage has given too much emphasis to dramatic dialogue. For him, the Ibsenian tradition should be enhanced, if not replaced, by other dramatic traditions such as those of Brecht, Artaud, Chekhov, Gorky, and especially the classical Chinese theatre, which employed singing, acting, dancing, and speaking in order to provide its audiences with theatrical experiences rather than mere concepts and ideas.

12. By "misunderstanding" — in quotation marks — I mean a view of a text or a cultural event by a "received" community that differs in important ways from the view of that same phenomenon in the community of its own "origins." I do not mean to suggest the preexistence of an epistemologically grounded "proper" or "correct" understanding of the text to which a "misunderstanding" can be applied.

13. For a recent study in Western scholarship on the receptions of this Yuan drama in the West, see, for example, Aldridge (1986). Aldridge's conclusions are telling in the light of the present study: "Voltaire's source was a translation of 1731 by a French Jesuit, Joseph Henri Premare, which was later included in a famous compilation by another Jesuit, Jean Baptiste Du Halde, under the title *Description geographique, historique, chronologique, politique, et physique de l'empire de la Chine et de la tartarie chinoise* (1735). Among the essential ingredients of the original Chinese work were song and music, but these were completely eliminated from Premare's translation and from Voltaire's adaptation as well. Since Voltaire's neoclassical drama departed from both the form and the substance of his Chinese source, one would be justified in asking whether his work should really be considered as an example of the penetration of Chinese culture. Should it instead be dismissed as mere Chinoiserie? The answer is that Voltaire himself understood a great deal more about Chinese civilization than his play reveals, but that he was prevented by the prevailing taste of the times from closely following his model" (p. 145).

14. For more information on the paradoxical relationship between Brecht and Mei Lanfang's theories of theatre, see Sun (1987). For a more general article on the reception of Mei Lanfang's performance in the Soviet Union in 1935 on the part of European theatre artists such as Stanislavsky, Meyerhold, Craig, Brecht, Eisenstein, Piscator, Tairov and Tretiakov, see Banu (1986); Huang (1982).

REFERENCES

Aldridge, A. Owen (1986). *The Reemergence of World Literature: A Study of Asia and the West.* Newark: University of Delaware Press.

Artaud, Antonin (1958). *The Theater and Its Double*. Trans. Mary Caroline Richards. New York: Grove Press.

Balakian, Anna (1990). "Literary Theory and Comparative Literature." In Valdes, ed. (1990), Vol. 3, pp. 17–24.

Banu, George (1986). "Mei Lanfang: A Case Against and a Model for the Occidental Stage." Trans. Ella L. Wiswell and June V. Gibson. *Asian Theater Journal*, Vol. 3, No. 2 (Fall), pp. 153–178.

Barmé, Geremie (1983). "A Touch of the Absurd — Introducing Gao Xingjian, and His Play *The Bus-stop*." *Renditions*, Nos. 19 & 20 (Spring & Autumn), pp. 373–377.

Baum, Julian (1985). "Peking's *Wild Man* Jolts Theater Goers." *The Christian Science Monitor*, 24 June, p. 9.

Boubicek, Bruno, trans. (1990). *Wild Man. Asian Theater Journal*, Vol. 7, No. 2 (Fall), pp. 195–249.

Fan Xiheng 范熙恆 (1987). "Chong *Zhaoshi gu'er* dao *Zhongguo gu'er* — shang" 從《趙氏孤兒》到《中國孤兒》—— 上 [From *The Orphan of Chao* to *Orphelin de la Chine* (Part I)]. *Zhongguo bijiao wenxue* 中國比較文學 [Comparative literature in China], Vol. 4, pp. 159–195.

Gao Xingjian 高行健 (1983). "Lun xiju guan" 論戲劇觀 [On dramatic theories]. *Xiju jie* 戲劇界 [The dramatic circle], No. 1, pp. 27–34.

—— (1985a). "Guanyu yanchu de jianyi yu shuoming" 關於演出的建議與説明 [Suggestions for the performance of the play] (in *Yeren* 野人 [Wild man]). *Shiyue* 十月, No. 2, p. 169.

—— (1985b). *Yeren* 野人 [Wild man]. *Shiyuan* 十月, No. 2, pp. 142–168.

—— (1985c). "*Yeren* yu wo" 《野人》與我 [*Wild Man* and I]. *Xiju dianying bao* 戲劇電影報 [Drama and film newspaper], 12 May, p. 2.

Goldblatt, Howard, ed. (1990). *Worlds Apart: Recent Chinese Writing and Its Audiences*. Armonk, NY: M. E. Sharpe.

Hsia, Adrian (1982). "The Reception of Bertolt Brecht in China and Its Impact on Chinese Drama." In Tatlow and Wong, eds. (1982), pp. 47–64.

Hsu, Tao-Ching (1985). *The Chinese Conception of the Theater*. Seattle: University of Washington Press.

Huang Zuolin (1982). "A Supplement to Brechts 'Alienation Effects in Chinese Acting.'" In Tatlow and Wong, eds. (1982), pp. 96–110.

Primeau, Ronald, ed. (1977). *Influx: Essays on Literary History*. Port Washington, NY: Kennikat Press.

Pronko, Leonard Cabell (1967). *Theater East and West: Perspectives Toward a Total Theater*. Berkeley: University of California Press.

Sun, Cecile Chu-Chin (1986). "Problems of Perspective in Chinese-Western Comparative Literature Studies." *Canadian Review of Comparative Literature*. Vo. 13, No. 4, pp. 531–548.

Sun, William Huizhu (1987). "Mei Lanfang, Stanislavsky and Brecht on China's Stage and Their Aesthetic Significance." In Tung and MacKerras, eds. (1987), pp. 137–150.

Tatlow, Antony (1973). *Brechts chinesische Gedichte*. Frankfurt am Main: Suhrkamp, 1973.

Tatlow, Antony, and Tak-wai Wong, eds. (1982). *Brecht and East Asian Theatre*. Hong Kong: Hong Kong University Press.

Tay, William (1990). "Avant-garde Theater in Post-Mao China: *The Bus-Stop* by Gao Xingjian." In Goldblatt, ed. (1990), pp. 111–118.

Tung, Constantine, and Colin MacKerras, eds. (1987). *Drama in the People's Republic of China*. Albany, NY: State University of New York Press.

Wang Xining (1985). "An Unconventional Blend." *China Daily* (Beijing), 21 May 1985, p. 5.

Weisstein, Ulrich (1968). *Comparative Literature and Literary Theory: Survey and Introduction*. Bloomington: Indiana University Press.

Yu Qiuyu (1989). "Some Observations on the Aesthetics of Primitive Chinese Theater." *Asian Theater Journal*, Vol. 6, No.1 (Spring), pp. 12–30.

The Myth of Gao Xingjian[1]

By means of just three plays, two kinds of myth have been created around Gao Xingjian. In China he is seen as the most avant-garde, creative and stimulating playwright of his time. An older generation of academics and theatre professionals, frustrated by a theatre which had been deployed solely in the service of various political power battles for nearly forty years and a younger generation who also yearned for a fundamental renewal in theatre, clung to Gao as a new kind of dramatist writing a new kind of theatre. In the West, both China experts and theatre scholars have unquestioningly adopted him as "the most advanced new dramatist in China in content and form."[2] For most European commentators, the interest in Gao's work stems mainly from the connection they like to make between Gao and some of the great dramatists of modern European theatre, such as Ibsen, Beckett, Artaud and Grotowski. In fact, Gao probably stands somewhere between these two poles, as we shall show.

Much of Gao's work is said to be censored or under the threat of being banned and both Chinese and Western audiences greedily await the sensation of a new play. One of his early works, *Bi'an* 彼岸 [The other side, 1986],[3] however, which breaks all boundaries of modern Chinese theatre, has not progressed beyond the rehearsal room. On publication, it proved to be too abstract for the younger generation of theatre goers who instead began to turn their attention and hopes of renewal towards a group of younger authors writing more radical and controversial plays such as *Women* 我們 [We, 1985] by Wang Peigong and *Mofang* 魔方 [Rubic cube, 1985] by Tao Jun. Relieved from the burden of expectation, Gao turned towards dramatic theory, painting and the novel. At the same time, his earlier plays were maturing towards recognition in the publication of *Gao Xingjian xiju ji* [Plays by Gao Xingjian]. It would seem appropriate therefore to re-examine Gao's position beyond the myth — as someone who stands between the classic writers of Chinese spoken drama such as Cao Yü, Tian Han and Lao She — and the more radical alternative dramatists in the late 1980s. At the same time, we would like to analyze his overestimated relationship to modern European theatre, and to explore his part as a classic playwright in a deeply Chinese tradition.

ALARM SIGNAL — A SUCCESSFUL FIRST MODEL

Among modern Chinese dramatists, Gao Xingjian is unique in that he comes from a literary, and moreover international literary background. His status in China is that of an intellectual, a man who through his studies and contacts abroad has been exposed to European philosophy and ideas. In the late 1970s and 1980s, with the study of foreign literature and even foreign languages strictly controlled, Gao's position was at once exciting and dangerous; the reputation of his work quickly spread.

Gao studied French at the Beijing Institute of Foreign Languages from 1957 to 1962. When he graduated, he joined the Foreign Languages Press as translator. It was in this capacity as interpreter that Gao travelled for the first time to Paris in 1979 accompanying the novelist Ba Jin. Gao was transferred to the People's Art Theatre in 1981 and has travelled again to France on three other occasions since 1980, and in 1985 to Britain, Berlin and Vienna in conjunction with the London International Festival of Theatre (LIFT) and Horizonte Theatre Festival in Germany. Both Chinese and Western observers, knowing Gao's background in European drama and literature, and the extent of his exposure to the Western stage, have made the assumption that his own work is an absorption, or at worst a simple copy of the European dramatists. Gao's work is barely mentioned without an ancillary name-tag — Brecht, Beckett, Artaud, Kantor, Grotowski. The impression was deepened after Gao's theoretical treatise, *Xiandai xiaoshuo jiqiao chutan* 現代小説技巧初探 [A preliminary exploration of the techniques of modern fiction, 1981] was circulated.[4] Barmé accurately points out that this work is rather more "… a loose collection of jottings and reflections on Western and Chinese fiction." (Barmé, 1983a, p. 139).

Gao's first acclaimed play, *Juedui xinhao* 絕對信號 [Alarm signal, 1982] — in fact it is his eleventh play, since he had written eight plays at university as well as one opera and one television/film script, though none of these were performed beyond a student level — was produced in November 1982. It ran to over one hundred successful performances in a back street theatre before being transferred to the Capital Theatre — the home of the People's Art Theatre and Beijing's largest, most prestigious theatre. *Alarm Signal,* different in style from any other play then on the Chinese stage, was at once hailed as a theatrical revolution, and the rumour soon spread that Gao was the first author to bring Western ideas of drama onto the Chinese stage: "Gao uses an uninterrupted drama in one movement in the style of Antonin Artaud and Kantor" (Barmé, 1983a, p. 139). In fact, *Alarm Signal* was co-written with Gao's colleague, Liu Huiyuan, and the director, Lin Zhaohua, had not a little influence on the final version of the performed play. Gao is consistently judged by the standard of the European counterparts he is assumed to be imitating, and once the idea of a new style of drama has been recognised and named — in this case "psychological" — the myth of Gao is given out and feeds off itself. The critics were unanimous in their conclusion that *Alarm Signal* is "a psychological play about an unemployed young man" (Barmé, 1983a, p. 139), "a deft psychological study of an unemployed youth" (Barmé, 1983b, p. 373) and "the play examines the psychological make up of an unemployed youth" (Roubicek, 1986, 1990, p. 11).

Gao himself is somewhat enigmatic in his response when questioned about the "patron saints" of his work. When it is said that his plays are protected by the reputation "Brechtian," "Beckettian" and so on, he responds, "Yes, they say that" (Riley, 1987). Whether or not the reputation saved the performance at the time, giving it credence as a new, innovative style, now, from a distance, the play should be re-examined on its own terms. *Alarm Signal* seems to be a first-run, a first attempt that sows the seeds of many innovative elements of his later plays, while leaning on the conventional framework of theatrical presentation.

Alarm Signal is basically a well-made thriller. It concerns a train journey of several hours in a guard's carriage to the town Caojiapu, where two carriages are to be robbed. The dramatic line of the play is clear, as the train nears the town the tension rises inside the guard's carriage. The play makes a slow start until all the protagonists are gathered in the carriage: a Guard (56 years old), an Apprentice Guard (*Xiaohao* — "Trumpet," 21 years old), a Girl (*Mifeng* — "Honey Bee," 20 years old), an Unemployed Youth (*Heizi* — "Moleface," 21 years old), and the Train

Robber (37 years old). The Youth, Heizi, is pulled into the action by the robber, whom he must help when the time comes. During the journey, Heizi contemplates what he is about to do. The Guard is a positive figure who gives long speeches about the role of man in society and his duties; while the Train Robber presents a contrasting destructive role. The Girl once knew the Apprentice Guard, so Heizi has an opportunity to contemplate feelings of jealousy, and self-pity, and Heizi is, we are told, unemployed, which allows him to explore the need to find a role for himself in life. The "psychology" of the play is presented directly. Using spotlights, three distinct phases of time are evoked — the past, as they remember what has been, the present, and the imagination, the hopes and fears of the future.

In this way, the writers have worked with a very straightforward plot and in their presentation on stage broken with at least fifty years of Chinese stage convention. This was perhaps the first time an author had presented feelings, dreams, and memories in a direct way — mixing them indeterminably with present emotions. Gao himself suggests that *Alarm Signal* was an experiment to try and show three periods of time at once. The times are not divided or separable; all seem present. Gao says: "… it should be realistic. If you speak of a time, then you are in that time" (Riley, 1987).

For Gao, a theatre performance is a process, a movement, presented all at once in the present. All aspects of the different times come together only in the head of the viewer; the process is completed by the audience who is witness to all the times being presented. The critics stressed only the cathartic progress of the play (as the train nears the town and Heizi is persuaded not to comply with the Train Robber) which is perhaps only a surface interest and does not take into account the actual dynamic of the play. Gao claims the focus is centered on the Chinese language itself. The Chinese language can circumvent any expression of tense. "To smile" may also be "to have smiled": "please smile" is also "did smile" (Gao, 1981, p. 22). All times are expressed as one. For Gao, the heart of the play is very much rooted in Chinese soil, and does not follow any particular European dramatic theory. It is this concept of the nature of the Chinese language, and therefore how this language works in a dramatic presentation, which consistently appears in all of Gao's works, and in that sense, *Alarm Signal* is truly a working model for his later plays.

Gao founds his theatrical process on the complexities and ambiguities of the Chinese language. His comment, "If you speak of a time, then you are in that time" reveals the total trust Gao places in the spoken word, which links him very firmly to his Chinese forerunners and distances him from modern European dramatists and their mistrust and destruction of language. *Alarm Signal* is similar to a moral lesson, told in a rather direct way. As Gao turns inside thoughts into present actions, so he brings out every feeling, every thought and underlines it. The Guard seems to represent one aspect of the Heizi's conscience. He is an extremely positive character, one who impresses on Heizi the duty of work. Work is not a privilege as Heizi thinks, but a duty to the rest of society, a service. He has worked twenty-six years without a holiday and barely sees his wife. His pride glistens as he assures Heizi of man's positive role in life among other men. The Train Robber, who stands as evil temptation on the one hand in contrast to the righteous self-sacrificing Guard on the other, is the blacker side of Heizi's conscience. He dares Heizi to destroy the society he feels has let him down, to break out, to make a mark. The conflict is finally resolved in the words of the upright Guard — that those who strike out against society in fact strike out against their own hearts. The symbolism of the Guard and the Robber; the direct presentation of their roles and words can make the play seem rather melodramatic, especially to Western eyes. The train carriage itself is a society in little, and its progress towards possible disaster is saved by the new found heroic hope of youth which Heizi represents.

As a first play, *Alarm Signal* already shows Gao's attempts to create a new style of Chinese drama. The play is totally different in presentation from any of its contemporary "scar" plays, where the subject of unemployed youth is dealt within a rough, abrasive way. It is also far from being a model play based on any particular European drama or dramatic theory. Artaud's concept of drama with whom Gao is persistently linked by Western critics, demands *une sorte d'evenement* (a kind of happening) which can shake the audience and have a cathartic effect on them. This has little to do with the representation of a moral dilemma as a young man explores his relationship to the rest of society. A wild pistol shot in the final denouement of the play as Heizi saves the train he was to have robbed is not the cathartic effect of which Artaud dreamed.

THE BUS-STOP — "IT IS BETTER, AFTER ALL, TO MOVE ON"

Following the success of *Alarm Signal*, Gao wrote his next play in 1981–82, again, for the People's Art Theatre — *Chezhan* 車站 [The bus-stop]. The play was received with the same excitement as its predecessor, and the reputation of Gao as a radically new kind of playwright was increased when *The Bus-Stop* was banned during the few months of the "Anti-Spiritual Pollution Campaign" in August 1983. From the point of view of content, *The Bus-Stop* was immediately labelled absurd and, since the play involved characters waiting endlessly at a bus stop where busses never stop, the comparison with Beckett's *Waiting for Godot* was made. *The Bus-Stop* was seen to be about "the Chinese brothers and sisters of Beckett's Vladimir and Estragon."[5]

Like *Alarm Signal, The Bus-Stop* begins with an apparently straightforward situation, waiting for a bus at the bus stop. *Alarm Signal* is set inside a carriage on a moving train. The characters, once assembled, are left to play out their fates through discussion, argument, and especially through the realistic representation of past memories and future hopes on stage. *The Bus Stop* also begins with a fixed world — a rigid framework — only in this play there is no build up towards a goal, a denouement. *The Bus-Stop* is about not going anywhere, it is about waiting.

The set for *Bus Stop* arranges the bus stop in the shape of a cross. Two V-shaped barriers face each other at the narrowest point and the bus stop is fixed where the two Vs meet. There is space for people to wait inside the V, but if they go forward they are prevented by the barrier. It is obvious there is no way forward. Certain characters come to fill the space and wait for the bus: A Silent Man, an Old Man, a Lout, a Girl, a student named Glasses, a Mother, a Carpenter and a lower level cadre called Director Ma. Their appearance on the stage is almost cartoon-like, in that once assembled, the audience has a finished tableau of the playwright's intention. Although the passing of time creates something of a climax, as does the sudden rainfall, the general process of the play is that there is no progress, no sense of movement. Gao seems to be working with director Lin Zhaohua towards a visually very distinct, direct style. But the fixed and apparently hopeless space he gives his characters is quite unlike Beckett's concept of man who is caught in an intolerable limbo-like state where the awful tragedy of having been born relentlessly chases the terrible end of death, or worse — not death.

The Bus-Stop in fact has little to do with the European concept of absurd drama. All the characters in Gao's play have real and ordinary aims in town to be fulfilled — to play a game of chess with a master, to visit family, to try out yoghurt that has just appeared in the city, to make a piece of furniture or to keep a blind date. The difficulty lies in their obtaining their goals, since the busses run by without stopping. Time passes, and still they wait, until finally they *assume* that a half-torn notice still sticking to the bus stop was supposed to have informed them that the route was no longer in service.

> Director Ma: (to Glasses) Look at the bus sign, what station is this? And now what time does it say on your quartz watch? Write it all down, we'll get even with the bus company yet!
>
> Glasses: (Looking at the bus sign) What? The bus stop doesn't have a name?
>
> Old Man: That's odd.
>
> Director Ma: What's the use of a bus stop without a name? Look again, properly.
>
> Girl: There isn't one.
>
> ...
>
> Lout: (runs round to the other side of the sign. To Glasses) Look here, it seems as if there was a piece of paper stuck on it, only there's only a bit of it left.
>
> Glasses: It was probably an announcement.   (Gao, 1986, p. 136)

The language of the characters as they talk to each other is logical, sometimes amusing, sometimes boring — the little details of life, sometimes quite sad — the continual, frustrating little disappointments in life. But nowhere is there a feeling of the uselessness of language, or the purposelessness of life. Gao states this clearly in his comments on the play. "Beckett ...," he says, "writes about the absurdity of life, and for him, it's a tragedy. Although his works have jokes, the end is the pointlessness of life, the lack of sense in living. My play is also absurd — an unreal situation — but it's not so serious. It's more a comedy ..." (Riley, 1987). This aspect is perhaps carried over from his play *Alarm Signal* where the conversion of Heizi into a contributing member of society saves the train.

Gao's play probably had enough social message to be criticized heavily. The critic He Wen says, "it is possible that the play contains abstruse doctrines such as "freedom of choice" deriving from existentialism, but the direct impression it creates is that the bus company and the fate of those waiting would-be passengers symbolise the general condition of our present life" (1983, p. 387). Yet this play is not the tragedy of paralysis or inaction, nor the tragedy of any social mismanagement within China, nor a questioning of man's individual relationship to life. The play has a strong message to convey the energy of forward movement. The play encourages its characters "to move on." From the Silent Man, the only one to walk into town, to Director Ma as he bends to tie his shoelace before moving on, the message is clear "Go On." The exit of the Silent Man is echoed repeatedly by music which is at first lyrical and then march-like, the passing busses seem to encourage the idea that perhaps those who only stand and wait should go on. That they do not prolongs the energy of the message, the volume and direction of the message must increase until finally all six voices are calling different theories of going at the same time (Gao, 1983, pp. 137–138). The only word the audience will catch again and again is "go."

Although we do not know if the characters on stage do go in the end or not, Gao's treatment is clear. In fact, his intentions are perhaps too clear for those who wanted to see more radical ideas in Gao's plays. While Gao is as dissimilar to younger playwrights of his time as he is to the "scar" writers and other literary companions such as Bei Dao 北島, Gao is equally far from Beckett. Nor does he make any particular statement about the state of Chinese society. One of his characters, Glasses and the Girl discuss the meaning of life:

> Glasses: Ah, life, ah, life.
> Girl: What kind of life do you call this?
> Glasses: Even if you don't call it life, we still go on living it.
> Girl: We'd be better off dead.
> Glasses: Then why don't you end it?
> Girl: We come into the world for nothing — only to die. It's not worth it.
> Glasses: Life should have some meaning to it.
> Girl: And if you don't die, but just go on living like this, it's so boring.
>
> (Gao, 1983, p. 133)

The energy of motion is clearly hoped for in this passage. To stand still is certainly boring, a waste of time (the play itself had to be cut from an original three-hour script).

In contrast, the poet and novelist Bei Dao, writing as early as 1974 describes the despair of the Chinese youth,

"People are born unlucky."

"So why do you want to go on living?"

"Living is just a fact."

"Facts can be changed."

"The pity of it is that people have enough inertia to keep lingering on, eking out an existence to their last breath, and that's what passes for life force."

...

"In your life, what is there worth believing in?"

"Our country for example."

"Ha, that's an outdated tune."

"No ... I mean our common suffering, our common way of life, our common heritage, our common yearning ... all of these make up our indivisible fate: we have a duty to our country."

"Duty? The duty to be an offering after having been slaughtered?"

"Yes, if necessary."

"Forget it."   (Bei Dao, 1987, pp. 19–21)

The example of Bei Dao and others like him suggests that Gao is simply not interested in criticising, or changing society. Such things could be and were being written around him but this was not the theme of his work, which is more deeply personal, almost intimate.

The Bus-Stop is preluded by *The Passer-By* [Guoke] by Lu Xun. In performance, the role of the Passer-By was played by the same actor who then played the Silent Man, the only one to walk into town, and not wait for the bus. Originally Gao conceived the idea of the Silent Man as a piece of music only. The character did not exist in the script until director Lin Zhaohua suggested turning the energy Gao conceived of as a motion into a real character. Gao says the Silent Man was originally simply the hope, the desire to go on, and Lin manifested this sense of hope in the presentation of a real character. In fact, Gao's use of Lu Xun's *The Passer-By* has caused more comment than the rest of the play. Although Gao himself claims the idea came to him during rehearsals, and that as a prologue it simply expressed the idea of energy he wanted to convey, its inclusion invites comparison.

Lu Xun works through ideas of "going," or "wandering" in his book of collected pieces *Wild Grass* from which *The Passer-By* is taken. The two authors have quite different aims — Lu Xun explores the romantic ideal of wandering, searching, and the knowledge that going forwards means only towards the grave, yet to brave the darkness, to embrace the unknown is better than to be still:

> Old Man: Don't you even want to rest?
> Passer-By: I do.
> Old Man: Well then, rest here for a while.
> Passer-By: But I cannot.
> Old Man: You still think you had better go on?
> Passer-By: Yes, I had better go on.
> Old Man: Very well, you must go then.
> Passer-By: Good, I'll say goodbye then.
> ...
> Thank you both, I wish you luck (he hesitates thoughtfully then starts). But I cannot, I have to go on. I had better go. (Raising his head he walks resolutely towards the west. The girl helps the Old Man into the hut, then shuts the door. The Passer-By limps on towards the wilderness, and night falls behind him.)   (Lu Xun, 1956, p. 338)

Here, almost nothing can prevent the Passer-By from moving on, his impulsion forwards seems wholly unstoppable. In *The Bus-Stop*, however, there is a certain pragmatism, which qualifies the desire to move on. The characters are so ingrained with a certain way of life that they prefer to clasp to their comfortable daily routines rather than risk the unknown:

> Carpenter: Have you ever walked along the road at night? You're in the middle of the wilderness, and it's getting dark. There's only darkness in front of your eyes. The more you walk, the more you think the path might have forked off another way. You'd do better to wait until dawn. Once it's daylight, though, and you're still dithering, you've been quite stupid.   (Gao, 1983, p. 137)

In *The Bus-Stop* the audience is left to decide why the characters did not move on, or if they did, when they did, and why did they not move sooner. In this sense, Gao's play is similar in form to a learning play or *Lehrstück*, an intellectual discourse on the philosophy of "movement" and the "change" (or lack of change) implied with it. It does not take the example of unstoppable forward drive from the piece by Lu Xun as a prologue, but rather uses *The Passer-By* as another aspect of the discourse on movement, another contribution to the theatrical discussion on "going" and "staying still."

Gao has spoken of the importance of action in drama and contrasted the performance of ideas and psychology in the plays of Ibsen and Chekhov, for example, with the complete inaction of Beckett's plays (Riley, 1987). The idea expressed in *Alarm Signal* that the Chinese language can cope with presenting all tenses on stage in a direct, present way, is developed even further in *The Bus-Stop*. In this play, music and the "music" or "noise" of many voices in cacophony are part of the present action — the desire, or impulse to move on. The drama plays with the expectation or anticipation of energy, of being about to go, to be on the verge of going, and yet staying still. Finally the moment of possible movement is subsumed in a cacophony of mundane daily problems which the various characters face. While throughout the play, they have some ability to interact with one another, telling each other about themselves, and sharing opinions on subjects that affect them all such as the policy of advancement through backdoor pay-offs, the unhappiness of love, or the need (or not) to make an orderly queue (society), the characters barely seem to shift from their starting positions, and their language seems equally static, at most circular. When the rain suddenly falls, they all shelter under a piece of plastic sheeting, and there is a brief moment of intimacy, a brief sense of progress, of change, until the sun just as suddenly comes out again, and they return to the petty rumblings of conversation. The dialogue is static, repetitious, its only progression circular. The characters do not listen to what the others say, do not "move on" from their original views. In this way, Gao denies the language any of the impetus he creates in other ways such as the leitmotif music of the Silent Man. The verb "to go" is the same as "shall we go?" and as it is repeated in the dialogues like a piece of punctuation, a full-stop, losing energy and meaning the more it is used without being implemented. It literally loses meaning. The dramatic tension of the play seems to wind down rather than increase, and yet the constant positive message of moving on contradicts the stillness of the play. The contradiction between the forward energy of the music and the static, helpless state of the characters provides the play with intense dramatic power.

MYTH AS THEATRICAL SOURCE

The production of Gao Xingjian's next play, *Yeren* 野人 [Wild man, 1985], probably provoked more commotion than any of his earlier plays or than those of any other Chinese playwright till then. The critics considered it "controversial, original," "unconventional," "phantasmagorical," and "more unbridled both theatrically and thematically."[6] In his programme notes, Gao introduces the play as a "many voiced symphony, a modern epic drama." The time is "seven or eight hundred years ago till now" and the place, "the upper and lower reaches or a river, a city and a mountain area" (p. 142). This huge span of time, place and event caused many spectators and critics some difficulty:

> If someone tries to describe the fate of man from primeval times till now in the limited space of two hours, then the result may well be a string of events which do not seem to have any clear pattern and many ideas which seem rather superficial.... Finally, I could not understand everything. (Wang Yusheng, 1985, p. 13)

Yeren is generally translated "Wild man," but the Gao's use of the word *ye* also carries a meaning of "uncultivated," "natural" in a *positive* sense. The play explores the potential interchange between man and nature and concentrates on this aspect of "Something created in mystery/ Before heaven and earth/In silence and emptiness/Alone and unchanging/Always present, always moving" (Laozi, *Daodejing*, Chapter 25). The play seems to be a cosmological exploration of the concepts of movement, change and stagnation:

Man abides by Earth
Earth abides by Heaven
Heaven abides by Dao
Dao abides by what is natural.   (Laozi, *Daodejing*, Chapter 25)

The critics could not help themselves from bringing Artaud back into their critical repertoire, "it is perhaps undeniable that Gao is influenced by the French avant-garde dramatist Antonin Artaud's theory of 'total theatre' in which all theatrical elements — sound, music, costume, gesture and lights — all play a significant role" (Wang Xining, 1985, p. 5). The director, again on this occasion, Lin Zhaohua, calls it "a complete director's play ... a Chinese National Minorities play ... a contemporary drama all in one" (Riley, 1987b). Gao simply calls it "a multi-faceted play. It includes tragedy and farce at the same time" (Riley, 1987a).

The play does indeed follow several strands of different stories. One of the main figures, the Ecologist wants to propagate the idea of conservation, and presses for the saving of an ancient forest from timber cutting. He is at the same time separating from his wife, as she from him, but when he is attracted to a young peasant girl in the village by the forest, he is unable to detach himself enough to contemplate a new relationship. A storyteller, the Old Singer, functioning in part as narrator, in part as shaman, evokes many traditions and rituals celebrated by the peasants: he sings and chants the myths of civilisation, blesses the building of a new house with the blood of a chicken, and wriggles his way round officialdom when he is suspected of killing a bear, and practising Shamanism. The Forester plans the cutting of the forest in fine detail, only to be frustrated when he hears the forest is to become protected. At the same time, a group of scientists and explorers hunt the forest for the "wild man," a strange man-like being which supposedly inhabits the forest. In some senses, each of the main characters has his own play: the peasant girl is married off in the traditional rural way; a school teacher is researching the ancient songs of the story-teller; a little girl — witness to the appearance of the wild man — gets given a piece of chocolate she has never tasted before, and so on. Gao comments "scene and scene are sometimes interlocked and repeated again and again on top of one another, like the paper-thin skins of *hun tun* that are so glued together they cannot be separated, or individually identified" and "... of course, the play cannot avoid touching upon the bitter experience of a few characters."[7]

Within this multiplicity of characters and tales, the Old Singer is a central figure who binds and mediates the various worlds as a shaman might do in traditional *nuoxi* or exorcism theatre and ritual. He carries out an exorcist ritual to bring rain by dancing the magic nine-step Luo dance [tiao yubu] to send the drought-bringing devils to the four corners. He sacrifices a cockerel at the roof-raising scene, "Let my cockerel expel evil/Cock's blood flow into the earth, Good fortune and prosperity flow into the house" (Gao, 1985b, p. 149), he sings the myth of creation — Pan Gu swinging the axe to divide heaven and earth (Gao, 1985b, p. 161). However, the much needed rain turns into a disastrous flood, the cut of Pan Gu's axe is echoed in the cutting of the forest which has led to ecological ruin. The destructive power of Nature is as threatening as the authoritarian bureaucracy of the Party Officials, and the commercial, greedy journalists. Thus, it is the Ecologist, coming from one world and encountering this "other world" for the first time, who mediates both worlds, while the Old Singer has a key role to play in binding the events on stage to a cosmological pattern.

"Save the forest!" is more than a cry, a propaganda appeal. The frequent repetition of the call, the all-pervading sound of the axe, or the unending scenes of torrential downpour (we are told that the cutting of trees leads to soil erosion, and flooding) punctuate the whole action of the play with the concern for balance in the ecology. The Ecologist engages in lengthy speeches with the Forester, among others, on the need for control in using the earth's resources. On the one hand, rural man is too careless of his environment, and as he becomes educated, makes it worse by wanting to change the environment to suit his needs. On the other hand, the more education man has, the more he can rationalise concepts such as conservation. Each scene follows and overlaps its neighbours as in a collage, remains open-ended, ambiguous. Here is a scene which exposes the petty-mindedness of middle ranking cadres; there is a scene showing the confusion and hiatus of scientists and experts over fact and fiction (particularly experts from abroad, speaking different languages), another scene is added in between to show the grabbing, sensationalist nature of newspaper journalists.

The main emphasis of the play, according to Gao, is man's ruination of his environment, his lack of understanding of his own heritage, and this destruction and lack of understanding in turn denies him the possibility of understanding the present. Gao is by no means the only Chinese author to address this issue in the 1980s. In China there has been a revival of interest in China's ancient past, especially among writers and even politicians. A kind of neo-romanticism seems to have developed, and young writers such as Ma Zhongjun and, in particular, film-makers from the so-called Fifth Generation such as Zhang Yimo have even made special visits into the countryside to observe traditional ways and rituals, in an effort to recreate such scenes and reconfirm a specifically Chinese identity. Gao himself declares that he refers to traditional Chinese theatre (xiqu) rather than to Artaud, who, after all, founded his ideas on theatre after seeing the performances from a Balinese troupe.

Gao's house-building and wedding scenes have a power, vitality and sense of freedom which is not present in his earlier plays. The Old Singer evokes spirits to appear, and promises to show "the riddle, one of the four greatest riddles of the earth."[8] Similarly, on his first entrance, the actor playing the Ecologist warns the audience that other actors may come from behind or beside their seats. "Dear audience, you need not fear that the actors will appear from under your seats, do not be afraid on that score" (Gao, 1985b, p. 143). Thus speaks the actor playing the Ecologist. However, direct contact with the performers, or the feeling of being drawn into some kind of communal ritual is seldom ventured.

Gao presents almost a rational treatise, this time on the subject of man, his environment and heritage The image of chaos is a technical, director/choreographer's device. Gao invokes spirits from another world, but does not let them loose, nor can he be rid of them. In the end, man conquers the rape of his environment, and brings order to nature, respecting the harmony of *yin* and *yang*. While man may fail utterly to communicate with woman (Gao stresses man has no way of understanding the opposite sex — this *yinyang* constellation is a permanent cosmic battle) but man will go in harmony with his surroundings as long as he is aware enough of the need for control.

The control Gao speaks of in the play is perhaps also reflected in control in the performance. The anticipated multifaceted, vibrant living performance including music, dance and mime, is actually a well-controlled exercise, where dance, song, lights, costume, character are all part of the framework within which Gao sets forth his idea, just as traditional Chinese theatre also uses all these elements in performance. Lin Zhaohua, the director, calls this play the most typical or representative of Gao's works.

BEYOND THE BOUNDARY — *THE OTHER SIDE*

Gao's next play, *Bi'an* [The other side, or "the other shore"], was written in May 1986, but has so far not been performed in China. Perhaps the reason for this may have been the campaign against "bourgeois liberalization" which "re-imposed restrictions on artistic experiment experienced in 1983" (Roubicek, 1986, p. 20). Or, the dismissal of the Secretary General of the Chinese Communist Party, Hu Yaobang, and the expulsion from the party of some intellectuals and writers also caused a general lack of interest in performing this play. The play went into rehearsal at the People's Art Theatre, and only half of the play was ever rehearsed because it apparently proved difficult for the actors from a technical point of view. In any case, the play centres around the problem of the individual facing the masses — how the individual is tempted to-wards certain ways of behaving by the masses, how he may also be abused by the masses and forced into certain ways of behaving, and how rela-tionships of power are the key to understanding the individual in society.

The play *The Other Side* is quite unlike Gao's earlier plays in that it explores the nature of theatre and performance itself. Some actors en-ter an arena (it need not be a stage, according to Gao), and use a rope as the only prop to play games which explore the relationships of the ac-tors to each other. Holding one end of the rope, one actor explains, for example, how he can act as a satellite around another actor who holds the other end. One is the pivot around which the other turns, both are linked (and yet also bound) by the rope. In the same example, the situ-ation can be reversed, and the changes in the relations between people are shown to depend upon who has the most strength or power to domi-nate the pull of the rope. The actor/director in charge of these games goes on to explain that such changes and nuances of man's position among his fellow men can also be shown even without the rope, and the play proper proceeds, using voice and movement as the rope was used, as a prop or device to reveal the changing relations between the actors.

The play is loosely constructed and follows an explorative pattern which Gao names abstract play. The drama is perhaps the most extreme ex-ample of Gao's interest in examining man and his role in society, his role to other men for it goes beyond the framework of the fixed space of a railway carriage, or bus stop, for example, and operates in a make-believe environment (where a river or a temple are created by the actor's imagination only) and an unfixable, fluid environment is used. The play proceeds along the idea of game playing. One prop, a rope, is replaced by another, language, or music; all serve the actors' exploration of ways in which to express their positions to each other, to themselves and to the audience. After crossing to the other side of the Lethe-like river, language is totally eradicated and forgotten and has to be discovered anew. These innocent beings are taught a new language by a mother-like figure — yet even this new language quickly becomes contaminated with the familiar patterns of power grabbing and dependency.

In some senses *The Other Side* echoes Gao's earlier play *Alarm Signal* in that it interprets literally Gao's concept that "to speak of a place is to be in that place." The actors create a river for themselves, which they must cross to proceed further on in the play:

Man: Who are you?
Woman: I'm one of you.
Man: Where are we?
Woman: We're on the longed for, never to be reached, other side.[9]

Whether the passage to the other side is representative of the passage into death, the passage into liberation from the earthly body, or a passage into life, or has any other meaning, Gao leaves the audience to decide. The actors themselves are unsure, are simply searching — *going forward*. On the other side, the actors seem to lose all former knowledge. They sleep and are awoken by Woman who gently tells them the language of their bodies which they try to imitate:

Woman: This ... is a hand.
Crowd: Th ... thai ... i ... is ... hind ... hand ...
Woman: Hand.
Crowd: Hand, hund, hond, hand.
Woman: This is a foot.
Crowd: Th ... th ... this ... i ... is ... f ... fo ... foot.   (Gao, 1986, p. 158)

The actors slowly relearn spoken language. As they do so, they also touch and relearn the language or grammar of their bodies. The character Man (the actor who directed the rope games) wanders through the play relearning his status among the others, exploring himself and his relations to others. The character Woman sometimes appears as Earth Mother, teacher of souls, and at other times as a fallen woman who madly cries out against the rest of the group for their rejection of her, and who exposes their hypocrisy. Each scene seems almost a hypothesis of a scene. The character Girl makes believe she is enclosed in a transparent egg shell. The character Youth tries to pull her out of the shell, but she is too frightened. He turns and finds his father — or at least the character Father — and there follows a dialogue about the misunderstandings between youth and age. The boy turns round again to be met by a human wall and a woman who demands money for passage through. If he has none, she will take his watch and he can lie to his mother about the loss of it. Each scene barely explores one idea before it has, dream-like, metamorphosed itself into another scene.

Western critics were quick to draw the examples of the Polish director Jerzy Grotowski into discussion on *The Other Side*. For he has written that the aim of his theatre is to study what lies behind the everyday mask, to expose the innermost core of a personality in order to offer it up as sacrifice for the community. But in his notes, Gao suggests it is like a myth, a story in which each listener must find his own meaning — a story with no particular rationale in terms of development, a fantasy play. *The Other Side* can better be interpreted in the light of Buddhist philosophy, than any dramatic theory of Grotowski. While one would hesitate to claim that creating a play around the theme of "Otherness" or "another state of being," is intended in a solely Buddhist sense, Gao is certainly exploring such states on the stage — itself another world. One element of Buddhist philosophy can be seen in the search to "step beyond oneself," to reach a state of nothingness, of no-thought. No-thought is necessarily also no-language. Gao plays with words in some scenes to such an extent that the words themselves become empty of meaning, are reduced to sound only. It is not written in a scattered, nonsense way, as it might be in an absurd drama. Gao writes in a deliberately conscious way with repetition and pun on word sound and tone (the four tones in the Chinese language) to empty and contort the words and their meanings.

> Man: And if I don't want to look?
> Crowd: (speaking over each other, the words descend into nonsense.) If you don't want to, that's fine, we can't force you. But if you don't want to look it doesn't mean no one else can look, and if everyone's looking you can't not look, when no one's looking, then you can stop looking; if everyone is looking and you're not looking, everyone's looking for everyone, if you're looking everyone will be looking. Are you looking, if you're not looking everyone will be looking for if you're not looking everyone will not be looking but looking for you.
>
> (Gao, 1986, pp. 178–179)

The Buddhist elements of the play are perhaps most obvious in one scene which is set in a Buddhist temple to the sound of the Crowd chanting the Buddhist scriptures and incantations bent on reaching the state of Nirvana. The play is structured around the character Man who struggles with the sense of "belonging" which is so impressed upon him by the Crowd. From first clinging to and learning from the Crowd, he does finally stand apart from them, and establish his own sense of self. Prior to the scene above, the Crowd are all looking for something. Each one is looking on the ground for a specific thing, each knows what he is looking for. The Man finds himself also looking, but since he does not know what he is supposed to be looking for, he gives up and wants to pass by. The Crowd will not let him. They think that he must have found the thing he was looking for already, and that if he has, he has somehow out-smarted them.

> Man: But 1 haven't found anything!
> Crowd: Then you'd better go on looking. (Gao, 1986, p. 179)

Finally, Man calls out: "But I have nothing to do with you" (Gao, 1986, p. 178). He constructs a forest out of mannequins he finds lying around at the end of the play.

Of the four plays dealt with here, *The Other Side* is perhaps the hardest to understand. Certainly it is the hardest to perform. Perhaps it was too much ahead of itself for the Chinese actors let alone the audience. Kenneth Rea, from the Royal Shakespeare Company, who was working with drama students in Beijing at the Central Academy of Drama in 1984 highlights the problem of drama training in China. As Ken Rea says, "The final impression is usually one of confusion and frustration at not being able to know exactly what the Chinese actors one has worked with really think and feel, or indeed to what extent they can afford strong individual feelings at all" (1985, p. 33). Rea goes on to suggest that Chinese actors are not trained to risk exposure of the inner self, and this has to do with a long *xiqu* theatre tradition where the actor can also critically observe his own role as he performs it in order to be able to execute certain actions or movements with skill, as well as allowing — even inviting — the audience to appreciate the skill with which he performs. It is possible that the actors trained in spoken drama and not *xiqü* enforced certain limitations on the production of this play.

In conclusion, the myth that Gao has simply followed patterns of drama set by Western dramatists such as Ibsen, Beckett, Artaud, Kantor, or Grotowski has proved as fruitless as the idea that Brecht may have founded his theories of Alienation entirely on having seen some performances of *jingjü* in Moscow. In both cases, a companion dramatist or dramatic theory shadows original work. Gao's work is possibly so Chinese that we simply cannot understand it in the West properly. Yet, we have seen that the seeds of Gao's concepts of drama are deeply bound to certain potentials inherent in the Chinese language, which he fully exploits. For, the Chinese language can surpass all physical boundaries of time and space — according to Gao, "time and space are language" (Riley, 1987). In *Alarm Signal* language evokes three distinct times in the present time; in *The Other Side* a new concept of space is broken into through language — the deconstruction of language becomes "beyond language."

Gao uses another Chinese style in all his plays which seems to echo the message banners which hail the citizen from every possible building site, monumental hall, school auditorium, department store and so on. It is a style which is declamatory, terse, compact and finished within itself and it is found in the wise lectures of the old guard in *Alarm Signal*; the insistent musical leitmotif of the Silent Man in *The Bus-Stop*; the cries of "Save the forest" in *Wild Man* and the director/actor leading the rope games in *The Other Side*. The theatre in China has a long tradition of always having spoken out, and trusting the word to convey faithfully the right message. The exaggeration in *xiqu*, the turning outward of inner emotions such as anger, or fear, can also be seen in Gao's plays. The thoughts and feelings of his characters are embodied either as real characters on the stage, or spoken out as part of present speech. Gao certainly writes for a specifically Chinese audience. Vladimir and Estragon come from any (European) country, any (European) place, any (European) sense of time. Gao's figures are thoroughly Chinese — Director Ma in *The Bus-Stop,* the Girl Honey Bee in *Alarm Signal,* even Man in *The Other Side* and the Forester in *Wild Man*. These plays all explore the relation of man to his fellow men, to the rest of society, and how man is related to the world in one way or another. It makes Gao both an exciting challenge to a Chinese audience as well as a threat, if one considers the long years of suppression of the sense of self in favour of the community. Gao says of his drama that "in essence, the nature of drama is not to serve society [as the Communist ideal maintains] but to entertain both performers and audience alike. The loss of utilitarian aims in our art will bring about the self-liberation of art (Roubicek, 1986, p. 25). If we see his plays in this light, and understand his search to express a sense of identity, and position in the world, the plays can be interpreted beyond their superimposed Western shadows. Gao Xingjian can step beyond the myth determined by false comparison with European modern dramatists. His work must be seen in the light of its essentially classic Chinese nature. Gao seems to stand firmly among the ranks of established writers, such as Cao Yü and Tian Han, and the newer, perhaps more radical dramatists that have emerged.

NOTES

1. This is a revised version of an article with the same title published in *Haishi Zou Hao: Chinese Poetry, Drama and Literature of the 1980s* (Bonn: Engelhard-Ng Verlag, 1989), pp. 129–151.
2. For details, see Richter (1987), p. 7.
3. The title of the play has also been translated as *The Other Shore.*
4. Gao Xingjian, *Xiandai xiaoshuo jiqiao chutan* 現代小説技巧初探 [A preliminary exploration of the techniques of modern fiction].
5. For details, see Chang and Kubin (1987), in which there is a translators' endnote to *Die Busstation.*
6. See Barmé (1983b), p. 373; Che Xin (1986), p. 44; Wang Xining (1985), p. 5; Bogert (1986), p. 52.
7. See Programme notes to *Yeren* [Wild man].
8. See Programme notes to *Yeren* [Wild man].
9. Translated by Jo Riley, in Martha Cheung and Jane Lai, eds., *An Oxford Anthology of Contemporary Chinese Drama*, p. 159.

REFERENCES

Barmé, Geremie (1983a). "To Be or Not." *Australian Journal of Chinese Affairs*, Nos. 9–10, pp. 139–145.

—— (1983b). "A Touch of the Absurd — Introducing Gao Xingjian and His Play *The Bus-Stop*." *Renditions*, Nos. 19 & 20 (Spring & Autumn), pp. 373–377.

Bei Dao 北島 (1987). *Waves* 波動 [Bo dong]. Trans. Susette Cooke and Bonnie McDougall. London: Heinemann.

Bogert, C. (1986). "Playwrights Thrive on an 'Open' Peking Stage." *Far Eastern Economic Review*, 14 November, p. 52.

Chang Hsien-chen and Wolfgang Kubin, trans. (1987). "Endnote to Die Busstation." *Theater heute*, No. 2, pp. 9–13.

Che Xin (1986). "Original, Controversial Stage Plays." *China Reconstructs*, July, p. 44.

Cheung, Martha P. Y., and Jane Lai, eds. (1997). *An Oxford Anthology of Contemporary Chinese Drama*. Hong Kong and Oxford: Oxford University Press.

Gao Xingjian 高行健 (1981). *Xiandai xiaoshuo jiqiao chutan* 現代小説技巧初探 [A preliminary exploration of the techniques of modern fiction]. Guangzhou: Huacheng chubanshe 花城出版社.

—— (1982). *Juedui xinhao* 絕對信號 [Alarm signal]. *Shiyue* 十月, No. 2, pp. 17–36.

—— (1983). *Chezhan* 車站 [The bus-stop]. *Shiyue* 十月, No. 3, pp. 119–138.

—— (1985a). *Gao Xingjian xijuji* 高行健戲劇集 [Plays by Gao Xingjian]. Beijing: Qunzhong chubanshe 群眾出版社.

—— (1985b). *Yeren* [Wild man]. *Shiyue* 十月, No. 2, pp. 142–169.

—— (1986). *Bi'an* 彼岸 [The other shore]. *Shiyue* 十月, No. 5, pp. 238–251.

He Wen 何聞 (1983). "Postscript: On Seeing the Play *The Bus-stop*." Trans. Chan Sin-wai. *Renditions*, Nos. 19 & 20 (Spring & Autumn), pp. 387–392.

Laozi 老子. *Daodejing* 道德經 [The classic of virtues].

Lu Xun (Lu Hsun) 魯迅 (1956a). "The Passer-By." Trans. Yang Hsien-yi and Gladys Yang. In Lu Xun (1956b), Vol. 1, pp. 332–338.

—— (1956b). *Selected Works of Lu Hsun*. Trans. Yang Hsien-yi and Gladys Yang. 2 vols. Beijing: Foreign Languages Press.

Programme notes (1985) to *Yeren* [Wild man].

Rea, Kenneth (1985). "Search for the Inner Life of the Actor: The Problems of Acting in China Today" *Drama*, No. 156, pp. 30–34.

Richter, Almuth, trans. (1987). "Introduction to Gao Xingjian, 'Mein Verhältnis zu Brecht.'" *Theater heute*, No. 2, pp. 7–9.

Riley, Jo (1987a). Interview with Gao Xingjian, 15 June.

—— (1987b). Interview with Lin Zhaohua, 22 June.

——, trans. (1997). *The Other Side*. In Cheung and Lai, eds. (1997), pp. 149–183.

Roubicek, Bruno (1986). "*Wild Man* by Gao Xingjian — A Modern Chinese Drama." Unpublished thesis, Newcastle University. Revised as "*Wild Man*: A Contemporary Chinese Spoken Drama." *Asian Theater Journal*, Vol. 7, No. 2 (1990), pp. 184–249.

Wang Xining (1985). "An Unconventional Blend." *China Daily*, 21 May, p. 5.

Wang Yusheng 王育生 (1985). "Kanguo *Yeren* houde jidian zhiyi" 看過《野人》後的幾點質疑 [Some thoughts after seeing *Wild Man*]. *Wenyibao* 文藝報 [Literary gazette], 13 July, p. 13.

Gao Xingjian's *Monologue* as Metadrama

I am full of doubts, I even doubt all ideas and values in general. The only thing I do not doubt is life, because I am alive and kicking. Life has a meaning that transcends ethics and if I still have some value, then it lies only in this existence.

I write for myself, I do not set out to please other people, nor am I trying to remould the world or other people, because I cannot even change myself. The important thing for me is simply that it is I who speak, and I who write.

— Gao Xingjian, "Without Isms" (1993)

Critics generally agree that in the post-1978 era, in which artistic creation in China was still dominated by realism and steered by socialist doctrine, Gao Xingjian opened a new path in theatre art and intellectual inquiry, through his appropriation of modern Western forms as part of his process of intellectual inquiry and as a conscious challenge to the established modes of thinking. *Juedui xinhao* 絕對信號 [Alarm signal, 1982], his first play, departs from realist conventions through its externalization of interior activities, which was hitherto unfamiliar to a Chinese audience (Quah, 1997, pp. 13–14), through its exposition of the lighting equipment, which reminds the audience that it is drama and not real life, and through its performance in a small theatre, rather than in the proscenium stage, so as to shorten the distance between the actors and the audience (Quah, 1997, p. 16). In *Chezhan* 車站 [The bus-stop, 1983], the performance of which has been acclaimed as the first production of the Theatre of the Absurd in Mainland China (Quah, 1997, p. 14), not only are the sets of the play minimized for the sake of provoking the audience's imagination, but the performers also alienate

themselves from their dramatic personae, and resume their capacity as
actors to speak to the actual audience (Quah, 1997, p. 18). In *Yeren* 野人
[Wild man, 1985], the actor who plays the role of the ecologist goes even
further: apart from assuming the dual capacity of the actor and the
character, he speaks for the playwright/director as he explains the structure and style of the play, thus reaching out to the audience in the form
of the authorial consciousness (Quah, 1997, p. 19). All these, coupled
with Gao's requirement that his actors prolong the transitional state between themselves as performers and as personae, and that they possess
the consciousness of such a neutral state throughout their performance
(Chen, 1995, p. 4), enhance a more fervent interaction among the actors,
the characters and the audience. In short, they fall in line with Gao's
advocacy of "theatricality," adopted from Antoin Artaud's Total Theatre
and the Brechtian Epic Theatre, and with his belief in the function of
his theatre which aims, on the one hand, at getting the audience to "participate in a pleasant show, similar to that during a festival, feel entertained and joyful, physically and psychologically," and on the other hand,
at inducing them to be alienated from emotional involvement for "the
process of reception and reflection" (Gao, 1985, p. 169), so as to lead to
a more extensive influence on society.

THEATRICALITY AND THE FOURTH WALL

Curiously, *Du bai* 獨白 [Monologue], a one-actor play found in Gao's drama
collection published in Beijing in 1985, has not attracted much critical
discussion, especially when compared with *Alarm Signal, The Bus-Stop* and
Wild Man — better known as Gao's *Trilogy* — which are all found in the
same volume. Nevertheless, that the play is a dept illustration of the
dramatist's notion of theatricality, even more so than are his other plays, is
obvious enough at the first glance. At the beginning of the play, the Actor
proclaims his attempt to build a wall that separates him from his audience:

> Actor: (*He says to himself*) I want to place a piece of rope (He raises his
> head and faces the audience) and draw a line here. You are on the
> outside of the line, me on the inside.
>
> (*He faces the audience*) I want to build a wall along the rope (He bends
> over and makes gestures as if he is really constructing a wall), thus sepa-
> rating you — the audience, and me — the actor.   (Gao, 1985, p. 187)

Yet, he is soon aware of the necessity of the wall to be "transparent," reminiscent of the "transparent fourth wall" in realist drama,

> Yet I cannot build a real wall. (*He stops, while the imaginary wall has already reached his chest*) If a wall is built, then can you still watch what I'm doing? (*He looks out of the wall, before he looks inward again*) It won't be fun anyway, if I were to act for myself on the inner side of the wall. The wall must therefore be transparent, so as for you to observe what I'm doing, even though there's no need for me to be able to see you.
>
> (Gao, 1985, p. 187)

before he sets out to defend and describe the realist theatre, where the audience, separated entirely from the actors, watch the performance in total passivity, and where the actors, without paying the slightest attention to the audience, engage in their performance in a self-centred manner: "Now, I can live freely in the characters I portray. Your criticism no longer bothers me. Nor does your pricking gaze make my skin creep" (Gao, 1985, p. 188). Nevertheless, as he is describing with enthusiasm his profession as an actor, he inevitably discloses the artificiality of stage performance,

> (*With quite a lot of confidence and in a slightly exaggerating manner*) When I portray a physician, I'd act in a serious yet friendly manner, and speak in a muffled tone, due to the mask I'd be wearing. When I portray a street singer, I'd have to take on a coarse voice. When I portray a bookworm, I'd have to wear a pair of thick spectacles.
>
> (Gao, 1985, p. 188)

and it is not long before he is compelled to acknowledge the influence of the audience upon the actors: "Take us actors as an example. A successful actor is the one who becomes so popular that the audience will rush to buy tickets once they find your name on the theatre signboards. But that is easier said than done" (Gao, 1985, p. 189). In fact, throughout the one-act play, the line between the Actor as a performer and as a dramatic persona remains blurred. While the Actor, as he describes his profession to the audience, apparently assumes his identity as an actor, confusion concerning his dual role arises from time to time:

> (*He speaks softly to himself*) What do I have to say?
> (*He turns to the back stage*) I've forgotten my lines!   (Gao, 1985, p. 188)

As the monologue progresses, he somehow becomes the dramatist's mouthpiece, by acknowledging the transitional stage an actor has to cross over from his identity as an actor to that as a character:

> (*He walks freely, slightly raising his voice*) Moreover, he (the actor) has to portray those roles assigned to him, but which he does not like. A good actor has to control his emotions, move out from his own self, and like his audience, he has to step back and observe the role he is playing.
>
> (Gao, 1985, p. 191)

He even goes on to demonstrate the process by which an actor successfully engages with his assigned character:

> (*He sits on the edge of the stage*) [He's] refining his character. (*He looks at the circle of light at the stage centre*)
>
> (*He speaks softly*) He uses his hand to support his chin. (*He rests his chin on his hand*)
>
> No, now he drops his hand. (*He drops his hand*)
>
> He rests his hand on his knee, and looks as if he is thinking of something. (*His hand caresses his knee*)
>
> This is not fine. (*His hand stops caressing his knee*)
>
> That's right. He finally forgets to fumble with his hand, and deliberately takes on that pensive expression. Thus, he finally sinks into the character he's been trying to portray.   (Gao, 1985, p. 193)

As he has earlier described the influence of the audience upon the actor, he now confirms their inseparability and discusses the exchange between them during the theatrical performance:

> (*He gets excited and his words roll out turbulently*) You are you. You are an actor. You use your conscience, your personality and your knowledge, and exchange what you know about the character with the audience.
>
> (Gao, 1985, p. 191)

In order to elaborate on the necessity of the interaction among the actor, the audience and the character, moreover, Gao uses a metaphor that resonates with the "open-door" policy introduced in the post-

Cultural Revolution era, which had allowed the playwright to experiment with a new mode of aesthetics with its accompanying spectrum of possibilities and stimulations (Quah, 1997, p. 3):

> You grasp that moment while you're acting on the stage, and open a window to the audience. If the window is not big enough, then you'll have to open a door.
>
> (*He makes a gesture as if he is opening a door, which he walks across*) You walk over to the audience, and invite them to join you in the creation of your character. You are both your character and you yourself.
>
> (Gao, 1985, p. 191)

Therefore, he comes to realize the need to step across the "transparent fourth fall," one which he has advocated at the beginning:

> (*He raises his voice*) No matter how common and humble an actor's origin, once he steps across the fourth wall that separates the actors and the audience, and dares to gaze upon the audience with the gaze of the character he's playing, then he is a confident and bright actor.
>
> (Gao, 1985, p. 192)

In an ideal theatrical performance, not only the audience, but also the actor, are sustained in a state between cool detachment and active participation:

> Instead of being himself, he is now able to feel the solitude suffered by his character. He is able to laugh and cry as this character, even without the help of setting, props, costumes and make-up and sound effects.
>
> (Gao, 1985, p. 192)

> (*He resumes his voice as an actor*) Once an actor has a firm grasp of the character, he is able to act naturally, treating his performance as a creation, or even an enjoyment. On the one hand, he indulges in his character; on the other, he is able to alienate himself from the role he's playing, and like the audience, he observes himself playing the role of that particular character. (Gao, 1985, p. 193)

As the play begins with the Actor placing a rope on the stage, in an attempt to build a wall along it, the play now ends with his pointing out the paradox of a "transparent fourth wall," and thus his realizing the necessity of pulling down this "wall":

(*Loudly*) Who left the rope on the stage?

(*He reminds himself*) Wasn't it you?

(*Loudly*) Why left the rope on the stage?

(*Reminding himself*) Didn't you compare it to a wall?

(*Running out of patience*) what wall?

(*Impatient*) a fourth wall that separates you from your audience

(*Stubbornly*) but then, how can the audience see me?

Isn't the wall transparent?

But a transparent wall isn't a wall at all! Pull it down!

(Gao, 1985, p. 199)

"I," "YOU," "S/HE"

As Gao stresses the importance of both content and form, his works, despite their preoccupation with theatrical experimentation, which seem to have overshadowed their thematic ideas, do address the primary concerns of contemporary China. His earlier plays mainly deal with the estrangement of man, which is caused by a discrepancy between their aspiration and the disappointing reality, and call for the expression and realization of individuality alongside with the achievement of a collective vision for the country; his later works, especially those written after he was exiled in France, move toward the perennial phenomenon of human alienation, and scrutinize with a touch of spatial and temporal absurdity man's relationship with his environment, with his fellows, and with himself. What is remarkable about his later plays, moreover, is that they consist of much fewer characters than his earlier ones, and are sometimes delivered in the third, but not the first, person, as in *Shengsijie* 生死界 [Between life and death, 1991]. Through the filter of the subjectivity of a third-person narrator, the emotional characteristics of the character under description thus appear to be distorted, diluted or exaggerated, with the result that a psychological distance is established between the narrative text and the truth about the character; the formalization and externalization of the dialogic characteristic of utterance, in addition, serve to dramatize the tension between the self and the other, and consequently, the self is revealed as a fragmented, rather than as a holistic, self-contained, entity (Quah, 1999, pp. 140–142). Even the second person, "you," in *Yeyoushen* 夜遊神 [Nocturnal Wanderer, 1993] is highly ambiguous, through which the audience are psychologically mobilized to identify with the protagonist, and accordingly enter into a state of isolation, and the co-existence of the first and the third persons in *Duihua yu fangjie* 對話與反詰 [Dialogue and rebuttal, 1992] only serve to reinforce the fact that the characters are cocooned within their own subjectivities (Quah, 1999, pp. 146). In short, the dramatic narrative is no longer a means to achieve an alienation effect, but becomes the theme of alienation itself. It is therefore not surprising that the endings of these later plays also differ tremendously from those of the earlier ones: while *Alarm Signal*, *The Bus-Stop* and *Wild Man* all convey a sense of optimism by the end, which transform the reflective mood of the plays into a possibility for the future, in *Between Life and Death*, *Nocturnal Wanderer*, and *Dialogue and Rebuttal*, the quests by Gao's protagonists for a freer form of existence all end in failure. Their failure are accounted for by relating the playwright's concept of freedom to the Daoist idea of "Nothingness" which, according to Zhuangzi, refers to a higher level of subjectivity,

> A superior man has no self,
> A heavenly man has no need,
> A sagacious man has no name.

Thus the pulling down of boundaries allows man to interact freely with nature (Quah, 1999, p. 161). Gao's characters, unable to overcome their indulgent consciousness, are therefore helplessly entrapped within their subjectivity. In other words, not only do Gao's later works exemplify the modern predicament described by Marshall Berman, that the "public shatters into a multitude of fragments, speaking incommensurable languages," which renders the nature of utterance meaninglessness (Quah, 1999, pp. 163–165), but also offer the gloomiest pictures of those physically related, yet spiritually disconnected, individuals who inevitably undergo various forms of "self-deification" (Quah, 1999, p. 159): *Between Life and Death* closes in a dimly lit scene, in which a heap of clothing can be vaguely seen where the woman is lying prostrated; the characters degenerated into worms in *Nocturnal Wanderer*; as *Dialogue and Rebuttal* ends, the man and the woman, giggling, crawl around on the stage, twisted and distorted like two strange worms.

Interestingly, *Monologue*, written in April 1984, somehow bridges Gao's pre-exile and post-exile works, and is a more complicated piece of drama than it first seems to be. On the one hand, it does resonate with the post-exile works of Gao in terms of both theatrical techniques and thematic issues. To begin with, it is delivered throughout by a single actor and character in his fifties. This, coupled with his proclamation of his wish to be cut off from the audience, are reminiscent of the alienation suffered by the protagonists in the playwright's later works. On the other hand, there is the interchangeable use of the first, the second, and the third persons. Though the Actor, in a tone that smacks of egotism, begins his monologue in the first-person, it is not long before he is compelled to shift to the second person which, according to the playwright, is comparable to close-up shots in movies, and facilitates the emotional exchange between the narrator/character/actor and the reader/audience (Gao, 1981, pp. 13–14). He does so, firstly, as he addresses the audience, which in turn betrays his reliance upon them; secondly, as he "sincerely" expresses his views toward his life, and appeals to their empathy with the use of shared human experiences:

> (*He gets sincere, and without a touch of theatricality*) One day, you suddenly realize that you're old. You are your children's children. There's nothing sadder than becoming old. (Gao, 1985, p. 189)

> What I want to add is that you discover that you've getting too old before you find time to accomplish all your life-long goals. You have to retire, stay home and play with your grandchildren: if not your grandson, then your granddaughter.... Sure, by that time, you will be touched whenever your child calls you daddy, and your heart will be stirred by a mixed feeling of sadness and warmth. You feel, after all, that your life is not entirely without focus. Oh, where did I stop? (Gao, 1985, p. 189)

> I wonder if any of you, the audience, has similar experience. You wake up in the middle of the night, sweaty and your heart thumping, and can sleep no more. Are you that old already? Will you sink into a deep sleep one day and, without least expecting it, do not wake up the next morning? (Gao, 1985, p. 194)

As the play moves on, he, and thus the playwright, manage to balance the thematic with the technical by drawing the audience's attention to both the Actor's age (the fact that he is aging), and his profession (the fact that he is an actor):

> You must find a way out of it. You'll claim that there's no set limit on art. Rather than charming the audience as you used to when you were a young man, you now impress them with your performance. You pull down the fourth wall, and fall back on your acting. As you get older, you yearn for simplicity. (Gao, 1985, p. 194)

Then, he further conveys his appeal through a suppositional stage, one which is boiled down to a minimal set, make-up and costumes, thus showing how the essence of drama lies in the performance of actors:

> (*He speaks softly*) you tell the audience that this scene is set against a forest —
> [*The stage light gradually weakens, with his profile slowly revealed by his sidelights.*]
> (*He looks as if he sees it*) In the dark forest there is a little path.
> [*A strip of light appears dimly on the outer edge of the stage.*]
> He's reached old age, the autumn of ones life. (*He walks over into the strip of light*)
> Falling leaves. (*He raises his head*)   (Gao, 1985, p. 195)

In order to show the versatility of the stage, and to demonstrate the spontaneity of Gao's "Ideal Actor" in his/her creative process of constructing a unique theatrical experience, the Actor continues to play out the different periods of one's life. He also changes his perspective by switching his viewpoint to "you," who is both himself and the audience, as he appeals to his audience's sense of nostalgia for their childhood and adolescence:

> Then you remember the bygone days as a child and adolescent....
> [*A child singing a newspaper jingle, forlorn and intermittent.*]
> You were poor, but you never gave up....   (Gao, 1985, p. 195)

Still speaking in the second person, and with the minimum support of lighting and sound effects, he manages to break the boundary of time, to carry the audience over to the next stage of ones life, and to impress them with the energy and enthusiasm of youth:

> [*Yellow light casts on his face. He narrows his eyes looking for the origin of the song, but it stops suddenly. There comes the cracking of waves. The light on his face disappears, and is replaced by a glow of red light behind his body. He opens his arms wide, as if he's running toward the sea.*]
>
> You were so young, so full of enthusiasm. You are filled with excitement, and you long to embrace your life, in a way the sea embraces you!
>
> [*As the cracking of the waves mounts, he cries with excitement.*] Oh — oh —!
> Oh — ah —   (Gao, 1985, p. 196)

As he moves forward, mobilizes the audience's imagination, and helps them to relive the uncertainty, precariousness, despair they suffer in their middle-ages, he simultaneously transforms the limited stage into a free space:

> [*His scream mixes with the sound of the waves, both fading into the background. He stands still. Now, red and green lights flicker on both sides, and he looks sideways, puzzled. The hoots of vehicles, high-pitched microphones, whistles, and songs on both if his sides get mixed up and confuse him.*]
>
> You enter into the middle-age. You stand at the crossroad, get involved in an incident, and find yourself surrounded by crowds of people. You cannot see clearly, and don't know what fault you've done. It's as if you've trespassed the red lights and so have to learn a hard lesson.
>
> (Gao, 1985, p. 196)

He even appeals to such experiences as love, and he changes his perspective to that of the girl "she":

> (*He assumes the tone and expression of a narrator*) At this moment, she comes to you lightly, as if in a dream. Somehow you think you've met her before. She's like the girl who lived next-door, the one who came to play with you when you were a child. Yet you can't remember her face anymore. Anyway, you think it was she, and so you speak softly to her.
>
> (Gao, 1985, p. 198)

When he resumes the capacity of an aging actor, his being a man in his fifties, he does so in the persona of "you,"

> [*The music becomes louder. He appears in applause and cheers. The circle of light disappears, and the whole stage is in the limelight.*]
>
> (*He assumes the tone and expression of an outsider, and speaks rapidly*) Your performance is recognized once more. You become an authority figure. However, you know so well that your status cannot stay long. You are merely an actor, whose position is best on the stage. You feel uneasy and become sleepless. You realize that as an actor, you are way too old.
>
> (Gao, 1985, p. 197)

and finally, through the collective first person "we." As he now confesses to the audience that "we actors" cannot "stand loneliness," he is perhaps making a dual remark, indicating that they, as human beings, cannot endure solitude and alienation:

> (*He winks like an old man does, but speaks with enthusiasm*) We actors all prefer to have people around us. We love your applause, and we yearn to be loved by the audience. We cannot stand loneliness.
>
> (Gao, 1985, p. 198)

As Gao's trilogy all end in a tone of optimism, and in particular, the characters in *The Bus-Stop* arrive at the conclusion that they should start their journey by walking, in *Monologue*, the Actor finally pulls down the transparent fourth wall, replaces the rope, and even goes down the stage. Thus, while the playwright, through the Actor's final action, indicates what a "living drama" should be like, he also seems to be suggesting a possible way out of the cell of alienation in which protagonists of his post-exile plays are found to be trapped hopelessly, and that it falls within the power of the individuals to break down the wall that estranges them from their surroundings and separates them from their fellow beings:

> As you were the one who first set it (*the wall*) up, you should be the one who pull it down.
>
> Ok. (*He picks up the rope, puts it into his pocket, and walks down the stage*)
>
> (Gao, 1985, p. 199)

ART OF GAME-PLAYING

In the light of the above discussion, *Monologue*, as expected, is apparently more akin to Gao Xingjian's early works in its theme and mood. Nonetheless, the playwright himself asserts that, despite his "own political opinions and views on literature and art," he feels "no need to be trapped by any political or aesthetic framework," and since "literary creation is always an individual impulse of the writer," it "has nothing much to do with doctrine," but "always exposes, criticizes, challenges, subverts and transcends the current society" (Gao, 1996, p. 106). Accordingly, the differences between his works in the 1980s and 1990s, which have been attributed sociopolitically to the crackdown in Tiananmen Square on 4 June 1989, and Gao's subsequent exile in France, might have been dichotomized and overstated. Just as the optimism in Gao's *Trilogy* is

tinged with uncertainty, Gao claims that the Daoist notion of "wuwei" 無
為 [non-action] and Buddhist's renunciation of the world are, contrary
to what some critics might think, too "negative" to be applicable to the
interpretation of his post-exile works (Gao, 1996, p. 113). Thus, the ending of *Monologue* should be viewed with the same scepticism: even if the
Actor's crossing over to the audience is treated symbolically as his determination to break out from his previously isolated existence and to rel-
ish the sense of community offered by his fellow beings, there is yet no
indication of what exactly he will do, or of how he accomplishes it, after
he walks down the stage. This situation seems to prepare, if not predict,
what happens in *Bi'an* 彼岸 [The other shore, 1986], another play by
Gao. "To the other shore! To the other shore! To the other shore!" All
people want to cross over to the other shore, though they neither know
what it is like, nor foresee the conflicts and assaults that arise after their
arrival and their repossession of language, knowledge and consciousness.

If a short play like *Monologue*, which foregrounds the interaction among
the actor, the character and the audience, is to reassure us of anything,
it is perhaps, as Gao remarks, the idea that "self," which has hitherto
been worshipped as "god" in literature of the past, must inevitably be
subject to a vigorous questioning in the postmodern era (Gao, 1996,
p. 112), as we see how it splits into, and fluctuates among "I," "you" and
"s/he," and merge with other split selves to constitute "we" in this one-
actor play. In addition, what shines through the play, as shown by the
acting out of various stages of a person's life by the Actor, is a firm belief
in one's existence in the world, a conviction which has been stressed by
the playwright over and over again both in his interviews and articles.
Otherwise, *Monologue*, as the playwright's other works, is a cauldron of
contradictions. The play, particularly its subtly-conveyed motif of alienation and its associated ambiguities, is reminiscent of the paradoxes in
Gao Xingjian's works as well as of his life: though he claims to express
his ideas in his dramatic works, both performers and audience are made
aware of the unreality of his theatre, accept the "artifice of suppositionality" and to enjoy the "game of playing" (Quah, 1999, p. 110); despite the brilliance of his works, they have been banned and do not reach
the readers in China; through his self-exile and his solitary life in the
suburb of Paris, he has nevertheless enjoyed artistic freedom, as well as
taken the time to refine his use of language, thus allowing him to open
himself, through his writings, to the public.

REFERENCES

Chen Ganquan 陳敢權 (Anthony Chan Kam Kuen) (1995). "Cong *Shengshijie* kan Gao Xingjian de xiju lilun" 從生死界看高行健的戲劇理論 [A discussion of Gao Xingjian's dramatic theories with respect to his *Between Life and Death*." *Xiju yishu* 戲劇藝術 [Dramatic arts], No. 9, pp. 2–4.

Gao Xingjian (1981). *Xiandai xiaoshuo jiqiao chutan* 現代小説技巧初探 [A preliminary exploration of the techniques of modern fiction]. Guangzhou: Huacheng chubanshe 花城出版社.

—— (1985a). *Du bai* 獨白 [Monologue]. In Gao (1985b), pp. 187–199.

—— (1985b). *Gao Xingjian xiju ji* 高行健戲劇集 [Plays by Gao Xingjian]. Beijing: Qunzhong chubanshe 群眾出版社.

—— (1993). "Xiju: rouhe xifang yu zhongguo de changshi" 戲劇：揉合西方與中國的嘗試 [Drama: An attempt to blend the West with the East]. *Ershiyi shiji* 二十一世紀 [The 21st century], No. 21, pp. 62–68.

—— (1996a). *Meiyou zhuyi* 沒有主義 [Without isms]. Hong Kong: Tiandi tushu youxian gongsi 天地圖書有限公司.

—— (1996b). "Meiyou zhuyi" 沒有主義 [Without isms]. In Gao (1996a), pp. 8–17. Original work published in 1993.

Quah Sy Ren (1997). "Gao Xingjian and China's Alternative Theatre of the 1980s." M. Phil. thesis, University of Cambridge.

—— (1999). "The Theatre of Gao Xingjian: Experimentation Within the Chinese Context and Towards New Modes of Representation." Ph.D. thesis, University of Cambridge.

Wang Baolin 黃寶蓮 (2000). "Gao Xingjian sumiao" 高行健素描 [A portrait of Gao Xingjian]. *Kaifang zazhi* 開放雜誌 [Open magazine], No. 167 (November), pp. 32–33.

Yang Lian 楊煉 (2000). "Zhe shijie daodi hai you yanjing" 這世界到底還有眼睛 [The world is, after all, not blind]. *Kaifang zazhi* 開放雜誌 [Open magazine], No. 167 (November), pp. 25–27.

Gao Xingjian and the Idea of the Theatre

As a writer, Gao Xingjian is highly conscious of the crosscurrents of the Chinese and Western cultures interacting in his personal and artistic lives. It is important to point out that he always values the self, not in an egotistic manner, but in the knowledge of the imperative to comprehend the self, its relation to the world, and the value of existence. The key here is the Chinese concept of "jingguan" 靜觀 (Gao, 1996g, p. 20), or "peaceful observation," which encompasses the ideas of tranquillity, disinterestedness, and detachment. And it is through this concept that we can begin to understand his idea of the tripartition of the actor, that is, just as a writer should observe himself and society with the indifference of an outsider, an actor should also be able to observe his performance and the character he is portraying with the same degree of "coldness" and detachment.

Gao Xingjian's idea of dramaturgy affirms the importance of what he calls theatricality [juchangxing 劇場性]. When Aristotle talks about "action," Gao Xingjian claims, he is referring to action in its fundamental sense, that is, the kind of action that the audience can see and hear (Gao, 1996a, p. 254), unlike the "action" in contemporary drama which is limited to the conflict of ideas and concepts. This physical aspect of drama is what distinguishes it from poetry, which emphasizes lyricality, and fiction, which underlines narration. Drama is process, and while it may not necessarily be complete in itself, the changes, discoveries, and surprises in their course can be amplified and elaborated upon and made into elements of theatricality, thus generating dramatic action on the stage (Gao, 1996i, p. 133).

According to Gao Xingjian, stage language can be used to indicate harmony or disharmony as in a musical structure. Like the notes in a symphony, the phonic qualities of words often highlight their materiality, effectively transforming the utterances into a non-narrational medium. In this manner, stage language acquires the charm and the almost magical power of chanting, and produces a deeply felt compulsion in both actors and audience. Such is the difference between the new language of drama, with its emphasis on materiality and physical impact, and the semantically inclined language commonly used in other literary genres (Gao, 1996i, p. 133).

THE THREE IDENTITIES OF THE ACTOR

There is yet another aspect to the making of theatricality. Drama is nothing but performance, and the actions on the stage are meant for the enjoyment of the audience. In order to facilitate this communication and to enhance its directness, Gao Xingjian maintains that the actor has to be self-conscious of his craft, being aware not only of the character he is playing, but also of the fact that he is putting on a performance as a performer. This awareness is in contrast to Stanislavsky's total immersion method, and to an extent it is also distinguished from Brecht's "alienation," which breaks the illusion of realism and underlines the distance between performance and audience. To Gao Xingjian, there is no denying that drama is ostentation — the many attempts at realism by the modern theatre are nothing short of spurious and futile efforts to achieve impossibility. Ostentation is helpful and also essential to communicating with the audience: in fact, an actor should highlight the act of pretending, as if he is saying to himself and to the audience, "Look how well I can pretend to be somebody else!" As in Peking opera or the Japanese kabuki, even though the actor focuses his attention on how to perform his role, he still manages to retain his identity as an actor — his job is to give a good performance but not to live the life of the character (Gao, 1996h, p. 238). The pretending still exists, and is even accentuated, but it co-exists with a more direct and true-to-life actor-audience communication, in which the actor has become the centre and disseminator of artistic awareness. In other words, besides the character-centred and audience-centred theories of Stanislavsky and Brecht, Gao Xingjian has ventured his own actor-centred theory in an argument for a more self-conscious art.

How does one achieve self-consciousness and yet still be "in" the performance and be a good actor at the same time? The answer to this is Gao Xingjian's idea of the tripartition of acting. In traditional Chinese theatre, Gao Xingjian explains, when the actor gets ready for the role he is to play, he extracts himself from his everyday activities, relaxes his body and focuses his mind to go into his performance. During this time, he "purifies" himself into a "state of neutrality"; in other words, he is in transition between his everyday self and his role. This neutrality can be explained by looking at the convention of "liangxiang" 亮相 (literally "to reveal oneself") in Peking opera (Gao, 1996h, p. 238). At the time of "liangxiang," the actor freezes his movement for a few seconds to mark his entrance or the completion of a display of martial arts, dance sequence, etc., thus making himself "appear" before his audience, who applaud and voice their approval. The performance is briefly suspended, as the actor neutralizes his acting capacity and calls attention to the exhibition of his art.

Thus in any performance, there exists in the actor three identities — the self, the neutral actor, and the character. Neutrality is not tantamount to self-effacement; it demands a self-consciousness in the actor of his own make-believe. At the same time this also equips the actor with a "third eye" of inner vision which, because of the detachment from the character he is portraying, is capable of observing his performing self, the other actors on the stage, and more importantly, the audience. Neutrality then becomes a medium which enables the actor to control and adjust his performance, helping him to be in and out of his character not only before the performance but also many times during the performance. And because the actor is both experiencing (acting) and observing himself while performing, he is more able to project his feelings for the character and for the audience's enjoyment. In any theatre, what needs to be communicated is not reality but the feeling of reality. Embodying the three identities on the stage, the actor can challenge the character he is playing, empathize with him, pity, admire and even criticize him. The dramatic tension resulted from this kind of acting is beyond that of mere yelling and shouting which disguise themselves as theater. In this way, not only the plot but also acting itself can be interesting and become the focus of the audience's attention. And the actor, because his feeling for the character is not derived exclusively from his physical self, is awarded a high degree of satisfaction through an awareness of his own artistic creation.

Gao Xingjian is concerned about acting, but being first and foremost a writer, he is equally concerned about playwriting. He laments the demise of the playwright in the contemporary theatre. The playwright, according to Gao, has been forced to give up his former prominence to the director, who is now the absolute ruler of the stage. With the weakening position of playwriting, theatre increasingly relies on technology to support its predominantly visual presentation, and music, which is capable of generating tension through contrasts and variations (for example, in a symphony), has also been abused, given the task of covering up the inadequacies in performance. As the peripherals have taken over from real dramatic action, and abstraction, in the form of exegesis of ideas, emerges as the only objective, theater tends to become non-drama or even anti-drama and moves closer and closer towards the end of its road (Gao, 1996e, p. 14).

As a playwright, Gao Xingjian is motivated by the desire to wrestle the centre stage from the hands of the director. He insists on the dramatic, the "drama" [xi 戲] happening on the stage. His plays may not feature a well-made plot, and they may even resort to abstractions from time to time, but there has to be structural integrity — expositions, contrasts, conflicts, and discoveries, the essentials with which drama is made, and which are seen as "action" by the audience. The dramatic is not confined to externalities; most of Gao Xingjian's recent works feature internal conflicts, the psychological drama within a character's consciousness.

SHIFTS IN POINT OF VIEW

Gao Xingjian admits that his idea of the tripartite actor is not universally applicable to all kinds of scripts, and he remains unsure whether this theory of his has been the driving force behind his style of playwriting or vice versa. The idea is part of Gao Xingjian's scheme in search of a new language for the contemporary stage; the drama of the modern man's frenzied schizophrenia demand such acting as complement, or even prerequisite. His understanding of performance, namely, the co-existence of the self, the neutral actor, and the character in the actor, opens up new possibilities in playwriting. Just as consciousness is capable of being realized by the tripartite actor, it can also be interpolated on the discourse level to project different modes of perception.

It is evident that his latest works all feature his newly developed ideas on narrative modes in drama and put into use his demands on the actor. In these plays the characters not only speak in the first person, as is the case according to dramatic convention, they also speak and refer to themselves in the second and third persons, being in and out of their own selves in the same play or even in the same scene. For instance, in *Duihua yu fanjie* 對話與反詰 [Dialogue and rebuttal, 1992], the hero and the heroine speak in the first person in the first half, and then switch to the second and third persons respectively in the second half when they are languishing in apparent meaninglessness as spirits after they die.

Gao Xingjian's experiments in the narrative modes of drama may have been inspired by the special features in the Chinese language. Many times he has commented that the Chinese language, being an uninflected language, facilitates shifting the "angle" or perspective of narration. "As the subject in a Chinese sentence can be omitted and there are no verbal conjugations, it is quite elemental to displace the 'I' as the subject with a zero subject. The subjective consciousness can be transformed, achieving a pan-subjective consciousness or even self-effacement. And it is just as easy to change the 'I' into the second person (you) or the third person (he/she). The 'I' as 'you' is a case of objectification, and the 'I' as 'he/she' is detached observation, or contemplation. This really affords the writer tremendous freedom!" (Gao, 1996f, pp. 174–175)

Commenting on the new possibilities of his dramatic strategy, Gao Xingjian says:

> The character, which usually appears on stage in the first person, can be divided into three different points of view and speak in three different persons, and the same character will then have three psychological dimensions. The character as both agent and receptor is enriched by many perspectives, which enable a more complete mode of expression. And from his various observation platforms, the same character will be able to generate and express many different attitudes towards the outside world and towards his own experience of it.   (Gao, 1996b, pp. 262–263)

The shift in narrative mode is not a mere substitution of "I" by "you," "he" or "she;" it also has implications for the actor and the audience's point of view. With the "I" relating the story of "you," "he" or "she," the character is functionally divided into two separate roles of addresser and addressee, or narrator and narratee, even though they are both physically embodied in one person. The second or third person self functions as the observed, who operates in the external world made up of other characters. As the "I" is insulated from direct contact with the external world, he is equipped with a different perceptive from that of his divided double, and in his capacity as a non-participating narrator, he can be more objective in assessing his own consciousness as someone other than himself.

The discourse situation in Gao Xingjian's plays mostly point to the exploration of the self, the centre around which all the happenings revolve and towards which all the meanings gravitate. In combining the narrating and experiencing selves, the narrative situation is capable of generating tension among the divided selves of the same character, with the "you" being more intimate to the implicit "I," but not less confrontational than the third person self ("he/she"), who is further removed. According to Lacanian psychoanalysis, "otherness" can never be firmly grasped. The other is basically a locus of the subject's fears and dears; they do not belong to an external category, but are internal and unchangeable conditions of man's existence. Viewed in this perspective, the dreams and speeches, when they are expressed on the stage, illuminate the split in the subject's imaginary register and its elements.

The process opens up new venues of communication for the theatre. For instance, the "you" in *Yehoushen* 夜遊神 [Nocturnal wanderer, 1993], in its capacity as the observed self of the "I," is the main character in the play whose fate and emotions are on display. In this manner, the audience get to see the play's actions with an awareness of the non-experiencing "I" and his implicit judgement on the "you." They are thus given a comprehensive picture of the drama, the complexity of the character, his inner conflicts which have been externalized, and his relationship with the world at large. And in *Shengsijie* 生死界 [Between life and death, 1991], the heroine examines her own life in a series of narrated flashbacks. Here the implied "I" plays the role of narrator retelling the story of "she," who is the projected and experiencing self of "I." In this manner, a degree of objectivity is achieved because the narrating "I," detached from immediate experience, can be largely sheltered from self-pity. Thus on the level of expressiveness, shifting the narrative mode propitiates self-examination and makes it easier for the unconscious to reveal itself.

SELF-CONSCIOUSNESS THEATRE

The modern stage has gone a long way since the Stanislavsky method of realistic acting, that is, total identification and immersion in the character being portrayed. Brecht's epic theater introduces the third-person narrator, and highlights stage narratology by adding another dimension to communication in the theatre — the audience, made aware of the existence of a world outside the world of the play, are "alienated" from the performance and performers. For Gao Xingjian, his idea of the theater goes beyond alienation and invoking the audience's rationality. It is inherent in and grows out of his conception of the world of the play, a world focusing on the consciousness of both actor and character, self-contained in its ostentation, yet made expansive to involve the audience emotionally and intellectually. The key word is "self-consciousness." Gao Xingjian's self-conscious art reveals itself not merely in its self-reflexivity or in its relation to the world at large, that is, how the world looks at the self; it can only be understood as self-observation in an alienated and detached manner. The relationship between the first-person self and his "other" hangs in a delicate balance, covering the whole spectrum of subjectivity and objectivity. The resultant potential for dramatic tension and conflict is part and parcel of his idea of the theater, which encompasses both acting and playwriting.

Gao Xingjian insists that his ideas should not be regarded as technique for technique's sake, nor are they merely aimed at rhetorical purposes. His pursuit of a new theatre is intended to reveal the naked realities of the modern man and his living conditions privileging formalism would only bury the truth of these realities and conditions (Gao, 1996b, p. 191). Gao Xingjian is not a fan of the modern theatre (so-called "spoken drama" in Chinese) dominated by words and their meaning generation functions. Far more concerned with the unstated emotions in language and in performance, he aspires for a "modern language," akin to the language games found in *Zhuangzi* and in the *Diamond Sutra* [Jingang jing 金剛經], to express the feeling of detachment and a kind of "free and easy" contemplation as embodied in the Daoist and Buddhist texts (Gao, 1996f, p. 175). In this he finds an ally in the Chinese language, which he tries to rejuvenate and develop into an appropriate medium of expression for the stage:

... I am not at all a cultural chauvinist, and I don't have in me the

incomprehensible arrogance typical of the Chinese race. The only thing I
want to do is to rejuvenate this ancient language, so that it can be equally
conversant to express the bewilderment of the modern man, his pursuits,
his frustrations in not being able to attain them, and in the final analysis,
the sufferings and happiness of living, the loneliness and the dire need
for expression.   (Gao, 1995, pp. 68–69)

Gao Xingjian's language is largely lyrical and at times even gossipy,
yet it can be extremely powerful and moving in its indifference and apparent irrelevance, containing words of "unspoken wisdom." As with many
Zen Buddhist texts, his words "speak directly to the heart," striking at
the innermost core of the human soul. When they are most effective,
they are graced with an almost magical power derived from a spellbind-
ing rhythm akin to chanting, evincing a materiality beyond mere utterance and referentiality. The idea is to allow the mind of the audience to
"wander in contemplation" among the words to grasp their true spirit,
which resides as a sublimated effect outside the language being used
(Gao, 1996f, p. 175).

He does not resort to yelling and screaming in his writings. He is not
a revolutionary, and he refuses to fight other people's war except one
that resides in his heart. In concentrating on the self, Gao Xingjian's
writings can be regarded as subjective and individualistic. However, his
is a different kind of individualism that values the self but not at the
expense of others. As he says of his novel *Lingshan* 靈山 [Soul mountain]:

My perception of the self has nothing to do with self-worship. I detest
those people whose desire is to displace God with himself, the kind of
heroism which aspires to defeat the world, and the kind of self-purgation
which puts on the guise of a tragic hero. I am myself, nothing less, nothing more.   (Gao, 1996f, p. 174)

In this way he rejects Nietzsche and the individualism of the West,
which he considers destructive. His attitude is not unlike that of the traditional Daoist or Zen Buddhist who is bent on seclusion or exile from
society to cultivating his inner virtues and strength, and in his somewhat
aloof and detached position, he still casts an indifferent eye to observe
the world of humans. However, while Daoism and Buddhism aspire for
understanding the *Dao*, Gao Xingjian insists on knowing and studying
the self and its inner secrets in all its complexities; while the former

represents inner peace, Gao Xingjian finds only pain and suffering, and unfortunately, there appears to be no salvation. The individual is helpless in the face of this predicament, for he is impotent to change himself or his world. He can assert his existence only by way of thinking and the production of discourse, as he once proclaimed: "I discourse, therefore I am" (Gao, 1996c, p. 128); ironically they tend to become as ineffectual and meaningless as the world he finds himself in — therein reside the frustration and insoluble dilemma of the modern man.

REFERENCES

Gao Xingjian 高行健 (1995a). *Gao Xingjian xiju liuzhong* 高行健戲劇六種 [Six volumes of plays by Gao Xingjian]. Taipei: Dijiao chubanshe 帝教出版社.

—— (1995b). "Guanyu *Bi'an*" 關於《彼岸》 [On *The Other Shore*]. In Gao (1995a), Vol. 1, pp. 68–69.

—— (1996a). "Juzuofa yu zhongxing yanyuan" 劇作法與中性演員 [Playwriting and the neutral actor]. In Gao (1996d), pp. 253–266.

—— (1996b). "Lingyizhong xiju" 另一種戲劇 [Another type of drama]. In Gao (1996d), pp. 186–192.

—— (1996c). "Liuwang shi women huode shenmo?" 流亡使我們獲得什麼 [What have we got in exile]. In Gao (1996d), pp. 116–155.

—— (1996d). *Meiyou zhuyi* 沒有主義 [Without isms]. Hong Kong: Tiandi tushu youxian gongsi 天地圖書有限公司.

—— (1996e). "Meiyou zhuyi" 沒有主義 [Without isms]. In Gao (1996d), pp. 8–17.

—— (1996f). "Wenxue yu lingxue: Guanyu *Lingshan*" 文學與靈學・關於《靈山》 [Literature and metaphysics: On *Soul Mountain*]. In Gao (1996d), pp. 167–82.

—— (1996g). "Wo zhuzhang yizhong leng de wenxue" 我主張一種冷的文學 [I advocate a cold literature]. In Gao (1996d), pp. 18–20.

—— (1996h). "Wode xiju he wode yaoshi" 我的戲劇和我的鑰匙 [My drama and my key]. In Gao (1996d), pp. 235–252.

—— (1996i). "Yao shenmeyang de xiju" 要甚麼樣的戲劇 [What sort of drama do we need]. In Gao (1996d), pp. 230–234.

Space and Suppositionality in Gao Xingjian's Theatre

Gao Xingjian is one of the Chinese dramatists who launched a strong challenge to the realist drama in China during the 1980s. It was a time when the repression of intellectual life in mainland China was mitigated, and literary and artistic creation began to resume some vitality. As a professional playwright of Beijing People's Art Theatre, Gao, with Lin Zhaohua as director, produced three controversial plays, namely, *Juedui xinhao* 絕對信號 [Alarm signal, 1982], *Chezhan* 車站 [The bus-stop, 1983] and *Yeren* 野人 [Wild man, 1985]. After he left China in 1987 and later settled in Paris, Gao continues to write plays in an environment that provides him with more freedom.

In this essay, I intend to discuss Gao's experimentation, not only as a playwright, but also as one who has great knowledge of and ample experience in theatre practice. Although he has been perceived as a Chinese successor to the European tradition of the Theatre of the Absurd, Gao's theatre has its influence from both Western modern dramatists and Chinese traditional aesthetics. A detailed analysis of Gao's works, from his early texts to later plays, such as *Bi'an* 彼岸 [The other shore, 1986] and *Mingcheng* 冥城 [The nether city, 1991], will help us understand how Gao plays with and expands the concept of theatre as a representation of both the real and the unreal. With his idea of suppositionality, a form that becomes the subject content, Gao has constructed a new theatre, which is liberated from the restrictions of conventions and narrow political ideologies.

LIBERATING THEATRE BY LIBERATING THE SPACE

Gao discards the idea of drama as exclusively an art of words and thus negates the conventional notion of spoken drama. Then, he demolishes the fourth wall erected by the Chinese disciples of the Russian/Soviet dramatist Konstantin Stanislavsky (1863–1940). When this is done, he has experimented with a theatre that is neither restricted by words nor bound by walls. Gao Xingjian is thus left with nothing more than an *empty space.* This space is, however, not a theatre of emptiness but one stripped of conventions and ready to be imbued with new vitality. After obliterating the old, Gao gives himself the mission of establishing the new.

The theatre as an empty space, envisioned by Peter Brook (b. 1925), provides "the imaginative neutrality which allows the actor to move freely through the entire physical world and into subjective experience, not only presenting 'man simultaneously in all his aspects,' but also involving the audience collectively in a 'total experience'" (Innes, 1993, p. 126). Gao may not have been influenced heavily by Brook. At least he does not mention any such influence as he does of dramatists, such as Bertolt Brecht (1898–1956), Samuel Beckett (1906–1989) and Antonin Artaud (1896–1948). However, Brook, as well as Gao, uses Artaud's idea of representing intense physicality with powerful universal and primordial forces as a dominant component in his theatre. Interestingly, if not surprisingly, the vitality of theatrical space delineated by Brook is strikingly similar to that of Gao. Gao advocates "a return to the bare stage with sets and props reduced to a minimum," and "a return to acting itself as the tension asserted by acting is the essence of drama." An actor's powerful performance, Gao contends, "is to mobilize the audience's unlimited imagination and transform the limited and restrained stage into a free space" (Gao, 1996, p. 188).

It is apparent that in a theatrical space that has been set free, for both Gao and Brook, the main occupant of this space will be *the actor.* It is the actor who will inject life into the theatre by manoeuvring theatrical space and activating the audience's participation, both emotionally and intellectually. In fact, the revival of the active role of the actor has been the primary task of many great directors of the twentieth century. Each does so in a different way. Brecht perceives objectivity on the part of his actor-narrator as the way to provoke the audience's intellectual involvement. The intensity of Artaudian theatre is presented through physical language and movement of the actors. Jerzy Grotowski (1933–1999) eliminates all music, scenery, lighting and make-up, considering them external, and keeps only the fundamental spectator-actor relationship within the theatre.

Gao's knowledge of such traditions and the history of modern Western theatre, has helped him achieve a high level of awareness of the possibilities of theatrical space and actors. These Western playwrights are all significant in their capacity as directors; Gao is one of the very few contemporary Chinese playwrights who can direct as well as write. For the productions of his three plays by Beijing People's Art Theatre, he was a *de facto* co-director with Lin Zhaohua and also conducted actor training workshops prior to the actual rehearsals.[1] After he left China, he has been invited on several occasions to direct his own plays in Asian and European countries. The awareness of the theatre as a three-dimensional space with actors generating live dynamism is something he is able to bring into fruition in his capacity as director and trainer of actors.

I shall examine Gao's works, with an emphasis on his post-exile plays, from the perspective of his awareness of theatrical space and actor-spectator interactivity within such a space. In an article delineating the nature of his new theatre, Gao sums up the first stage of his experimentation with an extensive definition of his ideal drama, what he calls "drama of the future" [weilai de xiju 未來的戲劇], as follows:

> Drama of the future is a kind of total drama. It is a kind of living drama which features enhanced interactions among actors, between actors and characters, among characters, and between actors and audience. It is different from the drama which is bottled and canned in the rehearsal room. It encourages spontaneous acting which fills the theatre with vibrancy. It is like playing communal games. It fully develops every potential of the art. It will not be impoverished. It will collaborate with the artists of spoken language and avoid degenerating into mime or musical. It is symphonic and multi-visual. It will push the expressivity of language to its fullest capacity. It is an art which will not be substituted by another form of art. (Gao, 1988, p. 86)

We can extrapolate three characteristics of his "drama of the future" from this description. First, we have Gao's notion of total theatre which, since its inception in *Wild Man*, developed into a unique and vibrant form of modern Chinese theatre which has inherited a sense of carnivalesqueness and the ritualistic expressivity from traditional Chinese theatre. The subjects and motifs of Gao's total theatre usually derived from Chinese mythology and folk stories, especially those related to Daoist traditions. Second, this passage shows that the basis of Gao's theatre is the "suppositionality" of theatre [juchang jiadingxing 劇場假定性]. The idea of theatre as a suppositional space was discussed extensively in the debate stimulated by the notion of *xieyi* 寫意 drama, which the veteran Shanghai director Huang Zuolin 黃佐臨 (1906–1994) suggested in the 1980s.[2] Suppositionality also has its origins both in Chinese dramatic aesthetics and in the idea of stylized theatre advocated as an opposition to Stanislavsky's realist theatre by another Russian/Soviet dramatist Vsevolod Meyerhold (1874–1940) at the beginning of the twentieth century. Third, Gao makes clear in this passage that the theatre's suppositional nature revolutionizes the former actor-spectator relationship. With the rejection of theatrical illusions, the actors are required to adopt a different approach to the representation of characters. In this process, they assume a new type of free capacity to establish direct interaction with the audience and hence transform passive receivers into active players within theatrical space.

Gao's indebtedness to Chinese traditional theatre and culture is apparent. The following discussion will show that traditional dramatic aesthetics and the traditional conceptions of *xiqu* 戲曲 have been a great inspiration to Gao's theatre of the modern.[3] Interestingly, these characteristics of Gao's new theatre have also been mentioned by Meyerhold, one of the first dramatists who started searching for alternatives to Stanislavsky's method of representation. Suppositionality, the central idea of Gao's ideal theatre is, according to him, the basic characteristic of traditional Chinese theatre. However, it is also unmistakably the fundamental feature of Meyerhold's theatre, which he calls "stylization." In their challenge to naturalism and realism, Meyerhold and Gao arrive at their own quite different ideal theatres which have similar features, albeit inspired by different sources. In my discussion of Gao's theatre, it is necessary to refer to Meyerhold, a predecessor of many influential Western dramatists of the twentieth century, and one who has acted for Gao as a bridge from Stanislavsky to Brecht and Artaud in his early encounter with theatre in the early 1960s and later experimentation in the 1980s.

TOTAL ACTORS FOR TOTAL THEATRE

Gao Xingjian's notion of total theatre consists of two essential aspects.

First, it is an ideal form of theatre, which creatively appropriates elements from both modern Western and traditional Chinese theatres. Total theatre is an ideal that Gao has pursued throughout his career since the early and mid-1980s. *Wild Man* is the culmination of his idealism, which he calls the "modern Eastern theatre." His endeavour to realize the total theatre resumes in his later, post-exile works, such as *The Nether City* and *Shanhaijing zhuan* 山海經傳 [Story of the *Classic of mountains and seas*, 1993], in which he returns to the form and subject matter of Chinese folk and traditional arts.[4] Second, total theatre is a platform for the exploration and exploitation of the actors' potentiality. The theatre will, in his view, only be able to achieve totality, that is, to express and present all possible forms of performance, if the actors are well rounded in their presentation ability. After the production of *Wild Man*, Gao started with his second stage of experimentation in which he returned to what he perceived as the basis of performance, the actors, and began to place more emphasis on their training.

The Other Shore is Gao's first attempt at pursuing his second stage of experimentation. The play was written after Gao returned from his visits to Berlin and Paris, with the specific objective of training student-actors for the Beijing People's Art Theatre. Gao and his long-term working partner, Lin Zhaohua, planned to set up an Experimental Theatre Workshop where actors would receive a training different from the conventional Stanislavskian method practised in the Theatre and generally throughout China (Gao, 1996, p. 166).[5]

One of Gao's primary concerns during this period was to release drama from the restrictive notion of the art of words. He also envisaged "resuming all functions of drama," and, for that purpose, adopting a new concept of acting for the effective presentation of his modern drama. Gao has often made an analogy between his concept and the actors of traditional *xiqu* who are able to perform reciting, singing, acting and acrobatic skills. In the postscript of *The Other Shore*, Gao proclaims that the ultimate actor, which he wants his training to achieve, is one who is capable of assuming a role in the drama of "Shakespeare, Ibsen, Chekov, Aristophanes, Racine, Lao She, Cao Yu, Guo Moruo, Goethe, Brecht, Pirandello, Beckett, and even mime and musical" (Gao, 1995a, p. 64). Gao's ideal actor therefore possesses, besides well-rounded performing skills, greatest versatility that will enable him to creatively construct a unique theatrical experience. He should be able to perform all kinds of drama, Chinese or Western, classical or modern, realist or absurdist, as well as those that are not classifiable according to any conventional categorization. This training is intended to awaken the actor's capabilities so that he will not be confined to a single school of performing techniques. How can such an actor be fostered? How is Gao's training different from conventional methods? *The Other Shore*, the only play written by Gao specifically for such purposes, provides some answers.

The initial setting of *The Other Shore* is ambiguous. It is stated at the beginning of the play that the time is "undefinable," while the place is "from the real world to the hypothetical other shore" (Gao, 1995a, p. 3).[6] Without any specific delineation of time and place, Gao presents the theatre as an empty space; he requires the actors to establish the temporal and spatial specificities in their performance. The performers also appear on stage in their capacity as actors rather than as characters. They are supposed to display to the audience the process by which actors are transformed into characters. Far from imposing an illusory scene on the audience, Gao deliberately and overtly presents to them an experience of the theatre as it is being created. The play begins with an actor, playing with a rope, and leading a group of actors in a procession resembling a pre-performance warming-up exercise. The lead actor sets the contextual situation with his words and the ensemble follows his instructions by responding physically to what the former says. The lead actor begins:

> I have a rope with me. We are going to play a game. Take it seriously, just like children do.
>
> Right, you, please hold the other end of the rope. Now, there is a connection between us. Before this, I am I, and you are you. With the rope, we are connected, and it becomes you and me.
>
> [...]
>
> If we pull the rope hard, the situation will depend on who is stronger. The stronger will pull and the weaker will be pulled. Like a game of tug-or-war, it is a competition based on strength. Therefore, there will be a winner and a loser, victory and defeat.
>
> If I haul the rope, you will become a dead dog being dragged. On the other hand, if you have control over it, I will be driven by you like a horse or an ox. Therefore, our relationship is never stagnant.
>
> (Gao, 1995a, pp. 5–6)

With the lead actor's narration as a general guide, the ensemble is required to actualize the concept of relationship and present it in terms of physical action. It is a process of improvisation which Viola Spolin defines as "setting out to solve a problem with no preconception as to how you will do it" and "permitting everything in the environment (animate or inanimate) to work for you in solving the problem" (Spolin, 1973, p. 383). In such a process, the participants have to stretch their imagination, as well as be highly aware of their physical environment, in order to present those concepts set out by the leader in a creative manner with their physical actions and movements. Physicalization, as it is "a visible means of making a subjective communication" (Spolin, 1973, p. 387), will ultimately lead to the integration of the actors' subjectivity into the theatrical space.

As the actors are warmed up and the audience becomes used to such imaginative representation, the ensemble starts to display concepts which are more abstract such as conflict, intimacy, rejection, entanglement, abandonment, shadowing, avoiding, banishing, courting, revolving, flocking and breaking (Gao, 1995a, pp. 8–9). The gestures and movements of the actors become more sophisticated and portray a stronger suggestiveness. The physical display of these concepts demands a greater intricacy of interaction between the actors — two or more. At this juncture, one of the actors declares, "Now, what is in front of us is not a rope but a river. We have to cross over to the other shore" (Gao, 1995a, p. 9). A real object, in this instance, is transformed into a symbolic one. The interaction with fellow actors is thus extended to incorporate the physical, albeit imaginary, space. As the audience's imagination has been stimulated, and its members are guided into the space suppositionally constructed by the actors' performance, the philosophical motifs begin to be revealed.

In the process of crossing the imaginary river, the ensemble depicts various situations identified as "fishes are swimming through my thighs," "there is a whirlpool," "we are floating on the water, like a string of corks, like waterweeds," and "no isle, no light, in total darkness" (Gao, 1995a, pp. 10–12). At the same time, they are again supposed to display these situations using physical actions. By this time, the situation has transformed the smaller independent groups into an integrated ensemble in which each actor has to be aware of the interplay between himself and all the other actors. Gao describes how different elements of performance work together to achieve a unity,

> The ideal performance is a unity of physical actions, spoken words and
> psychology. The play attempts to search for a mode of artistic presenta-
> tion that will help the actors to achieve such unity. In other words, while
> searching for physical actions, actors are required to deliver spoken words;
> with both spoken words and physical actions, the psychological process
> will be realized.   (Gao, 1995a, pp. 64–65)

The three elements that make up the unity are not new discoveries.
As they are essentially the basic components cited in different schools of
acting, the crux of the idea is how these three are integrated and work
together to form a workable formula for different dramatists. It is therefore necessary to contextualize Gao's idea of performance unity in order to provide a clearer perspective on the nature of his approach as
compared to his predecessors.

In acting, physical actions and spoken words constitute the external
components of performance readily perceivable by the audience. The
psychological processes are, on the other hand, experienced internally
by the actor and are only perceivable through actions and words.
Stanislavsky suggests that psychological preparation of the actor is the
key to the success of his performance. To him, the fundamentals are
"the work of grasping the true nature of each emotion through one's
own power of observation, of developing one's attention for such a task,
and of consciously mastering the art of entering the creative circle"
(Stanislavsky, 1967, p. 92). The basic approach for an actor of
Stanislavsky's System is therefore to begin with internal creation although
some say that in the early stage of his career as an actor, Stanislavsky
worked successfully in the reverse way, that is, "from the body to the
mind by copying models for his characters" (Mitter, 1992, p. 23).

Whereas the Stanislavskian method focuses on the actor and his creation of a role by either immersing himself in the psychological aspects of
a character or imitating its external features, Gao suggests that the starting point of acting should be an understanding of theatrical space
through actions and words. The setting in the theatre is therefore not
constructed according to what is already physically present on stage but
consciously established by the actors' suppositional and suggestive
delineation. In this process, the actors are in control of their actions and
words, as well as the definition of that theatrical space. In the case of *The
Other Shore*, the place where the audience gathers does not automatically

present itself as a theatre until the actors gradually lay out the details which define it as a theatrical space, but not any other locale. When the actor declares that the rope is a river, he has elevated the physical and visible space into an imaginary and invisible one. When the ensemble has crossed over the river and reached the other shore, they have accomplished the transformation of a rehearsal venue into a *symbolic dimension*, which now becomes the specific attribute of that theatre.

In opposition to the Stanislavskian method of acting, Meyerhold proposes the employment of "plastic movement." Plasticity, according to Meyerhold, is the actor's physicalized presentation of movements and poses "which enable the spectator not only to hear the spoken dialogue but to penetrate through to the *inner* dialogue." Together with the presentation of speech, plastic movement supersedes naturalistic scenery as the sole focus of attention in the theatre. In order to capture this attention, Meyerhold proposes an iconic style of scenery and even suggests that scenery be "abolished altogether" (Meyerhold, 1998, pp. 56–57). However, Meyerhold's actor is not supposed to be confined within the enclosed imaginary circle of public solitude required by Stanislavsky. On the contrary, he has to acquire flexibility in his presentation,

> [W]e might see the dramatic theatre transformed into a kind of revue in which the actor appears now as a dramatic artist, now as an opera singer, now as a dancer, now as an equilibrist, now as a gymnast, now as a clown. Thus, by employing elements of the other arts the theatre can make the performance more diverting and deepen the spectator's comprehension of it.   (Meyerhold, 1998, p. 254)

It is apparent that Meyerhold, as a director, places his emphasis on the training of actors with respect to the exploration of theatrical space. The two essential characteristics of his actors are, first, that they are highly aware of the way they portray their actions and words as well as the different combinations such portrayal can attain, and, second, that they are equipped with various skills of presentation. This flexibility enables them to extend their relationship with the theatrical space.

Gao's notion of ideal acting has, apparently, developed in this direction. *The Other Shore* has effectively presented a situation in which it is clearly discernible how the training of actors takes its course. Everything starts from scratch. Both the ensemble and audience are guided through the process of the formation of a theatrical experience. The actor who plays with the rope, in this instance, is both a facilitator of improvisation training as well as a narrator who explains to the audience. With the rope as a medium, actors explore relationships and abstract concepts.

The act of exploration with actions and words helps to define the suppositional setting of the play with the establishment of what Gao calls the "psychological field" [xinli chang 心理場]. Gao defines his idea of psychological field with respect to theatrical space as follows:

> The flexibility of the theatrical space is in fact immense. If the actors are able to create a psychological field with their performance, the presentation of the director and designers can only be more variegated and versatile. For example, by imagining the relation of two characters or that of characters and audience placed within an eggshell, or dispersing the characters' internal experience among the entire theatre, there will be a lot of new possibilities....
>
> The theatrical space is physically fixed while the psychological field created by performance is strong. The establishment of dramatic space relies primarily on the latter. In this way, a dead space becomes alive.
>
> (Gao, 1996, p. 246)

In a way similar to a gravitational field or magnetic field, the psychological field is defined by the force exerted within a region, with the actors as the initiators of this energy. The actors are not only required to portray the characters they are playing, but are also supposed to be aware of and to maximize the potentiality of theatrical space. Obviously, the theatre will be lifeless without the actors' awareness of the psychological field. More significantly, as the construction of such theatrical space determines the theatrical experience to which Gao aspires, it is important to train actors who are capable of accomplishing such a task.

Another important quality necessary for the actors in their exploration of theatrical space is spontaneity. While he advocates learning from *xiqu* actors, Gao repeatedly cautions against the formalized acting found in *xiqu*. Formalization is the primary cause of the lack/loss of spontaneity in *xiqu* because every detail of acting is fixed and rigidified as it becomes formalized. In a performance, Gao suggests analogically, "the actor should be in the same state as an athlete, ready to enter the arena, or a cock in a fighting ring, ready to take up a challenge and respond to his opponent at all times" (Gao, 1995a, p. 67). Spontaneity is thus the ability to react to and interact with unexpected circumstances.

In Gao's view, the theatre is a space filled with spontaneity. The space is therefore not cut off from reality but one that resembles reality. By contrast, while conventional realist theatre manifests itself as a representation of the verisimilitude of real life, it paradoxically excludes spontaneity, an essential aspect of reality. Gao realized quite early — during the rehearsals of his first staged play, *Alarm Signal* — the need to release the actors from Stanislavskian acting. Lin Liankun 林連崑, a veteran actor who played the Senior Train Guard in *Alarm Signal*, came to the rehearsal with a pre-conceived character in his mind. Gao had to convince him to give up everything he had prepared and to start again with the other actors (Gao, 1998). Stanislavsky's "circle of attention" seems to squelch spontaneity as much as formalized *xiqu* acting.

As the most vital factor in the process of improvisation, spontaneity works together with intuitiveness. The latter, according to Spolin, is the ability to respond at unexpected moments. The person reacting with this intuition is able to "transcend the limitation of the familiar, courageously enter the area of the unknown, and release momentary genius within himself" (Spolin, 1973, pp. 3–4). The actor's intuitiveness thus enables him to exercise spontaneity not only as a passive means to deal with unforeseen circumstances but, on an active level, to enhance interaction with other actors and the audience. A group of actors carrying out improvisation experience, a process of what Brook calls "ensemble creation," in which unexpected situations lead to the emergence of something new. This process does not stop as the rehearsals come to an end before the actual performance, but continues to go on during the performance. Opposing the view implicit in Stanislavsky's book title, *Building a Character*, Brook argues that "a character isn't a static thing and it can't be built like a wall" (Brook, 1990, p. 128). The actor must continue to be spontaneous in the theatrical space where he has to react to and interact with those present in the same space, including the audience, the members of which are totally new in every performance.

There are two stages in which spontaneity is brought into play, first during rehearsals and later during performance. The way spontaneity works in these stages is quite different. In the rehearsal room, Gao suggests, "the actors are guided to attain their fullest potential in creat-

ing the roles together with their acting partners" (Gao, 1995a, pp. 66).
In other words, an actor's understanding of the character he is playing
does not arise solely from his own interpretation and creation; instead,
he has to make use of his senses to capture how his partners perceive the
character and react to it, then he has to react to them. In the course of
this interaction, the alertness of the actors and power of self-observation
will be challenged. What is presented is thus not individualized performance but integrated acting by the ensemble as a whole. The scenes of
actors representing abstract concepts and performing the crossing of
river in *The Other Shore* in particular demonstrate such an "ensemble
creation." Gao's theatre is therefore an interactive theatre. The
interactiveness begins at the first rehearsal.

Within the theatrical space, interaction extends to the relationship
between actors and the audience. With the demolition of the fourth wall,
the two spheres, on stage and off stage, that were previously separated,
have merged into one. In his plays, Gao continually and deliberately
attempts to maximize the potential of such interactivity. The direct revelation of internal emotions in *Alarm Signal* is only an initial attempt.
The multi-vocality in *The Bus-Stop* and *Wild Man* creates a multi-focal and
multi-directional situation where interaction with the audience illumi-
nates the structural sophistication of the plays. Gao's extensive employment of a narrator, whose first appearance is as the actor who plays the
Ecologist in *Wild Man*, is another evidence of his effort to promote such
interactivity. While Gao's narrator may have been influenced by Brecht,
it is clearly more akin to his own Chinese traditions.

Whereas Brecht's narrator is a means to achieve the effect of alienation,
Gao's narrator aspires to get the audience emotionally involved in a theatrical activity resembling a carnival. In *Story of the Classic of Mountains
and Seas*, the narrator does not double as a character, as is normal for
Gao's plays, but appears in his original capacity as a *shuochang yiren* 説唱
藝人 [a performer of storytelling and ballad singing]. A *shuochang yiren* is
different from the more commonly known *shuoshu ren* 説書人 [storyteller]
as he is not only able to recite stories from history and *yanyi* 演義 [historical
romances], and to portray the characters dramatically in those stories,
but also able to produce a more sophisticated art form that combines
singing and often playing a musical instrument with telling a story. More
significantly, he is highly responsive to the reception of his play by the
audience and his performance changes spontaneously in accord with

the situation. In the *shuochang yiren*, Gao has found a way to make interactivity work for his theatre.

In summary, Gao's total theatre requires actors who are equipped with an extensive spectrum of performing skills and, at the same time, have retained a high measure of intuitive spontaneity. Through their speeches and physical actions, the theatrical space is established and this occurs primarily through interactivity that takes place among the actors and with the audience. The physical space is less significant in such theatre as the theatrical space is defined by the actors' performance, rather than by its fixed physical dimensions. Emancipated from the restrictions of conventional perceptions of space and time, the actors have much greater freedom than in the conventional theatre to create a theatrical experience by activating the audience's imagination. It is through suppositional and suggestive delineation that the audience is able to perceive and understand what is represented in the theatre. Gao envisions a theatre founded on suppositionality and unbound imagination.

THE ART OF SUPPOSITIONALITY

Opposing the representation of reality, Gao Xingjian attempts to present his theatre as an aesthetic experience that establishes itself within the theatrical space. The most important characteristic of this theatre is its *suppositionality*. The idea of suppositionality suggests that every element in the theatre is artistically represented, subjectively imagined, and thus fundamentally unreal. Gao does not want his audience to perceive what is performed in the theatre as a reflection of the real but to participate in the creation of the theatrical experience. In proposing a theatre of suppositionality, Gao has in fact reiterated some significant ideas of the Soviet director Vsevolod Meyerhold and, more importantly, that of the traditional *xiqü*. However, he consciously avoids advocating the utilitarian employment of suppositionality to represent reality or to profess ideology. Instead, he wants to develop it into an autonomous mode of artistic representation.

Before discussing the notion of *jiadingxing* 假定性 [suppositionality], it is necessary to revisit two of Gao's key concepts, namely, *xijuxing* 戲劇性 [dramaticality] and *juchangxing* 劇場性 [theatricality], which he mapped out in his first articles on drama, published as a series in 1983. Fundamentally, Gao suggests, drama is an *art of actions*. Different types of drama, such as realist, naturalist, Brechtian and *xiqu*, are established through the dramatists' individual interpretation and practice of their arts. Each of them has a different emphasis on certain aspects of action, which he perceives as of primary importance. Actions, Gao further contends, can be expressed in the form of spoken language, physicality, narration of events, psychological activities and progression of discovery. More importantly, there are endless possibilities of form, as new means of presenting actions will always be created. It is essentially in the process of performing these actions that dramaticality is being defined within the theatre (Gao, 1988, pp. 15–21).

What makes drama a unique form of art, in Gao's view, is the direct interaction between performers and the audience. His idea of theatricality is illustrated with respect to this particular characteristic. First, in order to facilitate communication with the audience, dramatists experiment with different arrangements of the physical space of the theatre. Spectators are placed at two or three sides of the performance area, surrounding it or even within it. Although this physical space can, to a certain extent, be manipulated, its dimensions are invariably fixed. Second, more significantly, it is a psychological space (which Gao, in his later articles, defines with respect to what he calls the "psychological field") created from the interaction among the performers and the audience, which provides the energy and life within the theatre. Presenting illusions of reality restricts the establishment of such space. However, energy is created when imagination is evoked through the performance of actions. The notion of theatricality hence depends on the way this peculiar space is manoeuvred (Gao, 1988, pp. 8–14).

It is clear that two fundamental and related components in Gao's theatre are actions and imagination. He starts from the proposition that a theatrical performance should not attempt to achieve verisimilitudes but should take what is delineated within its boundaries as suppositional. But as I will go on to show, more significantly, Gao deviates from the conventional notion of representing reality with theatrical suppositionality, and treats suppositionality as *the subject* of his theatre.

The notion of suppositionality was widely discussed in China in the 1980s after Huang Zuolin's idea of *xieyi* drama, first advocated in 1962, was resurfaced in 1982. Although Huang did not mention the term *jiadingxing* in his article, it is apparent that *xieyi* drama is accomplished through non-realistic representation rather than the mimicry of reality.

One Chinese critic summarizes this situation by saying that Huang's *xieyi* drama "fully demonstrates the fascination of dramatic suppositionality and extensively develops the formal representation of the theatre's spatial and temporal dimensions" (Zhou, 1990, p. 9). While the idea of suppositionality in modern Chinese theatre may have emerged with Huang's advocacy of *xieyi* drama, it becomes a principal issue in the larger search for new modes of representation during the 1980s. In their exploration, Chinese dramatists and critics trace the idea of suppositionality to both Western and Chinese sources. Looking to the West, they realize that, besides Brecht, a similar idea had been advocated by an earlier dramatist, Meyerhold. Within the Chinese traditions, of course, the notion of suppositionality serves as the foundation of the art of *xiqu.*

The first systematic introduction of Meyerhold into China took place in 1981. In an article entitled "The Contributions of Meyerhold," Tong Daoming expounds the life of the Soviet dramatist and his innovations as a director. One of Meyerhold's important concepts is something he calls *jiadingxing* and suggests that the concept is inspired by Chinese theatre (Tong, 1981, p. 83). Although Meyerhold mentioned Chinese theatre as a source of reference for the training of his actors much earlier than the occasion when he watched Mei Lanfang's performance in 1935,[7] he explicitly states that the primary inspiration for his concept of theatre is from his European predecessors, the Belgian playwright Maurice Maeterlinck (1862–1949) and the Russian poet-director Valery Bryusov (1873–1924). He discusses their ideas extensively on several occasions (Meyerhold, 1998, pp. 33, 35–36, 37–39, 49).

The term for Meyerhold's concept, which the Chinese understand as *jiadingxing,* is translated into English by Edward Braun as "stylization." Meyerhold explains his usage of the term,

> With the word "stylization" I do not imply the exact reproduction of the style of a certain period or of a certain phenomenon, such as a photographer might achieve. In my opinion the concept of "stylization" is indivisibly tied up with the idea of convention, generalization and symbol. To "stylize" a given period or phenomenon means to employ every possible means of expression in order to reveal the inner synthesis of that period or phenomenon, to bring out those hidden features which are to be found deeply embedded in the style of any work of art.
>
> (Meyerhold, 1998, p. 43)

As Meyerhold emphatically declares, "Stylization is opposed to the techniques of illusion" (Meyerhold, 1998, p. 63). He perceives his attempt to establish a stylized theatre as a "campaign against naturalism" (Meyerhold, 1998, p. 34). By breaking away from the restrictions of stage properties and technical devices, he envisions creating a "three-dimensional area," in which "the creative powers of the actor" are prominently restored. He also stresses that the spectator is a "fourth *creator*, in addition to the author, the director and the actor," who "is compelled to employ his imagination *creatively* in order to *fill in* those details *suggested* by the stage action." Quoting from a letter from the Russian dramatist Leonid Andreev, he says, "the spectator should not forget for a moment that an actor is *performing* before him, and the actor should never forget that he is performing before an audience," and stresses "the more obvious the artifice, the more powerful the impression of life" (italics original) (Meyerhold, 1998, pp. 62–63).

Meyerhold's notion of stylization, advocated in the first decade of this century, in many respects reminds one of the *jiadingxing* vehemently embraced by many Chinese dramatists of the 1980s. They are similar in several aspects. First, their targets are similar. Second, they both encourage the involvement of the audience in a combined effort to create the theatrical experience. Third and most importantly, they envision a theatre which blatantly reveals the fact that it is not a mechanical reflection of reality, but aspires to invoke the audience's imagination with its formal representation.

I prefer not to adopt Meyerhold's term "stylization" in my discussion of the Chinese concept of *jiadingxing*. Instead, I have used the term "suppositionality" for the present discussion. This is because, first, any aesthetic notion, be it *jiadingxing* or stylization, without exception, has its own etymological and epistemological significance. Although, for the convenience of discussion, one term could be used for another similar concept, the meaning of the latter will not be fully illustrated in that term and will suggest unnecessary relations with it. Second, in addition to its resemblance to the Western concept, the Chinese notion of *jiadingxing* has its deeper roots in indigenous cultural and aesthetic traditions.

Discussions of the traditional concept of suppositionality can be carried out on two aspects, the practical and the theoretical. It is to be noted, however, that the term *jiadingxing* does not occur in the discussions of *xiqu* performance or in traditional dramatic aesthetics. It is a contemporary term adopted to explain a traditional Chinese concept. The traditional *xiqu* stage does not attempt to hide the fact that it is a venue for acting. A classic illustration is the common stage setting consisting simply of a table and two chairs. Different arrangements of these simple stage properties signify different localities, from the room of an ordinary family to a palace hall. They can also symbolize something other than furniture, such as a bridge or a hill. The actors are dressed in lavishly decorated costume, speak stylized language, singing rather than talking, and express their emotions with formalized actions and movements. None of these resembles real life. It is therefore a theatre founded on an elaborated system of conventions with which all members of the audience are well acquainted. The art of *xiqu*, as the famous *jingju* 京劇 actor of the Republican era Gai Jiaotian 蓋叫天 (1888–1970) proclaims, "has to be unreal, it won't be real if it isn't unreal, it won't be beautiful if it isn't unreal" (Hu, 1988, p. 75). In other words, *xiqu* is a performance of symbolic artifice. On the *xiqu* stage, it is always explicitly indicated that all that is represented is unreal. Contemporary dramatists have taken this acceptance of the unreal from *xiqu* and have further developed the notion of suppositionality, realizing that it provides a great deal of freedom for expression in theatrical art.

Within the discourse of traditional dramatic aesthetics, the dichotomy of the real and the unreal, albeit expressed in different ways, is often adopted to evaluate the merits of dramatic works and performance. The late Ming drama critic Wang Jide 王驥德 (1557?–1923) points out, "The way of drama [is that] the best [work] is founded on the real [shi 實] and expressed through the unreal [xu 虛]." In the view of the contemporary writer Yao Wenfang, that which is depicted should be based on real life while the vehicle of its depiction should express what is in the artist's imagination. Hence what is portrayed should both contrast with and be distant from reality (Yao, 1997, p. 47). Li Yu 李漁 (1611–1680), a prominent aesthetician and playwright of the early Qing, asserts, "The behaviour in life is completely natural [ziran 自然]; the behaviour on stage should be intentional [mianqiang 勉強, literally, to do with an effort]. Although intentional, it appears natural." Performance on stage, as Li suggests, should not be an imitation of reality, which is natural, but should represent it with artificial means (Yao, 1997, pp. 99–100). Both premodern dramatists can be said to have espoused theories that are

closely akin to suppositionality and to have thought that portrayal of this
kind is a higher realm of art. This is because it has transcended reality
and hence attained a greater sense of freedom and subjectivity.

Portrayal of reality in theatre does not mean solely representing its
physical appearance but also expressing its spirit, that is, its *shen* 神, a
term in traditional Chinese aesthetics. The idea of *shen* in the discussion
of theatrical representation is not the same as what is conventionally
translated into English as (internal) spirit as opposed to (external) attributes [xing 形], although the term has been at the centre of Chinese
aesthetic discourse in this connotation. *Shen* is, as Yao suggests, a unique
idea in classical Chinese aesthetics, which is roughly equivalent to the
contemporary notion of imagination. With respect to formal structuration, Yao further asserts, *shen* facilitates the search for innovation,
uniqueness and exquisiteness. The effect created by *shen* is intrinsically
rich and yet leaving much room for pondering (Yao, 1997, p. 335).

Representation is seldom treated independently in dramatic practice
or theory. Traditional *xiqu* has often been consciously utilised by the
authorities as a powerful didactic medium for the inculcation of political and moral values (Mackerras and Wichmann, 1983, pp. 4–5). And
even if this had not been the case, moral didacticism has been conven-
tionalized and internalized in the stories of *xiqu*. The contrast of the real
and the unreal in classical dramatic aesthetics reveals that the subject of
artistic representation remains the effective portrayal of reality. Such an
intrinsic relation between content and form continues to prevail in the
contemporary era among those who are attempting to search for new
theatrical forms. In her study of Huang Zuolin, Faye Fei summarizes
Huang's concept of the theatre as "sociopolitically realistic while technically non-*xieshi* 寫實 [non-realist] but *xieyi*" (Fei, 1991, p. 192). Her statement sufficiently sums up the contemporary Chinese dramatists' endeavour in formal innovations. While dramatists discover the freedom that
suppositionality brings, they still maintain that realism is the essence of
dramatic works. If we turn to the Western dramatists that are most celebrated by the Chinese dramatists, we notice that they too possess such a
characteristic. Meyerhold is a Marxist searching for new forms with which
to reveal the course of historical progression (Schmidt, 1981, p. xvi).
Brecht is also a Marxist, who has subverted the conventions of realist
theatre to effect his didacticism (Willet, 1977, p. 211). In other words,
for these dramatists, Chinese and Western alike, artistic representation

has never really gained full autonomy from the greater ideological structure.

Gao Xingjian differs from all these dramatists in that his search for artistic representation is not burdened by ideological baggage. He scarcely professes ideology of any kind; if he does, he unabashedly champions the ideology of no "ism" as manifested in a collection of his critical essays, entitled *Meiyou zhuyi* 沒有主義 [Without isms] (1995). In an article published in 1983, he suggests that "the realness in dramatic art is established on suppositionality" (Gao, 1983, p. 97). Interestingly enough, this line was deleted when the article appeared in the collected edition (Gao, 1988, p. 33). The act of deletion, at this point, may not be sufficient to prove that Gao has departed from the view of the theatre in a simplistic dichotomy of the real and the unreal. However, it is apparent, in the light of the following discussion, that the notion of suppositionality does not merely represent "the realness in dramatic arts," but possesses a more complex significance.

Gao suggests that knowledge of suppositionality has led to the understanding of drama as a game (Gao, 1988, p. 65). Semantically, the Chinese term "*xi* 戲" means both "drama" and "game," in a way corresponding to the English word "play" which refers to "a dramatic piece for the stage" as well as "the playing of a game." As Xu Weisen 許渭森, a Qing dynasty critic, once put it, "Drama [xi 戲] is all a game [xi 戲], as it is unreal [fei zhen 非真]" (Yao, 1997, p. 262). Underlining the awareness that what is on stage is an act of performance, Gao asserts that the objective of the theatre is to make both the performers and audience believe that it is suppositional and to join in playing the game (Gao, 1988, p. 66). Precisely, what Gao has proposed is not that suppositionality is a means to the ultimate end of creating an impression of reality, or, in his earlier words, the "realness in dramatic arts." On the contrary, he wants the audience to know and accept that the nature of theatre is suppositional and to enjoy the artifice of suppositionality.

The issue is then how suppositionality is to be achieved. We must return to the essential element of Gao's theatre — the actors. This is where his emphasis on the training of all-rounded actors displays its relevance:

> At a time when the contemporary theatre is flooded with sounds, lights, colours and properties, I propose to return to a bare stage and redefine suppositionality, the innate characteristic of the theatre, with the actor's

performance. Sets and props should be reduced to the minimum. Furthermore, not to create realness should be regarded as the highest mission.
In contrast, the employment of sounds, lights, colours and properties is
only meaningful if they become the support for, and extension of, the
performance.   (Gao, 1996, pp. 247–248)

Whereas many dramatists who acknowledge the idea of suppositionality
have attempted to utilize different theatrical means to achieve effective
representation, Gao perceives them as secondary and even unnecessary.
The theatrical experience, therefore, is stripped off everything except
two basic components, the actors and the audience. Such a conception
was first advocated by the Polish director Grotowski in his notion of Poor
Theatre in which he defines the theatre as "what takes place between
spectator and actor," stressing that "all other things are supplementary"
(Grotowski, 1969, p. 32). For Grotowski, as Shomit Mitter asserts, "the
actor becomes the sole vehicle of truth in the theatre" (Mitter, 1992,
p. 100). Gao's special focus on the actors' performance, in this context,
differentiates him from Meyerhold and Brecht, and reveals his kinship
to Grotowski.

But while he regards "the personal and scenic technique of the actor
as the core of theatre art" (Grotowski, 1969, p. 15), Grotowski requires
his actors to "play their characters by playing themselves" and "express
as fact the fiction of their narratives" (Mitter, 1992, p. 79). In contrast,
Gao not only explicitly reveals the fact that what happens in the theatre
is a conscious performance by the actors, but he also wants the entire
process of performing to be watched and appreciated by the audience
(Gao, 1996, p. 249). The representation of reality, in this instance, is a
non-issue. Suppositionality, as Gao conceives of it, is the subject, rather
than the means, of representation. As the basic component of Gao's
theatre, his actors have to possess the fullest ability to exhibit the richness and fascination of suppositionality.

Gao's training of actors, as seen in the earlier discussion, is intended
to evoke their spontaneity and to nurture comprehensive acting skills.
In the theatre, this well-rounded training is actualized in the actors' multi-
faceted and multi-layered performance. The three performers in *Alarm
Signal* portray distinctive aspects of the youthful characters in reality,
imagination and the recollection of the past. The actor who plays the
Ecologist in *Wild Man* assumes three different personae as narrator,

observer and character. Whereas in these plays the adoption of different roles by the actors is an integral part of the plays' narrative structure, in *The Other Shore* the change of roles becomes part of the performance *per se*. Initially, the ensemble performs the process of improvisation in the capacity of actors. When they reach the opposite shore of the river, the function of theatre as a rehearsal room has terminated and a suppositional theatrical space is established. As the play progresses, the actors take on new roles and each time they do this a different spatial and temporal dimension is being defined.

Besides their physically perceivable performances of various roles, the actors also portray abstract concepts and invisible objects through their speeches and movements. For instance, the river that the actors attempt to cross does not physically exist but the idea of the river is portrayed by the actors and accepted by the audience. Suppositionality is also achieved in a more intrinsic way as illustrated in a scene towards the end of *The Other Shore*:

> The Crowd: (*suddenly*) It's here!
>   It comes all of a sudden.
>   Get out of the way.
> (*The Shadow comes on stage walking backward. The Crowd makes way for him.*)
> The Man: (*feebly*) Who's that?
> The Shadow: Your heart.
> (*While the Crowd stares at the blind and deaf Heart hobbling across, the Shadow quietly drags the Man off stage. The Crowd, following the Man's old and weak Heart which is actually invisible, gradually leaves the stage.*)
> (Gao, 1995a, pp. 61–62)

In this context, it is not only the existence of an invisible object (the Heart) but the features of the object (blind and deaf, hobbling, old and weak) that need to be specified by acting. Furthermore, the performance also presents a process, from the Crowd's expectation of the Heart's arrival, to its appearance and, finally, its departure. In this particular example of suppositionality, there are several aspects to be noted. First, speech is minimal. Only the arrival and the object itself are briefly mentioned in words. Second, movement is also minimal. There is no exaggerated movement except for the Crowd walking off stage. Third, the invisible object is presented as if it is a character. Its features to be portrayed are not physically seen, even though the object has a life of its own. Fourth, as the process unfolds, not only spatial but also temporal dimensions are involved. The other closely related factor, imagination, plays a vital part in the successful presentation of this scene.

By isolating this scene from the rest of the play, it is quite impossible to portray the complex image of the Heart as delineated in the written text. Movement and speech, in this instance, have their limitations. But imagination will work if it is evoked earlier. This is established in the preceding context, in which the theatrical space is being defined, and extended later. Before this scene, the Man has arduously gone through a futile search for the significance of his being. In the process, as his alter ego, the Shadow, points out mercilessly that he is losing trust in others, his heart is becoming tired and feeble, and he is unable to love any more (Gao, 1995a, p. 60). When the Heart finally comes on stage, despite its invisibility, the audience will have no difficulties in exercising the intercontextual referentiality of their imagination. The crux is therefore that they have got themselves fully involved in the game, that is, the activity in the theatre, and accepted the rule of the game, that is, the suppositionality of the theatrical space. In the game of theatre, as suppositionality is its nature, imagination is indispensable.

From this perspective, we can see some similarities between Gao's theatre and traditional *xiqu*. First, they are both arts of suppositionality. They do not attempt to portray reality. On the contrary, they focus on the artistic representation of suppositionality. Second, in the artistic world of both genres, imagination is an essential element in the process of creating and appreciating the theatrical experience. Third, didacticism is not the primary concern of either of these types of theatre. Although traditional *xiqu* usually has moral messages, the artist's foremost interest is in displaying his/her skills in singing, reciting, acting and acrobatics. Hence, these two genres of theatre appeal more to the aesthetic sense than to the intellect. However, the two are not alike in that *xiqu*'s art of suppositionality is primarily founded on formalization and conventionalism, while Gao's is on spontaneity and originality. Clearly, Gao envisions his theatre to be a representation of art in its own right rather than a representation of reality or of ideology.

RECREATING CARNIVAL

In his theatre of suppositionality, Gao Xingjian uses various means to help the actors and audience to achieve an aesthetic experience. The creation of a carnival mood in the drama and the employment of clown characters, both inspired by traditional Chinese theatre, are the two most significant attempts. On the one hand, the carnival mood helps create an environment that encourages the audience's emotional participation. On the other, the clown characters complicate the relationship between the real and the unreal, and stimulates the audience to adopt a different perspective from that represented in the theatre. These two seemingly contradictory aspects of Gao's theatre are in fact integrated so as to present the theatre as a suppositional space in which the real and the unreal are interrelated, and art and life co-exist.

Although Gao opposes didacticism in theatre, his earlier plays, as we have seen, have not been totally devoid of messages of one kind or another. *Alarm Signal* depicts the frustrations of Chinese youth at a juncture of social transformation. *The Bus-Stop* portrays the collective anxiety about moving forward. *Wild Man* is an epic of paradoxes arising from the conflicts of tradition and modernization. Beginning with *The Other Shore*, however, Gao is less interested in theatre as a medium for didactic purposes than in theatre as an art itself. The transformation of theatre from an instructional means to an artistic mode of representation inevitably involves a recontemplation of its intrinsic qualities. From the Chinese traditional theatre, Gao has assimilated its spirit and also proposed that the actors should learn from the well-rounded training of *xiqu* performers. In the course of appropriation, however, he has always been careful to avoid adopting *xiqu*'s formalized conventions, which, in his view, is what causes *xiqu* to become a "dead art." By the same token, Gao has also borrowed modes from traditional and folk arts to enrich his modern theatre. One of them is the carnivalesque [youyi 遊藝] form. Inevitably, this form has also determined the content of his theatre.

In *Wild Man*, Gao, for the first time, proposes to "create a cordial and lively atmosphere within the theatre, and let the audience be involved in an enjoyable performance, as if attending a festive celebration. They will be delightfully entertained, both physically and spiritually" (Gao, 1985, p. 272). There are lively moments such as a wedding scene where young men are playing blaring percussion music and young women singing joyous nuptial songs. These carnivalesque elements are, however, juxtaposed against the tree felling motions of the lumberjacks upstage and loud noises of the falling timber filling the theatre (Gao, 1985, pp. 262–

265). The supposedly joyous scene, in actual effect, suggests an ironic situation in which the audience experiences intellectual alienation rather than emotional involvement. The motifs of *Wild Man* prove to be too heavy for the evocation of a lively, festive atmosphere. The many social issues earnestly raised in Gao's earlier plays impede his attempt to incorporate the carnivalesque form in his modern theatre.

In his later plays, Gao attempts to present the carnivalesque mood in a different way. Instead of having scenes of festive celebration with song and dance, he employs clown characters to create a carnival effect. Such a character first appears in *The Other Shore* as a Mountebank who sells dog-skin plaster. Before the Mountebank's appearance, the protagonist, in memory-like scenes, witnesses three particular occasions of his past, namely, his first encounter with a girl, his oppressive relationship with his father, and an instance which, being curious about what is happening on the other side of a wall, he trades a gift from his mother to an old woman who is collecting an entrance toll, only to see the girl he desires being raped. These are all perceived as turning points in the protagonist's life. Before these scenes begin and in between them, there are the chanting and reciting of Buddhist scriptures, creating a solemn, religious atmosphere which serves as a key to the main scene.

In such a context, the Mountebank enters, "with bare chest and tightened waist, he hits the gong while walking round the stage,"[8] hawking his dog-skin plaster which he boasts is a panacea to all illnesses:

> Dog-skin plaster for sale! Dog-skin plaster for sale! A secret prescription handed down in the family for thirteen generations. Internal wounds, external wounds, injuries from falls and contusions, stricken with heart attack, bitten by rabid dogs, and those infatuated men and oestrous women, sufferers of infantile convulsions and apoplectic stroke, those who are utterly heartless and mindless, those who are possessed by ghosts and spirits — just a single plaster and that's what you need to be fully recovered. If one doesn't work, use another one. Oh, dog-skin plaster for sale! Dog-skin plaster for sale! Those injected with chicken blood and those who've taken the wrong medicine, female sterility and male impotency, and all indecencies — take one and cure all! Hey, the one who stutters and the one whose mouth is lopsided, jealous women and revengeful men, unfaithful husbands and disrespectful sons, pockmarks on the face and ringworm on the foot — if one doesn't work, use another one. Don't pay if it

fails. Dog-skin plaster for sale! Those who want mustn't hesitate! That's
the one and only chance, miss it and you'll regret it!

(Gao, 1995a, pp. 44–45)

At first sight, the brief appearance of the Mountebank seems to have
little relevance to the scene. In the context of sombre reflection on the
protagonist's past, the hawking of the Mountebank seems strange and
awkward. Because of the character's short appearance, the critic Zou
Jiping has conveniently ignored its significance and focused his analysis
merely on the memory-like scenes which appears in accord with the general theme of the play (Zou, 1994, pp. 156–158). Another critic speaks
of his philosophical dimension, suggesting that the Mountebank is possibly a secular substitution for the failure of religious expiation (Huang,
2000). However, he has neither elaborated on his argument nor, more
importantly, perceived the employment of such character in the light of
its formal significance.

If we take a look at the past, since the Song dynasty if not earlier,
festive carnivals and theatre have been closely connected in the living
sphere of the Chinese, especially in the general rural regions. In the
predominantly agricultural society of premodern China, festivals and
the slack seasons are the time when the people rest and enjoy
entertainment. During this time away from work, *xiqu* performances are
among the principal items of entertainment. Because of *xiqu*'s close relation to the joyous nature of collective activity, one Chinese scholar has
pointed out, three of its important characteristics can be observed. First,
as *xiqu* is a type of entertainment enjoyed during a time of relaxation,
most of its repertoire is filled with joyfulness and excitement. Even if the
story begins with sorrowful incidents, it will usually end with a happy
reunion. Second, being a form of entertainment whose audience is largely
made up of illiterate peasants, the stories and dramatic lines tend to be
straightforward and easily understandable. Third, as it is the main attraction at the carnival ground, the audience expects it to provide a lively
atmosphere in which members can enjoy and participate. Hence, a *xiqu*
performance usually has bustling elements such as buoyant music and
acrobatics (Zheng, 1990, pp. 24–30). Viewed from this perspective, the
desire for festive atmosphere not only has influenced certain aspects of
xiqu, but *xiqu* has also become an integral part of the festive carnival. To
a great extent, the traditional theatre and the carnival are inseparable

and even inter-dependent. The liveliness of the traditional theatre hence fundamentally accords with the liveliness of the carnival ground.

Both the carnivalesque mood and the use of the clown character in Gao's plays further suggest connections with Mikhail Bakhtin's notion of carnival laughter. Although Gao seems not to have been influenced by Bakhtin, directly or otherwise, it is useful to observe how Bakhtin's interpretation of European folk culture and of Renaissance literature is relevant to the present study.[9] It should be noted, however, that Bakhtin's notion, with a different historical and cultural context, can be used only as a reference but not as a yardstick in the interpretation of Gao's works. My objective in adopting the Bakhtinian notion of carnival laughter as a point of comparison with Gao is to demonstrate the way in which Gao's employment of the carnivalesque form has defined a new theatrical space. I shall argue that Gao's carnivalesqueness is in fact more akin to the clown role [choujue 丑角] of Chinese traditional theatre.

According to Bakhtin, carnival festivities, comic spectacles and ritual constituted an important part of the life of ancient and medieval people. Before the Middle Ages, both serious and comic aspects of the world had an equally sacred and official status. However, this equilibrium changed as a result of the canonization of the serious ecclesiastical and political ceremonials. Carnival laughter and comic ritual were transformed to a nonofficial level, although people of all classes still participated. Bakhtin summarizes the significance of carnival in everyday life as follows:

> [C]arnival does not know footlights, in the sense that it does not acknowledge any distinction between actors and spectators. Footlights would destroy a carnival, as the absence of footlights would destroy a theatrical performance. Carnival is not a spectacle seen by the people; they live in it, and everyone participates because its very idea embraces all the people.... It has a universal spirit; it is a special condition of the entire world, of the world's revival and renewal, in which all take part. (Bakhtin, 1984, p. 7)

In the world of the carnival, social rank and status disappear, with all people considered equal. It is therefore a unique situation as it unites the utopian ideal and the realistic together in this carnival experience (Bakhtin, 1984, p. 10). By adopting the carnival spirit, works of Renaissance literature, such as those of Rabelais, portray a distinct aesthetic concept that Bakhtin calls "grotesque realism." The principle of grotesque realism, Bakhtin asserts, is degradation, in which all that is high, spiritual, ideal and abstract is lowered and demoted "to the material level, to the sphere of earth and body in their indissoluble unity" (Bakhtin, 1984, pp. 19–20). Such a process reveals "the people's unofficial truth" by overcoming the serious aspects of official and authoritarian culture: violence, prohibitions, limitations, fear and intimidation, and hence "clarifies man's consciousness and gives him a new outlook on life" (Bakhtin, 1984, pp. 90–91).

When he first introduces ritual and festive scenes in *Wild Man*, Gao requires his audience to become totally involved in the joyous mood. Members of the audience become participants in that performance. Perceived in the context of conventional Chinese realist theatre, it is apparent that Gao's objective is to create a new theatrical space in which performers and audience do not remain completely separate as two distinct and incommunicable communities. The presence of footlights, as Bakhtin argues, characterizes theatrical performances, but only conventional ones. Gao's removal of the footlights, in contrast, signifies a return from the enclosed space of realist theatre to the carnival ground of antiquity. Although he is not successful in his initial attempt in *Wild Man*, its significance cannot be disregarded.

First, in a formal aspect, despite the fact that *Wild Man* was written to be performed on a proscenium stage, the incorporation of carnival scenes in modern theatre is a vital step towards the adaptation of artistic forms from folk culture. The carnival is not artistically/artificially represented in the modern theatre. Gao's attempt is to present events with a carnival mood in its original forms, albeit often in fragmentary state. In so doing, Gao intends to introduce the mood and spirit of carnival as an entirety without distorting it with modern consciousness. Second, from an ideological point of view, as the carnival compels total and equal participation of both the performers and spectators, it transforms their existing relationship. It subverts the conventional status of the audience at the lower receiving end as a group that is to be educated and instructed. The audience has now been given freedom to express their sense of participation, both emotionally and intellectually. It has, furthermore, acquired a higher status in the performer-spectator relationship, which enables them to have not only a different level of participation but a totally different role within the theatrical space.

From this perspective, the employment of a clown character in *The*

Other Shore can be perceived as an extension of such an intention. Clowns, Bakhtin suggests, are not "actors playing their parts on a stage," but "representatives of the carnival spirit in everyday life" (Bakhtin, 1984, p. 8). The carnival laughter generated by such characters involves all the people and is directed at everyone. In addition, it has an ambivalent nature, "it is gay, triumphant, and at the same time mocking, deriding." As such, it expresses both the real and the ideal point of view of the world. In Bakhtin's words, "he who is laughing also belongs to it [that he is laughing at]" (Bakhtin, 1984, p. 12).

If the festive scenes in *Wild Man* are incorporated to get the audience involved in a carnival atmosphere, the attempt is made in a passive way. The stage and audience are separated, and the decision to participate or otherwise remains predominantly with the latter. In *The Other Shore,* by contrast, the Mountebank, as a character, is taking over the initiative in such a process. He takes on an aggressive role, breaking down the boundary between performer and spectator by assuming a status lower than that of the audience. The stereotyped image of a mountebank, with his contradictory and nonsensical utterance, elicits a higher status being adopted by the audience. The change of status, as Keith Johnstone explains it in terms of improvisation, facilitates the flow of space: high-status players will allow their space to flow into that of low-status players (Johnstone, 1989, pp. 58–59).

The Mountebank portrays himself initially as an object of ridicule. The audience laughs at him and his claims about the dog-skin plaster. When he says that the plaster can cure illnesses, wounds and injuries, the audience despises him as they do to any mountebank in the real world. When he boasts that it cures heart attack and apoplectic stroke, the audience is amused by his braggadocio. At this stage, the exchange of status between the performer and spectators is completed. However, the Mountebank does not stop at this point; he continues to propound the dog-skin plaster's effectiveness against infatuation and oestrus, jealousy and revenge, all of which far exceed the curative powers that could be expected in any medicine. Hence these are claims that go beyond normal rationality. By transforming a situation of laughter into one of farcical absurdity, Gao puts a final twist on the performer-spectator relationship, and the audience is led to scrutinize reality in the context of absurdity.

To a certain extent, the above-mentioned scene in *The Other Shore* reminds one of a somewhat similar dramatic effect achieved by the situational absurdity in *The Bus-Stop*. Whereas the latter is more concerned with the revelation of the dramatic characters' individual subjectivity, the scene of the Mountebank and his comic and absurd utterance presents a dramatic juxtaposition of forms which extends the theatrical space to include the audience as participants of the entire experience. Within the larger context of the reflection of one's past, the presence of the Mountebank establishes a stark contrast with the solemn religious atmosphere and the protagonist's self-indulgence. In the process of juxtaposing reality and laughter, the Mountebank has guided the audience towards a deeper participation in the search for the meaning of life.

The ability of carnival laughter in Gao's theatre to revive and renew the spirit in the audience works in a different way for Gao than it does for Bakhtin. Whereas Bakhtinian carnival laughter is an effect that literary works produce, for Gao, carnivalesqueness is a technique that he uses to create an extended theatrical experience. When he creates a carnival mood and uses clown characters in his theatre, Gao does not conceal the fact that within a common sphere, which is the theatrical space, reality and laughter are co-existing. It is exactly the juxtaposition of the real and the unreal that provides a different approach to reception and interpretation.

Interestingly, this approach is not unfamiliar to readers of traditional Chinese novels. The narrative structure of *Hongloumeng* 紅樓夢 [Dream of the red chamber] is in fact founded on the ambivalence of the real [*zhen* 真] and the unreal [*jia* 假]. In the introductory chapter, Zhen Shiyin 甄士隱, who is almost at the *cul-de-sac* of his life, meets a seemingly crazy and erratic Daoist priest. After listening to the priest's *Hao liao ge* 好了歌 [Song of worthiness and dissipation], a song which depicts poignant reality in a jocular tone, Zhen is suddenly enlightened with an understanding of the mortal world and insouciantly follows the priest, leaving all his secular possessions behind (Cao and Liu, 1990, pp. 10–12). Both the song and Zhen's encounter with the priest are appropriate footnotes to the thematic verse, "Reality becomes fiction when the fiction appears to be real; possession becomes emptiness when the emptiness appears to be possessed" [jia zuo zhen shi zhen yi jia, wu wei you chu you huan wu 假作真時真亦假，無為有處有還無] (Cao and Liu, 1990, p. 6).[10] In the aesthetic world of traditional Chinese novels, the real and the unreal are often inter-represented in order to present a more ambivalent and

sophisticated cosmic view. The traditional representation of the unreal in
jocularity emerges in Gao's theatre in the form of carnivalesqueness.
Significantly, carnivalesqueness becomes one of the fundamental elements in Gao's attempt to establish a theatre that integrates the real and
the unreal.

Apart from its affinity with Bakhtinian carnival laughter and the
jocularity that appears in traditional novels, Gao's clown character,
as a form of representation, closely resembles the role of *chou* 丑 of
traditional Chinese theatre. Among the four primary role categories of
traditional theatre, *chou* has the most flexibility in performance style.[11]
First, as the *chou* virtually appears in every play and is usually the sup-
porting role to *sheng* 生, *dan* 旦 or *jing* 淨, he is required to be familiar
with their performing styles and skills. Traditionally, other than his own
role, *chou* is also trained extensively to perform other roles. Second, the
chou plays a wide range of characters, from government officials to poor
scholars, from hooligans to old women. He has to speak in *jingbai* 京白
[local vernacular language of Beijing] as well as different kinds of dialects.
He also needs to have a good command of acrobatic skills. Third, the
chou is free to improvise his own lines on the spot in response to the
audience's reaction to the play, or to comment on current affairs not at
all related to the play (Liu, 1962, pp. 359, 368). In summary, *chou* is
"sanctioned to use colloquial speech, indulge in personal or topical
allusions, and identify himself with the crowd out in front" (Scott, 1983,
p. 126).

Although the performance of the *chou* is no less formalized than that
of the other three conventional role types, the fact that its antecedents
are the public storyteller and fairground entertainer (Scott, 1983, p. 125)
indicates that it has its roots in popular entertainment closely connected
with people's everyday life. Remarkably similar to the Bakhtinian clown,
the *chou* is not only close to the audience but also "serves a catalytic function" (Scott, 1983, p. 125) by satirically depicting negative characters
such as corrupt or stupid officials or petty criminals. With this understanding of the characteristics of the *chou*, it becomes apparent that Gao
is most interested in the *chou* among all four role categories and presents
it in different variations in his modern theatre because of its potentiality
to establish an experience of total participation.

Variations on the clown character are adopted more extensively in
The Nether City and *Story of the Classic of Mountains and Seas*, the only two

plays by Gao that are based primarily on Chinese classics. *The Nether City* is adapted from *Da piguan* 大劈棺 [Big smash of the coffin], a title from the traditional *xiqu* repertoire. First written as a dance drama and later reworked into a full-length play, the play is about Zhuang Zhou 莊周 [Zhuangzi 莊子] who disguises himself as a handsome young man to lure his wife and test her chastity. *Story of the Classic of Mountains and Seas* is based on pre-Qin records of primeval mythology. It depicts the genesis of the world as well as the resentment for each other among the ancient gods. With these plays Gao attempts to bring a new perspective to the conventional reception of Chinese folk stories and mythology, as well as to carry out more extensive experimentation with the forms of traditional Chinese theatre.

Most of the ghost characters in *The Nether City* bear the characteristics of the *chou* role. At the end of the first part, as Zhuang Zhou's wife realizes that her husband is not dead and the young man who has seduced her is in fact Zhuang Zhou in disguise, she is extremely horrified and is frightened literally to death. The second part of the play depicts the experience of Zhuang Zhou's wife in the nether city and especially of her judgement. Two ghostly runners escort her to the nether city. They argue and fight between themselves and sneer at her. In a later scene, the black and white ghosts [hei bai wuchang 黑白無常] and a crowd of female yakshas [mu yecha 母夜叉] sing, dance, and ridicule each other in a carnivalesque manner. The performance of these characters, Gao indicates, should be "exaggerated to the utmost extent," with bustling percussion music, heavy makeup, and variety and magic shows, "to achieve the entertaining and recreational effects which have previously been missing from the modern theatre" (Gao, 1995b, p. 68).

In *Story of the Classic of Mountains and Seas*, many of the gods are also portrayed in a farcical and jocular manner. Mythical emperors such as Huangdi 黃帝, Yandi 炎帝 and Dijun 帝俊 appear with worldly lust and sentiment. They are often surrounded by subordinate gods such as Wucainiao 五彩鳥, Chiyou 蚩尤, Shentu 神荼 and Yulei 鬱壘 who resemble the jesters. The heavenly gods are depicted as clowns. The heavenly palaces are transformed into carnival grounds. Again, Gao proposes that the play be performed in a "recreational style" so as to create a lively atmosphere comparable to that of a carnival during the temple festival [miaohui 廟會] (Gao, 1995c, p. 108). In order to attain the effect of carnivalesqueness, Gao has suggested two methods. First, performing techniques of traditional *xiqu* can be employed, such as the use of painted faces and masks, brandishing of swords and spears, stilt-walking, playing with dragon lanterns, somersaults, high-wire walking, and so on. Second, activities going on during the temple carnival other than those on the stage are also incorporated, such as hawking, selling dog-skin plaster, monkey show, acrobatics, puppet show and selling candies (Gao, 1995c, p. 108). Significantly, Gao has attempted to employ elements from the stage of traditional *xiqu*, as well as elements from off stage. He is not only trying to create a theatre within the carnival but one embodying the entire carnival event. The boundary between performance and the audience disappears, so does that between art and life.

Theoretically, Gao's theatre has already expanded beyond the performance sphere of traditional *xiqu*. Whereas *xiqu* continually renews itself by incorporating elements from other artistic genres such as folk dance and music, Gao boldly attempts to incorporate elements which are not conventionally considered as artistic. He aspires to a theatre which offers an experience larger than that of art, that is, one that involves total participation of the audience to the same immense extent as their participation in life. This experience of integrating art and life has its roots, apparently, much earlier than the emergence of proper theatrical performance. In this respect, Gao's theatre resembles religious rituals of the ancient eras, *xiqu* performance in a carnival ground during a festival, or what Bakhtin called the "ritual spectacles" of folk carnival (Bakhtin, 1984, p. 5), in which everyone is a participant.

In practice, the achievement of such an experience depends on two conditions. First, there should be virtually no physical distinction between the performers and audience, that is, they must be thoroughly mixed in a communal space. Second, the audience should not expect to watch a performance but be mentally prepared to participate in the whole process, be it part of the performance or otherwise. In a modern urban theatre, Gao's ambition may not be easily achieved. However, his attempt undoubtedly creates a theatre with a freer and more flexible spatial dimension as compared to the existing ones. In this suppositional space set free from restrictions, the adoption of carnival forms and clown characters not only enriches Gao's artistic representation, but also suggests that we take a new look at the notion of the real and the unreal.

THE AMBIVALENCE OF THE REAL AND THE UNREAL

Suppositionality, as previously discussed, has not only provided Gao Xingjian with flexibility for artistic representation but has also become the subject of his theatre. The employment of suppositionality as a form has given rise to the establishment of a new mode of theatrical aesthetics, which is opposed to the conventional way of representing reality. Employment of suppositionality has also, unavoidably, resulted in suppositionality's intervention in the narrative structure of the plays. Quoting as a reference, I suggested earlier that, with respect to form, the carnivalesqueness of Gao's theatre may be connected with the traditional notion of the real and the unreal in *Dream of the Red Chamber*. In the following discussion, I intend to illustrate further how suppositionality constitutes an integral part of Gao's narrative and is intrinsically involved as the subject of his plays.

Dream of the Red Chamber was probably the first Chinese novel to employ the idea of the real and the unreal as a form of fictional structuration, as it provides an appropriate point of reference.[12] Yu Pingbo 俞平伯, one of the early twentieth-century scholars who established the new textual criticism of *Dream of the Red Chamber*, points out that the unique representational mode of the novel is suggested from the very beginning: the real incidents are being hidden away [zhenshi yinqu 真事隱去], and represented by mendacious speech [jiayu cunyan 假語村言] (Yu, 1988, p. 635). The intention of the writer Cao Xueqin 曹雪芹, as Yu argues, was to present the unreal in an explicit manner and the real as the hidden truth. Quoting the *Fengyue baojian* [Mirror of lust 風月寶鑑] as an example, he suggests that the image of the beautiful lady Jia Rui 賈瑞 sees in the obverse side of the Mirror is actually the unreal while the skeleton in the reverse side is the real. Extending the metaphor to the structuration of the entire novel, Yu concludes, the obverse represents the unreal, as portrayed in prosperity and lustfulness and, in contrast, the reverse represents the real, as suggested by the hidden darkness (Yu, 1988, p. 811). Many scholars have adopted this interpretation of the novel, and further elaborated on it. Although the mode of inter-representation in *Dream of the Red Chamber* has exhibited some sense of ambiguity, a subjective truth is apparently present in the writer's cosmic view. What the writer has attempted is to present this truth, in a manner resembling a mirror reflection, through a spectrum of delusive images of reality.[13]

In Gao Xingjian's plays, the idea of the real and the unreal is articulated in different ways. Significantly, the representation of the unreal is intrinsically intertwined with the theatrical form of suppositionality. If we look at the Mountebank in *The Other Shore*, we can see that the unreal is represented at several levels. First, the Mountebank, as a character, and his dog-skin plaster, signify falseness although there is a certain sense of realness as there are such things in real life. Second, his boasting that the plaster is effective in curing all kinds of illness further dramatizes this characteristic of falseness. Third, as part of his jocular and exaggerated utterance, the Mountebank also enumerates human weaknesses and villainies, in a way that exceeds normal rationality, hence an additional level of unreality is suggested. In the process, the impression of unreality is gradually constructed and enhanced. However, in the most unreal and unbelievable instance, Gao reveals the deepest truth that what needs to be cured is not any kind of physical illness but vicious human nature itself. Such a revelation emerges from an inter-textual reading with reference to the protagonist's reflection of the past and the religious chanting. An awareness of suppositionality has been established from the very beginning, the audience should be conscious that everything presented is suppositional and unreal, and that they are being led to perceive the incident in a detached and objective manner.

Suppositionality, in this sense, provides an additional perspective of reality and unreality in the play. Where Gao's play is similar to *Dream of the Red Chamber* lies in his suggestion that reality is not to be perceived in a straightforward manner but that there is an ambivalent nature within it. His theatre differs from this novel in that its ambivalence is made more complicated by its unique form. There is not a single mirror that provides a particular image of reflection but, with the presence of suppositionality as another mirror, there are in fact *two* parallel mirrors facing each other, creating infinite images. Therefore, the seeming truth suggested in the play is not the absolute truth but only *one of the many appearances of truth*. As truth is represented in the theatre by means of suppositionality, it loses its status of absoluteness. Truth is only a representation and, by this logic, there can be different representations of truth. The hidden message is then that the reader/audience should not be deceived by any appearance, even if it is that of truth, because there are many aspects of reality which are not, and cannot be, fully represented.

This ambivalence runs through the entire play. *The Other Shore* begins

with the ensemble, in the capacity of real-life actors, explicitly presenting the process of constructing a theatrical experience with suppositionality. In so doing, it suggests that the actors are real while that which
is represented is unreal. The represented includes the relationships and
abstract concepts portrayed at the beginning, and also the entire world
of the other shore signified later. These are all suppositional and established with the effective operation of imagination. However, in this suppositional world of the other shore, the playwright presents incidents
which have astonishingly struck a chord with the audience's real-life
experience. When the actors cross over to the other shore, they assume
fictional characters which are members of the Crowd. At this moment, a
Woman appears and teaches them to speak and to express the feelings
of love. After they have gained the ability to express feelings, they begin
to create their own malicious expressions and use them on the Woman.
As the Crowd becomes more excited, they, as a collective, lose their moral
and intellectual judgement and kill the Woman (Gao; 1995a, pp. 14–21).

In another scene, a Card Player is leading a game with the Crowd.
One rule of the game is that whoever loses has to stick a piece of paper
on his/her face. As the game goes on, nobody wins but the Card Player.
The Man begins to suspect that the Card Player is playing a trick and
warns the Crowd not to submit to it. But the Crowd, manipulated by the
Card Player, continues to reject the Man's accusation. Under increasing
pressure from the collective, the Man finally gives in and submits to the
game of deception (Gao, 1995a, pp. 27–38). These incidents instinctively
remind one of the situation in the Cultural Revolution and thus are starkly
real to the audience. Yet because they appear on the suppositional other
shore represented in a suppositional theatre, there exists a distance, deliberately created by the playwright, in perceiving these incidents. In this
instance, moreover, the nature of the real and the unreal is blurred,
which accords with the fact that the miseries of the past, despite its
recentness, have become nebulous and even illusory.

Toward the end of the play, as all the stories of the other shore have
been told, the protagonists resume their initial capacity as actors. The
actors talk about things totally irrelevant to the previous scenes, such as
"I like sweets, especially yoghurt." "How do you go back? So boring. What
a lousy play it is!" "What's on tomorrow? How about lunch?" and so on.
The play ends with all sorts of sounds being heard: the cry of a baby,
starting and vrooming of cars, ringing of bicycle bell, flowing of tap water,

and distant siren of an ambulance (Gao, 1995a, pp. 62–63).[14] These
sounds, along with the actors' prattle, signify a return to reality and remind the audience that what they have just seen is only a play. The process
of the construction of suppositionality is thus completed with the
deconstruction of it. If there is any suggestion that the other shore is the
only truth amidst all unreality of life, the ending relentlessly breaks this
illusion. In a theatre of suppositionality, what is seen as real in one instance may turn out to be unreal in another. The many appearances of
the real may therefore not necessarily combine to form the truth. On
the contrary, to borrow and modify the verse in *Dream of the Red Chamber,*
"Reality becomes unreal when the *truth* appears to be real."

This notion of *the unreality of the real* reemerges and intensifies in *The
Nether City.* The real and the unreal are further intertwined as suppositionality intervenes deeper. Gao adapts the story of Zhuang Zhou test-
ing his wife and, with his unique mode of suppositionality, presents some
new perspectives on the familiar incident. In *The Nether City,* the actor
who plays Zhuang Zhou performs in several capacities.[15] Initially, he
appears on stage as an actor, who has no relation to the character and
directly addressing to the audience, tells the synopsis of the story:

> It happened in antiquity. It is an extremely outmoded story. It is about
> the ancient sage Zhuang Zhou who has played a prank on his wife, which
> is ridiculous, foolish and irremediable. That's why we have this play which
> is utterly unbelievable, thoroughly outrageous and extremely disastrous.
> It has even astounded the gods and the ghosts. Of course, it has absolutely
> nothing to do with people of today.   (Gao, 1995b, p. 6)

Similar to the artist of storytelling and singing in *Story of the Classic of
Mountains and Seas,* he makes it explicitly known to the audience that
what follows is fictional and unreal. Moreover, by alienating the audience from the temporal and spatial locality of the story, commenting in
an exaggerated manner, and reminding the audience of the story's irrelevance to the present, the actor has repeatedly instilled in the audience
the suppositional nature of what is being represented.

The actor then puts on his cloth hat [jin 巾][16] and assumes the role of
Zhuang Zhou. When he is playing the role, he does not fully enter the
character:

> Zhuang Zhou: This man is Zhuang Zhou. He has been away from home

> for years.... He doesn't trust his wife who is alone at home. An idea
> comes swiftly across his mind. He bribes the shaman and pretends to
> be dead. With some men carrying a coffin and playing mourning
> tunes, here he comes to relay the bad news.   (Gao, 1995b, p. 6)

Although he is already in the role, he partly maintains the capacity of
an actor to introduce the character. When the troupe arrives at Zhuang
Zhou's home, Zhuang Zhou disguises himself as a resplendently dressed
young man, the Prince of Chu:

> Zhuang Zhou: How grievous! How distressful!   (Gao, 1995b, p. 11)

He is lamenting to Zhuang Zhou's wife in his capacity as the Prince of
Chu, whom he is impersonating. In this instance, he has already assumed
the role of the Prince of Chu, leaving his former role of Zhuang Zhou.
Then he starts to seduce Zhuang Zhou's wife:

> Zhuang Zhou:(*asides*) This Zhuang Zhou is so wicked. He is seducing his
>   own wife.
>   (*to the wife*) Madam, you are so pretty!   (Gao, 1995b, p. 12)

These are the asides by which the actor comments on the character.
Swiftly, he resumes the role of the Prince of Chu, and carries on with the
acting in the story. From the above description, we can see that the actor
has taken up four capacities: as narrator, as Zhuang Zhou, as the Prince
of Chu, and as commentator while playing the role of Zhuang Zhou.

There are several levels on which we can see the representation of
the real and the unreal in this play. In the context of the story, Zhuang
Zhou is the real person while the Prince of Chu is impersonated and
therefore unreal. Zhuang Zhou's purpose of doing this impersonation is
to find out whether his wife is truly honest to him. His pursuit of truth is
embedded in untruthfulness. Thus before his quest for truth actually
begins, the truth has already been subverted by his untruthful act. As
Zhuang Zhou's wife gradually submits to the Prince of Chu's seduction,
she perceives the unreal as the real. What she sees and believes is a superficial appearance, which conceals the truth. It is thus inevitable that
she eats her own bitter fruit when the hidden truth is unveiled. The
tragedy is therefore the result of the subjective misapprehension of the
real and the unreal by *both* Zhuang Zhou and his wife. This is indeed the

message in the original story, which again echoes the saying in *Dream of the Red Chamber*, "Reality becomes fiction when *the fiction* appears to be real."

As suppositionality comes into play, the relations between the real and the unreal appear in a different light. The straightforward moral in the original story is deflected and a new angle of perception is offered. First, the actor's swift interchangeability between different capacities makes it plain that it is a story being acted out, and it continually reminds the audience of the theatre's suppositional nature. Nothing is to be perceived as real, not even the character of Zhuang Zhou. Second, the notion of unreality is enhanced by the actor's being alienated from the character to comment on it. In so doing, he is resuming capacity as a person in real life, someone who lives in the same world as the audience. Moreover, he stands with the audience on the one hand, and establishes a distance between him and the audience on the other, when he says that the story "has absolutely nothing to do with people of today." Once again, Gao Xingjian suggests that all the characters and incidents that appear to be real in the play, in fact, have a certain connotation of unreality. In Zhuang Zhou's final words: "Living is like death; death is like living. Life and death, no one ever knows [the truth]" (Gao, 1995b, p. 64). With the employment of suppositionality in the representation of his dramatic subjects, Gao does away with all possible illusions within the theatre as he eliminates all elements suggesting realness and reality.

NOTES

1. In an interview, Gao said he has directed three plays in China (Wu, 1995). Apparently, he is referring to the plays which actually have Lin Zhaohua as the named director. Gao has also stated explicitly how Lin and he conducted workshops during the rehearsal of *The Other Shore*, which stopped abruptly after a month (Gao, 1996, p. 223).

2. The term *xieyi* was used by Huang Zuolin as early as in 1962 to highlight the non-realistic style of Chinese theatre in contrast to the realistic [xieshi 寫實] style of Western realist drama. The idea did not receive much attention then, but became the focus of an extensive debate in the 1980s. See Quah (2000), pp. 46–47.

3. I have discussed the use of the term *xiqu* in Quah (2000), p. 61. *Xiqu* has often been translated as "Chinese opera" or "music-drama." The transliteral

form is nowadays more widely used as *xiqu*, as a genre of Chinese theatre, is essentially different from Western opera.

4. *Shanhaijing* 山海經 [The classic of mountains and seas], written between the 4th and 2nd centuries B.C., is an ancient record of Chinese geographical features and mythologies.

5. The aspiration of Gao and Lin was not eventually realised as the "Anti-Bourgeois Liberalisation Campaign" escalated in 1986. Chinese experimental theatre, however, continued to progress even in the unfavourable political atmosphere of the late 1980s. As compared to Gao's experimentation, experimental theatre of the 1990s has moved from the dependence on written texts towards emphasis on performances. Furthermore, most of the performances are not opened to the public. Practitioners and audience are mainly college students (for example, those from the Central Academy of Drama [Zhongyang xiju xueyuan 中央戲劇學院] and Beijing Academy of Film Studies [Beijing dianying xueyuan 北京電影學院]), and some professional theatre artists. Lin Zhaohua has been working closely with Performance Studio [Yanju gongzuoshi 演劇工作室]. Young directors such as Meng Jinghui 孟京輝 of Exposed Drama Society [Chuanbang jushe 穿幫劇社] and Mou Sen 牟森 of Drama Workshop [Xiju chejian 戲劇車間] are also important figures who have produced provocative experimental works. Wu (1998, pp. 78–102) and Lin (2000) have provided some details on these experimental theatre activities, while Salter has an interview with Mou Sen (Salter, 1996, pp. 218–228). However, as experimental theatre in China is always being marginalised, very few critics have paid much attention and hence the scarce literature about it.

6. Gilbert C. F. Fong has published an excellent English translation of Gao's later plays, including *The Other Shore, Between Life and Death, Dialogue and Rebuttal, Nocturnal Wanderer* and *Weekend Quartet* (See Gao, 1999). I did not use his translation because I have based on Gao's original Chinese version for my discussion. In this case, a translation that is as close as possible to the Chinese text is necessary.

7. In his Theatre-Studio, established in 1913, Meyerhold referred to actors of Chinese travelling companies performing without any stage conventions but remained attractive to the audience (the article was written in 1914). In another article written in 1916, he listed "stage and acting conventions in the Japanese and Chinese theatres" as one of the discussion subjects in a training programme for actors (Meyerhold, 1998, pp. 147, 154).

8. This paragraph describing the entrance of the Mountebank is missing from the later collection of his works (Gao, 1995a). The above is quoted from the text first published in *Shiyue* 十月, No. 5, 1985, p. 246.

9. When I asked Gao whether his idea of polyphony has been influenced by

Bakhtin, he said, "The translation of Bakhtin's work appears in China very late.... I don't agree with him. What he says is only complicated [fuza 複雜], not polyphony [fudiao 複調]" (Gao, 1998). Apparently, Gao is not very impressed by Bakhtin.

10. David Hawkes translated this couplet as "Truth becomes fiction when the fiction's true; Real becomes not-real where the unreal's real" (Hawkes, 1973, p. 55). Although Hawkes' translation of *Hongloumeng* is generally accepted, I do not use his version. In this case, he has condensed the meaning of the couplet and only translated the first line.

11. The characters in *xiqu* are normally categorised into several role types. In *jingju*, there are *sheng* [male], *dan* [female], *jing* [painted-face] and *chou* [clown].

12. It is to be noted that although the idea is first structurally employed in *Dream of the Red Chamber*, the representation of the real and the unreal in fictional writings has appeared much earlier. For example, short stories of the Tang dynasty such as Shen Jiji's 沈既濟 *Zhen zhong ji* 枕中記 [A dream in the pillow].

13. Many later scholars have presented illuminating discussions about the complex relations of the real and the unreal in *Dream of the Red Chamber*, for example, see Yu Yingshi (1978) and Anthony C. Yu (1997). I am not going into the details as my primary concern is to borrow the fundamental idea of the real and the unreal in *Dream of the Red Chamber* for the analysis of Gao's unique employment of suppositionality.

14. In the collected edition, the last two lines are missing. It is here quoted from *Shiyue*, No. 5, 1985, p. 250.

15. Capacity is a technical term referring to the actor's alternation between different identities. It is one of the key concepts in Gao's notion of neutral actor. I intend to further discuss this topic with reference to Gao's other works in another essay.

16. A hat for informal wear, *jin* is usually worn by *sheng jue* [male role] in *jingju*. The action of putting on the hat signifies the actor entering the role of Zhuang Zhou.

REFERENCES

Bakhtin, M. M. (1984). *Rabelais and His World*. Trans. Helene Iswolsky. Bloomington: Indiana University Press.

Brook, Peter (1990). *The Empty Space*. London: Penguin.

Cao Xueqin 曹雪芹 and Liu E 劉鶚 (1990). *Hongloumeng* 紅樓夢 [Dream of the red chamber]. Beijing: Renmin wenxue chubanshe 人民文學出版社.

Fang Zixun (Gilbert C. F. Fong) 方梓勳, ed. (2000). *Xin jiyuan de huawen xiju*

新紀元的華文戲劇 [Chinese drama in the new millennium]. Hong Kong: Xianggang xiju xiehui 香港戲劇協會 and Xianggang xiju gongcheng 香港戲劇工程.

Fei, Faye Chunfang (1991). "Huang Zuolin: China's Man of the Theatre," Ph.D. thesis, City University of New York.

Gao Xingjian 高行健 (1983). "Tan jiadingxing" 談假定性 [On suppositionality]. *Suibi* 隨筆, No. 29, pp. 96–103.

—— (1985). *Gao Xingjian xiju ji* 高行健戲劇集 [Plays by Gao Xingjian]. Beijing: Qunzhong chubanshe 群眾出版社.

—— (1988). *Dui yizhong xiandai xiju de zhuiqiu* 對一種現代戲劇的追求 [In search of a modern form of drama]. Beijing: Zhongguo xiju chubanshe 中國戲劇出版社.

—— (1995a). *Bi'an* 彼岸 [The other shore]. In Gao (1995b), Vol. 1.

—— (1995b). *Gao Xingjian xiju liuzhong* 高行健戲劇六種 [Six volumes of plays by Gao Xingjian]. Taipei: Dijiao chubanshe 帝教出版社.

—— (1995c). *Mingcheng* 冥城 [The nether city]. In Gao (1995b), Vol. 2.

—— (1995d). *Shanhaijing zhuan* 山海經傳 [Story of *The Classic of Mountains and Seas*]. In Gao (1995b), Vol. 3.

—— (1996). *Meiyou zhuyi* 沒有主義 [Without isms]. Hong Kong: Tiandi tushu youxian gongsi 天地圖書有限公司.

—— (1998). Interview by Quah Sy Ren, Paris, 2 and 3 May.

—— (1999). *The Other Shore: Plays by Gao Xingjian*. Trans. Gilbert C. F. Fong. Hong Kong: The Chinese University Press.

Grotowski, Jerzy (1969). *Towards a Poor Theatre*. Ed. Eugenio Barba. London: Methuen.

Hawkes, David, trans. (1973). *The Story of the Stone: A Chinese Novel by Cao Xueqin in Five Volumes*, Vol. 1. London: Penguin.

Hu Miaosheng 胡妙勝 (1988). "Zhongguo chuantong xiqu wutai yu xiandai xifang wutai sheji" 中國傳統戲曲舞台與現代西方舞台設計 [The design of Chinese traditional xiqu stage and modern Western stage]. In Xia and Lu, eds. (1988), pp. 66–97.

Huang Meixu 黃美序 (2000). "Shitan Gao Xingjian xiju zhong de seng dao renwu" 試探高行健戲劇中的僧道人物 [A preliminary discussion on the Buddhist and Daoist characters in Gao Xingjian's plays]. In Fang, ed. (2000), pp. 296–309.

Innes, Christopher (1993). *Avant Garde Theatre (1892–1992)*. London: Routledge.

Johnstone, Keith (1989). *Impro: Improvisation and the Theatre*. London: Methuen.

Lin Kehuan 林克歡 (2000). "Huangdan yu pintie — Jiushi niandai Zhongguo neidi de shiyan xiju" 荒誕與拼貼 — 九十年代中國內地的實驗戲劇 [Absurdity and collage: Chinese experimental theatre of the nineties]. In Fang, ed. (2000), pp. 235–242.

Liu Si 劉嗣 (1962). *Guoju juese he renwu* 國劇角色和人物 [Roles and personalities in the national drama]. Taipei: Liming 黎明.

Mackerras, Colin, ed. (1983). *Chinese Theatre: From Its Origin to the Present Day.* Honolulu: University of Hawaii Press.

Mackerras, Colin, and Wichmann, Elizabeth (1983). "Introduction." In Mackerras, ed. (1983), pp. 1–6.

Meyerhold, Vsevolod (1998). *Meyerhold on Theatre*, revised edition. Ed. and trans. Edward Braun. London: Methuen.

Mitter, Shomit (1992). *Systems of Rehearsal: Stanislavsky, Brecht, Grotowski and Brook.* London: Routledge.

Quah Sy Ren (2000). "Searching for Alternative Aesthetics in the Chinese Theatre: The Odyssey of Huang Zuolin and Gao Xingjian." *Asian Culture*, No. 24 (June), pp. 44–66.

Salter, Denis (1996). "China's Theatre of Dissent: A Conversation with Mou Sen and Wu Wenguang." *Asian Theatre Journal*, Vol. 13, No. 2, pp. 218–228.

Schmidt, Paul, ed. (1981). *Meyerhold at Work.* Trans. Ilya Levin and Vern McGee. Manchester: Carcanet New Press.

Scott, A. C. (1983). "The Performance of Classical Theater." In Mackerras, ed. (1983), pp. 118–144.

Spolin, Viola (1973). *Improvisation for the Theatre: A Handbook of Teaching and Directing Techniques.* London: Pitman.

Stanislavsky, Konstantin (1967). *Stanislavsky On the Art of the Stage*, 2nd ed. Trans. David Magarshack. London: Faber and Faber.

Tian Benxiang 田本相, ed. (1998). *Huawen xi hui* 華文戲薈 [Meetings of Chinese drama]. Beijing: Zhongguo xiju chubanshe 中國戲劇出版社.

Tong Daoming 童道明 (1981). "Meiyehede de gongxian" 梅耶赫德的貢獻 [The contributions of Meyerhold]. *Wenyi yanjiu* 文藝研究, No. 5, pp. 78–91.

Willet, John (1977). *The Theatre of Bertolt Brecht: A Study from Eight Aspects*, revised ed. London: Eyre Methuen.

Wu Wanru 吳婉茹 (1995). "Zhaoxun xinzhong de lingshan" 找尋心中的靈山 [Searching for the soul mountain in his heart]. Interview by Mei Xin 梅新. *Zhongyang ribao* 中央日報 [Central daily], 22–23 December.

Wu Weimin 吳衛民 (1998), "Lun dangdai Zhongguo wutai de 'xianfeng xiju'" 論當代中國舞台的"先鋒戲劇" [On "avant-garde theatre" of the contemporary Chinese stage]. In Tian, ed. (1998), pp. 78–102.

Xia Xieshi 夏寫時 and Lu Runtang (Yun-tong Luk) 陸潤棠, eds. (1988). *Bijiao xiju lunwen ji* 比較戲劇論文集 [Essays on comparative drama]. Beijing: Zhongguo xiju chubanshe 中國戲劇出版社.

Yao Wenfang 姚文放 (1997). *Zhongguo xiju meixue de wenhua chanshi* 中國戲劇美學的文化闡釋 [The cultural interpretation of Chinese dramatic aesthetics]. Beijing: Zhongguo renmin daxue chubanshe 中國人民大學出版社.

Yu, Anthony C. (1997). *Reading the Stone: Desire and the Making of Fiction in* Dream of the Red Chamber. Princeton: Princeton University Press.

Yu Pingbo 俞平伯 (1988). *Yu Pingbo lun* Hongloumeng 俞平伯論紅樓夢 [Yu Pingbo on *Dream of the Red Chamber*]. Shanghai: Shanghai guji chubanshe 上海古籍出版社; Hong Kong: Sanlian shudian 三聯書店.

Yu Yingshi 余英時 (1978). Hongloumeng *de liangge shijie* 紅樓夢的兩個世界 [The two worlds of *Dream of the Red Chamber*]. Taipei: Lianjing chuban shiye gongsi 聯經出版事業公司.

Zheng Baoyin 鄭寶寅 (1990). *Chuantong wenhua yu gudian xiqu* 傳統文化與古典戲曲 [Traditional culture and ancient xiqu]. Wuhan: Hubei jiaoyu chubanshe 湖北教育出版社.

Zhou Jie 周捷 (1990). "Cong *Zhongguo meng* kan xieyi xiju de shenmei texing" 從《中國夢》看寫意戲劇的審美特性 [Observing the aesthetic characteristics of xieyi drama from *China Dream*]. *Huaju* 話劇, No. 5, pp. 8–16.

Zou, Jiping (1994). "Gao Xingjian and Chinese Experimental Theatre." Ph.D. thesis, University of Illinois at Urbana-Champaign.

Gao Xingjian and the Asian Experimentation in Postmodernist Performance[1]

Any study of the postmodernist performance in theatre must begin with an examination of how the representational nature of drama, which is defined by Aristotle as imitation, has been affected and transformed by the globalized culture industry, which is a hallmark of postmodernity, and in which all images and representations cease to function as "promotional accessories to economic products" (Connor, 1989, p. 46). In the postmodern mode, images and representations are the products themselves and an end, rather than a means, in the process of representation.

In the modernists from Ibsen, Chekhov, Pirandello and Brecht to the Absurdists, there is a persistent struggle to break from the Aristotelian formulation of drama as imitation, that is, a means through which the representation of a reality as an end is made possible. This struggle to break away from the prison house of the Aristotelian structure is never complete in the modernist experiments. By replacing the scene of "resolution" with the scene of "discussion/confrontation," Ibsen has only modified the Aristotelian structure by injecting into it a sense of skepticism, which is still representational in function. Chekhov's directionlessness, Pirandello's cubism, Brecht's estrangement, and the Absurdists' plotlessness also fall within the realm of representational drama, which encompasses a structure with a modified beginning, middle and end. The modernist experimentation succeeds only in modifying the Aristotelian structure so that it can accommodate new and even conflicting perspectives on the reality to be represented. In other words, the experimentation in the modernist theatre has at its best questioned and challenged the formal aspects of Aristotelian drama, but has not gone beyond the function of the theatre as representation, and in this function representation serves no more than as a means.

PERFORMANCE IN POSTMODERNIST THEATRE

The postmodernist theatre can be defined, in Jean-Françoise Lyotard's term, as a theatre based on the "performativity" of a theatre language, which is completely divorced from its previous representational function in becoming a product of the culture industry. As an attempt to break away from the Aristotelian theatre based on a totalizing reason which believes in a reality that can be imitated, the postmodern theatre sees itself as concerned with the practices of representation. In his book, *The Idea of the Postmodern: A History,* Hans Bertens summarizes the major tenets of postmodernism as an attitude developed from the 1960s counterculture, which is both anti-representational and self-reflexive. By being anti-representational, postmodernist art is self-referential, with its significance lying not in any external referent, but in itself. And by being self-reflexive, postmodernist art is concerned with the metalanguage of its form. Put in this way, the postmodernist theatre is a theatre in which only performance remains, and this performance is meant to be deconstructionist.

Considering art as an institution, which involves the power of shaping in cultural formation, the postmodernist theatre with an emphasis on self-reflexivity explores the relation between discourse and power in the constitution of the subject and identity. It is this concern of postmodernist art with practices of representation, image and identity, and the formation of the subject that much of it has to do with cultural politics. As institution and as discourse, the postmodernist theatre itself can be seen as a matter of cultural practices that necessarily entail the power of constitution. Hence, in any study of the postmodernist theatre, the discursive function of the form must be discussed. And in so doing, any understanding of the postmodernist theatre must begin with an examination of subject formation in relation to the theatre arts as institution.

In terms of its art form, the postmodernist theatre lays great stress upon the contingency of performance, rather than upon an "abstraction of the idea of the work-in-itself" (Connor, 1989, p. 134). The Aristotelian structure of "beginning-middle-end" is thus seen in postmodernist performance as a process, the purpose of which, as Ihab Hassan says, lies in a poetics of "unmaking." The postmodernist theatre is a theatre which does not believe in the possibility of an essence, and in which only performance counts, as Joel Weinsheimer says: "The playing of the play is the play itself" (Weinsheimer, 1985, p. 109). In this way, it can be said that the postmodernist theatre has its origin in Antonin Artaud's Theatre of Cruelty, in that theatrical performance is given importance over ideas, and silence over language. The postmodernist theatre is a theatre of performance, rather than a theatre of the abstraction of idea, for performance itself is form, essence and idea. As Steven Connor comments, "The result of this is a theatre theoretically coiled in upon itself, in which work, performance and audience-effect fission together in a powerfully externalized unity" (Connor, 1989, p. 135). Hence, in the postmodernist theatre there is a heavy reliance on parody as a device to critique the practices of representation.

As a theatre depending on the contingency of performance, the postmodernist theatre is reflexive of its form and existence, "calling attention to the fact that it [is] being made and how it [is] made" (Brockett and Findlay, 1991, p. 430). It is a theatre of performance, as well as a theatre about itself. Considered in this way, the poetics of unmaking in postmodernism is particularly meaningful in that in the theatre the world is seen as being unmade into a world in the making, in which the human subject unfolds as a process of subjectivity in the making as well. Previous concepts of plot and characterization, no matter whether they are in the Aristotelian or modernist sense, no longer exist in the postmodernist theatre. Critical categories of psyche, dream, distortion and plotlessness in modernist poetics are no longer the defining qualities of the postmodernist theatre, which offers a new poetics of collage in playing with discontinuities and inconsistencies always in the making and unmaking.

GAO XINGJIAN AND THE CHINESE EXPERIMENTATION WITH THE POSTMODERN

A rethinking of the cultural formation of the subject can be found in the new Chinese theatre, which takes the form of a quest for cultural roots. The new dramatic forms experimented with on the Chinese stage are mainly attempts to break away from the Aristotelian tradition of realistic imitation. The contemporary theatre in China began in the 1980s with theatrical innovations in breaking from the Ibsenian theatre toward a loose structure and impressionistic style of acting. Yet toward the end of the 1980s, there already emerged signs of a new theatre. These new plays begin with the experimentation with a metalanguage that questions firstly the existence of reality, and secondly the relation between reality and representation.

The new theatrical forms which emerged in the 1980s serve not only as an oppositional cultural discourse to the state ideology and institution, they are also critical, skeptical and self-reflexive in nature and are therefore involved with an examination of the metalanguage of theatre. Almost all the new experiments in the 1980s attempted to break down the fourth wall between performance and the audience. On the surface, this seems to be indebted to the Brechtian aesthetics of critical estrangement, but in the context of Chinese theatre (which has a long *xiqu* tradition of critical estrangement) the cross-dialogue between the characters and the audience is an attempt to maximize the performance so that the audience can also participate in it, and to undermine the authority as well as the ideological shaping power, via the process of identification, of the performance.

The cultural politics of the new theatre can be seen in its provision of alternative perspectives and contrastive styles, which are reflexive upon the nature of performance. Examples of this new theatre can be found in *Chezhan* 車站 [The bus-stop, 1983], which is critical of both the theatrical practices of representation and the relation between theatre and time. The detachment of the actors from the characters at the end of the play, *The Bus-Stop*, is a device to provide a metatheatrical perspective which is meant to be critical of the form. At a philosophical level, the farcical performance, role playing, cross-dialogue, and debate in the play are devices of parody and critique that are meant to achieve a certain degree of postmodernist self-reflexivity. In the play, the nature of time as a linear scheme, in which human subjectivity is historicized, is challenged and questioned at both philosophical and psychological levels.

Being reflexive and cubist in experimentation, the new Chinese plays in the 1980s examine their own theatrical form as a metalanguage. In the "Notes for Production of the Play" appended to *Yeren* 野人 [Wild man, 1985], Gao Xingjian has the following observation on the use of overlapping counter-points in musical structure that can be experimented with in a play:

> Interwoven in the play are several different themes that produce multiple tones, so that they overlap to give a sense of harmony, as well as disharmony. The overlaps form counter-points, like those in a musical structure. Not

only are there multiple tones in language, when language overlaps with music and sound, they produce multiplicity that will form counter points with scenery. The effect is the same as the impression that a symphony attempts to achieve by means of overlaps and repetition in themes, language and sound.

Thematic multiplicity, as well as the polyphonic use of language, has to be realized in the multiple dimensions of performance. For example, before an actor enters, he may have some interaction with the audience. This is one dimension of performance. After he enters, the actor may, as an actor, recite to the audience. This is another dimension. The character that an actor plays may be a character living in the present, or he may also be a shadow in the background scenery. (Gao, 1985, p. 169)

The technique of overlapping and repetition produces an effect of collage and multiplicity not only in the depiction of the natural man as dehumanized and contaminated by culture, but also in its postmodernist representation of the fragmentation of the self. In the actor's various roles, the acting subject is split in its being both actor and character. Such a split in roles is also a split in subjectivity, a theme that the play presents and also an effect in the actor's self-reflexivity that Gao wishes to explore.

The self-reflexivity of the postmodernist theatre is further developed in Gao Xingjian's *Bi'an* 彼岸 [The other shore, 1986], which is a parody as well as a ridicule of the falsity and artificiality of the theatre in its realistic function of imitation. The play begins with a group of actors improvising on the stage by imagining various possible interactions with a rope which is used to symbolize human relationships. With a higher degree of abstraction, *The Other Shore* is a skeptical repudiation of human rationality and the totalizing reason. In the "Notes for Production of the Play," Gao Xingjian gives an idea about the essence of such performance, which is summarized as follows:

1. Drama should be liberated from the confinement of language;
2. The ideal performance should be a combination of the elements of body movement, language and psychology;
3. Through performance the actors can reach a state of sensory abstraction, rather than a state of philosophical abstraction;
4. The play does not need any elaborate props, except for a few pieces of furniture. The idea is to let actors interact with the environment;

5. Through performance the actors will build up a concrete relationship with imaginary objects on the stage;
6. Grotowski's method is to help the actors discover their selves.
   Through rehearsal, actors can assert their selves, which are self-
   reflexive selves.
7. The play requires the actors to break from the performance which
   is based on logical thinking. The most lively performance is based
   on intuition, empty presence, and improvisation;
8. The play is simply meant to train actors, rather than to present a
   new type of theatre; and
9. The purpose of the play is to maximize the expressive power of
   language, rather than to minimize it. Language includes all sounds
   that occur during the performance, and not just dialogue, which
   does not even have to be grammatical or bear meaning.

                                                    (Gao, 1986, p. 251)

These points can be considered as a manifesto of the new Chinese theatre,
which ushers in the postmodernist performance that has begun to take
shape since the mid-1980s.

CULTURAL FORMATION OF THE SUBJECT

A new perspective on the character as subject in cultural formation is
also explored by other playwrights in the postmodernist theatre in China.
While Gao Xingjian's *Wild Man* examines the cultural formation of the
human subject, Sha Yexin's 沙葉新 *Jiaru wo shi zhende* 假如我是真的 [The
imposter, 1979] probes the issue of identity as social belief not based on
any essence of the individual. In both plays, there is use of farce as performance style. Different from the presentation of characters from multiple perspectives in Brechtian drama, both plays attempt to explore the
multiplicity of human subjectivity. From a feminist perspective, Sha Yexin
further explores the relation between gender as a cultural construct and
the shaping power of the socialist discourse in China. The play *Xunzhao
nanzi han* 尋找男子漢 [In search of masculine man, 1986] explores the
cultural formation of masculinity and questions the social foundation of
political patriarchy in China. The play is presented on a minimal stage
with the female protagonist debating on repressed masculinity and
the repressive function of contemporary politics. The treatment of the

theatre as a forum for cultural critique and rethinking can further be found in Sha Yexin's play *Yeshu, Kongzi, pitoushi Leinong* 耶穌、孔子、披頭士列儂 [Jesus, Confucius and John Lennon, 1987]. The play is a good example of the postmodernist technique of collage, which juxtaposes different spatial and temporal dimensions into a new contradictory space. Sha's other play, *Yige sizhe dui shengzhe de fangwen* 一個死者對生者的訪問 [The dead's interview with the living, 1985], which experiments with the cultural values in psychology and social consciousness, can be read profitably with the Japanese playwright Abe Kōbō's 安部公房 *You, Too, Are Guilty* (which will be discussed below).

The "resistance" countering the dominant culture industry can be found in the theatre, television, film, music and other forms of media that has developed in China since the mid-1980s. A new form of theatre, the experimental theatre, has emerged in China (mainly in Beijing) over the past fifteen years as an alternative mode of cultural critique that has experimented with postmodernist styles of performance and concepts of representation. If the theatre in China in the pre-1980s can be characterized as the directors' theatre (for the predominance of the directors' influence in the stage style), the experimental theatre in China in the 1980s can be labelled as the actors' theatre, in which the playwrights have adopted the perspectives of the actors. The further experiments in the 1990s can be seen as an extension of the postmodernist project that began in the 1980s. The work of the two leading Chinese avant-garde dramatists, Gao Xingjian and Sha Yexin, has been further developed by young stage directors, in whose productions there is an emphasis on the sensational impact upon the audience through the performance which relies heavily on physical gesture and movement. This is a further development of the idea of a "Chinese poor theatre," which is inspired by Grotowski and put into form by Gao Xingjian. Take for instance the play *Wo ai XXX* 我愛XXX [I love something something, 1993], produced by Meng Jinghui 孟京輝. A Chinese major graduated from Beijing Normal University and received training in the theatre at the Central Academy of Drama, Meng is currently director of the Central Experimental Theatre. In the play there is rock music and dance, mixed with Chinese acrobatics, to produce visual effects of chaos, polyphony, repetition and disharmony. Yet after the scene of visual movement and chaos, the stage suddenly changes to a scene composed mainly of repetitive speeches constructed on a number of contradictory sentences based on the theme

"I love something something." The speeches are delivered by two actors against the backdrop of slide projections of scenes taken from documentary films about revolutions, wars, strikes and demonstrations that occurred in the 1960s and 1970s. This scene of speeches reminds the audience of the revolutionary speeches popular in the Cultural Revolution. It also creates a strong ironic effect which trivializes and negates what is meant to be great in revolution. At the metatheatrical level, the production explicitly shows that on the stage only movement and gesture remain to carry meaning, while dialogue is reduced to the function of punctuation or footnote.

In Wang Shuo's 王朔 screen plays published and produced in the 1990s, there is a great deal of political and cultural critique, which consists of obvious elements of parody delivered in both physical movement and dialogue. *Bianzi bu* 編輯部 [The editorial department, 1992], a screenplay serialized on the TV, is an example of this use of parody that skillfully makes fun of not only the characters, but also the audience. Similar to the productions in the style of the experimental theatre, the dialogue in the play is meant not only to carry verbal message, but also to support the parody function of the stage movements and gestures. Instead of relying on a debate or cross-dialogue with the audience, a technique widely used in the Chinese plays of the 1980s, the experimental plays in the 1990s make full use of the stage as a playground where both the actors and audience mock each other and are mocked.

THE POSTMODERN CONDITION AND ASIAN EXPERIENCE

To a considerable extent, the contemporary Japanese theatre since the 1960s, too, can be regarded as postmodernist. In the plays, Abe Kōbō's *Omae nimo Tsumi ga aru* お前にも罪があろ [You, too, are guilty, 1965] and Yamazaki Masakazu's *Fune wa Hobune yo* 舟は帆船よ [The boat is a sailboat, 1973], there are postmodernist attempts concerned with "unmaking" the basic situations of human existence in contemporary Japan. Both plays are set in a modern apartment, which is so ordinary that it may represent any apartment in Japan. Reminiscent of the room symbolism in Harold Pinter's plays, the apartment in the two plays is meant to bear a sense of universality through its ordinariness. The apartment may metaphorically also signify the human predicament in modern life.

You, Too, Are Guilty is a one-man play in which the audience is presented with the story of how a man reacts to an absurdist situation in life. The fact that the protagonist remains anonymous, but is just referred to as the Man, denotes his minimally reduced individual significance. None of the characters in the play has a name. They are not individuals, but universalized beings, whose identity can be interchanged. The dialogue between the Man and the imagined police detective reveals the Man's inner sense of guilt. The imagined police detective is in fact the other self of the Man, who is tormented by his inner sense of guilt. The absurdity of the situation, as well as the failure of the rational approach in argument, is evident of the collapse of a totalizing reason in contemporary Japanese life.

What is interesting in the play is not whether the murder is discovered, but the split self of the Man and the sense of sin inherent in him. A number of other things, which are of tremendously important thematic significance, can also be found in the play: the Man's principle of non-involvement, or self-centredness, the Dead Body's idea of social memory as a kind of insurance, the Man's confusion of his own identity, and inconsistencies. The conversation between the Man and the Dead Body reveals so much about life in contemporary Japanese society, in which the significance of individual existence is so absurdly and minimally reduced that an individual can only be identified in terms of his social connections.

The Dead Body's argument with the Man can be read as a ridicule of contemporary life and social conventions. Nationality, name and status no longer represent individual qualities, but serve merely as labels for an individual lost in an ocean of others. A contemporary man has no individuality. The apartment which he lives in is, unfortunately and ironically, the same as all the others in the same building and it can be opened by the same key. The Man's subsequent reaction to the Dead Body is a sign of his inner sense of insecurity. It is this sense of fear and insecurity which prompts him to act in a selfish way, trying to cover up the murder. Obviously, the play is not about murder, but about the psyche of a modern man facing a crisis.

In this play Abe Kōbō addresses questions of identity and individuality by placing the individual in a world of inconsistencies. Besides the *tatami,* there is nothing in the play, which is particularly Japanese. Like Abe's other works, *You, Too, are Guilty* is concerned with not only life in contemporary Japanese society, but also a general condition of human existence in the lack of individual essence. What is more interesting about this play is the use of performance in the Artaudian sense of the theatrical instead of "language and concepts of the rational mind" (Russell, 1987, p. 354). The play begins with a scene in a very Artaudian manner of performance. It focuses on interaction between two characters, the Man Next Door and the Woman Next Door. The scene is full of gesture and stage movement, but there is minimal dialogue only in the form of two monologue exchanges, which end with an ironic note: "if you trust society, there's nothing to be afraid of" (Abe, 1978, p. 3). Why? Because society is not a rational organization. The debate between the Man and the Dead Body is a way to show that rationality does not work in a situation of inconsistencies. The act of removing the corpse at the end of the play significantly and symbolically brings an end to a debate or dialogue: All language fails, and only action counts.

Yamazaki's *The Boat is a Sailboat* is not so much about an absurd situation in which rationality does not work. In this play, the problems of identity and subject formation among the new generation of Japanese are more specifically dealt with. The absent character, Murai, appears as a mysterious figure throughout the play. He is actually the personification of the general humanity in Japan. In this play, the author also makes use of an apartment to serve as a label for the person who lives in it. Having no individuality and being rootless, men's identities are taken by others as interchangeable, replaceable and are easily confused. Like a hole in the beehive, by which a bee is given its social place and degree of importance, the apartment in the play functions as a social centre for the role the person is supposed to play. Just because Tatsuno has moved to Murai's apartment, Tatsuno is treated by all the other characters as another Murai. In fact, the point is not whether it is Tatsuno or another person who has moved into the apartment. The other people are responsible for confusing Tatsuno's identity, for they themselves are all confused about it. At the end of the play, even Satomi seems not to be quite sure of Tatsuno's identity when he says that a criminal suspect has a marked resemblance with Tatsuno.

Presented in the two Japanese plays discussed above is a picture of the postmodern condition in Japan, in which there is the lack of self identity and the individual exists in isolation from society and in exchangeable identity. In this condition, as evidenced in the case of Tatsuno, only discourse matters, and it is discourse that institutionalizes and shapes people's thinking. In other words, postmodern identity is only a product of language. Tatsuno becomes Murai because everybody including himself believes that he is.

As seen in contemporary Chinese and Japanese theatre, the postmodernist mode of thinking can be discussed in terms of the quest for cultural roots for identity and subject formation in situations of dislocation and disintegration. In his book *The Location of Culture*, Homi Bhabha thinks that the sense of "homeness," or "sense of belonging," serves as the basis in the process of identity formation. Common to both the post-Cultural Revolution Chinese and the postwar Japanese, is their lack of a sense of "homeness," as well as their cultural alienation. As Homi Bhabha points out, "The unhomely moment relates the traumatic ambivalences of a personal, psychic history to the wider disjunctions of political existence" (Bhabha, 1994, p. 11). The social absurdities that occurred in post-Mao China and the Existentialist anxieties in contemporary Japan have shattered all beliefs in a totalizing reason. Traditionally both China and Japan are relatively stable societies with definable human relations. But as seen in *You, Too, Are Guilty*, *The Boat is a Sailboat*, *The Bus-Stop*, *Wild Man* and *The Other Shore*, nothing in society or in human relations remains stable or permanent. Whether they are Chinese or Japanese, contemporary people exist in dislocation, transience, and continual loss.

The parody and emptiness of language presented on stage is reflexive of this condition of the "Unhomed." The dramatists discussed present a world which is absurd and without essence. What remains is language as "discourse," which constitutes and positions the subject in relation to others. Yamazaki's play *The Boat is a Sailboat* vividly describes this condition in which the subject is shaped by language, rather than by any intrinsic qualities of a person. One is not what one is, but what other people perceive one to be. There is a similar exploration of this problem of subject formation in the Chinese experimental plays, such as Gao Xingjian's *The Other Shore* and Meng Jinghui's *I Love Something Something*. If the world is absurd and nothing has intrinsic qualities, then the theatre also does not have an essence of its own, except for the guarantee of a stage, which provides space for "the playing of a play" that presents rather than represents. In such a world, what a dramatist is left with is performance. As Gao Xingjian says, performance is make-believe and should not be replaced simply by the presentation of ideas and

philosophy, although ideas and philosophy cannot be absent from a
play.

NOTE

1. This is a revised version of the paper, "Postmodernist Performance in Contemporary Chinese and Japanese Theatre," which was first read at a conference on Asian Performance held in Hong Kong in 1994, later published in
   Lee and Ooi, eds. (1996), pp. 43–49, and reprinted in *Performing Arts International*, Vol. 3, Part 2 (1999), pp. 65–73.

REFERENCES

Abe Kōbō 安部公房 (1978). *Omae nimo Tsumi ga aru* お前にも罪があろ [You, too,
    are guilty]. Tokyo: Shinchōsha 新潮社. English translation in Takaya, ed. and
    trans. (1979), pp. 3–40.
Bhabha, Homi K. (1995). *The Location of Culture*. London: Routledge.
Bertens, Hans (1995). *The Idea of the Postmodern: A History*. London and New
    York: Routledge.
Brockett, Oscar C., and Robert Findlay (1991). *Century of Innovation: A History of
    European and American Theatre and Drama Since the Late Nineteenth Century*. 2nd
    ed. Boston: Allyn and Bacon.
Connor, Steven (1989). *Postmodernist Culture: An Introduction to Theories of the
    Contemporary*. Oxford: Blackwell.
Gao Xingjian 高行健 (1983). *Chezhan* 車站 [The bus-stop]. *Shiyue* 十月, No. 3,
    pp. 119–189.
—— (1985). *Yeren* 野人 [Wild man]. *Shiyue* 十月, No. 2, pp. 145–169.
—— (1986). *Bi'an* 彼岸 [The other shore]. *Shiyue* 十月, No. 5, pp. 238–251.
Lee, A. Robert, and Vicki Ooi, eds. (1996). *Old Worlds, New Worlds*. Hong Kong:
    International Association of Theatre Critics.
Lyotard, Jean-François (1979). *The Postmodern Condition: A Report on Knowledge*.
    Trans. Geoff Bennington and Brian Massumi. Manchester: Manchester Uni-
    versity Press.
Russell, Douglas A. (1987). *Period Style for the Theatre*. 2nd ed. Boston: Allyn and
    Bacon.
Sha Yexin 沙葉新 (1986). *Xunzhao nanzi han* 尋找男子漢 [In search of masculine
    man]. *Shiyue* 十月, No. 3, pp. 155–177.
Takaya, Ted T., ed. and trans. (1979). *Modern Japanese Drama: An Anthology*. New
    York: Columbia University Press.
Tam, Kwok-kan (1996). "Postmodernist Performance in Contemporary Chinese

and Japanese Theatre." In Lee and Ooi, eds. (1996), pp. 43–49. Reprinted in *Performing Arts International*, Vol 3, Part 2 (1999), pp. 65–73.

Weinsheimer, Joel C. (1985). *Gadamer's Hermeneutics: A Reading of* Truth and Method. New Haven: Yale University Press.

Yamazaki Mazakaru 山崎正和 (1971). *Fune wa Hobune yo* 舟は帆船よ [The boat is a sailboat]. Tokyo: Shinchōsha 新潮社. English translation in Takaya, ed. and trans. (1979), pp. 139–202.

Gender and Self in Gao Xingjian's Three Post-Exile Plays

As a playwright, Gao Xingjian has been known for his experimentation with Western avant-garde forms. In his pre-exile plays *Juedui xinhao* 絕對信號 [Alarm signal, 1982] and *Chezhan* 車站 [The bus-stop, 1983], for example, he tries various theatrical means to represent not just social reality but also psychological reality on the contemporary Chinese stage.[1] In his mid-1980s plays, Gao's effort to revive the declining contemporary Chinese theatre is characterized by his conscious attempt to explore various modes of theatrical performance. Thus in the plays, *Dubai* 獨白 [Monologue, 1985], *Yeren* 野人 [Wild man, 1985] and *Bi'an* 彼岸 [The other shore, 1986], he made attempts to address the problems of traditional forms of performance for a contemporary theatre. A close look at Gao's post-exile plays, however, reveals a clear departure from his earlier belief in saving the national theatre through theatrical experimentation, a mission that he comes to realize as too much of a moral and political burden for any playwright in contemporary China. The inclusion of traditional theatrical elements in the three plays, *Shengsijie* 生死界 [Between life and death, 1991], *Duihua yu fanjie* 對話與反詰 [Dialogue and rebuttal, 1992] and *Yeyoushen* 夜遊神 [Nocturnal wanderer, 1993], clearly marks a new orientation in Gao's experiments.

Gao finds the Chinese Zen Buddhist way of communication, which aims at conveying the message beyond the limit of human language, intriguing and attempts to explore the notion of language, subjectivity, self and gender on the stage. The dialogue in the form of *gong-an* story-telling is adopted to provide a space of "cross-subjectivity" communication between the characters. Story-telling is thus not simply a matter of form, but also of message. In such performances, the audience is led to think along the lines of "cross-subjectivity" dialogue. Hence, messages are communicated to the audience through a dialectical mode of question and answer between the characters. One may perhaps raise the question: Are Gao's later plays just another experiment with a new form? In postmodernist performance, form is of course message. In that case, can one conclude by saying that Gao's later plays amount to nothing, except form? Experimentation in form is extremely important if a playwright wishes to break new grounds or develop innovative theatrical techniques. Playwrights such as Henrik Ibsen, Bernard Shaw, August Strindberg, Eugene O'Neill, Bertolt Brecht, Arthur Miller and Samuel Beckett all have made significant contribution to drama through their innovations in form that can incorporate new elements in the representation of subjectivity. There is always a new vision, a new philosophy in each of the innovations made by these playwrights. In the case of Gao, it is necessary to go beyond the form to discover the significance of his theatrical experiments as well as to get a glimpse of the playwright's vision of life and human existence.

While the use of pronouns to represent the split selves and changing subject positions is nothing new, Gao extends the limit of such a technique. In modern drama, both Eugene O'Neill and Arthur Miller see it as a challenge to represent in visual theatrical terms the "stream-of-consciousness" of a person who is torn between his or her split selves. In doing so, the dramatist must overcome the difficulty of presenting the psychological states of a person in abstract terms and be able to render them into effects that are concrete and visible on the stage. In the case of Gao Xingjian, his method is considered innovative in that he allows the multiple facets of self in the character to be realized in various roles played by the same actor and these selves are registered by different pronouns of "I," "you," "he" and "she." It is worth noting that in the Chinese language, the use of pronouns to address multiple facets of self is not new, but to represent the self as split entails a psychoanalytical dimension. Such a representation, which is absent in traditional Chinese philosophical inquiry, re-orientates the way of perceiving the self as psychical processes.

THE SELF BEYOND PSYCHOANALYSIS

Notions of the self and its formation involve complex theorization. Broadly speaking, there are two large frameworks in which theories of the self can be placed for a critical re-examination, namely, social constructivism and psychoanalysis. Methodologically, both of these frameworks rely on the construction of the "other" as the "referent" for the construction of the "self" (Lacan, 1981, pp. 263–276). In the case of the "cultural self," the construction of the "cultural other" is particularly significant. In all existing paradigms, the "cultural other" is constructed on the assumption of culture as a community that is stable and fixed, and hence bound. Freud's attempt to define femininity as the opposite of masculinity is to place the "female self" in a dialectical relation with its "sexual other" (Freud, 1965). That is to say, female subjectivity has to be understood as psychoanalytical processes in opposition to its male counterpart. Such an approach, as well as all subsequent efforts in the psychoanalytic definition of gender, relies on the construction of a "gendered other." In the study of gender subjectivity, the construction of the "self" as an antithesis to the "other" thus betrays an inclination toward analytical philosophy in the Cartesian paradigm which, at its best, accounts for what constitutes "difference" and "duality" in the opposition between the subject and the object.

While Freud sees language as a tool for expression of the unconscious, Lacan focuses on the dialogical function of language in the constitution of the subject. In both theoretical orientations, language is seen as a manifestation of the unconscious. But they fail to shed light on the originary self, which is asexual in its primordial mode of existence. This self in its state of being is what Gao Xingjian calls "the self in chaos" [混沌 hundun], a state of non-distinction between subject and object, between self and other, between male and female, and between mind and body (Gao, 1996, pp. 250). Gao Xingjian's interest in the self is not just to show how the self can be understood through processes of detachment and objectification, that is, the use of pronouns. In his early works, he has already experimented with such processes. In the later plays, however, he seeks to return to the originary self as a way to explore human existence in its primordial state. Different from all existing paradigms, Gao does not simply situate the "self" in the context of gender/sexual opposition. He sees the role language plays in the formation of the self, but he attempts to go beyond language to uncover the preconscious mode of self that is lost in such a formation.

Gao believes that the true self lies in the prelinguistic state of human consciousness. Gao's approach is very much in line with the Daoist concept of intuition that emphasizes the non-linguistic and non-intellectual state of being. In the philosophy of Laozi and Zhuangzi, however, the self remains a perceiving subject that tries to go beyond the intellectual boundaries set by language. In Gao's theatrical experiments, the self is presented as both the perceiving subject as well as the perceived object. By adopting the method of "self-transcendent observation" [抽身靜觀 choushen jingguan], which he took from Chinese Zen Buddhism and used in his middle and later plays, Gao shows a prelinguistic state in which the self is presented in a state of primordial non-distinction. The self is thus represented in a dualistic state of being as both the subject and the object. In such a state, the self is at the same time "subject-in-object" and also "object-in-subject." This dualistic self as "subject-object" that transcends mere bodily experience is what Gao considers as the originary self.

Gao's exploration of the originary self begins with an inquiry into gendered subjectivity as informed by feminist psychoanalysis. Feminists have critiqued both Freud and Lacan for their lack of a theoretical account of the pre-Oedipal stage in the constitution of the subject (Kristeva, 1977, pp. 16–29). In post-Freudian psychoanalysis, the theorization of subject formation has rerouted its course from an interest in the Oedipal to a focus on the pre-Oedipal stage. Psychoanalysts, especially feminists, believe that the ungendered self exists only for a short period in the pre-Oedipal stage, in which "sexual difference does not exist" (Moi, 1985, p. 164). Yet, it is the pre-Oedipal stage that plays a crucial role in gender formation (Chodorow, 1978). Seen in this light, Gao Xingjian's later plays can be read as theatrical experimentations with (un)gendered subjectivity as well. It is this stage of human preconscious that Gao Xingjian finds most intriguing. His plays *Between Life and Death*, *Nocturnal Wanderer* and *Dialogue and Rebuttal* can thus be read as a trilogy in the deconstruction of gendered subjectivity, as well as an exploration of the originary self.

DECONSTRUCTING "FEMALE IMAGINATION"

Between Life and Death examines gendered subjectivity in relation to both language and the female body. By placing the female in opposition to the male, Gao presents at the beginning of his play a dream in which a middle-aged woman constructs her female self as the "other" of the male self. In a detached and neutral way, the actress narrates the Woman's imagination of her man, while the actor playing the role of the Woman's man attempts but in vain to respond to the Woman's remarks about their relationship. In the Woman's imagination, the Man is constructed but also reduced to a shadow without life. Throughout the play, the actor remains silent. In such a dream state, the Woman reveals her hidden desires, anxieties and frustrations. She complains about the Man's infidelity and non-commitment in love. As the play develops, the Woman's fear of losing her man is shown to be the cause of her possessiveness. In the process of imagining her idealized man, she has in effect demasculinized and negated her man, reducing him to merely "clothes on a hanger" (Gao, 1995c, p. 12). As the Woman admits, the male self is killed in her imaginary construction:

> Woman: (*She kneels on the ground before a pile of folded clothing. In front of the clothing lies a pair of men's shoes; on top of the shoes is a man's hat. Next to her is a leather jewellery box.*) She says she's never, ever in her life thought that it would end like this, that she would actually kill her man, her darling, her treasure, her little zebra, her sika deer, her sweetheart, her root in life.[2]   (Gao, 1995c, p. 13)

As the Man is constructed by the Woman in her imagination, he is only her other self and not a real "other." When the Woman wakes up from her dream, she is terrified by her own unconscious act, that is, the killing of the Man, who poses as her "other" and helps define her "self." It is interesting to note that in her dream construction, the Woman at the same time deconstructs herself as well as her imagination:

> Woman: (*Panting.*) No.... (*Beginning to feel terrified.*) She wants to know if her fear is also real. Maybe she only thinks she's afraid but actually she's not? She must experience death once to find out what death is and to feel its pain, in other words, a living experience of death, then, and only then can she prove that she is still alive, and then she'll know if life is worth living, if it's really necessary. She's suffering from a great pain in analyzing herself in desperate pursuit of her true self, to ascertain herself if her true self is a real woman or just a body without a self.   (Gao, 1995c, p. 15)

The Woman's only escape from this tautology is to flee from her self, from an analytical approach to her "self." Without the Man as her "other," the Woman comes to face her self in direct confrontation and the latter is presented in the image of another woman whom the Woman does not recognize:

> Woman: (*Quietly approaches.*) Who is this woman? She can't help wanting to know, but the woman keeps turning this way ... then that way.... No matter how she tries, she can't see her face clearly. (*Disappointed, she covers her face with her hands.*)   (Gao, 1995c, p. 18)

In one moment, the Woman wonders if she is alive with only a body and not consciousness. In another, when she sees in her hallucination death in the form of a coffin lying in front of her, she again wonders if she is physically dead and only her consciousness remains. In a desperate state, she searches for means to reassure herself of her own existence:

> Woman: (*She wobbles and feels her way along the wall, her head leaning against it.*) She doesn't know what this dream means.... No, she knows, she knows that right now her mind is not clear, she needs to sort things out, how did it all begin and where will it end? Nothing'll go wrong as long as she finds a clue. (*Turns, leaning against the wall.*) But she can't even remember a single incident from her childhood! Does this mean that she has never been alive, or is she just a shadow, the shadow of some nonexistent person? Is her existence just an illusion? No! She definitely had a childhood, she remembers! (*Determinedly gets away from the wall.*)
> (*The wall gradually disappears.*)   (Gao, 1995c, pp. 59–60)

The Woman attempts to reconstruct her self and reaffirms her life through her memory of things past. Her childhood experience with her mother and with a female doctor and the latter's lover surface as causes of her anxieties and sense of guilt. In her recollection, she sees sins in her past, in her own self. These sins are like ghosts haunting her, as in the case in Strindberg's *The Ghost Sonata*. She thus appeals to Buddha in an effort to redeem her self:

> Woman: She feels she's like gliding on a glacier and she can't stop. She sees only a big mass of blackness, any time now she's going to slip into the cracked icy layers and plunge into the deep dark water of death. After she dies all will vanish in an instant like snowflakes in water.

> The world is such a large place, she's not the only person living in it, she's not important, just let her vanish, let her be forgotten, ignored, and let her end in it once and for all.... But she can't free herself from the old grudges, the jealousy, the greed, the worries, and the anxieties. She knows what the Buddha has said about the four elements of life, which are mere emptiness, but she can't free herself from the vanities of human life. So she prays in a whisper, pleading the merciful Bodhisattva to look after her, to help her to sever her ties with the mortal world.   (Gao, 1995c, pp. 31)

The Woman comes to abhor her own body, which tends to confine her to an existence of desire and frustration. She feels fixed and bound incapable of being her true self, a self that remains unknown to her. She longs to be redeemed, to be saved from her physical being defined by her female body with its attraction and repulsion. She wants to free herself from all forms of gendered relationships that tend to weigh her down on earth and tie her to a life of dependence, suffering and unfulfillment. As she remarks,

> She says she sees her filthy body rolling in a puddle of muddy water, in broad daylight, on the side of the road, and in public view, everybody's trampling on her. She's covered with scabies, her voice hoarse, she's crawling and begging, but everyone's swearing at her and turns their back on her. (*Slowly opens her eyes.*)
>
> (*A nun with an iron-like grey complexion appears. She is enwrapped in a grey kasaya, a Buddhist robe, her eyes lowered and her hair worn in a bun. She is sitting up straight on a futon in a high place with her legs crossed and her palms clasped.*)
>
> Woman: She says she sees a Bodhisattva, her palms clasped together, sitting on top of a lotus flower platform.
>
> (*She approaches slowly and cautiously.*) She looks more closely, it's not a lotus flower.... She looks again, it's not Bodhisattva.... She looks even more carefully, it's a nun meditating with her eyes closed and her hands clasped together.   (Gao, 1995c, pp. 31–32)

The Woman's sight of a Buddhist nun cleansing her intestines brings a philosophical dimension to the discussion of self and gender. The Nun's insistence on cleansing her filthy intestines is symbolic of her conscious attempt to detach herself from mortal ties in the world. Yet, this conscious act itself reveals paradoxically her memory of the mortal world, her inability to abandon worldly cares to arrive at the metaphysical. It thus dawns on the Woman that she has to transcend her body, to arrive at a state of total abandonment and self non-assertion before redemption is possible. With this awakening, a new vision is born upon the Woman, who comes to experience a world of boundlessness in the finite world. The Woman's self finally reaches a state of transcendence when she comes to a better understanding of the world:

> Woman: This world has a form.... This world is elusive.... This world is like the wind.... This world is like a dream.... This world is crude.... This world is clamorous.... This world is lonely.... This world is monotonous....   (Gao, 1995c, p. 40)

"This world" referred to in the above speech is the human world as opposed to "the other shore" in Buddhist enlightenment. In its affirmation of a Buddhist self-transcendent state, in which language and human intellect are null, the play seems to negate the story it tells, for the audience is led to see that the very act of telling a story is in itself an intellectual activity. It is thus interesting to find the play ends with a metaphysical question posed by the Woman about the meaning of the play:

> Woman: Does it tell a story? A romance? A farce? A fable? A joke? An admonishment? Is it an essay because it's not a poem? Or is it a prose poem in the style of an essay but not quite an essay? It's not a song, as it has meaning but no vision. It resembles a riddle, but it has no answer. Is it an illusion, no more than the ramblings in an idiot's dream?
> (Gao, 1995c, p. 41)

When language fails to produce meaning, the speaker speaks without any reference, leaving only the self engaged in a soliloquy:

> Woman: Is this about him, about you, about me, about that her of the Woman, about that her who is not her, not you, not me, and not you or all of you? Just as the her you all see is not her, not me, and not you, it's merely the self, and the me you all see is not me, not her, it's only that so-called self looking at her, looking at me. What more can be said about the you-me?   (Gao, 1995c, p. 41)

At the end of the play, even the self is negated as an effect of "empty" language:

Woman: Again, what is the self? Besides these speeches in hollow words about nothing, what else can be left?   (Gao, 1995c, p. 42)

The irony hidden in the play is that the Woman, who constructs the Man in her imagination, is also the male playwright Gao's construction. Deconstructing the Woman thus necessitates deconstructing the playwright's male imagination.

DECONSTRUCTING "MALE FANTASY"

As in *Between Life and Death*, Gao focuses on the psychological reality of his characters in *Nocturnal Wanderer*. He employs the technique of a dream in a play, in which a young traveller on a train becomes a sleepwalker in his own dream. In the essay "Playwright's Suggestions on the Performance of the Play," Gao Xingjian succinctly states that the play is a "dramatic reinterpretation of some old themes, such as the battle between God and Satan, man and woman, good and evil, salvation and punishment, self and other, as well as consciousness and language" (Gao, 1995d, p. 124). The play seems to deal with the universal condition of human existence. However, when the play is read as a journey into the Sleepwalker's inner self, it can be considered as an inquiry into a man's sense of self and masculinity. In his encounter with the Tramp, the Ruffian, the Prostitute and the Thug, the Sleepwalker's self is tested against his wavering conscience between justice and injustice, courage and cowardice, compassion and indifference, as well as sexual temptation and moral integrity. In constructing the male self of the Sleepwalker, Gao does not rely merely on the female as a projection of the male's "sexual other." Instead, the Sleepwalker is placed in a wider web of social relations for an examination of his self. The Sleepwalker's encounter with the Tramp only affirms his desire to remain a wanderer and an observer of life:

Sleepwalker: (*Goes to the middle of the road.*) Everybody wants to give you a direction, everybody wants to run your life. (*Stops.*) You only want to take a leisurely stroll, without destination. What fun is there if you're told where to go? People like to tell you to do this, to do that and when trouble comes it's you who have to bear the brunt. What is called "destination" is as simple as this: people ask you to chase after a rabbit when it runs away. What about you? (*He turns his head but cannot find Tramp. He shouts.*) You have no destination, no direction. Just walk on and be anywhere.   (Gao, 1995d, p. 59)

The Sleepwalker's subsequent encounters with the Tramp and the Ruffian confirm his perception of the world as mad and of life as purposeless. The Sleepwalker wants to be free, to have peace of mind by being alone. He chooses to take a walk at night to avoid human contact. His encounter with the Prostitute, however, forces him to reexamine his self in relation to his sexual other as well as his masculine self:

Prostitute: She was killed by your imagination. You abused her in your imagination, and then you killed her. It's so typical of men.
Sleepwalker: You say you're not with them, you're entirely different!
Prostitute: But you're a man, all men are the same, they're so egoistic.
Sleepwalker: You say more or less you've got to have a bit of…. (*Hides the suitcase behind him.*)
Prostitute: A bit of what?
Sleepwalker: A bit of compassion … a bit of apprehension … a bit of conscience —
Prostitute: Don't talk about conscience!
Sleepwalker: What then?
Prostitute: The bit of conscience you had vanished a long time ago. That's right, there's only cowardice left in you, which is the difference between you and them, of course you know what's meant by "them." You don't have the courage to act, to do anything. Only in your imagination or in your fantasy can you let yourself go, being ever so wild and unruly, but you're absolutely a coward when it's real.
                    (Gao, 1995d, pp. 100–101)

The Prostitute serves first as an observer and later as a judge of the Sleepwalker's integrity in his interaction with other characters. In his contact with the Prostitute, the Sleepwalker begins to see himself in a new light. As an imagined woman, the Prostitute is a "mirror" for the Sleepwalker to see his self. In such a relationship, the Sleepwalker, who is a male, becomes the "gazed." What complicates the situation is that he is doubly gazed not only by the Prostitute but also by himself. That is why he appears even as a "you" to himself:

Sleepwalker: You say you can admit such difference, but you can't admit that you're a coward —

Prostitute: Don't worry, no one says that you're impotent. It's your so-called "thinking." You only talk to yourself, and you've been using your brain too much to know how to make love with a woman. That's why you haven't been able to get your woman, the kind you've been dreaming about.

Sleepwalker: What kind of woman?

Prostitute: Don't you know? A whore, one who can fulfill your sexual fantasies.

Sleepwalker: (*Hesitates.*) But the question is whether or not she can do it.

Prostitute: There's no way you can find one.

Sleepwalker: Why not?

Prostitute: Because even hookers are human beings and sex to them is only a way of making a living. Isn't it the same with you? You've got to have an occupation. You've got to work whether you like it or not. Aren't you also putting yourself up for sale?

Sleepwalker: (*Retorts.*) You say you're talking about her, and you're asking if she enjoys her work.

Prostitute: Are you talking about her body trade? Or the body she makes a living with? All women are the same, they're not necessarily cold or frigid, nor are they necessarily not wanton. The key is whether you can turn on that special nerve.

Sleepwalker: You ask is she after sensual pleasure?

Prostitute: Maybe it's just the opposite.

Sleepwalker: You ask is she going after emotional gratification but thinks that you're in it for pleasure?

Prostitute: You are wrong.

Sleepwalker: You say she also has spiritual needs, and she's not doing it just for money.

Prostitute: Wrong again.

Sleepwalker: You say then you don't understand.

Prostitute: You're a poor guy.

Sleepwalker: Is it money, or is it violence that women consider sexy?

Prostitute: You're a bore. It's so tiring talking to you. You don't know how to listen to a woman, how to listen to her voice, you never understand a woman.   (Gao, 1995d, pp. 101–102)

In this imagined dialogue, the Sleepwalker projects a woman who serves as his "sexual other" so that he can construct his masculine self. The Prostitute as a wanton female desiring sex is only a revelation, an externalization of the Sleepwalker's male fantasies, latent wishes and hidden desires. Gao presents the Sleepwalker as a coward whose sexual gratification exists only in his imagination of a woman:

> Sleepwalker: You say she covets the devil!
> Prostitute: You're far from being a devil.
> Sleepwalker: You say there's a devil in everyone's heart. The question is whether or not you set it free.
> Prostitute: Your problem is not whether you want to, or whether you're willing to, it's that you're incapable.
> Sleepwalker: You say she's only in it for the pleasure.
> Prostitute: Don't you also want your life to be wild and crazy?
> Sleepwalker: You say she is exactly a broken shoe.
>
> (Gao, 1995d, pp. 104–105)

In the imagined conversation, the devil in the Sleepwalker's unconscious is set free. As an imagined "other," the Prostitute is a device to deconstruct the Sleepwalker's imagination about women. His failure to hear the woman's voice makes him incapable of understanding the woman he has constructed.

The Sleepwalker's confrontation with the Thug further confirms the fact that the Sleepwalker exists as both the gazer-subject as well as the gazed-object in the sexual and moral sense. He feels trapped, with eyes watching him all the time. The Thug's manipulation shows him that it is difficult to be one's own master, that he is not free to wander about. In the process of preserving his self, he finds that he is forced to "kill" the Prostitute, that he is forced to resort to physical violence and "kill" the Thug. The Sleepwalker is led to see that he is basically a coward who dares not accept the Prostitute, not even in his dream, although he finds her sexually desirable, and he dares to kill only in his dream and fantasy and not in reality. His aloofness shows not so much his indifference to the world as his inability to love and to relate as a result of his sheer intellectual existence. While the Prostitute accepts any man with a heart, she rejects the Sleepwalker sexually for he remains an observer of life, a man of mere thoughts and no feelings.

UNSEXING AND UNGENDERING THE SELF

In *Between Life and Death* Gao presents a woman who speaks out her mind and fears and in *Nocturnal Wanderer* he again portrays a man who speaks aloud his mind and fantasies. In *Dialogue and Rebuttal*, however, Gao creates two voices as well as two perspectives, one of the male's and the other the female's. The play is presented in the form of a dialogue between a middle-aged writer and a twenty-six-year-old woman whom the writer met the night before in a bar. After a casual sexual encounter, the Man invites the Woman to stay in his apartment. Against such a background they engage themselves in a dialogue about love, life, self and gender relationship. In their dialogue, both the Man and the Woman seek to know each other through body contacts:

> Woman: You want me to say that I am a wanton woman.
> Man: You said it, not me.
> Woman: Don't you want every woman to be wanton?
> Man: Women are actually like that.
> Woman: It's you men's fantasy.
> Man: Men are like that too.
> Woman: Then what's there to be curious about?
> Man: They are only different in gender.
> Woman: Are all women the same to you?   (Gao, 1995a, p. 20)

While the Man and the Woman seem to be engaged in a dialogue, they are in reality preoccupied by their own thoughts. The dialogue can be rearranged into two monologue speeches, one by the Man and the other by the Woman, each imagining the opposite sex:

> Woman: You want me to say that I am a wanton woman.
> Woman: Don't you want every woman to be wanton?
> Woman: It's you men's fantasy.
> Woman: Then what's there to be curious about?
> Woman: Are all women the same to you?
>
> Man: You said it, not me.
> Man: Women are actually like that.
> Man: Men are like that too.
> Man: They are only different in sex.

In the Woman's monologue, the Woman asserts that women are not what the Man imagines, while the Man in his monologue insists that men and women share similar fantasies and they are only different in biological sex. As the conversation continues, both the Man and the Woman construct their selves as the "other" of the opposite sex. Yet, each is deconstructed by the other as mere imagination:

> Man: When we first started, we were talking in general terms, now it's different —
> Woman: How different?
> Man: Now it's you and me, and not men and women in the general sense. We're face to face with each other, we can see each other, and we've had some contact, I am not saying body contact, we're bound to have some feelings, some understanding of each other, we're two living human beings.
> Woman: But when you made love to me just now, you were treating me like your so-called women in the general sense, in other words, just a plaything.
> Man: Don't talk like that, because you and I were the same, weren't we? We were too passionate —
> Woman: Let me finish. You didn't even ask me my name, as soon as you entered the door, you....   (Gao, 1995a, pp. 21–22)

In the first part of *Dialogue and Rebuttal* the relation between body and gender is explored. Recent feminist theories show an anti-Cartesian emphasis on the body as the basis of gendered subjectivity and one finds the topic discussed in Gao's play, in which the sexual encounter is regarded as an affirmation of an individual's existence. As the Man observes, "Only feelings are real" (Gao, 1995a, p. 36). The Woman's remarks, however, seem to counter the Man's position in thinking that his being exists and is realized only in the sexual act: "You are crazy, you are sick! All you want is sexual excitement, your sexual fantasies, but not me" (Gao, 1995a, p. 44). Toward the end of the first part, both the Man and the Woman come to understand the plights of human existence arising from the imprisonment of the soul in the body:

> Man: The world has all gone crazy,
> Woman: (*Mumbling.*) Only because of loneliness,
> Man: (*Whispering.*) Only because of boredom,
> Woman: Only because of hunger and thirst,
> Man: Only because of desires,
> Woman: Unbearable desires,
> Man: Only because of unbearable desires,

Woman: Only because it's unbearable to be a woman,
Man: Only because it's unbearable to be a man,
Woman: Only because not only being a woman, but also being human,
Man: A living human being, a body of flesh and blood,
Woman: It's only for having feelings,
Man: It's only for having to resist death,
Woman: Only because of the fear of death,
Man: Only because of the yearning for life,
Woman: It's only for experiencing the fear of death,
Man: It's only for affirming the existence of one's self,
Woman: It's only a reason —
Man: Only because of a reason —
Woman: It's only for a reason because of a reason …
Man: No therefore, no purpose.   (Gao, 1995a, pp. 46–47)

An existentialist theme is put forth to the audience in this dialogue between the Man and the Woman, who finally merge in their voices to form one speech, lamenting over the meaninglessness of human existence in the absence of an essence. It is apparent that their sex game leads them nowhere but to a game of death, of consuming and destroying each other in the process.

The second part of the play thus deals with the Man and the Woman in their "death" state when they are left with an existence in pure consciousness after eliminating their bodies. In their state of "self-transcendent observation" — a state of being that Gao Xingjian advocates and attempts to attain, the selves are freed from their physical bodies of confinement. The Man and the Woman become bodyless, formless subjects. They are able to relate to their heads and bodies separately. In their dialogue with their dead bodies, they find that they are mere shadows of their existence:

Woman: What are you proud of? Now you've turned into a shadow, a slave
    at the feet of a woman?
Man: It doesn't matter. You and I are in the same boat, nobody can leave
    anybody. It makes no difference if you're my shadow or if I'm yours.
                                        (Gao, 1995a, p. 63)

With their bodies being cut off, the Man and the Woman have successfully unsexed themselves and become ungendered. In their dialogue with their cut-off bodies, they come to objectify themselves as "you" and "she" defined by their intellect with ability to speak, to remember and to think:

> Man: You say you're only talking to yourself.
> Woman: She says she's only left with memories.
> Man: You say you get a little bit of comfort only by talking to yourself.
> Woman: She says she can evoke a little bit of fantasy only through her memories.
> Man: You say you feel somewhat relaxed only when you're talking to yourself.
> Woman: She says she sees herself clearly only when she's fantasizing.
> Man: You say it's not that you don't want to get away from your self, but you're always talking to yourself, in that way the self will never go away and it'll never stop haunting you.
> Woman: She says only when she indulges herself in fantasies can she empty herself of her worries, be carefree and recall her past feelings. Even though they may have been scary feelings, they still manage to touch her heart.
> (Gao, 1995a, p. 67)

With their detachment from their bodies with their desires, the Man and the Woman find that they still need to deal with their consciousness with its fears and memory. They are eventually led to realize that only when they stop remembering, thinking, and using language will they be able to seek their true selves. Thus the Man says, "You need to forget completely your body, once and for all, get rid of it, thoroughly and forever" (Gao, 1995a, p. 67). This act of forgetting is a motif recurrent in many of Gao's works. And the "door" that the Man and the Woman refer to near the end of the play can thus be taken as an existentialist exit from the predicament of imprisonment in human existence. It can also be regarded as a Buddhist symbol signifying an entrance to the land of nothingness, where there is no self, no memory, no fantasy, no dream, absolutely nothing:

> Man: (*Softly, his back facing the Woman.*) That door, behind that door, there is nothing.
> Woman: (*Softly.*) And no memories.
> Man: Absolutely, absolutely.
> Woman: And no fantasies.
> Man: Absolutely, absolutely. (*Nods his head.*)

Woman: And no dreams either.
Man: Absolutely, absolutely.   (Gao, 1995a, pp. 73–74)

When they notice the door that may lead them to the land of nothingness, they are enlightened to the essence of existence. With this enlightened vision, whether or not the door exists is of no importance to them. What remains is how to deal with the human faculty of intellect, the ability of logical reasoning:

> Man: Is it is it not — is it winter fooling with teapot or teapot fooling with winter? (*Angrily.*) Or is it it is not winter fooling with teapot or teapot fooling with winter? Or it is it is not is it not winter fooling with teapot or is it it is teapot fooling with winter? Or is it winter fooling with teapot fooling with winter? Or it is it is not is it winter fooling with teapot and then fooling with winter? Speak, speak, speak, go on!
> (Gao, 1995a, p. 79)

At this point they find that the human intellect embedded in language fails to give meaning to existence, which in its essence does not follow the logic of thinking. Their acceptance of the "crack" on the ground without asking further questions about its possible meaning or implication symbolizes their break from reasoning and their final transcendence from logical thinking. It is clear from such an ending that Gao Xingjian is very much inspired by Buddhist thoughts, which hold up the importance of awakening and non-reasoning.

The Buddhist Monk in the play further complements this central message. He serves as a mirror to the Man and the Woman in their assertion of the human will. The Monk demonstrates his perfect control of his body through intense concentration of the mind in his acrobatic acts. His incessant attempts to put a stick in a standing position and then placing an egg on its top are symbolic of human will and human conscious effort to construct a relationship between things of very different nature. Read in psychoanalytical terms, the stick and the egg may signify the male and the female with highly sexual overtone. The Monk's failure to accomplish his set task until he lets go of his will and abandons his intellect and insistence is presented as an "answer" to the Man's and the Woman's inquiry about self and other. Only when the Man and the Woman succeed in abandoning their will can they be completely freed from human bondage characterized by distinctions between the self and the other, the male and the female, the living and the dead, as well as between things and non-things.

Through these theatrical representations, Gao succeeds in treating some highly philosophical themes and abstract concepts in drama; he shows through the tension in gender relations and subjectivity that ultimate awakening lies in the vision of non-distinction — in the "soul of chaos." It is apparent from these post-exile plays that Gao is in quest of enlightenment and transcendence that are only possible when human beings stop asserting their selves, stop exercising their faculty of intellect and stop making distinctions.

Viewed in this light, the three plays form a trilogy that begins with a female perspective and then a male one, and ends with a negation and deconstruction of both. Gao Xingjian's experiments with gender consciousness, body-soul opposition, the self and language, awakening and reasoning, and transcendence and wisdom seek to break down all categories of distinction and opposition. In doing so, the self is further deconstructed as linguistic constitution based on memory and fantasy. As one finds in these plays, redemption of the soul lies within the heart of non-distinction. To arrive at such a state, one's body must die in order to get rid of it and unsex oneself.

NOTES

1. Gao Xingjian left China for Germany in 1987 and then settled in Paris in 1988. His pre-exile plays refer those he wrote in China. In his early plays *Alarm Signal* (1982) and *The Bus-Stop* (1983), he experimented with Western techniques in the Chinese theatre. In his middle plays written while he was still in China, such as *Wild Man* (1995), *Monologue* (1995), *The Other Shore* (1986), *Nether City* (1987), *The Story of* The Classic of Mountains and Seas (1989), and some other short plays, he tried to incorporate elements of traditional Chinese theatre in the modern performance. His post-exile plays are those written in France. Examples are *Fugitives* (1989), *Between Life and Death* (1991), *Dialogue and Rebuttal* (1992), *Nocturnal Wander* (1993), *Weekend Quartet* (1995) and *Snow in August* (2000), many of which appeared first in French.

2. In our translation, we have followed Fong, trans. (1999), with minor modifications for special emphasis.

REFERENCES

Chodorow, Nancy (1978). *The Reproduction of Mothering.* Berkeley: University of California Press.

Fong, Gilbert C. F., trans. (1999). *The Other Shore: Plays by Gao Xingjian.* Hong Kong: The Chinese University Press.

Freud, Sigmund (1965a). "Femininity." In Freud (1965b), pp. 412–432.

—— (1965b). *New Introductory Lectures on Psychoanalysis.* Trans. and ed. James Strachey. New York: Norton.

Gao Xingjian 高行健 (1995a). *Duihua yu fanjie* 對話與反詰 [Dialogue and rebuttal]. In Gao (1995b), Vol. 6, pp. 1–84. Original work published in 1992.

—— (1995b). *Gao Xingjian xiju liuzhong* 高行健戲劇六種 [Six volumes of plays by Gao Xingian]. Taipei: Dijiao chubanshe 帝教出版社.

—— (1995c). *Shengsijie* 生死界 [Between life and death]. In Gao (1995b), Vol. 5, pp. 1–44. Original work published in 1991.

—— (1995d). *Yeyoushen* 夜遊神 [Nocturnal wanderer]. In Gao (1995b), Vol. 5, pp. 47–124. Original work published in 1993.

—— (1996). "Wo de xiju he wo de yaoshi" 我的戲劇和我的鑰匙 [My drama and my key]. In *Meiyou zhuyi* 沒有主義 [Without isms], pp. 235–252. Hong Kong: Tiandi tushu youxian gongsi 天地圖書有限公司.

Kristeva, Julia (1977). *About Chinese Women.* London: Boyars.

Lacan, Jacques (1981). *Four Fundamental Concepts of Psycho-analysis.* Ed. Jacques-Alain Miller; trans. Alan Sheridan. New York: Norton.

Moi, Toril (1985). *Sexual/Textual Politics: Feminist Literary Theory.* London: Routledge.

Pronouns as Protagonists: On Gao Xingjian's Theories of Narration[1]

Gao Xingjian's 563-page novel *Lingshan* 靈山 [Soul mountain][2] is fictionalized autobiography superimposed upon a documentation of his five-month journey through the Chinese hinterland from July to November in 1983. Interwoven into the fabric of the autobiography is the fact of his birth in early 1940 soon after the Japanese invasion of China and the rise to power of the Chinese Communist Party in the same period.[3] Several decades of China's social history are compressed into the pages of the novel. The coincidence of historical fact, however, is like the rice-paper on which Gao executes the unique ink paintings which have sustained his life as a writer in exile and provides immense space for audience creativity. The stark white spaces and configurations of black and grey of varying intensities convey startling dimensions of depth and light and evoke deep psychological associations from individual viewers.[4] The pages of *Soul Mountain* induce a similar effect in readers.

REFLECTING ON LITERATURE

Over the past two decades, Gao Xingjian's artistic sensitivities have found expression in works of drama, fiction and painting which, while demanding the absolute freedom of the individual as the author or painter, are characteristically dispassionate and command the participation of the reader/viewer. Gao Xingjian's fiction is not the result of undisciplined artistic genius, and fabricating stories to dispatch feelings of loneliness is a habit he had developed from childhood (Gao and Bourgeois, 1997, p. 5). He is a highly reflective thinker with an immense curiosity about all aspects of human existence within the context of its total environment, and this total environment is constantly changing. From the early years of the 1980s he began to address the issues raised for fiction as a genre in modern times, publishing his ruminations in the form of critical essays and embarking upon the writing of *Soul Mountain* which would allow him the space to experiment with various strategies to allow fiction as a genre to meet the challenge of a modern readership whose sensitivity and perceptions had radically changed with the irreversible developments since the advent of cinema, television and computers.

This article will review the ideas which Gao Xingjian presents in "Tan xiaoshuoguan yu xiaoshuo jiqiao" 談小説觀與小説技巧 [On fiction and the technqiues of fiction] (Gao, 1982, pp. 233–239). In it he enunciates the nature and scope of the problems for fiction writers in the present age. Written only months before he began to embark upon the writing of *Soul Mountain,* this essay constitutes a blueprint which anticipates the nature and scale of experimentation he envisaged in the novel. This article will also focus on Gao Xingjian's ingenious strategy of using pronouns as protagonists throughout the novel. These pronoun protagonists without faces dissect the author's self, subjecting its various facets to the scrutiny of the author and the reader. This is the most striking feature of the novel and Gao Xingjian's most radical experiment in artistic expression in a novel, which abounds in a plethora of experimentation with literary strategies to create an artistic reality with maximum creative space for both the author and the reader. The pronouns I, you, she, and later he (who swaps places with I) and another she, examine various facets of the author; it is a unique form of autobiographical depiction which is to some extent informed by Gao Xingjian's knowledge of drama. The pronouns speaking in soliloquies or dialogue, telling stories, dreaming, or reminiscing, succeed in providing many points of view even within the space of a paragraph.

The thematic substance of *Soul Mountain* may be traced to two traumatic and interrelated events in Gao Xingjian's life: his being targeted for criticism at a time when the memory of the persecution of writers during the Cultural Revolution was still palpable, and his being wrongly diagnosed as having lung cancer. His weeks of waiting while confronting imminent death induced a psychological review of his life, dislodging in the process large fragments of forgotten memory which re-surface in *Soul Mountain.* The disjointed, dream-like quality of these fragments is Gao's attempt to give linguistic expression, that is, to recreate his psychological state during this period of confrontation with death. Interspersed are observations and reflections from his five-month journey through remote parts of China.

PRONOUNS IN *SOUL MOUNTAIN*

In *Soul Mountain,* the protagonist "I" is the author who has fled the capital and is carrying out research on human society at the fringes of Han civilization. These chapters explore the impact of history on the human and natural environment of the places he visits. The protagonist "I" visits various remote villages, minority peoples, nature reserves with ancient forests and the giant panda, isolated monasteries and temples, and is witness to ancient folk and shamanistic practices. In Shennongjia 神農架, the "I" speaks with people who had sighted a "wild man" or encountered a "wild man" and listens to various stories told by the locals. Gao's interest in the "wild man" also resulted in his play of that name in 1985. The "I" chapters, which also contain large segments of conversation, folk songs and chants, examine how primitive instincts are repressed by civilization and how attempts during the Cultural Revolution to eradicate superstitious practices had been to a large extent superficial. The impact of tourism on the environment and the crass symbols of commercial development on historic sites in more recent times are also observed.

The protagonist "you" is on a quest to visit *Soul Mountain.* The author distances himself from this protagonist by calling him "you," hence enabling him to observe as a bystander, like a fly on the wall, his own behaviour and thoughts as well as that of the people "you" encounters. By the creation of "you" the author is given immense freedom to explore his own past relationships with women as well as his own past. The protagonist "you" encounters "she" who accompanies him on the first part of his journey. The "you" chapters are fast-moving: dialogues constitute a number of whole chapters as "you" and "she" discuss life, reminisce, talk about people they know, invent stories to tell each other. Chapters containing their first sexual encounter are at times sensitive and beautiful erotic depictions, and at other times graphic grey and black representations of the primitive instincts and sensations "you" experiences. "She" who suffers from hysteria and has suicidal tendencies even when "you" first encounters her becomes possessive and finally the couple torment each other as "you" the individualist seeks to extricate himself from the relationship. The author's perceptions of hatred, fear of loneliness, anguish, jealousy, mistrust, the desire to kill, the fear of being killed are all portrayed in Chapter 50. The protagonist "you" continues on his journey to *Soul Mountain* alone. The "you" chapters also reconstruct the author's forgotten past: his childhood years, family, and friends. The recurring motif of the little boy running barefoot on cobble stones instantly projects the reader back through time along with the author as he recalls past incidents. Distanced from the author as "you," the little boy is at the same time brought closer to the reader.

By Chapter 52 Gao Xingjian perceives that the distance between "I" and "you" has narrowed, that "you" is merging with "I." Another protagonist "he" is introduced. This "he" is the back of "you," after "you" turns and walks away. At this juncture, the author announces his intention to reintroduce the protagonist "you" to swap places with the protagonist "I": their swapping places is aimed at further increasing the vantage points from which to scrutinize the self's thoughts and actions. By distancing the author in these various ways, the author enjoys the aesthetic freedom he desires for the exploration of his self in this fictionalized autobiography. However, while being fictionalized autobiography, the strategy of using pronouns as protagonists compels reader involvement at many levels. Most importantly, the reader is given the sense of knowing the author at a personal level, liking him, and trusting what he has to tell. Other strategies employed in the novel further allow the reader to travel with the author through time and space, sharing his experiences, curiosity, thoughts, emotions and his search to understand himself as an individual in human society and as a writer of fiction.

As in each of his creations, *Soul Mountain* is a conscious search for Gao's personal aesthetic fulfillment: Gao demands absolute freedom of artistic expression in whatever medium he has chosen.[5] *Soul Mountain* is infused with Gao's perceptions of the individual's place within the totality of nature, a totality including personal and social relationships, and the relationship of human beings to the natural environment. Gao Xingjian's pondering on human existence is not a static one of the present and he examines the artifacts of past generations with the academic precision of the anthropologist, ethnologist, ethnographer, local historian and botanist.

As it has been maintained above that *Soul Mountain* is fictionalized autobiography, Gao Xingjian's involvement with literature in the context of China must now be considered, for it was in China that he completed the manuscript for the novel. In the late 1970s, as China opened its gates to the outside world after decades of isolation, half a century of literary creations from all parts of the globe gradually "slipped in" (Pollard, 1985, pp. 641–656) alongside the financial, management, engineering and scientific texts seen as essential for fast-tracking the process of scientific and technological modernization. Gao Xingjian had early access to developments in world literature through his knowledge of French. He had majored in French at the Beijing Institute of Foreign Languages and, on graduating in 1962, was assigned to work as a translator, a job he held until 1981 (apart from the period 1970–1975 which he spent working as a peasant). In 1979 he travelled to France as a translator with a delegation of Chinese writers and his knowledge of French and interest in French literature allowed him to establish contacts with the French diplomatic world, personal contacts which would later develop and shape his future life.

AVANT-GARDE WRITER

From 1980, Gao Xingjian's name began to appear in publications.[6] Guangzhou in South China, because of its proximity to the outside world, responded first to the lifting of publication restrictions. Geographically distant from the strict bureaucratic constraints of Beijing, a lively literary scene developed. *Huacheng* 花城, one of the major literary magazines to emerge soon after the beginning of liberalization, published his short story "Hanye de xingchen" 寒夜的星辰 [Stars on a cold night] in its second volume and the monthly magazine, *Suibi* 隨筆, began to serialize his *Xiandai xiaoshuo jiqiao chutan* 現代小説技巧初探 [A preliminary exploration of the techniques of modern fiction]. The latter work, published as a slim volume in 1981 and reprinted in 1982, was targeted for criticism in the debate oven modernism and realism which raged through literary circles during 1982.

In 1981 three more of Gao's short stories were published and he was assigned to work as a writer with the Beijing People's Art Theatre. In 1982 and 1983 two of his plays were staged as "experimental plays," for despite some incipient signs of liberalization in the literary and art world, the authorization process for publications, public exhibitions and performances was long and difficult, and works which failed to conform with official guidelines inevitably fell foul of the censors. The first of the plays, *Juedui xinhao* 絕對信號 [Alarm signal], performed twelve times to capacity audiences from the theatrical world. Public performances followed and led to a review in the French magazine *Cosmopolitan;* its announcement that *avant-garde* theatre had arrived in Beijing brought international notice to Gao Xingjian (Lee, 1995; Barmé, 1983; He, 1983). The second play *Chezhan* 車站 [The bus-stop] was staged ten times, again as an "experimental play" with audiences restricted to the theatrical world. The Party Secretary of the Chinese Writers' Association appeared uninvited at the last of these performances. He was decidedly unimpressed and before long it was rumoured that the Head of the Propaganda Department had declared *The Bus-Stop* to be "more Hai Rui baguan than *Hai Rui Baguan*"[7] and that it was the most poisonous play written after the establishment of the People's Republic of China. Immediately a paranoiac nervousness spread among writers that there would be a return to those times of extreme repression and the silencing of creative endeavours. Such fears were reinforced by the growing momentum of the Anti-Spiritual-Pollution Campaign: the theatre was instructed to put on two more performances of *The Bus-Stop* to facilitate the writing of criticisms by the appropriate work-units. Gao Xingjian was singled out for further criticism (Gao, 1996g, pp. 79–81).

Gao Xingjian had been under surveillance since the publication in 1981 of *A Preliminary Exploration of the Techniques of Modern Fiction.* The work was seen as promoting "modernism" which according to the authoritative 1965 edition of the *Cihai* dictionary was: "A general name for various decadent schools and tendencies of bourgeois literature and art in the period of imperialism; characterized by a distortion of reality, undermining the established forms and basic laws of literature and art, and negating tradition and typicality; it preaches cosmopolitanism and other reactionary ideologies ..." (He, 1992, p. 279). The added stress of being the author of *The Bus-Stop*, in the political uncertainties of Beijing, took its toll. A routine health check showed a shadow on his lung X-rays taken at two separate hospitals on different days: he was diagnosed with lung cancer, the disease which had killed his father a couple of years earlier. The doctor who had correctly diagnosed his father, had him arrange an appointment for a further X-ray: this was to take place some weeks later. While waiting he resigned himself to imminent death: he treated himself to the finest foods he could afford, sought out an old graveyard in an outlying suburb where the air was less polluted, and spent his time reading the *Book of Changes*. Although he was one of the main targets for attack in the literary debates at the time it was as if he were merely a bystander. The final X-ray indicated that he had been wrongly diagnosed but his weeks of waiting had brought him to a confrontation with death and hence a re-assessment of his life. For him, the reprieve from death meant a rebirth: living from that point was a highly conscious act.

However, the transcendental state of imminent death vanished as Gao Xingjian returned to confront reality. A part of that reality was the rumour that he was to be sent to Qinghai for "retraining." Some of his friends had been sent there but only one in ten had ever returned. He did not intend to wait around; and taking an advance royalty payment on a proposed novel, he reported to his work-unit that he was off to get first-hand experience of the lives of the woodcutters of the southwest. He headed for Chengdu and then into the ancient forests of Sichuan where he had been sent to a cadre school during the Cultural Revolution. From Sichuan he travelled to the east coast, in all passing through eight provinces and seven protected nature reserves, a journey of 15,000 kilometres over a period of five months. It was impossible for the authorities to track him down but he knew from his friends that he had been black listed. He returned to Beijing later in the year when political tensions had relaxed after Hu Yaobang reasserted his political authority.

The first performance of his play *Yeren* 野人 [Wild man] at the Beijing People's Art Theatre in 1985 again stirred up a controversy. 1985 was also a critical juncture for his future creative life. It was becoming clear that his creative instincts were at odds with the political reality of China. He travelled to Germany under the DAAD arts programme. While in Germany, the French Foreign Office and the Ministry of the Arts invited him for two visits to Paris where the Théâtre National de Chaillot held a conference on his plays and at which he presented a paper. He also travelled to England on the invitation of the London International Drama Festival and to Vienna on the invitation of Alte Schmide Cultural Centre where he held a solo exhibition of his paintings and presented readings from his fiction; several German universities and one in Denmark also hosted visits.

In 1986 Gao Xingjian's play *Bi'an* 彼岸 [The other shore] was published in China. Translations of his writings also began to appear in significant literary magazines in Europe. In France, *L'Imaginaire* published his article "Yao shenmeyang de xiju" 要甚麼樣的戲劇 [What sort of drama do we need?] and *Le Monde* published Paul Poncet's translation of his short story "Gongyuan li" 公園裏 [In the park]. Peter Polonyi's Hungarian translation of *The Bus-Stop* was published in the journal *Foreign Literature*. In the following year, 1987, excerpts of *The Bus-Stop* were published in German in *Drama Today* and Paul Poncet's French translation of the short story "Muqin" 母親 [Mother] was published in the contemporary fiction journal *Bréves*. Professional performances of Gao's plays also began in Europe: Göran Malmqvist's translation of *Duo yu* 躲雨 [Hiding from the rain] was directed by Peter Wahlqvist and performed at the Kungliga Dramatiska Teatern in Stockholm.

Gao travelled for a third time to Europe on the invitation of the Morat Institut für Kunst und Kunstwissenschaft to Germany. This time in Europe, he made the decision to seek residence in Paris, which he successfully obtained. Living in Paris he found the creative freedom he failed to find in China and his creative output increased dramatically. For a decade his audiences and readers — aided by translations where necessary — have been international. For Gao Xingjian the last writing of *Soul Mountain* for the publishers exorcised lingering vestiges of homesickness and he was aware of such feelings casting adrift in the process. In Paris, he has dedicated himself to literary and art creation and the writing of literary and art criticism; his recent publications include three plays which were first written in French, *Shengsijie* 生死界 [Between life and death], *Yeyoushen* 夜遊神 [Nocturnal wanderer] and *Zhoumo sichongzou* 周末四重奏 [Weekend quartet].

EXPERIMENTATION WITH LANGUAGE
AND TECHNIQUE

The issues raised in *Soul Mountain* challenge the reader on many fronts but their impact is intensified by Gao Xingjian's conscious attention to technique and language, for in his literary endeavours he is single-minded in his quest for authentic linguistic expression of his perceptions of reality. Gao Xingjian's attention to language involves all the senses and he draws on an extensive knowledge of aesthetics. For him literary creation is art in the medium of language; his approach is holistic and the result is a rich variety of sensual images. In Gao Xingjian's literary creations he consciously seeks to remove the silence of the written language (Gao, 1996f, p. 33), "to breathe new life into dead words" (Gao and Bourgeois, 1997, p. 52); he strives to appeal to the auditory senses so that virtually each word is chosen as in poetry. His literary creations are written for reading aloud. Consider for example this excerpt in Chapter 1 of *Soul Mountain:*

> The sun is about to set. The deep orange disc is infused with light but there's no glare. You gaze into the distance at the hazy layers of jagged peaks where the two sides of the valley join. This ominous black image nibbles at the lower edges of the glowing sun which seems to be revolving. The sun turns a dark red, gentler, and projects brilliant gold reflections onto the bend of the river: the dark blue of the water fusing with the dazzling sunlight throbs and pulsates. As the red disc seats itself into the valley it grows serene, awesomely beautiful. And there are sounds. You are aware of elusive sounds distinctly emerging from deep in your heart and radiating outwards. Trembling, the sun seems to prop itself up on its toes, stumble, and then sink into the black shadows of the mountains, scatter-ing glowing colours throughout the sky. An evening wind blows noisily by your ears and cars drive past, as usual sounding their deafening horns. You cross the bridge and see there a new stone with engraved characters painted in red: "Yongning Bridge. Built in the 3rd Year of the Kaiyuan reign of the Song dynasty and repaired in 1962. This stone was laid in 1983." This no doubt marked the beginning of the tourist industry here.
>
> (Gao, 1990, pp. 8–9)

By the time he had written his second major critical work on fiction, "On Fiction and the Techniques of Fiction," Gao Xingjian had already isolated specific techniques he saw as essential to revitalizing fiction as a literary genre and had experimented with some of these in a number of short stories. In the same year, he began to work on his novel *Soul Moun-tain* to give concrete form to the ideas on fiction he had developed over many years of writing for himself (when he knew he would not be able to communicate with readers), and pondering on the genre itself in the context of the challenges offered by the modern age. These ideas would develop further and grow in the process of his writing of the novel and they are essential for understanding the scope of the artistic experimen-tation he envisaged in *Soul Mountain.*

THEORIES OF NARRATION

The following paragraphs are a summary of "On Fiction and the Techniques of Fiction," which, for those early years of post-Mao China, constitutes one of the most important analytical studies of fiction as a literary genre in the modern world. Cogently argued and unambiguously based on the premise of freedom for the writer, reader and characters, "On Fiction and the Techniques of Fiction" was clearly a rebuff to the upholders of the literary orthodoxy inherited from Mao Zedong's "Yan'an Talks" of 1942, despite the apparent gentleness characteristic of Gao Xingjian's writings. For himself it was a blueprint of the issues he would deal with in his novel *Soul Mountain.*

Gao critiques the genre known as fiction in both China and the West and in the process provides his own definition. Existing translations and textbooks all defined the essentials of fiction as plot, characterization and setting but there had in fact been a deterioration in fiction after the May Fourth period. Even the writer Lu Xun (1881–1936) was aware that what he wrote did not conform to the definitions of the so-called "general outlines of literature." Yet, Gao Xingjian argues, Lu Xun's works are acknowledged and studied as fiction, despite their lack of deep characterization. He goes on to argue against adhering rigidly to any fixed pattern or to use definitions to stifle and suffocate fictional art, for the general outlines of literature are simply the summaries of past writings.

Artistic creations which are full of life have never started off with definitions. Fiction may tell narratives, write about characters or give scenes from life like genre paintings; or it can simply focus on an event, an emotion, a perception. As long as the work is well written it can vividly depict social life and the feeling of the times. However, fiction does not have to describe social life, it can simply write about people's psychological worlds. Through the analysis of people's psychological worlds, readers can come to understand human life and gain a better understanding of themselves. Time is a long flowing river and human life is forever changing: as fictional art reflects human life it should not be a mechanistic craft. As human perspectives are continually changing and developing, from the advent of fiction, the art of fiction has in fact been continually changing.

Fiction does not need to portray characters; characters can be simply implied meanings. With this type of characterization, the central concern of the work is the writer's own understanding and perceptions of life rather than true-to-life sketches of social life. The plot in fiction, too, is not necessary. Gao observes that while plots are taken from life, life is not solely constituted of plots. In fact, the larger part of life consists of non-plot elements. Therefore in order to fully reflect real life, the writer has to search for new structures and techniques to encapsulate these non-plot elements of life which are more widespread, for example, social customs and people's inner spiritual lives, including psychological activities, consciousness and the unconscious, thoughts and feelings. In Gao Xingjian's analysis, the plot is a structure derived from a relatively primitive knowledge of social life, that is, a cause-effect relationship. Cause and effect are a linked circle, but the world is not circularly constructed; nor is it simply linear so that the writer can keep narrating until a point is reached where the story comes to an impasse and two lines of development occur. This structure is still such that the two lines finally have to join and to re-form a circle, that is, the conclusion.

However, Gao argues, in the modern age people do not have such a simplistic view of life. They know that developments in life are not just circular: there are parabolas and trajectories. Hence even while taking plots from life, modern fiction does not necessarily have a conclusion. In modern fiction, characters may come and go, meet and separate; some depart without a farewell and there is no indication of what happens afterwards. The characters are not all linked from beginning to end, and in the conclusion not all are dealt with. Instead, the reader is left to feel, understand, imagine and evaluate life as it is presented in the work of fiction, based on the incidents in the work and on one's own personal experiences and knowledge. In life there are in fact some complete incidents, but even more that are incomplete. Hence the larger numbers of incomplete incidents do not have to be artificially brought to conclusions in fiction, and are a valid part of fiction.

In the modern world, as the potential for knowledge is raised and the art of fiction develops, writers have devised techniques other than plots to entertain readers. Modern fiction can either have plots or not, or it can merge plots with other artistic devices. In a work of fiction a specific narrative angle may be taken: the work may start off with a specific narrator or look at the world through the eyes of a particular person. This has greater authenticity than that told in the voice of the story-teller. Through stream-of-consciousness, the reader is submerged in the inner worlds of the characters and is able to follow their psychological activities. However, the use of stream-of-consciousness throws the traditional linked plot into chaos; it is thus replaced by a more complex structure woven of complex visual and auditory perceptions as well as various psychological perceptions.

The development of cinema technology has had a great impact on the aesthetic potential of readers; readers have been unconsciously affected by aesthetic habits fostered by the cinema. They become bored with long descriptions of settings and the passive narration of feelings; they want literary works to provide living pictures. They are impatient with detailed psychological analysis and demand that the psychological activities of characters be provided instantly. The modern reader's powers of perception are also more highly developed than those of their predecessors and their sensitivity to moods is not necessarily inferior to the writer's. Thus the writer should not assume a position of superiority or that of the teacher.

Tempo and rhythm, borrowed from music to convey mood, have been imported as techniques in fiction writing, and have brought demands on the structure of fiction. To deal with this, fiction writers have introduced into the structure of fiction the technique of montage from cinema and the arrangements of stanza and movements in music. Such complex structures are not possible with the primitive plot. The narrative method of "Once upon a time there was…" is incapable of capturing the high speed and rhythm of modern life and modern readers cannot tolerate this sort of static treatment and description. As soon as they open a book, they want to come face to face with the characters, be able to get right into the book, and moreover to immediately perceive the setting and mood of the book. Static description and narration is minimal in modern fiction and this increases the amount of memories and flashback insertions, which destroy linear sequence. The same incident can appear and reappear in a character's memory, and the jumping back and forth and different locations also destroy fixed three-dimensional space.

Recurrence and intensification of images is more expressive than description, analysis and explanation. By replacing the static descriptions of settings with mental images, the reader's mental activities will permeate the setting so that an unmoving setting will flow like time. Memory is not restricted by time sequence and can move about freely, so by constructing time and incidents in the memories of the characters fiction achieves a high degree of freedom. As it is possible to make the impact of a minute's meeting longer than ten years of separation and at the same time compress ten years into a moment, the complexities and the time of an incident can no longer be directly apportioned. This raises the issue of psychological time. The pushing, pulling, shaking, and stilled scenes of the movie camera are all artistic methods for extending psychological time within a short time span and give viewers more powerful images and emotions. For literature, which works in the medium of language, with corresponding devices such as short sentences with quick tempo and long sentences with slow tempo, the process of psychological time can be speeded up or extended.

There are many ways for the artist who works in the medium of language to recreate temporal and spatial relationships. Psychological time can be manifested in imagery, visual images and the tempo of narrative language. Imagery and visual images can be the objective world and can also be impressions, imagination or the dream images of the inner mind. In narrative language, there is treatment of characters and incidents, as well as the characters' perceptions and the narrator's comments. By weaving all of these together, the writer can throw into chaos objective temporal relationships and restructure them according to the needs of a particular work. In modern fiction, the completeness of temporal and spatial relationships is of little significance, and in employing these devices, the writer's intention is not the representation of incidents and scenery from reality but instead is focused on the spiritual world of the characters. Structure or form is the external manifestation of the content of fiction. The obsessive search for form divorced from content is futile, as is racking one's brains to find new forms. As long as the writer has in mind living characters and really has something to tell readers, then there is no need to be bound by old regulations: the writer should freely search for means of adequate self-expression. However, if one wants to moan about nothing or if what one has to say is insubstantial, then no form or artistic efforts will help.

Gao Xingjian is keenly aware of the importance of stream-of-consciousness as a modern narrative method, noting its use by writers of world acclaim dating back to Marcel Proust (1871–1922). In China, however, the experimentations by Wang Meng had stirred up a controversy. Gao saw that Wang Meng's critics did not in fact understand the meaning of stream-of-consciousness. He points out that "stream-of-consciousness is not an independent literary school nor can it be considered a method of artistic creation. It is simply a relatively new narrative method that transcends literary schools. All literary schools and writers using different methods of artistic creation can to a certain extent employ this narrative method" (Gao Xingjian, 1981, p. 26). And he further elaborates on the relation between psychology and the techniques of fiction:

> Stream-of-consciousness is related to the development of psychological research. As people investigated the rules of the external world, they searched for rules of the subjective activities of the human body itself. The conscious and subconscious activities of the human body have been the important content of modern psychological research and it was discovered that the psychological activities of human beings do not always accord with what can be logically deduced. Thinking, feelings, the conscious and subconscious, volition and impulse, lust, memory, etc., are like a dark river flowing endlessly from birth to death; even in sleep it is not interrupted. Rational thoughts are simply lights which serve as navigation markers on this dark river. When modern literature portrays man's inner world it must grasp this special aspect. This is the basis of the narrative language of stream-of-consciousness. However, the rules of psychological activities are not exclusive to the English, French, Germans, the Russians, Japanese, or to the Americans who speak English: these rules of course also apply to the Chinese who speak in Chinese and whose modes of thinking and perception are not substantively different. Workers and capitalists, presidents and rickshaw pullers may have demarcations as far as class consciousness and political attitudes are concerned but the patterns of their psychological activities are finally the same. The narrative language of stream-of-consciousness may be used for all of them to depict their inner worlds and to relate their spiritual activities. The narrative language of stream-of-consciousness is like other forms of literary language and is also organized. However, the ordering of it is not based on logical development and rational analysis. It accords with what is being depicted, that is, the natural patterns of psychological activities of a particular character in a work. The psychological activities of a person are extremely rich, full of life, full of vibrancy and these psychological activities are like an endlessly flowing river. Hence when this method is used for describing a person's inner world, what are provided are not just rational conclusions and analysis nor the state and outcome of action but the whole process of thought activities during rational conclusions and analysis, or a series of concrete and detailed perceptions during a particular action. Figuratively speaking,

it does not provide one or two points but the line between two points, and moreover it is often a curved line. Hence if one looks at a few points on the curve, they seem to have been put in according to the whims of the author, that is, free association. It can also be illustrated from an example in painting: the stream-of-consciousness language is not like classical painting where lines construct the painting, instead it employs the technique of oil painting where stroke after stroke of paint is applied. Close up one just sees patches of colour but from a distance the outlines can be seen.

As stream-of-consciousness language follows the psychological activities of a person it continually tells of the person's physiological perceptions: gustatory, olfactory, auditory, tactile and visual images, hence linking up the spiritual and the external world. Even though the external world is being described, it is the external world as perceived via the perceptory senses of the person. *In other words, stream-of-consciousness language is no longer objective description divorced from the perceptions of the self.*

The starting point of stream-of-consciousness consists of the concrete perceptions of the self of the character. When the writer grasps these authentic perceptions of the character being described, it will not be hard to feel the pulse of the character. This sort of language has a unique attraction and can summon the reader to go and experience the activities of the character's inner mind. Stream-of-consciousness is therefore an artistic language, which induces the reader to go and experience the self. This sort of narrative language is not concerned with time sequence, can mix memory and reality, the past, and imagination. Naturally it breaks through fixed spatial constraints, and in the same chapter, even the same paragraph, hallucination, dream, and real environment can be woven together.

(Gao Xingjian, 1981, pp. 27–32)

In Gao Xingjian's analysis, the general thrust of the conceptual changes in modern literature and the experimentation with new literary techniques indicate the striving for greater authenticity in literary works to win the trust of readers. Because the level of education in modern times has been universally raised, educated modern readers will not tolerate falsehoods and preaching. They do not look to the writer to tell them who is good and who is bad and what they should do and not do. They want the writer to bring forth convincing artistic images which can be felt and thought about, and which will actually help them understand the complexities of real life and themselves. Gao Xingjian approvingly quotes Lu Xun: "The valuable thing about literature is not because it instructs. If fiction is a textbook for moral cultivation how can it be called literature?"

Gao Xingjian's conclusion is that writers need to have a deep understanding of life and be continually raising the level of their writing technique. Literature must have thought content but whether or not though content is profound does not depend on the preaching of the protagonists. The theme of a work should come from something about which the author has some understanding in real life, even if it is something everyone knows about. The writer must start out from real life and write about some unique perceptions on it in order to have any impact on readers. Ideas grow from personal experiences and the theme in a work always takes shape, grows and matures spontaneously along with the artistic form.

A NEW FORM OF NARRATION

Having written *Soul Mountain* with the essay "On Fiction and the Art of Fiction" as a blueprint, even while in the process of writing it, Gao Xingjian is mindful that it is different from what is normally called fiction. In anticipation of his critics, in Chapter 72 he deals with this issue. The protagonist "he," who from Chapter 52 had changed places with the protagonist "you/I," meets a critic who has read the manuscript:

"This isn't a novel!"

"Then what is it?" he asks.

"A novel must have a complete story."

He says that he has told many stories: some with endings and some without.

"They are all fragments without any sequence, the author doesn't know how to organize them into connected episodes."

"Then may I ask how they can be organized?"

"You must foreshadow, then build towards a climax and have a conclusion. That's common knowledge in writing fiction."

He asks if fiction can be written without conforming to the method which is common knowledge. It would be just like a story: parts told from beginning to end and parts from end to beginning; parts with a beginning and an end and others with only a conclusion or are fragments which aren't followed up, parts which are developed but aren't completed, parts which are left out or don't need to be told any further, or about which there's nothing more to say can all be considered stories.

"No matter how you tell it, there has to be a protagonist in the story. In a long work of fiction there must be several important characters, but this work of yours ...?"

"But surely the I, you, she and he in the book are characters?" he asks.

"These are only different pronouns, to change the point of view of the narrative. This can't replace the portrayal of characters. These pronouns of yours — even if they are characters — don't have clear images, and can barely be said to have been described."

He says he isn't painting portraits.

"Right, fiction isn't painting, it's linguistic art. But do you think that petulant exchanges can replace the creation of the personalities of characters?"

He says that he doesn't want to create any personalities for the characters and moreover doesn't know if he himself has a personality, so to speak.

"Why are you writing fiction if you don't even understand what fiction is?"

He then politely asks for a definition of fiction.

(Gao, 1990, pp. 502–503)

Instead of answering, the critic accuses him of being modernist and trying unsuccessfully to be Western. To his retort that the work is Eastern, the critic berates him:

"Eastern literature is not as messy as what you've written! You've slapped together travel notes, moralistic ramblings, feelings, jottings, irrational discussions, unfable-like fables, copied down some folk songs, added some legend-like nonsense of your own invention, and called it fiction!"

(Gao, 1990, p. 503)

He is accused by the critic of being a nativist and a nihilist in turn. But he rejects all of these labels. He wrote because he could not bear the loneliness and to amuse himself. He had not expected to fall foul of the literary world. "Fiction for him was a luxury that transcended earning money and making a livelihood" (Gao, 1990, p. 504). He admits to a small amount of nihilism but this for him is not the same as absolute nothingness: "It's just like in the book where you is the reflection of I and he is the back of you — the shadow of a shadow, although there's no face it still counts as a pronoun" (Gao, 1990, p. 504).

In the long soliloquy of Chapter 52 he explains his use of pronouns as protagonists as well as his need to write *Soul Mountain*:

You know that I am just talking to myself to alleviate my loneliness. You know that this loneliness of mine is incurable, that no one can save me, that I can only talk about it to myself as the partner of my conversation.

In this lengthy soliloquy you are the target for what I relate, an I who listens intently to what I say, you are simply my shadow.

When I am listening to the you of myself, I let you create she, because you like me cannot bear the loneliness, and also have to find a partner for your conversation.

So you talk with her just like I talk with you.

She was born of you and yet affirms my self.

You who are the partner of my conversation transform my experiences and imagination into a relationship between you and her, and it is impossible to disentangle imagination from experience....

She who is the creation of experience and imagination transforms into various illusions which beguile and seduce you because this creation you also wants to seduce her, neither of you want the loneliness of your selves.

I am on a journey — life, good or bad, is a journey — and wallowing in imagination journey into my inner mind with you who are my reflection....

... the further we travel the closer we come, unavoidably merging, unable to separate. At this point there is a need to step back, to create a little distance. That distance is he. He is the back of you after you have turned and left me.

Neither I nor my reflection can see his face, it is enough to know that he is a person's back.

You who are my creation, created her so why must one insist on describing her face? She is of course a hazy image of associations induced by memories and is essentially indefinite, so let her remain indistinct, moreover her image seems to be changing endlessly.

It is only by getting rid of you that I can get rid of myself. However, having invoked you, it's impossible to get rid of you. So, I've got this idea: What will happen if you and I were to change places? In other words, I will be your shadow, and you will become the concrete form of I, this will be an interesting game. If you listen carefully to the I from the position of I, I will then become the concrete expression of your desires, and it will be a lot of fun.   (Gao, 1990, pp. 340–343)

In this chapter, Gao Xingjian also draws attention to the fact that in *Soul Mountain* the use of "we" is absent. "This word is anathema to him. The issue of the manipulation of the individual by group politics is explored in his two-act play *Taowang* 逃亡 [Fugitives] (Gao, 1995c, pp.

41–64). He states that he had been invited to write a play about the events of June 4th 1989 in Tiananmen. The resulting work has no specific references to the events and there are no heroes; it is coldly indifferent and contains no impassioned rhetoric for either the demonstrators or the authorities. He had written the work as a politico-philosophical play: "The Americans wanted me to change it, so I withdrew the manuscript and paid the translation fee myself. When I write, I have what I want to say, I do not pander to anyone's tastes. The solitary and independent writer confronts society and speaks and expresses himself in the voice of the individual, it is this voice which is more authentic" (Gao, 1996c, p. 15). It is clear in his mind that he will not sacrifice his writing for a political cause (Gao and Bourgeois, 1997, p. 17).

For Gao there is a clear distinction between politics and literature. He argues that a writer as an individual may be politically active but in literature there should be an absence of political passion and rhetoric: he advocates the writing of "cold literature" (Gao, 1996d, pp. 18–20). For patriotic reasons, many writers, notably Lu Xun, had sacrificed their creative lives, but this was a matter of choice (and of talent). Gao Xingjian clearly acknowledges that he lacks the talent required for politics and prefers instead to stand as an observer at the fringes or in the cracks of society (Gao, 1993, p. 114). The issue of patriotism, and its impact on the Chinese writer during the past century in particular, is discussed in his essay, "Guojia shenhua yu geren diankuang" 國家神話與個人癲狂 [The myth of nation and insanity of the individual] (Gao, 1993, pp. 114–121). However, for Gao Xingjian it is not only the myth of nation, which can exert a controlling influence on the writer: the slavish worship of money, fashions, trends, and theories are all enemies of literature. He defines his basic stance in literary creation as "meiyou zhuyi" 沒有主義 [without isms]; this stance is not new and is probably one adopted by writers throughout the world throughout the ages but he perceives the need to reiterate it in the present age (Gao and Bourgeois, 1997, pp. 36):

> To be "without isms" is more positive than nihilism, it adopts an attitude towards events, people and the self. This attitude does not acknowledge the existence of incontrovertible general truths. It may be regarded as a form of reasoning … which at least does not acknowledge blind superstitious belief, whether for a religion or for a brute force; there is no need to

follow after some authority, trend, or fashion, so that others will lead one by the nose; or to be spiritually shackled by some ideology so that one will be confined within its prison.   (Gao. 1996b, p. 1)

Although Gao Xingjian did not coin the term "without isms" until the mid-1990s, this unambiguous stance is already apparent in the essay, "On Fiction and the Techniques of Fiction," which he wrote in February 1982, and sustained him in the writing of *Soul Mountain,* from its inception in summer of that year to its completion in September 1989.

NOTES

1. This is a revised version of the paper, "Pronouns as Protagonists: Gao Xingjian's *Lingshan* as Autobiography," *China Studies*, No. 5 (1999), pp. 165–183.
2. In 1987 when Gao Xingjian left China, he took with him the manuscript of *Lingshan*, which he began in Beijing during the summer of 1982. He completed the manuscript in Paris in September 1989 and *Lingshan* was subsequently published in Taipei by Lianjing, 1990. Göran Malmqvist's Swedish version of the novel, *Andarnas berg*, was published in 1992 and Noel and Liliane Dutrait's French version, *La Montagne de l'Âme*, in 1995. Mabel Lee's English version, *Soul Mountain* was published by HarperCollins, Sydney, 2000.
3. Born 1940 in Jiangxi province during the wake of the Japanese invasion, Gao Xingjian started writing fiction as a youngster. In the ensuing years of harsh censorship during the 1960s and 1970s, he burned some hundreds of unpublished works, fearing the reprisals which had effectively silenced creative writers.
4. This was clearly evident in Gao Xingjian's solo exhibition at the Taipei Municipal Gallery during December 1995. However, most photographic reproductions fail to capture the startling depths achieved in the actual paintings.
5. Gao Xingjian demands absolute freedom in literary creation; even if it means that the writer must sometimes flee in order to escape interference with that freedom. He regards the debates over ideology and creative methodologies as interference and of little relevance in creative writing: "Literary creation is essentially solitary and no movement or group can help it." See Gao (1996d, pp. 20–21).
6. During 1980 Gao Xingjian also made a second trip to Europe (France and Italy), this time as a member of the Chinese Writers' Association.

7. A decade and a half earlier, the criticism of the historical play, *Hai Rui Baguan* 海瑞罷官 [The dismissal of Hai Rui] by Wu Han, had announced the beginning of the Cultural Revolution.

REFERENCES

Barmé, Geremie (1983). "A Touch of the Absurd — Introducing Gao Xingjian and His Play *The Bus-stop.*" *Renditions*, Nos. 19 & 20 (Spring & Autumn), pp. 373–377.

Davis, A. R., and A. D. Stefanowska, eds. (1982). *Austrina: Essays in Commemoration of the 25th Anniversary of the Founding of the Oriental Society of Australia.* Sydney: Oriental Society of Australia.

Gao Xingjian 高行健 (1981). *Xiandai xiaoshuo jiqiao chutan* 現代小説技巧初探 [A preliminary exploration of the techniques of modern fiction]. Guangzhou: Huacheng chubanshe 花城出版社.

—— (1982). "Tan xiaoshuoguan yu xiaoshuo jiqiao" 談小説觀與小説技巧 [On fiction and the techniques of fiction]. *Zhongshan* 鍾山, No. 6, pp. 233–239.

—— (1990). *Lingshan* 靈山 [Soul mountain]. Taipei: Lianjing chuban shiye gongsi 聯經出版事業公司.

—— (1993). "Guojia shenhua yu geren diankuang" 國家神話與個人癲狂 [Myth of nation and insanity of the individual). *Mingbao yuekan* 明報月刊 [Ming Pao monthly], No. 8, pp. 114–121.

—— (1995a). "The Voice of the Individual." Trans. Lena Aspfors and Torbjörn Lodén. *The Stockholm Journal of East Asian Studies*, Vol. 6, pp. 71–81.

—— (1995b). *Gao Xingjian xiju liuzhong* 高行健戲劇六種 [Six volumes of plays by Gao Xingjian]. Taipei: Dijiao chubanshe 帝教出版社.

—— (1995c). *Taowang* 逃亡 [Fugitives, 1990]. In Gao (1995b), Vol. 4.

—— (1996a). *Meiyou zhuyi* 沒有主義 [Without isms]. Hong Kong: Tiandi tushu youxian gongsi 天地圖書有限公司.

—— (1996b). "Zixu" 自序 [Preface]. In Gao (1996a), pp. 1–6.

—— (1996c). "Meiyou zhuyi" 沒有主義 [Without isms, 1993]. In Gao (1996a), pp. 8–17.

—— (1996d). "Wo zhuzhang yizhong lengde wenxue" 我主張一種冷的文學 [I advocate a cold literature]. In Gao (1996a), pp. 18–20. Original work published in 1990.

—— (1996e). "Bali suibi" 巴黎隨筆 [Jottings from Paris]. In Gao (1996a), pp. 21–28. Original work published in 1990.

—— (1996f). "Lun wenxue xiezuo" 論文學寫作 [On literary creation]. In Gao (1996a), pp. 29–85. Original work published in 1993.

—— (1996g), "Geri huanghua" 隔日黃花 [Stale chrysanthemums]. In Gao (1996a), pp. 158–166. Original work published in 1991.

Gao Xingjian and Denis Bourgeois (1997). *Au plus Prés du réel: Dialogues sur l'écriture* (1994–1997). Paris: Editions de l'Aube.

He Wen 何聞 (1983). "Postcript: On seeing the play *The Bus-stop*: He Wen's Critique in *Literary Gazette*." Trans. Chan Sin-wai. *Renditions*, Nos. 19 & 20 (Spring & Autumn), pp. 387–392.

—— (1984). "Huaju *Chezhan* guan hou" 話劇《車站》觀後 [On seeing the play *The Bus-Stop*]. *Wenyi bao* 文藝報, No. 3, pp. 21–25.

He Yuhuai (1992). *Cycles of Repression and Relaxation: Politico-Literary Events in China 1976–1989*. Bochum: Universitatsverlag Dr N Brockmeyer.

Lee, Mabel (1982). "Suicide of the Creative Self: The Case of Lu Hsun." In Davis and Stefanowska, eds. (1982), pp. 140–167.

—— (1995). "Without Politics: Gao Xingjian on Literary Creation." *The Stockholm Journal of East Asian Studies*, Vol. 6, pp. 82–101.

—— (1997). "Gao Xingjian's *Lingshan/Soul Mountain*: Modernism and the Chinese Writer." *Heat*, No. 4, pp. 128–157.

Lodén, Torbjörn (1993). "World Literature with Chinese Characteristics: On a Novel by Gao Xingjian." *The Stockholm Journal of East Asian Studies*, Vol. 4. pp. 17–39.

Pollard, David (1985). "The Controversy Over Modernism, 1979–84." *China Quarterly*, No. 104, pp. 641–656.

World Literature with Chinese Characteristics: On a Novel by Gao Xingjian

Gao Xingjian's novel *Lingshan* 靈山 [Soul mountain], which appeared in December 1990, is a work of art and should first of all be judged as such. But this exceedingly rich and complex piece of literature also gives expression to ideas and attitudes which merit the study of philosophers and intellectual historians, and it contains a wealth of information of interest to the historian and social anthropologist about the customs and traditions of the Han Chinese as well as of various national minorities.

This article focuses on the philosophical outlook and on some of the attitudes to Chinese tradition which the *Soul Mountain* reflects and which we may take as one representation of the *Zeitgeist of* post-Mao China. The fact that they are expressed in a work of literature rather than in a theoretical treatise does not make them less amenable to interpretation and analysis. In *Soul Mountain*, the difference between literature and philosophy is described in the following way:

> The novel differs from philosophy in that it is a living perceptual product. Your own arbitrarily coded message is soaked in a solution of desire. To watch the breeding and growth take place when this procedure results in the formation of cells is more interesting than art intellectual game, it is more similar to life and has by no means a final purpose.[2]
>
> (Gao, 1990, p. 344)

This coded message, although soaked in desire, should still be possible to interpret and analyze in terms of beliefs and attitudes.

My own interest in examining ideas and attitudes about tradition in *Soul Mountain* draws nourishment mainly from two sources: first, the meaning and implications of "world literature" and, second, the preoccupation with redefining cultural traditions as a central aspect of "the

Great Chinese Revolution," to borrow John Fairbank's term, that is, the break-up of the imperial order and the efforts to build a modern Chinese state and sodety (Fairbank, 1986).

WORLD LITERATURE

A kind of "world literature" that integrates elements from different cultures into an organic whole which transcends the sum-total of its constituent parts is now emerging as a major literary current, teeming with life and growing rapidly. The writings of V.S. Naipaul, Kenzaburo Oe 大江健三郎, Salman Rushdie, or Derek Walcott may be cited as prominent examples of this current. In a thought-provoking review, Stephen Owen discusses the poetry of Bei Dao 北島 in terms of "world literature" and argues that Bei Dao writes with his Western readers in mind and so refrains from using a Chinese idiom that would not be understood outside the Chinese cultural sphere (Owen, 1990, pp. 26–32). In Owen's view, Bei Dao has been relatively successful in his attempt to create world literature, but for this he has paid a high price: in order to reach out beyond China, Bei Dao constrains his creativity and sacrifices potential poetic qualities. I do not regard Bei Dao's poetry in this way. In my view, his poetry should be seen as an attempt to write good poetry rather than as an attempt to please Western readers. I find his poems highly original, often artistic in form and profound in content, not bleak copies of Western poetry. Still, Owen's argument raises an important issue well worth pondering.

While Owen finds that Chinese poets who write for the world cut themselves off from indigenous cultural sources, the prominent Japanese writer Kenzaburo Oe maintains in a different vein that it was only after reading Rabelais, Bakhtin and others that he could describe his own Japanese home village (Oe, 1992, pp. 1–16). Western techniques provide the key to doors to Japanese reality that have hitherto been shut. In Oe's perspective, to write world literature is not to place some constraint on one's creativity but the opposite: integrating techniques, experiences and data from different cultures opens up new literary vistas.

Whether we feel worried or encouraged by the prospects of the globalization of literature, the trend is clear: in a world which is shrinking as a result of technological advancement and economic integration, literary creation is breaking the confines of national boundaries. To study how this trend affects the development of different national literatures is a fascinating task, and the arguments of Owen and Oe raise interesting questions: to what extent does the globalization of literature constrain literary creativity, and to what extent does it provide new sources from which writers may draw nourishment?

REDEFINING CULTURAL TRADITIONS AND CHINA'S MODERNIZATION

To define tradition and, more importantly, to determine the position to take vis-a-vis tradition have been paramount concerns in Chinese intellectual life since the Opium War in the 1840s. The humiliating encounter with the Western Powers and with Japan seemed to make a re-evaluation of Chinese culture necessary. The foreign aggressors were not only interested in overturning the Chinese rulers, but they also rejected the basic tenets of the Chinese ethos — the rites and rituals and ideas which for more than two millennia had been conceived of as pillars of "all under heaven."

Conceiving of China's predicament in these terms, intellectuals and statesmen came for the first time in history to ask themselves if perhaps China must be saved at the expense of traditional Chinese culture, or at least aspects of traditional Chinese culture. The emergence of this question, which Joseph Levenson analyzes in terms of a transition from culturalism to nationalism, marks one of the turning-points in the intellectual history of China (Levenson, 1968). Throughout modern Chinese history, it has remained a focal point of discussion in the social and human sciences as well as in literature and art. In the final analysis, it is in this perspective that we must seek for the explanation of "the obsession with China" as a central feature in modern Chinese culture.[3]

1840–1919

In an early phase of the re-evaluation of traditional Chinese culture roughly lasting until the May Fourth Movement of 1919, the attitudes to indigenous tradition in that segment of the Chinese intelligentsia that determined the agenda of the discussions became, by and large, increasingly critical of traditional Chinese culture.

To be sure, before the New Culture Movement of 1915, most scholars argued that the solution to China's predicament must first of all be sought in the indigenous Confucian tradition. But this tradition seemed to have degenerated, so a Confucian regeneration was considered necessary. This kind of attitude we may see epitomized by the scholar-official Zeng Guofan 曾國藩 and those representing what Mary Wright calls "the last stand of Chinese Conservatism" (Wright, 1966). But it also nourished interest in the New Text School of Confucianism among intellectuals of a more reformist bent, such as Kang Youwei 康有為 and Liang Qichao 梁啟超. Even Zhang Taiyan 章太炎, who in some ways was politically very radical, was convinced that the Confucian tradition contained the basic answers to the Chinese predicament, although he differed from Kang and Liang in seeking for these answers in the tradition of the Old Text School rather than the New Text School.[4]

Some of those who sought the solution to China's predicament in the indigenous Confucian tradition re-interpreted Confucianism in the light of Western thought. For example, Kang Youwei's New Text Confucianism bears the imprint of European evolutionary ideas. Some even went so far as to suggest that the seeming success of Europe could largely be attributed to Chinese influence exerted by early Confucian thought.[5]

While clinging to indigenous Chinese high culture as the core of Chinese civilization, an increasing number of scholars and officials came to regard the adoption of Western techniques as a "means" to preserve the "essence" of traditional Chinese high culture. This formula of Chinese culture as essence and Western culture as means may be interpreted differently; the emphasis may be placed on the means or on the essence. In the landscape of late nineteenth and early twentieth century Chinese thought, it appears with the face of Janus: on the one hand, it was a defensive concession on the part of the cultural conservatives designed in order to safeguard the core of traditional Chinese high culture; on the other hand, it paved the way for the rejection of traditional Confucian ideology.

The rejection of the Confucian tradition in favour of Western culture became a major tenet of the New Culture Movement and the May Fourth Movement.[6] The cultures of China and the West were contrasted in a totalistic fashion and the Chinese cultural radicals found the culture of China inferior. In their eyes, the patriarchal culture of China, characterized by stifling rituals underpinned by a strict hierarchy in the family as well as in public life, lacked the vigour and the dynamism of Western culture. In their vision the teachings of Darwinism ought to be applied to society. Unable to foresee the full consequences of this conception, they became instrumental in introducing the ideas and attitudes of Social Darwinism into China. Some of the cultural iconoclasts even questioned the viability of the Chinese language as a means for communicating the ideas of modern scholarship (Qian, 1918, pp. 141–145). While even at the time, this was an extremist viewpoint, the notion that the *classical* written language was not fit for communicating modern ideas to large numbers of people was shared by the cultural radicals. Thus, the literary revolution proclaimed by Chen Duxiu 陳獨秀 and Hu Shi 胡適 was to a great extent a language revolution. The classical written language *wenyan* was abandoned in favour of the vernacular *baihua,* which was based on the language used in the classical vernacular novels but which was, in fact, Westernized to a considerable extent both in vocabulary and in syntax.

However, if we look more closely at the writings of cultural radicals such as Cai Yuanpei 蔡元培, Chen Duxiu or Hu Shi, we shall see that their rejection of Chinese culture was by no means as complete as the manifestoes of the time would often have it. Essentially, the target of their criticism was the patriarchal, stifling Confucian culture that they had themselves experienced rather than the original ideas of thinkers in the Confucian tradition. Hu Shi, for one, even found a scientific method in the writings of Neo-Confucian philosophers.

Moreover, and perhaps more interestingly, a close analysis of the writings of the cultural iconoclasts of the May Fourth Movement may reveal that their rejection of tradition bears the imprint of that tradition. Lin Yu-sheng 林毓生 has focused on the predilection for totalism as a basic traditional feature of their thought (Lin, 1978).

To sum up, the most striking aspect of this early phase of the re-evaluation of Chinese tradition was the separation of China as a state or a nation on the one hand and Chinese culture on the other: China became for the first time in history conceivable without the traditional Chinese high culture. The salvation of China was given the highest priority; if need be, China must be changed at the expense of Chinese culture.

1919–1949

In a second phase of the re-evaluation of Chinese tradition, beginning around 1919 and lasting until the establishment of the PRC in 1949, the picture is diverse and exceedingly complex.[7] Many ideas first formulated in the earlier phase were now followed up and developed. In the new literature that emerged in the wake of the May Fourth Movement, we find innumerable examples of main characters who rebel against the stifling tradition of patriarchal Confucianism. Ba Jin's *Jia* 家 [Family] trilogy stands out as the most widely known and probably most influential of all literary writings with this tendency.

As part of the revolt against tradition, individualism was exalted as a major value. Literature became for many writers essentially a vehicle for the manifestation of the self. Yu Dafu 郁達夫 and Guo Moruo 郭沫若 are both examples of writers who were greatly preoccupied with manifesting the self (Liu, 1985, pp. 110–118).

Western culture was introduced on a large scale, and many Chinese writers and artists tried deliberately to absorb Western ideas arid Western techniques. In some cases, such as Qian Zhongshu's 錢鍾書 *Wei cheng* 圍城 [Fortress besieged, 1947], Western influence is obvious; in other cases, such as the writings of Shen Congwen 沈從文, it is much more concealed, but still unmistakably there (Huters, 1982; Kinkley, 1987).

Innumerable "isms" and styles were introduced, but underlying most if not all of these attempts at renewal was a concern with China. Even the *l'art pour l'art* of the early Creation Society was motivated in terms of its believed value as a means to regenerate China (Guo, 1959, pp. 83–88).

With the ascendancy of so-called revolutionary thought came the call for ideological unity: individualism, freedom, objective scholarship became brandished as bourgeois values. Literary works should be written from the point of view of "scientific socialism." Again, literature became a "vehicle of the Way" [wen yi zai dao 文以載道] — the Way now being Communism, not Confucianism.

If leftist thought diverted attention away from individualism, not to speak of modernist forms of expression, in favour of serving the needs of the revolution as these needs were defined by the Communist Party leaders, it did on the other hand encourage the study of popular forms of Chinese culture as expressions of the thinking of the oppressed classes. Many works of literature produced according to the official Party line, such as the novels and short stories of Zhao Shuli 趙樹理, obviously draw on traditional story-telling (Prusêk, 1955). However, at the same time popular cultural traditions confronted the Communists with a dilemma:

expressions of the consciousness of the oppressed should, according to the Marxist textbooks, be "progressive," but the greater bulk of popular culture as preserved did not meet the ideological standards set by the Party. Therefore, the Party tried to make use of some of the old popular forms of culture, such as story-telling, but give them a new, politically correct, content. In this process the Party in fact killed much of the traditional culture.

To sum up, during the second phase of the re-evaluation of Chinese tradition, which was a period of great cultural vitality and variety, national salvation remained the primary concern. The upsurge of interest in the 1920s in the Enlightenment values of individualism, objective scholarship and democracy gradually gave way to a unified communist ideology focusing on classes and class consciousness, as defined *a priori* by the Party orthodoxy. The need to distinguish between traditional high culture and popular culture was recognized, and traditional popular forms began to be inculcated with the ideological messages of the day.

1949–1976

In a third phase of the re-evaluation of traditional Chinese culture, lasting from the establishment of the PRC in 1949 until the death of Mao Zedong in 1976, attitudes to traditional culture were strictly regulated by the Communist orthodoxy. The content of "Marxism-Leninism and Mao Zedong Thought" did vary but invariably provided intellectuals, writers and artists with the right questions and correct views. With few exceptions, there was no way to operate outside the framework of the orthodoxy.

During this phase the classical vernacular novels, and in particular *Hongloumeng* 紅樓夢 [The story of the stone; also known as "Dream of the red chamber"], were hailed as splendid manifestation of traditional Chinese culture. Of course, the question of their interpretation was highly politicized: to embrace a "mistaken" interpretation was to commit an ideological error.

Attempts were made to inculcate the form of the traditional Peking Opera with new, "revolutionary" content, and also other forms of traditional culture such as ballads and story-telling were mobilized to serve the revolution. These attempts were *not* all failures, but in the process most authentic forms of traditional culture that were still alive perished.

Throughout this phase the focus was on China, rather than on the individual man, who was a means for the regeneration of a strong and prosperous China led by the Communist Party; "individualism" and "freedom" were words of abuse.

1976–

A fourth phase in the re-evaluation of traditional culture began after the death of Mao Zedong. Much of the old orthodoxy was dissolved and this resulted in an upsurge of cultural creativity and variety. In a way that resembles and probably surpasses the 1920s, new ideas were introduced, often to be soon rejected, at a fierce speed. After the massacre in Beijing in 1989, the Party ideologues tried to slow down the process, but these efforts have proved largely abortive.

In the early 1980s the so-called New Confucianism was introduced into China and attracted much interest. Leading protagonists of this line of thought, such as Tu Wei-ming 杜維明, toured Chinese universities and argued that the fundamental tenets of Confucian thought, which had been largely distorted when usurped by the rulers of imperial China as instruments of ideological control, are indeed not incompatible with modernization and democratization but just the opposite: modernization and democratization make it possible for the first time in history to realize the fundamental Confucian values. Tu Wei-ming and others also argued that the Chinese people should define their identity in terms of their own culture and that the Confucian heritage may play an important role in this regard (Tu, 1989).

Another trend in the 1980s was to reject in a rather totalistic fashion indigenous Chinese tradition as inhuman. The television serial *He shang* 河殤 [River elegy] projected an image of Chinese history closely akin to Wittfogel's hydraulic society: the natural conditions of the North China plain had given rise to a monstrous oppressive bureaucratic social order and culture which saw men only as tools to be used for the collective good (Cui, 1988; Wittfogel, 1957). Fang Lizhi 方勵之, while being much more cautious than the *River Elegy* script writers as far as abstract historical generalizations are concerned, called for "total Westernization."[8] In literature also, several important writers such as Bei Dao wanted to break away from Chinese tradition arid assimilate Western techniques arid Western ideas as the core of a new and "modern" Chinese literature.

A third tendency in the 1980s was to combine a rejection of Confucian high culture, which was often seen as representative of the Northern Yellow River culture, with an interest in folk culture, in particular the folk cultures of southern China with some of their roots in the ancient kingdom of Chu.[9]

Thus, during this phase of the re-evaluation of Chinese tradition the concept of Chinese tradition has begun to be problematized and analyzed in new and interesting ways. In addition to the Confucian culture of the imperial ruling elite, several smaller traditions have been identified. The focus has largely remained on the destiny of China, but there have also been some notable signs of a shift of attention away from China's predicament towards the human condition. In this regard, Gao Xingjian appears as an important forerunner.

GAO XINGJIAN

Gao Xingjiani was born in 1940 in Ganzhou in Jiangxi province, but his ancestors came from Taizhou in Jiangsu province. In 1962 he graduated from the Beijing Institute of Foreign Languages, with a major in French. During the Cultural Revolution, he spent five years in the countryside. For almost twenty years he wrote without publishing. Only in 1979, and as a result of the cultural thaw after the death of Mao and the fall of the Gang of Four, could he begin to publish.

A playwright and a writer of novels and short stories but also a painter and a cultural critic and theoretician, Gao Xingjian's works span a wide spectrum.

In 1981 his book *Xiandai xiaoshuo jiqiao chutan* 現代小説技巧初探 [A preliminary exploration of the techniques of modem fiction] added fuel to the debate in China about modernism and realism in literature. The book was condemned by the orthodox critics and thereafter modernism was again considered a heresy.

In 1982 his play *Juedui xinhao* 絕對信號 [Alarm signal] was staged in Beijing. This play, which attracted much attention, marked the beginning of new experimental drama in China.

In 1983 his absurd drama *Chezhan* 車站 [The bus-stop] was banned, and he himself became a target of the campaign against the so-called spiritual pollution.

In 1985 his play *Yeren* 野人 [Wild man] was staged in Beijing, again attracting attention outside China and giving rise to a heated debate among Chinese critics.

In 1986 his play *Bi'an* 彼岸 [The other shore] was banned, and after that none of his plays has been staged on the Chinese mainland.

Since 1987 Gao has been living in Paris. In 1989 after the massacre in Beijing he announced his withdrawal from the Chinese Communist Party, and after the publication of his play *Taowang* 逃亡 [Fleeing; also known as "Fugitives," or "Absconding"] he has been condemned by the authorities, who searched and scaled his flat in Beijing and prohibited all his writings. Gao himself has stated that he will not return to China as long as totalitarian rule prevails.

Some of Gao's works have been translated into several languages (English, Flemish, French, German, Hungarian, Italian, Japanese, and Swedish), and some of his plays have been performed around the world (in Austria, France, Germany, Hong Kong, Sweden, Taiwan, the United Kingdom, the United States, and in former Yugoslavia). In 1992 he was awarded the prestigious French order *Chevalier de l'Ordre des Arts et des Lettres.*

SOUL MOUNTAIN

Beginning in 1982, it took Gao seven years to complete *Soul Mountain* which, in spite of numerous other writings, must be considered his main work so far. To refer to *Soul Mountain* as a "novel" is to use this term for want of a better one. It contains dialogues and stream-of-consciousness monologues, as we may expect from a novel, but also pieces, which look like journalistic reportage, anthropological reports, philosophical essays and historical treatises. This combination of themes is in some way reminiscent of classical Chinese writings, but the technique and intellectual content is also informed by Gao's deep insights into Western culture. Both in terms of form and content, the result clearly transcends any conceivable Chinese or Western source of inspiration.

At the simplest level, *Soul Mountain* is about a writer who, after being informed that he has lung cancer and most probably only a few months left to live, decides to say good-bye to the metropolitan life of Beijing in order to travel in Southern China and learn more about the cultures of some minority peoples as well as the culture of the Han people. Soon the cancer disappears without leaving any trace, but he still fulfills his travel plans. The journey takes him to the provinces of Sichuan and Qinghai in the Southwest of China and then along the Yangzi River to the provinces of Jiangsu and Jiangxi in the East. In broad outline, this frame story coincides with Gao Xingjian's personal experience.

Much of what the writer sees and experiences on his journey can be verified by scholarly methods. Places and reported customs of different peoples can be identified. But some things will not be found by a journalist or by a scholar doing field work. For example, Soul Mountain — the spiritual mountain — the elusive goal that the traveller searches for, cannot be found on any map.

The main character in the first chapter is a "you," but in the second chapter the focus shifts to an "I" — "I" also being the narrator. Throughout most of the 81 chapters of the book, there is this alternation between "I" and "you." Soon the reader discovers that "you" and "I" are actually one and the same person, so the shift in focus is a shift in perspective. From the different perspectives, different aspects of the person become visible. Already in chapter 2 we are informed that "while *you* searched for the way to Soul Mountain, I wandered along the Yangzi River, searching for this truth" (Gao, 1990, p. 13, italics added). The Soul Mountain is elusive and defies the efforts that this "you" makes to reach it. The "truth" [zhenshi 真實], on the other hand, is to be found here and now.

Perhaps we may see "the Soul Mountain" as representing fantasy, the dream of reaching out beyond the confines of what is, and "the truth" as representing reality, authentic living here and now.

The "you" meets a woman — "she" — whom he desires and conquers sexually. Having escaped from her family, she, too, is an outsider seeking fulfillment. This woman, who first turns up in chapter 5, becomes a main character, associated with the "you" rather than with the "I" (Gao, 1990, chapters 5, 11, 21, 27, 31, 32, 44, 56, 64). On the other hand, many different "hes" that emerge throughout the book seem to be associated with the "I" rather than with the "you" (Gao, 1990, chapters 10, 20, 22, 49, 72). In the last few chapters the "you," "I," "shes," and "hes" are then mingled in a way that makes it difficult to identify a main character.

The intricate structuring of the personages in *Soul Mountain*, which gives expression to the unity underlying their differentiation, represents a philosophical outlook, which permeates the book. This outlook, which we may refer to in terms of "subjectivism," is beautifully formulated in chapter 52. Here I will quote a short passage:

> You know that I am only talking to myself, in order to alleviate my sense of loneliness. You know that there is no cure for this sense of loneliness, there is no man who can save me from it, and so the only thing I can do is to take myself as an interlocutor.
>
> In this long monologue, you are the object of my discourse, you are me listening to myself, you are only my shadow.
>
> When I listen to you who are myself. I let you create a she, because just like me you cannot endure loneliness, and so you seek an interlocutor. […]
>
> In your spiritual journey, you, just like myself, search for your own ideas and the farther you travel the closer you get to me, and finally it cannot be avoided that you will come so close to me that we cannot be separated, and then it becomes necessary to take one step back and open up, a distance, and that distance is he, he is the shadow of you when you turn around and leave me. […]
>
> The different "hes" are also numerous images, which he produces of himself. Everything in this world, all strange and wonderful things, exists outside of me and you. In other words, they are projections of my shadow, which I cannot get away from, and if I cannot get away from them, why should I try?   (Gao, 1990, pp. 340–341)

Basically, man cannot reach out beyond himself, and so the "you" is just a projection of the "I," who in turn creates "she." And "he" and his numerous manifestations are the self's shadow. In the final analysis, each and every being and thing is a projection. The world is the world of the self — there is no way to get out of the self and reach the *Ding an sich.*

SOUL MOUNTAIN AND TRADITION

In order to locate the vision of *Soul Mountain* in the context of the re-evaluation of Chinese tradition, six tenets of this vision may be identified.

1. The Recreation of a Literary Language

In an essay about *Soul Mountain*, Gao says that "a writer is responsible only to his language" (Gao, 1992, pp. 203–215). He wishes to free the Chinese language from the shackles of political ideology and to create a literary medium fit to "produce modern literature imbued with an Asian spirit." The new literary language that Gao envisages must break away from the influence of the grammar and syntax of European Languages and return to some of the basic characteristics of the traditional Chinese language.

In arguing that liberating the Chinese language from some of the Western influence to which it has been subjected during this century would make it more suited to "produce modern literature imbued with an Asian spirit," Gao breaks radically with the conventional wisdom that has long prevailed. No doubt, his ideas in this regard will remain controversial. However, it seems difficult to dispute that the language of *Soul Mountain* is remarkable: with its archaic features it still seems very modern.

2. Alienation

Before he embarked on his tour of Southern China, searching for the spiritual mountain, the urban life of intellectuals in Beijing had left the main character of *Soul Mountain* with a sense of alienation — although I have not found the Chinese equivalent to this word in the book. Therefore, his travel and exploration of Southern China becomes a search for a sense of unity and of true life:

> I should have left that contaminated environment long ago and returned to nature, seeking true life. [...] In that environment people kept telling me that life is the source of literature, that literature must be loyal to life, loyal to the truth of life. But my mistake was precisely that I estranged myself from life, and so I betrayed the truth of life, for the truth of life is not equivalent to the outer manifestations of life, and this truth of life, or shall we say essence of life, in fact ought to be in a certain way rather than in another way, and the reason that I betrayed the truth of life was that I only enumerated a series of the phenomena of life, and then of course I was not able to reflect life correctly, but could only tread the path of distorting reality.   (Gao, 1990, p. 13)

The journey and the exploration of the main character being a search for true life, the focus is on the human being, not on China; man is an end, *the* end, not a tool for the regeneration of China. In this regard, *Soul Mountain* represents a fundamental departure from the "obsession with China" and the ensuing utilitarian, not to say Social Darwinist, view of man that characterizes so much of twentieth-century Chinese culture.

3. Primitivism

The search for "true life" becomes an attempt to *return* to the true life, which the main character finds in the life style of national minorities such as the Qiang 羌 and the Miao 苗 peoples, but which he believes were also original to the Han people. On this ground, we may speak of a primitivist streak in the book. Consider for example the reflections of the "I" on the naturalness of the mating habits among the Miao people: "I was suddenly enveloped in the sentiments of spring and I reflected that this must have been how man originally sought love, and later when so-called civilization caused a clear separation of the sexual impulses and love ... this was actually a stupidity of mankind" (Gao, 1990, p. 241). In this primitivist vein, we may also see the exaltation of the natural and spontaneous. For example, in chapter 60, the "you" of the novel discourses to the "she" about art and says: "Art in comparison with nature is bleak and lacking, only a fool will think that art transcends nature" (Gao, 1990, p. 414).

4. Anti-Confucianism

The originally true life had been spoilt by the forces of so-called civilization, in particular Confucianism. We may indeed speak of a decidedly anti-Confucian tendency. In chapter 59, a collector of folk songs makes the following comment about one song: "This is a folk song that has not been spoilt by any scholars! A folk song springing from the soul! Do you understand? You have rescued a culture! Not only the national minorities but also the Han people have a true folk culture that has not been contaminated by the ethical teaching of Confucianism" (Gao, 1990, p. 390).

5. Scepticism

Soul Mountain projects an image of Chinese history as rich and varied. But in line with the philosophical subjectivism that permeates it, the I finds it impossible to determine the true nature of Chinese history, *wie es eigentlich gewesen ist*. Reflecting on the illegible characters on a stele erected in memory of Emperor Yu 禹, the "I" reflects:

> [It] may be read thus: history is a riddle
> it may also be read thus: history is a lie
> it may again be read thus: history is nonsense
> moreover it may be read thus: history is prediction
> furthermore it may also be read thus: history is a sour fruit
> in addition it may be read thus: history clangs as iron
> again it may be read thus: history is a lump of dough
> also it may be read thus: history is grave clothes
> further it may be read thus: history is a sudorific
> further it may be read thus: history is a wall erected by devils leaving no
>   way out
> similarly it may be read thus: history is an antiquity
> even: history is reason
> still more extremely: history is experience
> more extremely yet: history is a proof
> and also: history is scattered pearls on a plate
> even: history is a series of causes and effects
> also: history is a metaphor
> or: history is a state of mind
> again thus: history is history
> and: history is nothing
> as well as: history is a sigh
> Actually, history may be read however you like, this is indeed a tremen-
>   dous discovery!   (Gao, 1990, pp. 500–501)

The kind of scepticism that this view of history manifests may be seen as a plea for plurality and a warning against orthodoxy. Reality is infinitely complex and cannot be understood in all its complexity. The meaning of an object cannot be understood in isolation; meaning is something that a subject attaches to an object. There is no such thing as the only true meaning. The pretension to define the correct meaning must be seen as a pretension to power.

The formulation of this scepticism seems informed by the insights of Buddhist philosophy but also by quantum mechanics and modern psychology. Discussing the self, the "I" remarks in chapter 26:

> I then go on to observe other people, and when doing so I discover that

my omnipresent repugnant self also sneaks in, not letting any face escape its infiltration. This is actually a nuisance. When I observe others I am still observing myself. I seek for a face that I like, or an expression that appeals to me, but they do not really move me, I cannot identify with the masses of people who pass by in front of me, I observe them but I do not see them, no matter where, in the waiting hall, or in the train compartment or on a ship deck, in a restaurant or in a park, or when strolling around in the streets, I always try to capture faces or bodies which resemble a face and a body I am familiar with, or look for some hint which may awaken some latent memory. When I observe other people, I always make them mirrors in which I may observe myself, and this kind of observation is always determined by my state of mind at the time. Even when I see a woman, I use my sense organs to figure her out and use my experiences to form my ideas of her before I make a judgement. As a matter of fact, my understanding of other people is both shallow and arbitrary, also when it comes to women. The women that I see are all illusions made by myself which I then use to delude myself, this is my tragedy. Therefore, in the end I always fail in my relations with women. If I were a woman, it would be the other way round and I would have the same trouble being together with a man. The problem emanates from the consciousness of this inner self, this monster which torments me. Narcissism, self-contempt, inhibitions, arrogance, contentedness and grief, jealousy and hatred have all their origin in this. The self is in fact the root of the unhappiness of man. Does then the solution of this unhappiness lie in the elimination of this conscious self?

Buddha spoke to Subodhi and said: All forms are illusory, and what has no form is also illusory.   (Gao, 1990, pp. 161–162)

6. Chinese and Western Myths

Soul Mountain contains numerous references to Chinese as well as Western myths and symbols. There are references to the Chinese Pangu 盤古, who used his axe to separate heaven and earth, and Nüwa 女媧, who created man, but also to the Western "prince on a white horse," etc. (Gao, 1990, pp. 125, 381, 364). This again is a testimony to Gao's ability to combine elements from different cultures into an integrated whole.

GLOBALIZATION AND TRANSNATIONALISM

Soul Mountain is a tale squarely set in China, containing descriptions of the geography of China and habits and customs of the Han Chinese and of various national minorities. However, in developing each of these six themes just identified in *Soul Mountain*, Gao Xingjian has drawn on the cultural traditions of both China and the West. The result is highly original and constitutes a whole that transcends by far the sum-total of its integral parts. I think we are therefore entitled to look upon *Soul Mountain* as a piece of "world literature with Chinese characteristics."

Of course, world literature may take many various forms. In some cases, such as Naipaul's *Enigma of Arrival,* the encounter of Western and non-Western culture is a major theme. But in other cases, such as Gao's *Soul Mountain,* it is the writer's perspective and his method, and not so much the theme, that are part of a modern world culture transcending the boundaries of traditional national cultures.

The globalization of culture and the emergence of world literature are basically the results of the expansion and integration of the world economy, that is, of factors outside the realm of culture as such, but this trend raises some important questions of cultural values. For example, if we consider, as I think we should do, variety and pluralism as fundamental values, then the question whether the globalization of culture will lead to a higher degree of uniformity or to greater variety becomes a crucial one.

In the long run the globalization of culture and the development of world literature is, I believe, an irreversible trend, but its course of development is an open question, to be determined by the conscious efforts of each and every one of us. If the process of globalization were to be guided solely by the forces of economic development, which are blind to cultural values, I fear that it would lead to impoverishment and the final extinction of most smaller cultures and languages in the world. But consciously guided, I am convinced that this process may also greatly enrich and vitalize the cultural reservoir at mankind's disposal. To see to it that individual cultures and languages do not all perish in the process of globalization, we need, to use Walcott's word, stubbornness: "Survival is the triumph of stubbornness, and spiritual stubbornness, a sublime stupidity, is what makes the occupation of poetry endure [...]" (Walcott, 1992).

The writings of V.S. Naipaul, Kenzaburo Oe, Salman Rushdi, Derek Walcott and others provide good reasons for cherishing the hope that variety will survive, and indeed be enriched, by the globalization of world culture.

For the culture of China which, no matter how illustrious, suffers from the ills of insularity, few things could be more promising than the appearance of first-rate writers of world literature. Gao Xingjian has now joined these ranks. So has Bei Dao. And many more are coming.

NOTES

1. This is a revised version of an article with the same title published in *The Stockholm Journal of East Asian Studies*, Vol. 4 (1993), pp. 17–39. In the original version, there is an appendix, "A Bibliography of Gao Xingjian's Published Writings in Chinese 1980–1992" (pp. 37–39), which is now omitted.

2. Page references are given to the Chinese edition published by the Lianjing chuban shiye gongsi 聯經出版事業公司 in 1990. My translations are based on the Chinese original, but I have also consulted Göran Malmqvist's Swedish translation: *Andarnas berg* (Malmqvist, 1992).

3. For details, see C. T. Hsia (1971), pp. 533–561; Long Yingtai (1992), pp. 46–49.

4. For a good introduction to these themes, see Charlotte Furth (1983), pp. 322–405.

5. For example, Wei Yuan asserted that Jesus had the Confucian classics translated into Latin. See Ch'en (1979), p. 65.

6. The standard work on the May Fourth Movement remains Chow Tse-tsung (1960).

7. For excellent introductions to the intellectual and literary currents of this time, see Schwartz (1983), pp. 406–450; Lee (1983), pp. 452–504; Lee (1987), pp. 421–491.

8. Concerning Fang Lizhi's conception of "total Westernization," see, for example, the speech he gave in Anhui on 27 September 1986, in Fang (1988). For a selection of Fang's writings in English translation, see Fang Lizhi (1991).

9. Interview with Han Shaogong, in Martin and Kinkley, eds. (1992), pp. 147–155.

REFERENCES

Ch'en, Jerome (1979). *China and the West: Society and Culture 1815–1937*. London: Hutchinson.

Chow Tse-tsung (1960). *The May Fourth Movement: Intellectual Revolution in Modern China*. Cambridge, MA: Harvard University Press.

Cui Wenhua 崔文華, ed. (1988). *Haiwai* Heshang *da taolun* 海外《河殤》大討論 [The great discussion overseas on *The River Elegy*]. Harbin: Heilongjiang jiaoyu chubanshe 黑龍江教育出版社.

Fairbank, John K. (1986). *The Great Chinese Revolution 1800–1985*. New York: Harper & Row.

——, ed. (1983). *The Cambridge History of China*. Cambridge, MA: Cambridge University Press.

Fang Lizhi 方勵之 (1986). "Tan zhengzhi tizhi gaige" 談政治體制改革 [On the reform of the political system]. In Fang (1988), pp. 222–230.

—— (1988). *Fang Lizhi zixuanji zhi er* 方勵之自選集之二 [Selected writings by Fang Lizhi, 2]. Singapore: World Scientific Publishing Co.

—— (1991). *Bringing Down the Great Wall: Writings on Science, Culture, and Democracy in China*. Ed. James H. Williams. New York: Knopf.

Furth, Charlotte (1983). "Intellectual Change: From the Reform Movement to the May Fourth Movement, 1895–1920." In Fairbank, ed. (1983). pp. 322–405.

Gao Xingjian 高行健 (1990). *Lingshan* 靈山 [Soul mountain]. Taipei: Lianjing chuban shiye gongsi 聯經出版事業公司.

—— (1992). "Wenxue yu xuanxue: Guanyu *Lingshan*" 文學與玄學·關於《靈山》 [Literature and metaphysics: On *Soul Mountain*]. *Jintian* 今天 [Today], Vol. 18, No. 3, pp. 203–215.

Guo Moruo 郭沫若 (1959a). *Moruo wenji* 沫若文集 (Collected writings of Guo Moruo), 10 vols. Beijing: Renmin wenxue chubanshe 人民文學出版社.

—— (1959b). "Wenyi zhi shehui de shiming" 文藝之社會的使命 [The social task of literature and art]. In Guo (1959a), Vol. 10, pp. 83–88.

Hsia, C. T. (1971a). *A History of Modern Chinese Fiction*, 2nd ed. New Haven and London: Yale University Press.

—— (1971b). "Obsession with China: The Moral Burden of Modern Chinese Literature." In Hsia (1971a), pp. 533–561.

Huters, Theodore (1982). *Qian Zhongshu*. Boston: Twayne Publishers.

Kinkley, Jeffrey C. (1987). *The Odyssey of Shen Congwen*. Stanford: Stanford University Press.

Lee, Leo Ou-fan (1983). " Literary Trends I: The Quest for Modernity, 1895–1927." In Fairbank, ed. (1983), Vol. 12, pp. 452–504.

—— (1987). "Literary Trends II: The Road to Revolution, 1927–1949." In MacFarquhar and Fairbank, eds. (1987), Vol. 13, pp. 421–491.

Levenson, Joseph (1968). *Confucian China and Its Modern Fate. A Trilogy*. Berkeley and Los Angeles: California University Press.

Lin Yu-sheng (1978). *The Crisis of Chinese Consciousness: Radical Anti-Traditionalism in the May Fourth Era*. Madison: University of Wisconsin Press.

Liu Zaifu 劉再復 (1985a). *Lun Zhongguo wenxue* 論中國文學 [On Chinese literature]. Beijing: Zuojia chubanshe 作家出版社.

—— (1985b). "Woguo xiandai wenxueshi shang dui ren de sanci faxian" 我國文學史上對人的三次發現 [Three discoveries of man in the history of modern Chinese literature]. In Liu (1985a), pp. 110–118.

Long Yingtai (Lung Yingtai) 龍應台 (1992). "Chengman 'Zhongguo Zhongguo Zhongguo' de pingzi" 盛滿"中國中國中國"的瓶子 [A bottle filled with "China China China"]. *Mingbao yuekan* 明報月刊 [Ming Pao monthly], No. 8, pp. 46–49.

MacFarquhar, Roderick, and John K. Fairbank, eds. (1987). *The Cambridge History of China*, Vol. 13. Cambridge, MA: Cambridge University Press.

Malmqvist, Göran (1992). *Andarnas berg* [Swedish translation of *Lingshan*]. Stockholm: Forum.

Martin, Helmut, and Jeffrey Kinkley, eds. (1992). *Modern Chinese Writers Self-Portrayals*. Armonk, NY: M. E. Sharpe.

Oe, Kenzaburo (1993). "Speaking on Japanese Culture Before a Scandinavian Audience." *The Stockholm Journal of East Asian Studies*, Vol. 4, pp. 1–16.

Owen, Stephen (1990). "What is World Poetry?" *The New Republic*, 19 November, pp. 26–32.

Prusêk, Jaroslav (1955). *Die Literature des befreitne China and itre Volkstraditionen*. Prag: Artia.

Qian Xuantong 錢玄同 (1918). "Zhongguo jinhou zhi wenzi wenti" 中國今後之文字問題 [The question of the future of the Chinese script]. In Zhao, ed. (1935–36), Vol. 1, pp. 141–145. Original work published on 14 March 1918.

Schwartz, Benjamin J. (1983). "Themes in intellectual history: May Fourth and After." In Fairbank, ed. (1983), Vol. 12, pp. 406–450.

Tu Wei-ming 杜維明 (1989). *Ruxue di san qi fazhan de qianjing wenti* 儒學第三期發展的前景問題 [The prospects of Confucian learning in its third phase of development]. Taipei: Lianjing chuban shiye gongsi 聯經出版事業公司.

Walcott, Derek (1992). *Nobel Lecture 1992*. Mimeo. Stockholm: The Swedish Academy.

Wittfogel, Karl A. (1957). *Oriental Despotism. A Comparative Study of Total Power.* New Haven and London: Yale University Press.

Wright, Mary C. (1966). *The Last Stand of Chinese Conservatism: The T'ung Chih Restoration, 1862–1874*. New York: Atheneum.

Zhao Jiabi 趙家壁, ed. (1935–36). *Zhongguo xin wenxue daxi* 中國新文學大系 [A comprehensive anthology of modern Chinese literature]. Shanghai: Shanghai liangyou tushu gongsi 上海良友圖書公司.

Gao Xingjian's Dialogue with Two Dead Poets from Shaoxing: Xu Wei and Lu Xun[1]

Gao Xingjian travelled to Germany on the invitation of the Morat-Institut für Kunst und Kunstwissenschaft in 1987. This was his third visit to Europe and while there he applied for residence in France. Before leaving China, he had already decided to take this course of action for he had with him his most precious possession: the manuscript of *Lingshan* 靈山 [Soul mountain], a novel he began to write in Beijing during the summer of 1982 and subsequently completed in Paris in September of 1989.

In the novel *Soul Mountain*, Gao Xingjian documents his observations of Chinese society and history during his five months of travel in the south. Juxtaposed against this backdrop are his reflections on human existence, and on his own past life. The 563 pages of *Soul Mountain* provide the space he requires for the large scale experimentation he sought to carry out with narrative technique and language. The result is a fictional autobiography employing pronouns as protagonists, each reflecting a facet of Gao Xingjian's self (Lee, 1995).

DIALOGUES ON LITERATURE IN *SOUL MOUNTAIN*

Chapter 71 of *Soul Mountain* tells of Gao Xingjian's visit to Shaoxing, a town in Zhejiang province, which is renowned both for its rice wine and for the eminent historical figures it has produced, amongst them the Ming dynasty poet, playwright and artist Xu Wei 徐渭 and the poet and fiction writer Lu Xun 魯迅. Shaoxing is also the birthplace of Gao Xingjian's mother, so he too has a link with this town. In this study, I have used Shaoxing as an artificial construct. It is simply a starting point for what I have construed as Gao Xingjian's conversations with the two dead poets: naturally they cannot respond but their literature and their lives constitute statements of what they stood for. Gao Xingjian's literature and life, too, are statements of his self; these statements are responses to the two dead poets of Shaoxing. First, Gao Xingjian's sparse comments on the two poets in the chapter are extrapolated, then the meaning of creative literature for them in their respective historical times is discussed. The final section will examine some of Gao Xingjian's recent essays which may be thought of as addressing the two dead poets, for they are symbolic of a conception of literature closely approximating Gao Xingjian's own. The two dead poets and their writings are embedded in the fabric of Gao Xingjian's literary and intellectual heritage: the voice of the self to which he is committed in his creative life is that of a self nurtured by that Chinese heritage and enriched since the 1950s by Gao Xingjian's access to Western literature.[2]

At the beginning of *Soul Mountain*, Gao Xingjian is already in Sichuan province, having fled the Beijing authorities and the possibility of being sent to one of the notorious prisons in Qinghai. By Chapter 71 (pages 497–501), he is in Shaoxing where he notes that the local grain temple, which had for one night provided shelter for Ah Q (immortalized by Lu Xun's novel of that name), has been renovated and now bears a sign with an inscription by a famous contemporary calligrapher. Gao Xingjian cannot help thinking: "When Ah Q was beheaded as a bandit he certainly wouldn't have imagined that such an honour would be bestowed upon him after his death." Gao Xingjian concludes that it is difficult even for minor characters to escape being put to death in this small town. Then there is the example of the revolutionary martyr Qiu Jin 秋瑾 whose photograph now hangs in her former residence: a woman of refinement and elegance, education and literary talents. "She was just over twenty when they trussed her up, paraded her through the crowds, and beheaded her."

By association, Qiu Jin's patriotic fervour and self-sacrifice takes Gao Xingjian's mind back to the "great writer" Lu Xun whose life "was spent in hiding and on the run. Fortunately he moved into the foreign concessions otherwise he would have been killed long before illness brought an end to his life." Gao Xingjian recalls that as a student he used to recite a line of one of Lu Xun's poems: "I offer my blood to the Yellow Emperor" (Lu Xun, 1981d). However, he now has reservations. "The Yellow Emperor is the legendary first emperor of China and can refer to one's country, race or ancestors." But, he asks: "Why must one glorify one's ancestors with blood? Is spilling one's own blood glorious? A person's head is one's own, why must it be chopped off for the Yellow Emperor?"

The questions raised here are critical for Gao Xingjian, both because of his commitment to literature of the self and his Chinese ancestry. They are obliquely answered when he ruminates on the dubious nature of both legend and history later in the chapter. At the tomb of Yu the Great [大禹 Da Yu] in the vicinity of Shaoxing, he recounts the reference in the *Shanhai jing* 山海經 [Classic of mountains and seas] to the animal ancestry of Yu the Great. When Yu the Great reveals his bear appearance to his new bride, the young virgin flees in panic. Crazed with lust, Yu the Great chases after and demands that she comply. "For his wife Yu was a bear, for the ordinary folk he was a god, for the historian he was an emperor, for those who write fiction he can be described as the first person to kill another to achieve his own ambitions." Just as the script on a stone slab at the tomb of Yu the Great continues to defy deciphering by the experts, so it seems to Gao Xingjian that all history is like this and is open to any number of interpretations.

These reflections on nation, race and ancestry, and the individual are developed further elsewhere in *Soul Mountain* but the pointed reference to the sacrifice of the self for the nation is not fully articulated again by Gao Xingjian until after 1990. However, in Shaoxing Gao has already affirmed his faith in the self and the individual and renounced his former readiness for self-sacrifice for nation, race, and ancestors. Here also Gao Xingjian debunks the supernatural aura surrounding the legendary hero Yu the Great, said to have curbed the floods by dredging the Yellow River. Gao Xingjian's reference to Yu's brutish animal instincts presents Yu as characteristically human. This leads him to express reservations about Yu's having dredged the Yellow River to curb the floods as is generally believed. Instead he indicates support for the thesis that Yu the Great had fought his way down to the east from the source of the Yellow River, subjugating all that lay in his path. As to the flood, Gao suggests that this may simply be repressed memory of amniotic fluids of the womb.

LITERATURE OF THE SELF: XU WEI

A visit to Xu Wei's old residence pushes Gao Xingjian's thoughts towards literature. More appealing than the thought of Lu Xun's self-sacrifice is Xu Wei's couplet: "The world is a false illusion created by others./What is original and authentic is what I propose." Gao argues that if the world is in fact a false illusion, "Why are others allowed to create it?" However, for Gao Xingjian at this time, originality and authenticity are less relevant than "whether or not it can be proposed." At that very time, the play *The Bus-Stop* and he as author were under criticism in Beijing.

> His [Xu Wei's] Studio of Green Vines is tucked away deep in the little lane: a small courtyard with several old vines and a hall with bright spotless windows, said to be the original building. These peaceful surroundings nevertheless sent him mad. Perhaps the world is not meant for human habitation, still human beings insist on existing in it. If one seeks to exist while retaining the authenticity one has at birth, one will either be killed or go mad, otherwise one will constantly be on the run. I cannot remain in this small town and quickly flee.   (Gao, 1990, p. 498)

Here in Shaoxing, Gao has already stated the choices he sees for the writer who would seek to be faithful to the authentic self. Later, he will make these choices clearer in his post-1990 essays. However, before turning to these, let us consider in turn Xu Wei and then Lu Xun who, as in the case of Gao Xingjian, were committed to the writing of literature of the self. The course of the respective lives of the two dead poets of Shaoxing are starkly different but it is argued here that severe limitations were imposed by their historical times and accidents of fate. On the other hand, their creative works, and even the manner in which the two addressed their personal circumstances, possess an artistic beauty which induces instinctive admiration.

Xu Wei was born in Shanyin 山陰 (present Shaoxing) and wrote under various style-names, including Daoist of the Green Vines. At the age of twenty, he graduated at the county level of the state civil service examination but several subsequent attempts at the provincial level of the examination were unsuccessful. Nevertheless his literary talents came to the notice of Hu Zongxian, Minister of the Board of War, who had been sent to supervise actions against repeated Japanese incursions on the southern coastline. Hu Zongxian engaged Xu Wei as his secretary and seems to have been impressed to such an extent with his writings that the latter's frequent bouts of drunkenness were tolerated.

When Hu Zongxian was later indicted for treason and committed suicide in prison, Xu Wei was terrified that he would be implicated. He wrote his own obituary and tried unsuccessfully to commit suicide three times: he hacked at his head with an axe, pierced his ear with a long spike, and mashed his testicles with a hammer. During this period of apparent madness, he accused his wife of infidelity and beat her to death. For this he was imprisoned but released after seven years through the interventions of a fellow native of Shaoxing, the Hanlin Academician Zhang Yuanbian. In the later part of his life he sustained himself by selling his calligraphy and painting. Cai Jingkang 蔡景康 describes him as possessing extraordinary skill in poetry, prose, drama, painting and calligraphy. But for the Japanese and Western world he is perhaps better known for his painting and calligraphy and his work in these fields of endeavour have been studied and collected with great enthusiasm.[3]

However, our concerns here are Xu Wei's views on literature. Xu Wei is generally regarded as having an unrestrained nature; while he revered what he understood to be loyalty and righteousness, he showed disdain for ritual and law. Xu Wei proclaimed that he "was not fettered by Confucianism," and attacked the traditional rituals of the late Ming. He was in the vanguard for advocating progressive thinking and established a new style in literature. Xu Wei lived in a period when the "restoration of the old" movement in literature was at its height. While writers formed factions and groups, Xu Wei vowed that he would not participate even in a faction of two. Writers who promoted restoration of the old, encouraged imitation: they attribute their ancestry to the Western Han capital but fail to produce a single word which originates from their own hearts (Cai, 1993, p. 195; Xu, 1993a, p. 198).

For Xu Wei, literature is original and its starting point is what has been personally perceived by the self. For authenticity, literature should express, the "feelings" (emotions, sensations and perceptions) of the self of the individual. However, for those who advocated a return to the literature of the Han dynasty, literature is distanced from "feelings;" instead it is either written by contriving "feelings," or else by "merely stealing others' words." The caustic tone of Xu Wei's indictment of contemporary Ming literature can be seen in the two passages below:

> The poetry of the ancients derive from feelings and not through contriving feelings, hence there was poetry but no poets. However, in later ages poets came into existence. Poems grew in vast numbers as did the styles;

as poetry these did not derive from feelings but instead were written by contriving feelings. The writing of poetry by contriving feelings smacks of working at poetry. Working at poetry inevitably leads to the stylistic imitation of poetry and the pilfering of excellent words in poetry. If this is in fact the case, then the essence of poetry is lost and it may be called a situation wherein there are poets but no poetry.   (Xu, 1993d, p. 196)

There are people who imitate the speech of birds: they make bird sounds but they are still human in nature. There are birds which imitate the speech of humans: they make human sounds but they are still birds by nature. This is how humans and birds are differentiated. Those who write poetry at present are similar to this; it does not derive from what they themselves perceive but stealing the words that others have previously uttered, they go on to say that this work is in this style and that piece is not; or this sentence is similar to this person's while that one is not. Although they are clever approximations they are inevitably still human sounds made by birds.   (Xu, 1993f, p. 197)

Xu Wei was conscious of how literature and politics had become enmeshed over time and lamented that while in the Tang period the state civil service examinations were based on poetry, poets such as Du Fu 杜甫 and Li Bai 李白 nevertheless failed in the examinations held in the capital; and while in the Yuan dynasty the examinations were based on opera, Wang Shifu 王實甫 whose arias are still sung by everyone also met with failure (Xu, 1993c, pp. 201–202). He recalled that when he commented on the collections of Han Yu and Feng Su, those works he thought were good were rated by others as poor. When he himself practised writing in the required style, the more ashamed he was of something the better it was assessed. This caused him to doubt others' assessments and when he saw people with these books which were the basis for the civil service examinations, he knew that what they wrote did not derive from their hearts. Although "often disgusted by what others considered to be good ... due to his own insignificance and lack of power ..." (Xu, 1993b, p. 202),[4] by passing the examinations on Han Yu and Feng Su he succeeded in gaining an official position.

Xu Wei lived in Ming times, when society was nurturing itself after the alien rule of the Yuan conquerors: this was a period of re-affirmation of traditional Han culture. His fight was within the indigenous culture, against the prevailing literary and intellectual trends which stultified and distorted the perceptions and judgements of the individual. Xu Wei's unswerving belief in literature of the self of the individual brought him in direct conflict with the constraining influence of the movement to restore the old in literature and the direct influence of linking this literature with politics.

SELF-SACRIFICE: LU XUN

Separated by some 300 years and more, Xu Wei was a part of the literary tradition of both Lu Xun and Gao Xingjian. And Lu Xun, who died a few years before Gao Xingjian was born, has in turn become embedded in China's recent literary history. All three writers nevertheless were committed to the idea of the unfettered self in creative writing.

Lu Xun admired the literature of traditional anti-orthodox writers of the past. In the early years of the 20th century, as a student in Japan he was further inspired by Western anarchist writings and Nietzsche, both of which extolled the worth and value of the individual.[5] However, historical fate had decreed that the unfettered self of Lu Xun should live at a time when China was threatened with progressive loss of sovereignty by the industrialized nations of Europe and later Japan.

Lu Xun was a writer by instinct and inclination but he had been endowed by personal experiences, including the revolutionary times in which he lived, with a deep sense of social responsibility (Lee, 1977; Mills 1977).[6] During the Cultural Revolution lines 1 and 2 of the second stanza cited below of Lu Xun's poem "Self Ridicule" were printed in the title pages of books, cited in prefaces, and made into posters to inspire the individual's self-sacrifice for the sake of the nation (and the will of the Chinese Communist Party). Lines 3 and 4, however, went unacknowledged as did the poems of Lu Xun's *Yecao* 野草 [Wild grass] collection; the latter work was dismissed as having been written while Lu Xun was still influenced by Nietzsche, and misconstrued as Lu Xun's farewell to the baneful influences of the German philosopher who promoted unabashed individualism and despised the collective will.[7] A close look at the lines below reveals a Lu Xun unlike the simplistic portrait of the revolutionary hero who sacrificed himself for the cause promoted by party ideologues:

Resolutely I calmly face a thousand pointing fingers,
Head bowed I willingly serve as an ox for the children;

But in the refuge of my small room I am myself,
Impervious to the changing of the seasons.   (Lu Xun, 1981e, p. 147)

Lines 1 and 2 clearly refer to Lu Xun's self-sacrifice for the youth of the nation: this is the public *persona* he had chosen to project. However lines 3 and 4 refer to his private life and to his unchanging commitment to literature of the self. It is this that he has had to publicly sacrifice and it is only in the privacy of his "small room" that he reverts to writing classical poems which was the only solace for his creative self after his decision to abandon creative writing for publication.[8]

Lu Xun's choice to abandon creative writing was an agonizing process and is graphically documented in the 23 poems written between April 26, 1924, and April 10, 1926, which were subsequently published as the collection *Wild Grass* ("Preface," 1927).[9] He was aware that the sacrifice of his creative self for patriotic reasons would leave him like the corpse in "The Epitaph":

... I gouged out my heart to eat it, wanting to know how it would taste. The pain from the wound was terrible, how could I know how it tasted?

... After the pain settled I began to slowly eat it. However it had already begun to deteriorate, so how could I know how it would have tasted? ...

... Answer me. Otherwise go away! ...   (Lu Xun, 1981c, pp. 202–203)

He realized that he would have to endure the pain of his sacrifice. In "Revenge II," the creative writer is symbolized as Christ at the crucifixion (Lu Xun, 1981a, pp. 174–175). It is not Lu Xun's physical self, which will perish, so like Christ, who refused to drink the wine mixed with myrrh, he is to feel the full extent of the agony of his sacrifice of his creative self. He will be fully conscious as he experiences the agony of his sacrifice, just as Christ fully experienced pain on the cross. However, Lu Xun charges those who have forced him to abandon creative writing with a crime more heinous than those who crucified Christ for he is but the mere son of man and must thereafter exist as a spiritual corpse.

ABSCONDING AS A MOTIF FOR A MODERN LITERATURE OF THE SELF: GAO XINGJIAN

Following the death of Mao Zedong and the fall of the Gang of Four, the frozen silence of literature of the self began to thaw. For Chinese writers, since the 1980s there have been substantive changes from Lu Xun's times. Like Lu Xun, Gao Xingjian had come to a conscious affirmation of the individual and the notion of literature of the self through his exposure to Western literature and philosophy. The foreign threat of Lu Xun's times no longer existed but had been replaced by other more insidious challenges for the individual and the notion of literature to which Gao Xingjian was committed. His return from the brink of death (after learning that he had been wrongly diagnosed with lung cancer) had made him acutely aware of life, his life and the creative expression of his self was integral to his life. He would suffer no compromise, even if it meant that he would constantly be on the run to escape the imposition of the will of any other extending beyond himself. Absconding is a recurring motif in his writings and the play bearing the title *Taowang* 逃亡 [Absconding; or "Fugitives," 1990] is an artistic exploration of some of the uncomfortable implications of group thinking and action.[10] Symbolic of his strongly individualist stance both as an individual and as a creative writer, is his repugnance for the use of the pronoun "we." In *Soul Mountain* he declares his anathema for using the pronoun "we": if he uses the pronoun "we" it is only when he is trying to be hypocritical or to ingratiate himself (Gao, 1990, p. 343).

When the staging of his play *Yeren* 野人 [Wild man, 1985] again caused a controversy, Gao Xingjian knew that he had no choice but to "abscond" to an environment which was more hospitable for what he was determined to achieve in his life. Having "absconded" to Paris he has found the creative freedom he was denied in China; his background in French language and literature has allowed him to move with considerable success into the European literary milieu and in 1992 he was awarded the *Chevalier de l'Ordre des Arts et des Lettres*. Gao Xingjian's large abstract ink paintings which have been collected by various galleries in various parts of the world have guaranteed him economic independence and therefore the freedom to devote himself to a form of literary creation which is subservient only to his own artistic instincts and intellectual dictates. He is a prolific writer and his recent publications include three plays which he first wrote in French and then in Chinese.

The 40 short epithets of Gao Xingjian's "Bali suibi" 巴黎隨筆 [Jottings from Paris, 1990] resonate with the language and texture of Zarathustra, each refuting the imposition of the collective will which leads to the annihilation of the self. To preserve the integrity and autonomy of the self against the encroachments of tyrannical political authorities, public opinion, ethical preachings, party or group advantage, the only solution is to abscond. If even this is not possible it will mean death for the being. "To abscond is therefore a means to self preservation. Otherwise one will either rot in gaol or perish through the criticism of the masses, or oblivious to the reason for one's existence drown in the great flow of established practices or be tormented endlessly by vain glory" (Gao, 1996a, p. 21).

> Becoming a recluse or feigning madness in ancient times were both forms of absconding, methods of self-preservation when there was no other option. Present society is not necessarily much more civilized and continues to kill people and moreover in even more ways: "self-confession" is one of these. If one will neither submit to making a confession nor conform to the custom then one has no option but to maintain silence. But silence is in itself suicide, a sort of spiritual suicide. For those who refuse to be killed or to suicide, there is only the option of absconding. To abscond is the only means of self-salvation — in the past or in present times.
>
> (Gao, 1996a, p. 21)

In Gao Xingjian's analysis, patriotism has distorted China's literary development in modern times. From the May Fourth period Chinese intellectuals, including writers, have regarded themselves as spokespersons for the masses: in doing so they abnegated their rights as individuals. While Chinese intellectuals had the courage to oppose traditional ethics and the political power of the bureaucracy they have found themselves helpless when confronted with the modern superstition (or myth) of nation. This superstition is founded in a national collective unconscious which is more deeply entrenched than ethical phenomena and its strength is derived from the primitive instinct for survival. With the collapse of the imperial system, feudal ethics based on loyalty to the ruler transformed into a patriotic nationalism which possessed moral and ethical powers (Gao, 1993). Gao Xingjian sees the creative Lu Xun as a victim of the superstition of nation: "That the writer Lu Xun was crushed by the politician Lu Xun is a tragedy for literature; of course for Lu Xun this may not have been a tragedy but it was probably a cause for regret" (Gao, 1996b, p. 27).

As in the case of Lu Xun, Gao sees politics and literature as being diametrically opposed and argues that while a writer as an individual may and should be politically active, in a creative work there should be an absence of political passion and rhetoric (Gao, 1996d, pp. 18–20). Despite his love for creative literature, Lu Xun found that he had no option but to totally abandon creative writing in order to devote himself fully to polemical essays which would bestir his compatriots to political action.

Gao Xingjian, however, is of the conviction that he himself lacks the talent for politics and he chooses to stand as an observer at the fringes or in the cracks of society (Gao, 1993). However, it is not only the myth of nation which can exert a controlling influence on the writer: the slavish worship of money, fashions, trends, and theories are all enemies of literature. He defines his basic stance towards literary creation as "without isms." He is aware that this stance is not new and that it is probably one adopted by writers throughout the world and throughout the ages. Nevertheless, he perceives the need to re-iterate it in the present age. This is Gao Xingjian's guiding philosophy in creative activities:

> "Without isms" is more positive than nihilism, it adopts an attitude towards events, people and the self. This attitude does not acknowledge the existence of incontrovertible general truths. It may be regarded as a form of reasoning … which at least does not acknowledge blind superstitious belief, whether it be in a religion or in an authority; there is no need to follow after some authority, trend, or fashion, so that others will lead one by the nose; or to be spiritually shackled by some ideology, so that one will be confined within its prison.[11]

With total freedom of artistic expression and the benefit of clarity which comes with distance and maturity, Gao Xingjian has been able to formulate and to fully articulate his reflections on China's recent literary history as well as what it means to be a Chinese writer living in the present age. His thoughts on literary creation voiced by the protagonists of his creative works and in his critical essays, enunciate a conception of literature and life closely approximating that of the dead poets Xu Wei and Lu Xun: literature is in a constant state of flux and depends on the ever-evolving consciousness and sensitivity of the self. The creative self of Gao Xingjian resides in the globalized world of present times, yet this statement on literature by Gao Xingjian written in Paris on the 18 July 1995, resounds with the echoes of the two dead poets of Shaoxing:

To be without isms is nothing more than a form of resistance to death by a life infused with vitality. It may not resolve any problems, yet it is still a stance. Artistic creations are traces left by such a stance but of course there are other traces resulting from the choice of the individual.

(Gao, 1996b, p. 5)

NOTES

1. This is a revised version of an article with the same title published in R. D. Findeisen and R. H. Gassmann, eds. *Autumn Floods: Essays in Honour of Marián Gálik* (Bern: Peter Lang, 1998), pp. 401–414.
2. In 1962 Gao graduated with a major in French from the Beijing Institute of Foreign Languages and was assigned to work as a translator. In 1981, he was reassigned to work as a writer with the Beijing People's Art Theatre.
3. For a short biography and selection of Xu Wei's essays on literature, see Cai Jingkang 蔡景康 (1993), pp. 195–205; see also Yu Jianhua 余劍華 (1979), pp. 1–35, which contains a detailed documented study of Xu Wei's life and achievements in art, poetry and drama.
4. Xu Wei also writes of how his evaluations of literature differ from others and the sense of isolation he feels: "Alas, with whom can I speak! What everyone ignores I alone scrutinize, what everyone likes I alone spit upon. Alas, with whom can I speak" (Xu, 1993e, p. 205).
5. See Lee (1985). Gao Xingjian (Gao, 1995) also examines the development of individualism in China in "The Voice of the Individual," translated by L. Aspfors and Torbjörn Lodén.
6. See discussions of Lu Xun's family background and years of study in Japan and their impact on his writings in Lee (1977) and also Mills (1977).
7. Marián Gálik's "Nietzsche in China (1918–1925)" (Gálik, 1971) was for some years the solitary work presenting a substantial examination of the influence of Nietzsche on Lu Xun until Yue Daiyun broke the silence with her "Nicai yu xiandai Zhongguo wenxue" 尼采與現代中國文學 [Nietzsche and modern Chinese literature] (Yue, 1980). This article by Yue Daiyun, together with her *Waiguo xuezhe yanjiu Lu Xun lunwenji* 外國學者研究魯迅論文集 [Collection of research papers on Lu Xun by foreign scholars], were in the forefront of works representing the beginning of greater academic freedom in China in the post-Mao period. I have addressed the issue of Lu Xun's alleged rejection of Nietzsche's influence in two articles: "From Chuang-tzu to Nietzsche: On the Individualism of Lu Hsun" (Lee, 1985) and "May Fourth: Symbol of Bring-It-Here-ism for Chinese Intellectuals" (Lee, 1990).

8. See my discussion of Lu Xun's classical poetry in "Solace for the Corpse with Its Heart Gouged Out: Lu Xun's Use of the Poetic Form" (Lee, 1982a), where I argue that after Lu Xun's decision to end his creative writing with the publication of *Wild Grass* (1927), he reverted to writing classical poetry to console himself.

9. Lu Xun's preface to *Wild Grass* is critical for understanding the collection of poems as a dedication to his notion of literature. For patriotic reasons he believed he had no choice but to use his writing talents for polemical writings. For a detailed discussion of the *Wild Grass* poems and the background to Lu Xun's decision to abandon creative writing, see my article, "Suicide of the Creative Self: The Case of Lu Hsun" (Lee, 1982b).

10. Gao was commissioned to write a play on the events of June 4th 1989. In the resulting work, *Absconding* [Fugitives], heroes are conspicuously absent. It is a coldly indifferent politico-philosophical play and contains no impassioned rhetoric for either the students or authorities: "The Americans wanted me to change it, so I withdrew the manuscript and paid the translation fee myself" (Gao, 1996c).

11. See Gao Xingjian's preface to *Meiyou zhuyi* 沒有主義 [Without isms] (Gao, 1996b, p. 1). See also his essay "Meiyou zhuyi" 沒有主義 [Without isms] (Gao, 1996b, pp. 8–17) and Mabel Lee, "Walking Out of Other People's Prisons: Liu Zaifu and Gao Xingjian on Chinese Literature in the 1990s" (Lee, 1996, pp. 98–112).

REFERENCES

Barmé, Germie (1983a). "A Touch of the Absurd: Introducing Gao Xingjian, and His Play *The Bus-stop*." *Renditions*, No. 19 & 20 (Spring & Autumn), pp. 373–377.

———, trans. (1983b). *The Bus-stop. Renditions*, No. 19 & 20 (Spring & Autumn), pp. 379–386.

Cai Jingkang 蔡景康 (1993). *Mingdai wenlun xuan* 明代文論選 [An anthology of Ming essays on literature]. Beijing: Renmin wenxue chubanshe 人民文學出版社.

Davis, A. R., and A. D. Stefanowska, eds. (1982). *Austrina: Essays in Commemoration of the 25th Anniversary of the Founding of the Oriental Society of Australia*. Sydney: Oriental Society of Australia.

Gálik, Marián (1971). "Nietzsche in China (1918–1925)." *Nachrichten der Geseclschaft für Natur-und Volkerkunde Ostasiens*, No. 110, pp. 5–47.

Gao Xingjian 高行健 (1990a). *Lingshan* 靈山 [Soul mountain]. Taipei: Lianjing chuban shiye gongsi 聯經出版事業公司.

—— (1990b). *Taowang* 逃亡 [Fugitives]. *Jintian* 今天 [Today], No. 1, pp. 41–46. Reprint, 1995. *Gao Xingjian xiju liu zhong* 高行健戲劇六種 [Six volumes of plays by Gao Xingjian], Vol. 4. Taipei: Dijiao chubanshe 帝教出版社.

—— (1993). "Guojia shenhua yu geren diankuang" 國家神話與個人癲狂 [The myth of nation and insanity for the individual]. *Mingbao yuekan* 明報月刊 [Ming Pao monthly], No. 8, pp. 114–121.

—— (1995). "The Voice of the Individual." Trans. Lena Aspfors and Torbjörn Lodén. *The Stockholm Journal of East Asian Studies*, Vol. 6, pp. 71–81.

—— (1996a). "Bali suibi" 巴黎隨筆 [Jottings from Paris]. In Gao (1996b), pp. 21–28.

—— (1996b). *Meiyou zhuyi* 沒有主義 [Without isms]. Hong Kong: Tiandi tushu youxian gongsi 天地圖書有限公司.

—— (1996c). "Meiyou zhuyi" 沒有主義 [Without isms]. In Gao (1996b), pp. 8–17. W. Lau, D. Sauviat and M. Williams, trans. "Without Isms." *Journal of the Oriental Society of Australia*, Nos. 27 & 28 (1995–96), pp. 105–114.

—— (1996d). "Wo zhuzhang yi zhong leng de wenxue" 我主張一種冷的文學 [I advocate a cold literature]. In Gao (1996b), pp. 18–20. Original work published on 30 July 1990.

—— (2000). *Soul Mountain*. Trans. Mabel Lee. Sydney: HarperCollins.

Goldman, Merle, ed. (1977). *Modern Chinese Literature in the May Fourth Era*. Cambridge: Harvard University Press.

Lee, Leo Ou-fan (1977). "Genesis of a Writer: Notes on Lu Xun's Educational Experience 1881–1909." In Goldman, ed. (1977), pp. 161–188.

Lee, Mabel (1982a). "Solace for the Corpse with Its Heart Gouged Out: Lu Xun's Use of the Poetic Form." *Far Eastern History*, No. 26, pp. 145–173.

—— (1982b). "Suicide of the Creative Self: The Case of Lu Hsun." In Davis and Stefanowska, eds. (1982), pp. 140–167.

—— (1985). "From Chuang-tzu to Nietzsche: On the Individualism of Lu Hsun." *The Journal of the Oriental Society of Australia*, No. 17, pp. 21–38.

—— (1990). "May Fourth: Symbol of Bring-It-Here-ism for Chinese Intellectuals." *Papers on Far Eastern History*, No. 41, pp. 77–96.

—— (1995). "Without Politics: Gao Xingjian on Literary Creation." *The Stockholm Journal of East Asian Studies*, Vol. 6, pp. 82–101.

—— (1996). "Walking Out of Other People's Prisons: Liu Zaifu and Gao Xingjian on Chinese Literature in the 1990s." *Asian and African Studies*, Vol. 5, No. 1, pp. 98–112.

Lodén, Torbjörn (1993). "World Literature with Chinese Characteristics: On a Novel by Gao Xingjian." *The Stockholm Journal of East Asian Studies*, Vol. 4, pp. 17–39.

Lu Xun 魯迅 (1981a). "Fuchou II" 復仇 (其二) [Revenge II]. In Lu Xun (1981b), Vol. 2, pp. 174–175. Original work published on 20 December 1924.

—— (1981b). *Lu Xun quanji* 魯迅全集 [Complete works of Lu Xun]. Beijing: Renmin wenxue chubanshe 人民文學出版社.

—— (1981c). "Mujie wen" 墓碣文 [The epitaph]. In Lu Xun 魯迅 (1981b), Vol. 2, pp. 202–203. Original work published on 17 June 1925.

—— (1981d) "Ziti xiaoxiang" 自題小像 [Self portrait]. In Lu Xun 魯迅 (1981b), Vol. 7, p. 423. Original work published in 1903.

—— (1981e) "Zizhao" 自嘲 [Self ridicule]. In Lu Xun (1981b), Vol. 7, p. 147. Original work published on 12 October 1932.

Mills, H. C. (1977). "Lu Xun: Literature and Revolution — From Mara to Marx." In Goldman, ed. (1977), pp. 189–220.

Xu Wei 徐渭 (1993a). "*Hu dacan ji* xu"《胡大參集》序 [Preface to *Collected Works of Hu Dacan*]. In Cai (1993), p. 198.

—— (1993b). "*Hu gong wenji* xu"《胡公文集》序 [Preface to *Collection of Writings by Hu Zongxian*]. In Cai (1993), p. 202.

—— (1993c). "Ti zi shu *Du shiyi shi hou*" 題自書《杜拾遺詩後》[Postscript to *An Anthology of Uncollected Poems by Du Fu*" in my own calligraphy]. In Cai (1993), pp. 201–202.

—— (1993d). "*Xiao Fu Shi* xu"《蕭甫詩》序 [Preface to *Poems by Xiao Fu*]. In Cai (1993), p. 196.

—— (1993e) "*Xixiang* xu"《西廂》序 [Preface to the *Western Chamber*]. In Cai (1993), p. 205

—— (1993f). "*Ye Zisu Shi* xu"《葉子肅詩》序 [Preface to *Poems by Ye Zisu*]. In Cai (1993), p. 197.

Yü Jianhua 余劍華 (1979). *Lidai huajia pingzhuan: Ming* 歷代畫家評傳：明 [Critical biographies of painters through the ages: Ming]. Hong Kong: Zhonghua shuju 中華書局.

Yue Daiyun 樂黛雲 (1980). "Nicai yu xiandai Zhongguo wenxue" 尼采與現代中國文學 [Nietzsche and modern Chinese literature]. *Beijing daxue xuebao* 北京大學學報 [Peking University journal], No. 3, pp. 20–33.

—— (1981). *Waiguo xuezhe yanjiu Lu Xun lunwenji* 外國學者研究魯迅論文集 [Collection of research papers on Lu Xun by foreign scholars]. Beijing: Beijing daxue chubanshe 北京大學出版社.

—— (1989–90). "Nietzsche and Modern Chinese Literature." Trans. C. Poon. *Journal of the Oriental Society of Australia*, Nos. 20 & 21, pp. 199–219.

Language as Subjectivity in *One Man's Bible*

Gao Xingjian has been known to the literary world first as an experimental playwright. In his dramatic works written before the mid-1980s, there is the experimentation with various Western modernist techniques, which is meant to present in new visions the social and political conditions of China in the 1980s. In all these works from *Juedui xinhao* 絕對信號 [Alarm signal, 1982] to *Yeren* 野人 [Wild man, 1985], he has demonstrated the art of a master in his representation of China in modernist, as well as postmodernist terms. However, in his works, both drama and fiction, written after the mid-1980s, he has brought in new modes of representing the Chinese tradition and in showing his tremendous creative energy in such attempts. Beginning with *Bi'an* 彼岸 [The other shore, 1986], he shows the first signs of an ongoing experiment to re-present the aesthetics of traditional Chinese dramatic arts in modern contexts. This experiment has continued with remarkable success in his later works written during his residence in France.

Yige ren de shengjing 一個人的聖經 [One man's bible, 1998], Gao Xingjian's latest work of fiction, can be read in the context of his experiment with a new mode of narrative. Although the novel was written in the late 1990s, the theory on which its mode of presentation is based can be found in Gao's earlier theoretical treatise, *Xiandai xiaoshuo jiqiao chutan* 現代小説技巧初探 [A preliminary exploration of the techniques of modern fiction, 1981], a work that had given rise to a debate on modernism in China and was taken as a target of critique for its effects of "spiritual pollution" (Gao, 1987, p. 99). As the title of this little book suggests, it is an exploration of the various possible forms that fiction can take, for example, a merger with drama and the use of cinematic techniques in fiction. As demonstrated in the book, the need to use modernist techniques arises from the fictional construction of the subject, whose psychological complexities are revealed in the stream of consciousness, which renders all objects in reality as subjective experience in memory, dreams, and psychological projection.

SUBJECTIVITY AS STREAM OF LANGUAGE

In his article, "The Politics of Technique in Modern Chinese Fiction," Leo Lee points out that the introduction of modernist techniques in modern Chinese fiction is heavily loaded with dissident ideology (1985, p. 187). It is in this context that Gao Xingjian's discussion of techniques in modern fiction can be seen as a breakthrough, not only in Chinese literary theory, but also in the ideological representation of the subject. In *A Preliminary Exploration of the Techniques of Modern Fiction*, Gao argues that the first and foremost duty of a writer is to express his own feelings toward certain events and certain people, but not to take himself as someone who is superior and has the duty to educate the reader (Gao, 1981, p. 4). In discussing the language of creative writing, Gao further states the point that a writer has to develop his own style. In this sense, the critique of Gao as a "polluted" modernist in China can also be seen as a political reaction against his advocacy for individuality in creative writing.

Considering the political climate of China in the early 1980s, the idea of individuality in creative writing is not only unorthodox, but also anti-tradition. One characteristic of traditional Chinese culture is its emphasis on the subordination of the individual "small self" 小我 [xiaowo] to the nationalist "greater self" 大我 [dawo].[1] This definition of the Chinese self has its origin in Confucian ethics which, when combined with the socialist emphasis on the collective self, forms the ideological basis for restricting the realization of the individual to his various roles under the supremacy of the state. Thus when Gao Xingjian proposed the idea of individuality, both as the style of a modern writer and as the central concern in characterization, in the early 1980s, he was actually calling for a reorientation in the portrayal of characters as psychical beings, as opposed to the description of characters externally in action. With this as his focus, Gao further deliberates his view on a number of issues pertaining to fiction writing in *A Preliminary Exploration of the Techniques of Modern Fiction*. They can be summarized in the following:

(1) Fiction may be plotless;

(2) Narrative language must be able to express the inner feelings
      of either the narrator or the character;

(3) Narrative point of view needs not be confined to that of a single
      perspective. It needs not be consistent and may shift and move
      among that of the first, second and third persons;

(4) The protagonist has to be represented as a psychological being,
      regardless of his/her social class and race;

(5) Stream of consciousness, as free association of thoughts, is a
      preferable mode to show the inner action of the character;

(6) The absurd as a mode of writing reflects the ideal of questing
      for the perfect;

(7) Life does not follow logic; to present the illogical is a way of
      questing for the rational;

(8) Symbolism may serve as a means to integrate philosophy and
      poetry with fiction;

(9) Literature as an abstraction of art is embedded with the author's
      worldview;

(10) The character as a complex and multidimensional subject;

(11) Literary language should be able to capture the psychological
       complexities of characters;

(12) Modern fiction should be constructed on the principle of
       structure, and not of plot;

(13) Fiction may borrow techniques from other forms of art, for
       example, the use of montage and musical structure;

(14) Time and space as psychological dimensions; and

(15) Fiction of the future will go beyond its boundary to embrace
       other forms of art and other literary genres.

What Gao Xingjian proposes in this theoretical work is principally the
use of more sophisticated techniques that can capture the multiple identities and complex psychology of the modern character. The idea of a
merger with other forms of art and literary genres, especially the use of
cinematic techniques and musical structure, sows the seeds of his thinking in later experiments.

In his other later theoretical works, Gao Xingjian repeatedly emphasizes the need to search for new modes of expression. In the afterword
(1987) to his collection of short stories, *Gei wo laoye mai yugan* 給我老爺買

魚杆 [Buy my grandfather a fishing rod, 1989], Gao Xingjian once again
draws the readers' attention to his intentional use of the three narrative
voices, that is, the use of "I," "you" and "he," to provide multiple points
of veiw in depicting the mental processes of characters. Gao believes
that the character as subjectivity realizes himself in the "stream of language" 語言流 [yuyan liu], which is an idea similar to that found in Julia
Kristeva's view of the "speaking subject" (Kristeva, 1980). Hence, Gao
says in *One Man's Bible*: "You express yourself, therefore you are" (Gao,
2000, p. 143).

In his essay, "Wenxue yu xuanxue: guanyü *Lingshan*" 文學與玄學 · 關
於《靈山》[Literature and metaphysics: on *Soul Mountain*, 1991], Gao further elaborates on the relation between the "stream of language" and
the shifting of narrative voices:

> In modern Western literature, stream of consciousness refers to the pro-
> cess of registering the subject's inner experience, which in creative writ-
> ing is realized in the stream of language. I would call this type of writing
> *the stream of language.* However, I believe such use of language may be
> more fully explored by deploying different narrative points of view in the
> description of the subject's mental processes. For example, the narrative
> point of view may be changed by replacing the first-person with the sec-
> ond-person, or even by substituting the second-person with the third-
> person. The subject is the same, but the mood of the mental processes
> presented will alter as the narrative voice changes.[2] (Gao, 1991a, p. 173)

The distinction between the narrator and the character, which is based
on narrative function, has been upheld by Western writers from Jane
Austen to Henry James as a device to achieve consistency in point of
view. In Gao's view, this distinction no longer works in the depiction of
contemporary subjecthood.

CUBISM AND FRAGMENTATION OF THE SUBJECT

The use of a single perspective to guarantee consistency in composition
and proportion has been held as the highest achievement of premodern
Western art. What constitutes a turning point from tradition to modernity in Western art is the shift from outer portrayal of the "object-as-
object" to the inner delineation of the "object-as-subject." The experimentation with the presentation of mood in impressionistic paintings is
an effort to capture the mood of the painter and his impressions of the

object. In Van Gogh's post-Impressionist self-portraits, for example, this tendency to gaze inward has taken a further step in portraying the subjectivity of the subject, which is at the same time the object in the very act of painting. Such a process of "objectifying the subject" presents a paradox in the portrayal of the subjectivity of the subject. Added to this paradox is the further difficulty of portraying the inner qualities of the subject, which are three-dimensional in nature, but have to be presented in two dimensions on the canvas. That is why post-Impressionism is incomplete in its project to resolve the paradox of objectifying the subject.

With the experimentation of cubism in the early twentieth century, the use of multiple perspectives emerged. The experimentation with multiple perspectives in such a movement as cubism signifies "an attempt to *conceive* the world in new ways" (Sypher, 1960, p. 265). Wylie Sypher states that such an attempt to break down "the three-dimensional space constructed from a fixed point of view" is an effort to represent objects that are "in multiple relations to each other and change their appearance according to the point of view from which we see them — and we now realize that we can see them from innumerable points of view, which are also complicated by time and light, influencing all spatial systems" (Sypher, 1960, pp. 264–265). By breaking down an object into two-dimensional geometrical planes and re-representing these planes in multiple relations, the cubist seeks to approach the object by deconstructing it, and hence undermining the illusion created in realistic representation. Such an effect is achieved by means of collage, which makes possible the presentation of multiple perspectives that will illuminate one another. Picasso's *Nature morte á la Cafetiére* (1947) is a good example to illustrate the adoption of multiple perspectives made possible by the collage of two-dimensional planes deconstructed from a three-dimensional object. In the cubist approach, deconstruction is achieved in the interest of total representation of the object through geometrical analysis.

The reader is reminded of the cubist revolution when he/she reads Gao Xingjian's later experimentation with different narrative voices of the split subject. The first thing that the reader is confronted with when reading Gao's *One Man's Bible* is the alternating narratives between the protagonist as "he" and also as "you," which are sometimes presented as two voices arguing with each other. But most of the time the "he" and "you" narratives represent two different structural lines that are co-referential and co-implicated. A similar case can be found in Luigi Pirandello's play *Six Characters in Search of an Author* (1921), which is one of the earliest experiments with cubist deconstruction of the dramatic subject into "character," "actor," and "real living persons." In contemporary Chinese fiction, the reader, who is familiar with the works by Zhang Xianliang 張賢亮 and some other writers, will notice that in the late 1980s there was already the experiment with split selves in the portrayal of the protagonist as "he" and "I." In *Xiguan siwang* 習慣死亡 [The habit of death, 1989] by Zhang Xianliang, the protagonist is presented as a split character with two selves: the "he" of the past and the "I" of the present. In both *Six Characters in Search of an Author* and *The Habit of Death*, the cubist deconstruction of the subject is used mainly to achieve a confrontational effect among the different perspectives. In Gao Xingjian's *One Man's Bible*, however, one finds more than the confrontation of different perspectives. At the psychoanalytical level, "he" is represented as the dream state and the projection of "you." As the dream psychoanalyzes the subject, the "he" deconstructs the "you."

In reading *One Man's Bible*, the reader will find that such an experiment with split selves is elevated to a level of experience in memory, history, imagination and translation of experience, which can be discussed in relation to the Chinese diaspora in the late twentieth century. Eva Hoffman's book, *Lost in Translation: A Life in a New Language* (1990), studies how the subject's experience can be lost when it is expressed in the language of another person's, especially in the case of writing about one's self. Thus the use of a single voice will only confine the presentation of experience to one plane of subjectivity and one dimension of experience. *One Man's Bible* successfully avoids such restriction by adopting an alternating double-voice structure. Writing the self between lives of the present and the past is a process that involves the translation of experience from one life into that of the other. In this process, one plane of experience is necessarily *discoursed* by that of the other. In the novel, the passage that describes how one's experience is determined by the discoursal function of language succinctly sums up Gao's view:

> To retell the story of that era, you find it so difficult. Even he has become incomprehensible to you. To reexamine the past, it is necessary to interpret first the vocabulary of that era and restore its exact meaning.
>
> (Gao, 2000, p. 150)

It is in language that subjectivity flows; it is also in language that time present is connected with time past and time future. Continuity in subjectivity surfs through the stream of consciousness and resurfaces in language. Meaning becomes possible only in the continuity of the subject. At the beginning of the novel, the German lady Marguerite presented as a wandering Jew is a "she," who serves as a psychical projection of "you," a contemporary Chinese exiled and lost in dislocation. Instead of saying that the experience of dislocation in a wandering Chinese is the same as diaspora in a wandering Jew, which represents a different, yet comparable, plane of experience, Gao Xingjian adopts the method of dialogic exchange of experience provided by the "you" and the "she":

> You said, China was, for you, very remote. She said she understood. You said you didn't have motherland. She said although her father was German, her mother was Jew. She also didn't have motherland, but she couldn't erase her memory. You asked her why she couldn't? She said she was not like you; she was woman. You said Oh, and nothing else.
>
> (Gao, 2000, p. 16)

In such exchanges of experience between the "you" and the "she," there is a shift of the interpretive point of view, which has been a strategy used for communication and for enlightenment of the mind in the tradition of Chinese Zen Buddhism. While in Chinese Zen Buddhism the *gong'an* 公案 strategy of story-telling is used for indirect communication by implication, in *One Man's Bible* the use of such a strategy has one more purpose, that is, to dissolve the subject "you" into vignettes of a floating life oscillating between the present and the past, between China and Euorpe.

The "he" and the "you" in the novel are not just two narrative points of view that complement and comment on each other, they are two voices that speak the split mind of the protagonist. This aspect of *One Man's Bible* is apparently inspired by Marguerite Duras's *Hiroshima mon amour*, in which the split minds of the male and female protagonists are interspersed with memories of the past and the present, in Japan and in Europe. Throughout *One Man's Bible*, most of the chapters are divided into narration by the "he" and the "you" in an alternating pattern. The double-voice structure of narration serves to illustrate "the psychological double" inside the protagonist, who has a split self and split identity.

In an article, "Wo de xiju he wo de yaoshi" 我的戲劇和我的鑰匙 [My drama and my key] written in 1991, Gao provides his reader with a key to his philosophical reconceptualization of the self:

> I have only got some experience about freeing the self in the course of training actors. For example, actors can adjust their breathing rhythm by doing *taizjiquan* 太極拳 and basic *gongfu* 功夫 exercises; they may also reach a state of non-thinking by doing free movements. When their bodies are fully relaxed, I will let them do some games of language consciousness. The actors will switch among the perspectives of "I," "you" and "he" so that they can observe themselves beyond the confines of the self. Through "the eyes" hidden behind themselves, they will interact with their opponents. When they treat their selves as their opponents, they are observing an object of their imagination by reliving it. All these games of language consciousness about the self are my keys.
>
> The so-called self is a matter of primordial non-distinction 混沌 [hundun]. Freudian psychoanalysis fails to explain what the self is. Modern psychoanalysis and linguistic approaches to the psyche are analytical in methodology. Though they have offered different methods to studying the self, they fail to provide a solution to the problem of what the self is. The Oriental approach to the self is basically a cognitive process of self-contemplation, which leads only to metaphysical speculation. The eight approaches to the self in Buddhism do not go beyond mysticism. I do not intend to explain what the self is, but only to provide one example of experience in stage performance.
>
> ... I believe humans up to now are still relying on language to understand their consciousness. Even if the distinctions among "I," "you" and "he" are not considered as the beginning of human self-awareness, they can still be taken as explicit tangible signs. Human behaviour as a cognitive process is inseparable from the subject positions that the "I," "you" and "he" take. The distinction between subject and object and the construction of the self are first based on the language the cognitive subject uses.
>
> (Gao, 1991b, p. 250)

The above passage sums up Gao's theory of the self as stream of language, in which one's identity shifts among the perspectives of "I," "you" and "he." By shifting the identity from "I" to "you" and to "he," the subject becomes the object, while the object also assumes its role as the subject. By shifting from "I" to "you" and to "he," the subject is presented as a matter of language in "inter-subjectivity."

FLOWING PERSPECTIVES IN THE STREAM OF LANGUAGE

Gao's advocacy of using shifting narrative points of view in the representation of subjecthood is perhaps inspired by the use of flowing perspectives in traditional Chinese painting. Being a painter himself, Gao is fully aware that effects of multiple perspectives are achieved not analytically, but intuitively. Take landscape painting as an example. The subject has to act as a participant in the creative process. The painting follows a flowing perspective as the subject interacts with various objects in his mental registration of the landscape. In his article, "Dui huihua de sikao" 對繪畫的思巧 [My thoughts on painting, 1995], Gao has the following observation about flowing subjectivity:

> When a person closes his eyes and translates the visual picture into mental images, he sees them flowing before his eyes, without depth and not following the perspectivism of proportion....
>
> Let me call the sense of depth in these mental images "pseudo-perspective," which arranges objects into different layers and with different points of view that, nonetheless, form a picture with organic unity. This is an improvised space, and it does not follow the principle of perspective. It may not have a focus, or it may have random focuses.
>
> (Gao, 1995, p. 292)

Such an idea of flowing perspectives in painting helps explain Gao's concept of flowing subjectivity. Although in the article cited above Gao mainly expresses his view on painting, the same principle of flowing perspectives is used in his novel *One Man's Bible*. In painting, the use of perspectives has to be realized in concrete terms of proportion in composition. In fiction, the question becomes a matter of how flowing points of view can be realized in the narrative structure.

In *Hongloumeng* 紅樓夢 [Dream of the red chamber], the use of the story of the stone as a mythical framework to inform the larger significance of the story of Jia Baoyu 賈寶玉 represents one method of juxtaposing two perspectives so that they can shed light on each other. However, such a method is still based on the use of two fixed, rather than flowing, perspectives. In film, the earliest experimentation with cinematic representation of stream of consciousness can be found in Ingmar Bergman's *Wild Strawberries* (1957), which bears a rudimentary form of flowing perspectives. Like in *Dream of the Red Chamber*, life is taken to be a journey in *Wild Strawberries* and is divided into two parts: one in the present, and the other in the past. In *Wild Strawberries*, there is a physical journey, in which Isak Borg, a bacteriologist, travels to Lund to receive the honour of Jubilee Doctorate. In the physical journey, time moves forward from the present to the future. However, there is also a mental journey taking place when Borg's mind goes back in time to the past. At every point of the physical journey set in the present, Borg looks back in time and turns inward to examine his inner life. While the physical journey shows Borg reaching out to meet other characters that remind him of various stages of his life in the past, his mental journey leads him closer to his emotional existence. Thus the physical journey is an external one, while the mental journey an inner one. Not only are these two journeys parallel to each other, they also intersect at times to yield an intricate web of past impressions and present memories. In presenting emotions in the past that intersect with those in the present, Ingmar Bergman has to invent a new style of narrative in order to overcome the structural limitations of linear narrative, for within the mind a person's past is inseparable from his present, and the same applies to emotions.

The structure Ingmar Bergman uses in *Wild Strawberries* is one that integrates the two journeys, as well as the two planes of experience, past and present. How is this integration achieved? How does this help one understand Gao's structural innovation in *One Man's Bible*? The following narration by the "you" in the novel offers an essential clue:

> You begin to think of Bergman's old, black-and-white film *Wild Strawberries*, which captures so subtly the anxiety of an old man facing the imminence of death. Probably you are also approaching old age. His other film, *Cries and Whispers*, portrays three sisters and a plump-looking maid suffering from loneliness, passion, illness and fear of death, all of which appeal to your sympathy. Can there be an integration between literature and art? This needs not be discussed, but there are people who do not think they can be integrated. Can Chinese literature be understood? By whom? By the West? Or by the Chinese living on the mainland and overseas? What is Chinese literature? Does literature have national boundary? How should Chinese writers be defined? Are mainland Chinese, Hong Kong Chinese, Taiwanese Chinese and Chinese Americans all Chinese?
>
> (Gao, 2000, pp. 296–297)

In this passage, the mind of the "you" flows from thoughts about film to those about literature, life, nation and identity. It is in the flow that both the subject and object are integrated. In other words, it is the flowing subjectivity expressed in the stream of language that unifies various facets of the subject's life, as well as the different points of view.

TEMPORALIZATION/SPATIALIZATION OF THE SELF

In *One Man's Bible*, there are also many instances bearing the imprint of stream of consciousness. When these instances are read in the light of Gao's envisioning of the fiction for future, they form scenes of montage that construct, while at the same time also deconstruct, life into flimsy moments of dream:

> You put your feelings, experience, dream-cum-memory-cum-imagination, thinking, speculation, premonition, intuition, etc., into language, give them music and rhythm, and link them up with the conditions of living people. Reality and history, time and space, concepts and consciousness all disappear in the process, in which language realizes itself, leaving the illusion created by language.   (Gao, 2000, p. 201)

Such an idea of language flow is concretized into film sense in Gao's experiment with montage as the basic structural principle of narrative in *One Man's Bible*. The reader notes that the cubist breakdown of the subject serves a larger function, not only to illustrate the fragmentation of identity, but more importantly to diffuse the self into a flowing narrative in which both time and space are given a new dimension.

Gao Xingjian's idea of relating language to music deserves more serious consideration. The use of musical structure in fiction has been experimented with by many writers. In the 1920s, the playwright Hong Shen 洪深 already showed in *Zhao yanwang* 趙閻王 [Yama Zhao, 1922] how stream-of-consciousness in a character can be represented in the counterpoint structure in music. The Hong Kong writer, Xi Xi 西西, has also used the musical structure in her novel, *Shao lu* 哨鹿 [Deer hunt, 1983], in which the narrative is divided into four symphonic movements with two themes that complement and counter each other.[3] In Aldous Huxley's musicalized novel, *Point Counter Point* (1928), he explains the form of a narrative as follows:

The musicalization of fiction. Not in the symbolist way, by subordinating sense to sound. (*Pleuvent les bleus basiers des astres taciturnes. Mere glossolalia.*) But on a large scale, in the construction. Meditate on Beethoven. The change of moods, the abrupt transitions. (Majesty alternating with a joke, for example, in the first movement of the B flat major quartet. Comedy suddenly hinting at prodigious and tragic solemnities in the scherzo of the C sharp minor quartet.) More interesting still the modulations, not merely from one key to another, but from mood to mood. A theme is stated, then developed, pushed out of shape, imperceptibly deformed, until, though still recognizably the same, it has become quite different. In sets of variations the process is carried a step further…. Get this into a novel. How? The abrupt transitions are easy enough. All you need is a sufficiency of characters and parallel, contrapuntal plots.

(Huxley, 1955, pp. 297–298)

Huxley's main concern is how the musical structure can be translated into the form of a novel. But for Gao Xingjian, the question becomes how such a structure can be realized in the stream of language. In *One Man's Bible*, Gao's innovation is concretized in the use of contrapuntal plots, which structurally and semantically serve as a dialogue between the "he" and the "you" within the monologue of the absent but implied "I." The "I" is the narrator, as well as an observer of life, whose present lies in the "you," and past in the "he." As an absent but implied subject, the "I" has to see his self, as well as objects outside his self, through the eyes of "he" and "you," whose roles and perspectives may be exchanged:

Perhaps the perspective can be changed. You sit among the audience and see how he climbs up the stage, an empty stage. Standing naked under the bright light, he has to have some moments to adapt himself so that he can, through the bundles of rays that have lit up the stage, distinguish the you who sit amidst the red velvet seats in the back rows.

(Gao, 2000, p. 253)

This exchange of perspectives is a psychological exchange within the self, so that the subject may be distanced from his self and reach a state of Chinese Zen Buddhist "self-transcendent contemplation" 靜觀 [jing guan] (Gao, 1991, p. 175). In psychoanalytical terms, however, this exchange of perspective is a function of the Lacanian "mirror stage," in which the subject is displaced by being objectified so that it may transcend itself and become a cognitive subject. Such a state of Chinese

Zen Buddhist "self-transcendent contemplation" in the cognitive subject is not the same as the Western notion of psychoanalytical transference. It is very Chinese and is based on the concept of subjecthood as language positions, which are reducible to what Julia Kristeva characterizes as Chinese psychical imaginary: "sign repetition and variation ... of transcription" (Kristeva, 1992, p. 296).

The two threads of narrative in *One Man's Bible*, one historical and the other personal, thus serve more than as narrative functions. On the social level, the historical narrative recounts the history of contemporary China as a process of nation building, which is deconstructed as a process of dehumanization in its ultimate attempt in undermining the individual. On the personal level, the "you" denotes a wandering self, in which only language and the body remain intersected with the historical narrative to produce a sense of continuity. The German lady is a "counterpoint" to the subject's body self, which provides a starting point for recounting the past and projecting into the future. In this process of temporalization, the self is also spatialized, merging memory with reality, dream with meaning:

Dimensions	Counter-Points	Montage/Effects	Counter-Points
Temporalization	Past-in-present	Present-in-past/ Present-in-future	Future-in-present
	Historical narrative	Jew/Chinese (Historical/ personal)	Personal narrative
	Persecution before 1987	Before/after 1997	Exile/Dislocation since 1987
	Flashback	self-transcendent contemplation	Foreshadowing
Spatialization	Mental journey	Stream of Language	Physical journey
	Inside China	Hong Kong	Outside China
	Reality	Stage	Life
	Reconstruction	Cubist breakdown	Deconstruction
Subjectivity	"He"	Self in primordial non-distinction [hundun 混沌]	"You"

Dimensions	Counter-Points	Montage/Effects	Counter-Points
Subjectivity (cont.)	Memory	Consciousness/ Body	Dream/Nightmare
	Outer self	Language	Inner self
	Repressed self	Psychic self	Wandering self

In Gao's novel, temporalization works synchronically with the spatialization of the self so that memory sequences are presented as visual scenes
freed from the division of time and space. In this way, effects of montage
are created between "an identical past and present" (Karl, 1992, p. 194).
The subject in such a state is what Gao calls "the self in chaos" [hundun
混沌], in which all categories of distinction are absent, leaving only a
mind of intuition.

The narrative of the novel thus takes a scene-structure, which breaks
down time into segments. As a playwright-novelist, Gao Xingjian demonstrates in *One Man's Bible* the technique of dramatizing narrative in fiction.
One may regard this as an experiment in a reverse Brechtian style that
he has discussed in *A Preliminary Exploration of the Techniques of Modern
Fiction*. This spatialization of time in his novel further shows Gao's successful use of multidimensional composition in Chinese painting for novel
writing. Such a new mode of novel writing in a painterly style makes
possible the presentation of the subjecthood of a wandering Chinese as
made up of memory and dream sequences. When the past self is juxtaposed and intersected with the present self, the subject is temporally
presented as caught in a state of discontinuity in continuity, which is
spatially represented as dislocation in location. Such a temporalization/
spatialization of the subject is reminiscent of the *nouveau roman* style
of Marguerite Duras's *Hiroshima mon amour*, in which characters are
presented as memories in soliloquies.

THE UNNAMABLE SUBJECT IN SPIRITUAL
AUTOBIOGRAPHY

One Man's Bible can be read as the spiritual autobiography of a wandering Chinese incessantly trying to flee from political persecution and from
the pressure of a collectivistic morality. It is an attempt of self-analysis
"to uncover both traumas and spontaneous sexual activity," and "to make

associations of earliest feelings with present attitudes" (Karl, 1985, p. 172). In the novel, protest against political persecution in China is welded with confessions of the protagonist's split selves. As Frederick Karl points out in the study of modern autobiography in his book, *Modern and Modernism*, "The archetype of spiritual autobiography is Rousseau's *Confessions*, in which the subject observing the subject while writing about himself and what is being observed becomes a kind of phenomenology of self" (Karl, 1985, p. 175). Gao Xingjian has also made a similar point in his concept of Chinese Zen Buddhist "self-transcendent contemplation": by turning outward into "he" and "you," the subject goes more inward in his quest for the true meaning of self. In this sense, *One Man's Bible* can thus be read as spiritual autobiography alongside the works of Hesse, Gide, Wilde, Joyce, Proust and Mann. Frederick Karl has the following observation about the emergence of modern spiritual autobiography in Europe, which allows the reader to read Gao's novel in a new light:

> The traditional *Bildungsroman*, which was nearly always a form of disguised autobiography, now becomes far less disguised as matter shifts to spirit. The shift is from physical well-being, happiness, stability to intangibles like mental health, sexual discovery, and, chiefly, spiritual needs. The protagonist, now a mere shadow figure of the author, no longer shapes himself into a social unit, but exists only for himself, a cell without reference to any group or person unresponsive to his needs. Narrative itself would reflect the change, with linear becoming convoluted, incidents occurring simultaneously or in memory, present tense giving way to past, ends implicit in beginnings.   (Karl, 1985, p. 171)

The reader will certainly notice similar features in Gao's novel, in which the protagonist goes beyond the Chinese complex of suffering during the Cultural Revolution and speaks of modern people's isolation and spiritual loss at a universal level. Living in diaspora and being spiritually alienated, the protagonist finds anchorage only in his personal writing: "You wrote this book for yourself, this book about fleeing, your one-man's Bible. You are your own God and your own disciple. You don't sacrifice yourself for other people, and don't ask other people to sacrifice themselves for you. Nothing is more fair than this" (Gao, 2000, p. 202).

While the modern mode of European spiritual autobiography is based on the model of the *Doppelgänger* "with a second face in addition to the first" (Karl, 1985, p. 177), Gao Xingjian's protagonist is a "three-faced subject," with an implied "I" shifting between the "he" and the "you." His use of split selves, unlike that in the European mode, is not to disguise the autobiography, but to see the subject from the subject's other points of view, in the way of "Chinese Zen Buddhist self-contemplation." Such a method has been extended to the study of the subject in language psychology. The subject is made known to the subject himself only through the effects he produces when he is objectified (Parker, 1992, p. 8). In *One Man's Bible*, this objectification of the subject is achieved by splitting the subject into two selves, the "you" of the present and the "he" of the past, so that each is perceived through the eyes of the other. In this process of objectification of the subject, the object is at the same time subjectified, so that there appears no distinction between subject and object. This is a state which Gao calls "primordial non-distinction," by which the subject comes to a full realization of his true self. In Gao's novel, the subject is seen through the eyes of his other selves in his passage through various stages of life. In such a process, everything objective is displaced by the self so that the deeply hidden unconscious is uncovered. Physical objects, characters, political persecution and women all become images and symbols of desire and repression within the subject. These images and symbols are effects of psychical projections of the subject. Yet, when these images and symbols emerge in dreams or in reality, they tend to negate and cancel out each other so that in the end the subject is left in uncertainty even of his self:

> You are not a dragon; nor are you a worm. Neither this, nor that. That which is not you is you. That which is not you is not a negation. Well, it can be said that it is one kind of reality, one trace, one process of being exhausted, one end product. Before being exhausted, that is, before death, you are no more than a news of life, a presentation or expression of that which is not you.   (Gao, 2000, p. 202)

The self depicted is in a process of unfolding into endless negations. Even in sexual relationships with women, the subject is not sure of what his self is, except for the physical feelings in his body. Gao's idea of the subject as his own God, and with himself as disciple, reveals a philosophy of "me-ism." For the subject, consciousness is a stream of language, nothing more. However, when language negates itself, the subject becomes unnamable and unspeakable. The unnamable and unspeakable subject flows in the double negation of language as a non-self between "he" and "you." If one understands Gao's philosophy of language, one will understand his experimentation with the "he," "you" and the implied "I" that may represent not only the three faces of the protagonist's split selves in temporal terms, but also other possibilities. Since the "I" is implied and absent, rather than explicitly stated, it may serve a double function by referring to both the protagonist and the reader. Hence, in the reading process the same "he" and "you" may become voices of the reader, a textual strategy that invites ironic identification.

NOTES

1. In my article, "Self-Identity and the Problematic of Chinese Modernity" (1995), I have argued that the definition of the self as its roles in traditional Chinese culture plays a pivotal function in the formation of Chinese identity even up till today. In such an approach, the individual has no self, except by identifying with its roles in the larger web of society and state.
2. All translations are mine.
3. Xi Xi's [西西 Hsi Hsi] *Deer Hunt* as a musicalized novel has been discussed in Soong (1986).

REFERENCES

Gao Xingjian 高行健 (1981). *Xiandai xiaoshuo jiqiao chutan* 現代小説技巧初探 [A preliminary exploration of the techniques of modern fiction]. Guangzhou: Huacheng chubanshe 花城出版社.

—— (1989a). "Ba" 跋 [Epilogue]. In Gao (1989b), pp. 260–261. Original work published in 1987.

—— (1989b). *Gei wo loaye mai yugan* 給我老爺買魚杆 [Buy my grandfather a fishing rod]. Taipei: Lianhe wenxue chubanshe 聯合文學出版社.

—— (1996a). "Chi dao de xiandaizhuyi yu dangjin Zhongguo wenxue" 遲到的 現代主義與當今中國文學 [Belated modernism and contemporary Chinese literature]. In Gao (1996c), pp. 98–107. Original work presented as a paper in 1987 at the Conference on Modernism and Contemporary Chinese Literature, Hong Kong.

—— (1996b). "Geren de shengyin" 個人的聲音 [The voice of the individual]. In Gao (1996c), pp. 98–107. Original work published in 1993. Lena Aspfors and Torbjörn Lodén, trans. (1995). "The Voice of the Individual." *The Stockholm Journal of East Asian Studies*, Vol. 6, pp. 71–81.

———— (1996c). *Meiyou zhuyi* 沒有主義 [Without isms]. Hong Kong: Tiandi tushu youxian gongsi 天地圖書有限公司.

———— (1996d). "Wo de xiju he wo de yaoshi" [My drama and my key]. In Gao (1996c), pp. 235–252. Original work published in 1991.

———— (1996e). "Wenxue and xuanxue: Guan yu *Lingshan*" 文學與玄學 · 關於 《靈山》 [Literature and metaphysics: On *Soul Mountain*]. In Gao (1996c), pp. 167–185. Original work published in 1991.

———— (2000). *Yige ren de shengjing* 一個人的聖經 [One man's bible]. Hong Kong: Tiandi tushu youxian gongsi 天地圖書有限公司. Original work published in 1998.

Hoffman, Eva (1990). *Lost in Translation: A Life in a New Language*. New York: Penguin.

Huxley, Aldous (1955). *Point Counter Point*. Middlesex: Penguin. Original work published in 1926.

Karl, Frederick Robert (1985). *Modern and Modernism: The Sovereignty of the Artist, 1885–1925*. New York: Atheneum.

Kinkley, Jeffrey C., ed. (1985). *After Mao: Chinese Literature and Society 1978–1981*. Cambridge, MA: The Council on East Asian Studies/Harvard University.

Kristeva, Julia (1980). *Desire in Language: A Semiotic Approach to Literature and Art*. Ed. Leon S. Roudiez; Trans. Thomas Gora, Alice Jardine, and Leon S. Roudiez. New York: Columbia University Press.

———— (1992). "Psychoanalysis and the Imaginary." In Levine, ed. (1992), pp. 285–297.

Lee, Leo Ou-fan (1985). "The Politics of Technique: Perspectives of Literary Dissidence in Contemporary Chinese Fiction." In Kinkley, ed. (1985), pp. 159–190.

Levine, George, ed. (1992). *Constructions of the Self*. New Brunswick, NJ: Rutgers University Press.

Parker, Ian (1992). *Discourse Dynamics: Critical Analysis for Social and Individual Psychology*. London: Routledge.

Soong, Stephen C. (1986). "Made in Hong Kong: A Writer Like Hsi Hsi." Trans. Kwok-kan Tam. *Asian Culture Quarterly*, Vol. 14, No. 4 (Winter), pp. 43–60.

Sypher, Wylie (1960). *Rococo to Cubism in Art and Literature*. New York: Vantage Books.

Tam, Kwok-kan (1995). "Self-Identity and the Problematic of Chinese Modernity." *The Humanities Bulletin*, No. 4, pp. 57–64.

Zhang Xianliang 張賢亮 (1989). *Xiguan siwang* 習慣死亡 [The habit of death]. Hong Kong: Mingchuang chubanshe 明窗出版社.

A Chronology of Gao Xingjian

This chronology follows the usual style of arrangement in a chronological order, which is supposed to give a sense of historical development. Our sense of time is linear in structure and many people believe that history should give accounts of events from the beginning. But I would like to suggest to readers that they begin with the end of this chronology, and read it backwards so that it follows the method of "archaeology of knowledge" as advocated by Foucault. In this way of reading, the readers will perhaps know more about why Gao Xingjian was awarded the Nobel Prize in Literature 2000.

CHRONOLOGY

1940
Born on 4 January 1940 in Ganzhou 贛州, Jiangxi Province, China. His father was a bank officer and his mother was an actress before she married. It was she who cultivated Gao's interest in the theatre and writing.

1948
Started painting. Encouraged by his mother, he started to write diary.

1950
Wrote his first story with his own illustrations.

1952
Studied at Nanjing No. Ten School (the Middle School Section of the previous Ginling University).

Started to learn sketches, water painting, oil painting and pottery.

1957

Graduated from high school. He was encouraged by his teacher to study painting at Central Institute of Fine Arts in Beijing but the idea was dropped. Instead, he was admitted to the Department of French at Beijing Institute of Foreign Languages. He organized a student drama group and wrote, directed and performed in his own plays.

1962

Graduated from Beijing Institute of Foreign Languages, majoring in French. Assigned to work as a translator at the Foreign Languages Press until 1980.

1966–67

Cultural Revolution began and he burned all his manuscripts to avoid possible persecution. He was later sent to a special cadre school for re-education.

1970

Spent five years (1970–1975) labouring in the countryside. During his leisure time he practised photography and secretly continued his creative writing.

1975

Returned to Beijing and resumed his work as a translator at Foreign Languages Press. He kept his interest in photography and photo-developing and started to paint again.

1977

Assigned to work as a translator at the Foreign Affairs Unit of the Writers' Association of China.

1978

Started to experiment with the novel form.

1979

Travelled to France and Italy. His exposure to great paintings prompted him to abandon oil painting and turn to Chinese ink painting.

Novella: "Hanye de xingchen" 寒夜的星辰 [Stars on a cold night] was published in *Huacheng* 花城 (Guangzhou), No. 3, 1979.

Essay: "Guanyu Ba Jin de chuanshuo" 關於巴金的傳說 [Rumours about Ba Jin] was published in *Huacheng* 花城 (Guangzhou), No. 6, 1979.

1980

Short story: "Pengyou" 朋友 [Friend] was completed in Beijing in March, 1980 and later published in *Mangyuan* 莽原 (Zhengzhou), No. 2, 1981.

Essay: "Xiandai xiaoshuo jiqiao chutan" 現代小説技巧初探 [A preliminary exploration of the techniques of modern fiction] was published in *Suibi* 隨筆 (Guangzhou), No. 1, 1980. This was the first installment of the serialized version of his study on the theory of modern fiction.

Essay: "Falanxi xiandai wenxue de tongku" 法蘭西現代文學的痛苦 [The agony of modern French literature] was published in *Waiguo wenxue yanjiu* 外國文學研究 [Studies in foreign literature] (Wuhan), No. 1, 1980.

Essay: "Faguo xiandaipai renmin shiren Puliewei'er he ta da *Geciji*" 法國現代派人民詩人普列維爾和他的〈歌詞集〉 [The French modernist poet Jacques Prévert and his *Paroles*] was published in *Huacheng* 花城 (Guangzhou), No. 5, 1980.

Essay: "Menghai" 夢海 [Dream of the sea] was published in *Huacheng* 花城 (Guangzhou), No. 6, 1980.

Essay: "Ba Jin zai Bali" 巴金在巴黎 [Ba Jin in Paris] was published in *Dangdai* 當代 (Beijing), No. 1, 1980.

Travelled to France as translator for a delegation of Chinese writers led by Ba Jin in 1980.

Assigned to work as a writer with the Beijing People's Art Theatre in 1980.

1981

First collection of essays on literary techniques: *Xiandai xiaoshuo jiqiao chutan* 現代小説技巧初探 [A preliminary exploration of the techniques of modern fiction] was published in book form by Huacheng chubanshe 花城出版社 in Guangzhou in 1981. It led to a violent polemic on "modernism."

Novella: "You zhi gezi jiao hongchun'er" 有隻鴿子叫紅唇兒 [A pigeon called red beak] was published in *Shouhuo* 收穫 (Beijing), No. 1, 1981.

Short story: "Pengyou" 朋友 [Friend] was published in *Mangyuan* 莽原 (Zhengzhou), No. 2, 1981.

Essay: "Yidali suixiangqu" 義大利隨想曲 [Capriccio of Italy] was published in *Huacheng* 花城 (Guangzhou), No. 3, 1981.

Transferred to the Playscript Division of the Beijing People's Art Theatre and became a full-time playwright.

1982

Play: *Juedui xinhao* 絕對信號 [Alarm signal] was his first play. It was published in *Shiyue* 十月 (Beijing), No. 5, 1982 and performed in the same year at Beijing People's Art Theatre. Directed by Lin Zhaohua 林兆華.

Short story: "Yu, xue ji qita" 雨、雪及其他 [Rain, snow and others] was completed in Beijing in February 1982 and published in *Chou xiaoya* 醜小鴨 (Beijing), No. 7, 1982.

Short story: "Lushang" 路上 [On the road] was published in *Renmin wenxue* 人民文學 (Beijing), No. 9, 1982.

Short story: "Ershiwu nian hou" 二十五年後 [After twenty-five years] was completed in June 1982 and published in *Wenhui yuekan* 文匯月刊 (Shanghai), No. 11, 1982.

Short story: "Huadou" 花豆 [Flower buds] was completed in Beijing in July, 1982.

Reprint of book: *Xiandai xiaoshuo jiqiao chutan* 現代小説技巧初探 [A preliminary exploration of the techniques of modern fiction] was reprinted in 1982.

Essay: "Tong yiwei guanzhong tan xi" 同一位觀眾談戲 [A conversation with an audience on drama] was published in *Suibi* 隨筆 (Guangzhou), No. 6, 1982.

Essay: "Tan xiaoshuoguan yu xiaoshuo jiqiao" 談小説觀與小説技巧 [On fiction and techniques in fiction writing] was published in *Zhongshan* 鍾山 (Nanjing), No. 6, 1982.

Started to write the novel *Lingshan* 靈山 [Soul mountain] in Beijing in the summer of 1982. The novel was later completed in Paris in 1989.

Performance: *Juedui xinhao* 絕對信號 [Alarm signal] was performed at Beijing People's Art Theatre in 1982. Directed by Lin Zhaohua 林兆華. It was a favourite play for production by about ten other drama groups throughout the country.

Video-recording: The production of *Juedui xinhao* 絕對信號 [Alarm signal] by Beijing People's Art Theatre was video-recorded.

1983

Play: *Chezhan* 車站 [The bus-stop] was published in *Shiyue* 十月 (Beijing), No. 3, 1983. It was also staged as an "experimental play" at Beijing People's Art Theatre in Beijing, China. Directed by Lin Zhaohua 林兆華. It was soon banned and Gao was severely criticized during the "spiritual pollution" campaign. But Gao was recognized by Mainland drama critics as one who started the experimental theatre on the Mainland.

Learned that the government intended to send him for political reform. To avoid harassment he undertook a five-month tour from July to November of the forest and mountain regions of Sichuan Province, tracing the course of the Yangzi River from its source to the coast, covering a distance of close to 15,000 kilometres.

His first play *Juedui xinhao* 絕對信號 [Alarm signal] was banned and he became the target of criticism in the debate over modernism and realism.

Short story: "Haishang" 海上 [At sea] was completed in March, 1983 and published in *Chou xiaoya* 醜小鴨 (Beijing), No. 9, 1983.

Short story: "Huahuan" 花環 [Garland] was published in *Wenhui yuekan* 文匯月刊 (Shanghai), No. 5, 1983.

Short story: "Yuan'en si" 圓恩寺 [Yuan'en temple] was published in *Haiyan* 海燕 (Dalian), No. 8, 1983.

Short story: "Muqin" 母親 [Mother] was published in *Shiyue* 十月 (Beijing), No. 4, 1983.

Short story: "He nabian" 河那邊 [On the other side of the river] was published in *Zhongshan* 鍾山 (Nanjing), No. 6, 1983.

Short story: "Xiejiang he ta de nü'er" 鞋匠和他的女兒 [The shoemaker and his daughter] was published in *Qingnian zuojia* 青年作家 (Chengdu), No. 3, 1983.

Essay: "Lun xijuguan" 論戲劇觀 [On dramaturgy] was published in *Xijujie* 戲劇界 (Shanghai), No. 1, 1983.

Essay: "Tan xiandai xiaoshuo yu duzhe de guanxi" 談現代小說與讀者的關

係 [On modern fiction and its relation with the reader] was published in *Qingnian zuojia* 青年作家 (Chengdu), No. 3, 1983.

Essay: "Tan leng shuqing yu fan shuqing" 談冷抒情與反抒情 [On cold lyricism and anti-lyricism] was published in *Wenxue zhishi* 文學知識 (Zhengzhou), No. 3, 1983.

Essay: "Zhipu yu chunjing" 質樸與純淨 [On simplicity and purity] was published in *Wenxuebao* 文學報 (Shanghai), May 19, 1983.

Essay: "Tan duoshengbu xiju shiyan" 談多聲部戲劇試驗 [Experiments with multi-vocality in drama] was published in *Xiju dianying bao* 戲劇電影報 (Beijing), No. 25, 1983.

A series of essays on drama was published in *Suibi* 隨筆 (Guangzhou), Nos. 1–6, 1983. They included:
"Tan xiandai xiju shouduan" 談現代戲劇手段 [On tactics of modern drama], No. 1;
"Tan juchanxing" 談劇場性 [On the theatrical], No. 2;
"Tan xijuxing" 談戲劇性 [On the dramatic], No. 3;
"Dongzuo he guocheng" 動作和過程 [Action and process], No. 4;
"Shijian yu kongjian" 時間與空間 [Time and space], No. 5; and
"Tan jiadingxing" 談假定性 [On suppositionality], No. 6.

Started to devote his time to ink painting.

He was wrongly diagnosed as suffering from lung cancer.

1984
Plays: "Xiandai zhezixi" 現代折子戲 [Highlights of modern Chinese opera] were published in *Zhongshan* 鍾山 (Nanjing), No. 4, 1984. They included:
Mofang zhe 模仿者 [The imitator];
Duo yu 躲雨 [Hiding from the rain];
Xinglu nan 行路難 [Tough walk]; and
Habala shankou 哈巴拉山口 [The pass at Mount Habala].

Filmscript: *Huadou* 花豆 [Flower buds] was published in *Renmin wenxue* 人民文學 (Beijing), No. 9, 1984.

Essay: "Wo de xijuguan" 我的戲劇觀 [My views on drama] was published in *Xiju luncong* 戲劇論叢 (Beijing), No. 4, 1984.

Performance: *Chezhan* 車站 [The bus-stop] was performed in Yugoslavia in October, 1984.

Radio broadcast: *Chezhan* 車站 [The bus-stop] was radio broadcast at the National Broadcasting Station in Hungary.

Translation: Excerpts of *Chezhan* 車站 [The bus-stop] were translated into English by Geremie Barmé and published in *Renditions*, Nos. 19 and 20 (1983). Actual date of publication in 1984.

Translation: Ng Mau-sang 吳茂生 translated into English Gao's "Xiandai jiqiao yu minzhu jingshen" 現代技巧與民族精神 (a chapter from *A Preliminary Exploration of the Techniques of Modern Fiction*): "Contemporary Technique and National Character in Fiction" in *Renditions*, Nos. 19 & 20 (1983). Actual date of publication in 1984.

1985
Play: *Dubai* 獨白 [Monologue] was published in *Xin juben* 新劇本 (Beijing), No. 1, 1985.

Play: *Yeren* 野人 [Wild man] was published in *Shiyue* 十月 (Beijing), No. 2, 1985. It gave rise to heated domestic polemic.

Collection of plays: *Gao Xingjian xiju ji* 高行健戲劇集 [A collection of plays by Gao Xingjian] was published by Qunzhong chubanshe 群眾出版社 in Beijing, 1985. Plays included in the collection are:
Juedui xinhao 絕對信號 [Alarm signal];
Chezhan 車站 [The bus-stop];
Yeren 野人 [Wild man]
Dubai 獨白 [Monologue]; and
Xiandai zhezixi 現代折子戲 [Highlights of modern Chinese opera].

Collection of novellas: "You zhi gezi jiao hongchun'er" 有隻鴿子叫紅唇兒 [A pigeon called red beak] was published by Beijing Shiyue wenyi chubanshe 北京十月文藝出版社 in 1985.

Short story: "Wuru" 侮辱 [Insult] was published in *Qingnian zuojia* 青年作家 (Chengdu), No. 7, 1985.

Short story: "Gongyuan li" 公園裏 [In the park] was published in *Nanfang wenxue* 南方文學 (Guangzhou), No. 4, 1985.

Short story: "Chehuo" 車禍 [A car accident] was published in *Fujian wenxue* 福建文學 (Fuzhou), No. 5, 1985.

Short story: "Wuti" 無題 [Untitled] was published in *Xiaoshuo zhoubao* 小説周報 (Tianjin), No. 1, 1985.

Filmscript: *Huadou* 花豆 [Flower buds] was republished in *Chou xiaoya* 醜小鴨 (Beijing), Nos. 1 and 2, 1985.

Essay: "Tan ge xiju liupai de tedian he chuanzuo fangfa" 談各戲劇流派的特點和創作方法 [On the characteristics and techniques of various types of drama] was published in *Zhongguo jushi xinchaoliu* 中國劇視新潮流, No. 2, 1985.

Essay: "*Yeren* he wo"《野人》和我 [*Wild Man* and I] was published in *Xiju dianying bao* 戲劇電影報 (Beijing), No. 19, 1985.

Essay: " Wo yu Bulaixite" 我與布萊希特 [Brecht and I] was published in the special issue of *Qingyi* 青藝 (Beijing), 1985.

Criticism: Juedui xinhao *de yishu tansuo* 絕對信號的藝術探索 [Alarm signal: An artistic inquiry] was edited by Juedui Xinhao Drama Group at the Beijing People's Art Theatre and was published by Zhongguo xiju chubanshe 中國戲劇出版社 in Beijing in 1985.

Performance: *Yeren* 野人 [Wild man] was performed at Beijing People's Art Theatre in May, 1985. Directed by Lin Zhaohua 林兆華. It gave rise to a heated debate in the country but it also won high international acclaim.

Video-recording: The production of *Yeren* 野人 [Wild man] by Beijing People's Art Theatre was video-recorded.

Exhibition (with Yin Guangzhong 尹光中): He held his first painting and pottery exhibition at Beijing People's Art Theatre in 1985. His ink paintings were highly praised by such writers as Ai Qing 艾青, Cao Yu 曹禺 and Wu Zuguang 吳祖光.

Invited by D.A.A.D. and gave lectures at a number of universities in Germany, including Bönn University, Berlin Free University and Heidelberg University, in 1985.

Travelled to France to attend a seminar on his drama at Théâtre National de Chaillot in 1985. He presented a paper on "Yao shenme yang de juzuo 要甚麼樣的劇作 [What sort of drama do we need], which was later included in a collection of essays on literature and art entitled *Meiyou zhuyi* 沒有主義 [Without isms] published in Hong Kong by Tiandi tushu youxian gongsi 天地圖書有限公司 in 1996.

Travelled to Austria and Denmark in the same year for exhibitions of his ink paintings.

Exhibition (solo): Berliner Kunstlerhaus Bethanien, Berlin, Germany.

Exhibition (solo): Alte Schmied in Vienna, Austria.

1986
Returned to Beijing and started his career as a painter.

Play: *Bi'an* 彼岸 [The other shore] was published in *Shiyue* 十月 (Beijing), No. 5, 1986. He was rehearsing the play when the order came to ban the performance of the play in China. Since then, none of his plays has been performed on Mainland China. The play had its world premiere in Taiwan in 1990. It was subsequently included in *Gao Xingjian xiju liuzhong* 高行健戲劇六種 [Six volumes of plays by Gao Xingjian], Volume 1, published in Taipei by Dijiao chubanshe 帝教出版社 in 1995.

Short story: "Gei wo laoye mai yugan" 給我老爺買魚竿 [Buy my grandfather a fishing rod] was published in *Renmin wenxue* 人民文學 (Beijing), No. 9, 1986.

Essay: "Yong ziji ganzhi shijie de fangshi lai chuangzuo" 用自己感知世界的方式來創作 [I create with my senses] was published in *Xin juben* 新劇本, No. 3, 1986.

Essay: "Yao shenme yang de juzuo" 要甚麼樣的劇作 [What sort of drama do we need] was published in *Wenyi yanjiu* 文藝研究 (Beijing), No. 4, 1986. Also appeared in *Lianhe wenxue* 聯合文學, No. 41, 1988. It was subsequently included in *Meiyou zhuyi* 沒有主義 [Without isms] published in Hong Kong by Tiandi tushu youxian gongsi 天地圖書有限公司 in 1996.

Essay: "Cong minzu xiju chuantong zhong jiqu yingyang" 從民族戲劇傳統中汲取營養 [Nurtured by the tradition of national drama] was published in *Xin juben* 新劇本, No. 5, 1986.

Essay: "Ping Geluotuofusiji de 'Mai xiang zhipu xiju'" 評格洛托夫斯基的

〈邁向質樸戲劇〉[A critique of Grotowski's *Toward a Poor Theatre*] was published in *Xiju bao* 戲劇報 (Beijing), No. 7, 1986.

Essay: "Tan xiqu yao gaige yu bu yao gaige" 談戲曲要改革與不要改革 [On music-drama: Reform or no reform] was published in *Xiqu yanjiu* 戲曲研究 (Beijing), No. 21, 1986.

Performance: *Chezhan* 車站 [The bus-stop] was performed by Horizonte 第四線 at Hong Kong Art Centre and Fringe Club in Hong Kong in March, 1986. Directed by Gu Tiannong 古天農.

Exhibition (solo): Department of Culture in Lille in France, 1986.

Translation: The magazine *L'Imaginaire* in France published Gao's essay "Yao shenme yang de juzuo" 要甚麼樣的劇作 [What sort of drama do we need] in French in 1986.

Translation: Paul Poncet translated into French his short story "Gongyuan li" 公園裏 [In the park], which appeared in *Le Monde* on May 19, 1986.

Translation: Peter Polonyi's translation of *Chezhan* 車站 [The bus-stop] appeared in the journal *Foreign Literature* in Hungary in 1986.

1987
Visited Hong Kong to present a paper at the conference "Modernism and Contemporary Chinese Literature" jointly organized by the Departments of English at The Chinese University of Hong Kong and University of Hong Kong in 1987. His paper "Chidao de xiandaizhuyi yu dangjin Zhongguo wenxue" 遲到的現代主義與當今中國文學 [Belated modernism and Chinese literature today] was later published in *Wenxue pinglun* 文學評論 (Beijing), No. 3, 1988.

Invited by Morat Institut für Kunst und Kunstwissenschaft to visit Germany but he could not get a visa because he was not a member of the Artists' Association of China and thus not considered a professional artist. With the help of Wang Meng 王蒙, the Minister of Culture then, he eventually succeeded in getting the visa from the government. From Germany Gao later went to France.

Play: *Mingcheng* 冥城 [Nether city] was written in Beijing in 1987. The final version was completed in Paris in 1991. It was subsequently included in *Gao Xingjian xiju liuzhong* 高行健戲劇六種 [Six volumes of plays by Gao

Xingjian], Volume 2, published in Taipei by Dijiao chubanshe 帝教出版社 in 1995.

Essay: "Jinghua yetan" 京華夜談 [Night talk in the capital] was published in *Zhongshan* 鐘山 (Nanjing), 1987.

Performance: *Duoyu* 躲雨 [Hiding from the rain], which was translated by Göran Malmqvist was performed at Kungliga Dramatiska Teatern in Sweden, 1987. Directed by Peter Wahlqvist.

Performance: *Chezhan* 車站 [The bus-stop] was performed by Litz Drama Workshop in England, 1987.

Performance: *Xiandai zhezixi* 現代折子戲 [Highlights of modern Chinese opera] was performed by Horizonte 第四線 in Hong Kong in 1987. *Mofang zhe* 模仿者 [The imitator] was directed by Qiao Baozhong 喬寶忠; *Duo yu* 躲雨 [Hiding from the rain] was directed by Ye jiali 葉家禮; *Xinglu nan* 行路難 [Tough walk] was directed by Qiao Baozhong 喬寶忠; and *Habala shankou* 哈巴拉山口 [The pass at Mount Habala] was directed by Gu Zuwei 谷祖威.

Performance: *Shengshengman bianzou* 聲聲慢變奏 [Variations on the tune: Shengshengman] was composed for performance in 1987. It was performed at Guggenheim Museum Theatre in New York, USA in 1989. Directed by Jiang Qing 江青.

Performance: *Mingcheng* 冥城 [Nether city] was written as a dance play in 1987 and performed by the Hong Kong Dance Company in Hong Kong in 1989. Directed by Jiang Qing 江青.

Translation: Excerpts of *Chezhan* 車站 [The bus-stop] were published in German in *Drama Today* in 1987.

Translation: Paul Poncet's French translation of the short story "Muqin" 母親 [Mother] was published in the journal of contemporary fiction *Brèves*, No. 23, 1987.

1988

Gao sought and obtained residence in Paris. He worked as a professional painter and writer.

Second collection of essays on theatre and dramatic representation: "Dui yizhong xiandai xiju de zuiqiu" 對一種現代戲劇的追求 [In search of a

modern form of drama] was published by Zhongguo xiju chubanshe 中
國戲劇出版社 in Beijing, 1988.

Collection of short stories: *Gei wo laoye mai yugan* 給我老爺買魚竿 [Buy
my grandfather a fishing rod] was published by Lianhe wenxue
chubanshe 聯合文學出版社 in Taipei in 1988.

Play: *Bi'an* 彼岸 [The other shore] was republished in *Lianhe wenxue* 聯合
文學 [Unitas: A literary monthly], No. 41, 1988.

Essay: "Chidao de xiandaizhuyi yu dangjin Zhongguo wenxue" 遲到的現
代主義與當今中國文學 [Belated modernism and Chinese literature today]
was published in *Wenxue pinglun* 文學評論 (Beijing), No. 3, 1988.

Performance: *Chezhan* 車站 [The bus-stop] was performed in England in
1988.

Performance: *Yeren* 野人 [Wild man] was performed at Thalia Theatre in
Hamburg, Germany. Directed by Lin Zhaohua 林兆華.

Performance: *Yeren* 野人 [Wild man] was rehearsed at Royal Lyceum
Theatre in Edinburgh, UK in 1988.

Play reading: *Yeren* 野人 [Wild man] was read at Théâtre National de
Marseilles, France, 1988.

Exhibition (solo): A personal painting exhibition was organized by
L'Office Municipal des Beaux Arts et de la Culture in Waterloo in France,
1988.

Translation: *Chezhan* 車站 [The bus-stop] was translated into German by
Wolfgang Kubin and Chang Hsien-chen and published by Brockmeyer
in 1988.

Translation: *Yeren* 野人 [Wild man] was translated into German by Monica
Basting and published in *Yeren: Tradition und Avantgarde in Gao Xingjians
Theaterstück "Die Wilden"* by Brockmeyer in Bochum, 1988.

Translation: Göran Malmqvist's translation of *Gei wo laoye mai yugan* 給我
老爺買魚竿 [Buy my grandfather a fishing rod] in Swedish was published
by Forum in Sweden in 1988.

Translation: Danièle Crisa translated *Chezhan* 車站 [The bus-stop] into
Italian and published it in the journal *In Forma Di Parole* in 1988.

Invited to give lectures at the Drama Camp in Singapore in 1988.

1989

Play: *Taowang* 逃亡 [Fugitives] was completed in Paris in October, 1989. It was published in *Jintian* 今天 (Stockholm) in 1990. The play was singled out for criticism by the authorities in China and since then Gao's plays have not been seen on the Mainland stage. It was subsequently included in *Gao Xingjian xiju liuzhong* 高行健戲劇六種 [Six volumes of plays by Gao Xingjian], Volume 4, published in Taipei by Dijiao chubanshe 帝教出版社 in 1995.

Revoked membership of the Chinese Communist Party in reaction against the government's suppression of the people in the June 4 (Tiananmen Square) Incident in Beijing.

Declared *persona non grata* by the Beijing government and all his works were banned in China.

Novel: *Lingshan* 靈山 [Soul mountain], which he started in Beijing in 1982, was completed in Paris, 1989.

Collection of short stories: *Gei wo laoye mai yugan* 給我老爺買魚竿 [Buy my grandfather a fishing rod] was published in Taipei by Lianhe wenxue chubanshe 聯合文學出版社 in 1989.

Play: *Mingcheng* 冥城 [Nether city] was published in *Nüxingren* 女性人 (Taipei), February, 1989.

Play: *Shanhaijing zhuan* 山海經傳 [Story of *The Classic of Mountains and Seas*] was completed in Paris in February, 1989. It was revised in January 1993 and subsequently included in *Gao Xingjian xiju liuzhong* 高行健戲劇六種 [Six volumes of plays by Gao Xingjian], Volume 3, published in Taipei by Dijiao chubanshe 帝教出版社 in 1995.

Invited by Asia Foundation to visit the United States in 1989.

Performance: *Mingcheng* 冥城 [Nether city] was written as a dance play in 1987 and performed by the Hong Kong Dance Company 香港舞蹈團 in Hong Kong in 1989. Directed by Jiang Qing 江青. The text was revised in 1990 and the final version appeared in 1991.

Performance: *Shengshengman bianzou* 聲聲慢變奏 [Variations on the tune: Shengshengman] was performed as a dance play at Guggenheim Museum in New York, 1989. Directed by Jiang Qing 江青.

Exhibition (with Huang Chunli 王春麗): Paintings were exhibited at Krapperus Konsthall in Malmö in Sweden, 1989.

Exhibition (with Huang Chunli 王春麗): Exhibition of their paintings was held at Ostasiatiska Museet in Stockholm in Sweden, 1989.

Exhibition (collective): Painting exhibition at the Grand Palais, Figuration Critique, Paris, 1989.

Interviews: Gao accepted interviews by the Italian newspaper *La Stampa*, by Radio Five of France and by the magazine *Le Sud*.

Translation: Almut Richter translated *Chehuo* 車禍 [A car accident] into German and published it in the magazine *Die Antenne*.

1990
Novel: *Lingshan* 靈山 [Soul mountain] was published in Taipei by Lianjing chuban shiye gongsi 聯經出版事業公司 in 1990.

Excerpts from the novel: *Lingshan* 靈山 [Soul mountain] appeared in *Lianhe bao* 聯合報 (Taipei), November 23–24, 1990.

Play: *Shengshengman bianzou* 聲聲慢變奏 [Variations on the tune: Shengshengman] was published in *Nüxingren* 女性人 (Taipei), No. 9, 1990. It was subsequently included in *Gao Xingjian xiju liuzhong* 高行健戲劇六種 [Six volumes of plays by Gao Xingjian], Volume 1, published in Taipei by Dijiao chubanshe 帝教出版社 in 1995.

Play: *Taowang* 逃亡 [Fugitives] was published in *Jintian* 今天 (Stockholm), No. 1, 1990. It was subsequently included in *Gao Xingjian xiju liuzhong* 高行健戲劇六種 [Six volumes of plays by Gao Xingjian], Volume 4, published in Taipei by Dijiao chubanshe 帝教出版社 in 1995. The play was singled out for criticism by the authorities in China and since then his plays have not been seen on the Mainland stage.

Essay: "Yao shenme yang de juzuo" 要甚麼樣的劇作 [What sort of drama do we need] was published in *Guangchang* 廣場 (Princeton), No. 2, 1990.

Essay: "Wo zhuzhang yizhong leng de wenxue" 我主張一種冷的文學 [I advocate a cold literature] published in "Shidai wenxue 時代文學," a supplement of *Zhongshi wanbao* 中時晚報 (Taipei), August 12, 1990.

Essay: "Taowang yu wenxue" 逃亡與文學 [Exile and literature] was

published in "Shidai wenxue 時代文學," a supplement of *Zhongshi wanbao* 中時晚報 (Taipei), October 21, 1990.

Performance: *Bi'an* 彼岸 [The other shore] had its world premiere at the National Institute of the Arts in Taipei, Taiwan in 1990. It was directed by Chen Ling Ling 陳玲玲 and performed by the staff and students of the Institute.

Performance: *Chezhan* 車站 [The bus-stop] was performed at Wiener Unterhaltungs Theater in Vienna, Austria in 1990. Directed by Anselm Lipgens. Translated by Wolfgang Kubin.

Performance: *Yeren* 野人 [Wild man] was performed by the Seals Theatre Company 海豹劇團 in Hong Kong in 1990. Directed by Luo Ka [Law Kar] 羅卡.

Exhibition (solo): Centre culturel de lumière de Chine in Marseilles in France, 1990.

Exhibition (collective): Grand Palais, Figuration Critique in Paris, 1990.

Exhibition (collective): Trejiakov Galerie, Figuration Critique, Moscow, Russia, 1990.

Translation: Bruno Roubicek's English translation "*Wild Man*: A Contemporary Chinese Spoken Drama" appeared in *Asian Theatre Journal*, Volume 7, No. 2 (Fall), 1990.

Translation: "Yao shenme yang de juzuo" 要甚麼樣的劇作 [What sort of drama do we need] was translated into English and included in *Nobel Symposium*, No. 72, 1990.

1991

Taowang 逃亡 [Fugitives] was banned on Mainland China. Gao was criticized by the Chinese government and dismissed from the Chinese Communist Party in 1991. The government closed down his residence in Beijing.

Short story: "Shunjian" 瞬間 [An instant] was published in "Shidai wenxue" 時代文學, a literary supplement of *Zhongshi wanbao* 中時晚報 (Taipei), No. 74, September 1, 1991. It was later included in *Chao lai de shihou* 潮來的時候 [Tide rise] published by Taiwan wenhua shenghuo xinzhi chubanshe 台灣文化生活新知出版社, 1992.

Play: *Shengsijie* 生死界 [Between life and death] was completed in 1991 and appeared in French first and then in Chinese. It was published in *Jintian* 今天 (Stockholm), No. 2, 1991. It was subsequently included in *Gao Xingjian xiju liuzhong* 高行健戲劇六種 [Six volumes of plays by Gao Xingjian], Volume 5, published in Taipei by Dijiao chubanshe 帝教出版社 in 1995.

Attended a seminar on *Lingshan* 靈山 [Soul mountain] at Stockholm University in which he read a paper on "Wenxue yu xuanxue: Guanyu *Lingshan*" 文學與玄學：關於《靈山》 [Literature and metaphysics: On *Soul Mountain*] in 1991.

Essay: "Guanyu *Taowang*" 關於《逃亡》 [On *Fugitives*] appeared in *Lianhe bao* 聯合報 supplement (Taipei), June 17, 1991. It was based on a statement made at the Royal Dramatic Theatre in Stockholm.

Essay: "Bali suibi" 巴黎隨筆 [Jottings from Paris] appeared in *Guangchang* 廣場 (Princeton), No. 4 (February), 1991.

Essay: "Wo de xiju he wo de yaoshi" 我的戲劇和我的鑰匙 [My drama and my key] was presented at a conference on Asian contemporary literature and drama held at University of Paris-VII in 1991.

Play reading: In a reading session and seminar on *Taowang* 逃亡 [Fugitives] and *Dubai* 獨白 [Monologue] organized by the Kungliga Dramatiska Teatern in Sweden in 1991, Gao declared that he would not return to China as long as the country was under totalitarian rule.

Play reading: Invited by D.A.A.D. to participate in Sino-German cultural exchange activities in which *Shengsijie* 生死界 [Between life and death] was read in 1991.

Performance: *Juedui xinhao* 絕對信號 [Alarm signal] was performed by Horizonte 第四線 at Sai Wan Ho Cultural Centre in Hong Kong in March, 1991. Directed by Lao Shuangsi 勞雙思 and Ling Guosheng 凌國生.

Exhibition (solo): Espace d'Art Contemporain Confluence in Rambouillet, France, 1991.

Exhibition (collective): Grand Palais, Figuration Critique in Paris, France, 1991.

Exhibition (collective): Galerie de l'Association des Artistes, Figuration Critique, St. Petersburg, Russia, 1991.

Translation: "Shunjian" 瞬間 [An instant] was translated into Japanese and published by JICC Press in 1991 in a collection of short stories.

1992

He was awarded *Chevalier de l'Ordre des Arts et des Lettres de la France* by the French government.

Play: *Duihua yu fanjie* 對話與反詰 [Dialogue and rebuttal] was written by invitation from Maison des Auteurs de Théâtre Etrangers, Saint-Herblain in 1992. It was subsequently included in *Gao Xingjian xiju liuzhong* 高行健 戲劇六種 [Six volumes of plays by Gao Xingjian], Volume 6, published in Taipei by Dijiao chubanshe 帝教出版社 in 1995.

Essay: "Geri huanghua" 隔日黃花 [Stale chrysanthemums] appeared in *Minzhu Zhongguo* 民主中國 (Princeton), No. 8 (February), 1992.

Essay: "Zhongguo liuwang wenxue de kunjing" 中國流亡文學的困境 [The predicament of Chinese exile literature] was published in *Mingbao yuekan* 明報月刊 [Ming Pao monthly] (Hong Kong), October, 1992. It was based on a paper Gao presented at London University in 1992.

Essay: "Wenxue yu xuanxue: Guanyu *Lingshan*" 文學與玄學・關於《靈山》 [Literature and metaphysics: On *Soul Mountain*] appeared in *Jintian* 今 天 (Stockholm), No. 3, 1992. It was based on a paper Gao presented at Stockholm University in 1991.

Essay: "Xiju chuangzuo xu kuansong tiaojian" 戲劇創作需寬鬆條件 [Creative drama writing needs flexible conditions] was published in *Mingbao yuekan* 明報月刊 [Ming Pao monthly] (Hong Kong), December, 1992.

Essay: "Wo de xiju" 我的戲劇 [My drama] was read at Leeds University in England in 1992.

Essay: "Haiwai Zhongguo wenxue mianlin de kunjing" 海外中國文學面 臨的困境 [The predicament of Chinese literature overseas] was a paper presented at Lund University in Sweden in 1992.

Essay: "Hanyu de weiji" 漢語的危機 [The crisis of the Chinese language] was presented at a conference on contemporary Chinese literature held at University of Heidelberg in Germany in 1992.

Play reading: Invited by Institute of Contemporary Arts in London to read his play *Taowang* 逃亡 [Fugitives] in 1992.

Play reading: *Taowang* 逃亡 [Fugitives] was read at the Festival International des Francophonies in Limoges in 1992.

Performance: *Taowang* 逃亡 [Fugitives] was performed at Kungliga Dramatiska Teatern in Sweden, 1992. Directed by Björn Granath.

Performance: *Juedui xinhao* 絕對信號 [Alarm signal] was performed at Godot Theater in Taipei, Taiwan, 1992.

Performance: *Taowang* 逃亡 [Fugitives] was performed at Nürnberg Theater in Nürnberg, Germany, 1992. Directed by Johannes Klett.

Performance: *Duihua yu fanjie* 對話與反詰 [Dialogue and rebuttal] was performed at Theater des Augenblicks in Vienna, Austria, 1992. Direected by Gao Xingjian.

Radio broadcast: *Taowang* 逃亡 [Fugitives] was broadcast on radio by British Broadcasting Corporation in London, UK, 1992.

Radio broadcast: *Shengsijie* 生死界 [Between life and death] was broadcast on Radio France Culture in Paris, France, 1992.

Exhibition (solo): Espace d'art contemporain le cercle bleu in Metz, France, 1992.

Exhibition (solo): Centre culturel de l'Asie in Marseilles, France, 1992.

Translation: Göran Malmqvist's Swedish translation of *Lingshan* 靈山 [Soul mountain], entitled *Andarnas berg*, was published by Forum in 1992.

Translation: *Taowang* 逃亡 [Fugitives] was translated into French by Michèle Guyot and Emile Lansman and published by Lansman in Belgium in 1992. The French title is *La Fuite*.

Translation: *Taowang* 逃亡 [Fugitives] was translated into German by Helmut Foster-Latsch and Marie-Luise Latsch and published by Brockmeyer in 1992.

Translation: *Taowang* 逃亡 [Fugitives] was translated into Swedish by Göran Malmqvist.

Translation: *Shengsijie* 生死界 [Between life and death] was translated into German by René Mark and published in the German journal *Hefte für Ostasiatische Literatur*, No. 13, 1992.

1993

Play: *Shanhaijing zhuan* 山海經傳 [Story of *The Classic of Mountains and Seas*] was published in Hong Kong by Tiandi tushu youxian gongsi 天地圖書有限公司 in 1993. It was subsequently included in *Gao Xingjian xiju liuzhong* 高行健戲劇六種 [Six volumes of plays by Gao Xingjian], Volume 3, published in Taipei by Dijiao chubanshe 帝教出版社 in 1995.

Play: *Yeyoushen* 夜遊神 [Nocturnal wanderer] was completed in Paris in November 1993. The paly was first published in French and then in Chinese and Gao entitled it *Le Somnambule*. It was published by Carnières-Morlanwelz (Belgium): Editions Lansman in 1995. The Chinese version was subsequently included in *Gao Xingjian xiju liuzhong* 高行健戲劇六種 [Six volumes of plays by Gao Xingjian], Volume 5, published in Taipei by Dijiao chubanshe 帝教出版社 in 1995.

Play: *Duihua yu fanjie* 對話與反詰 [Dialogue and rebuttal] was published in *Jintian* 今天 (Stockholm), No. 2, 1993. It was subsequently included in *Gao Xingjian xiju liuzhong* 高行健戲劇六種 [Six volumes of plays by Gao Xingjian], Volume 6, published in Taipei by Dijiao chubanshe 帝教出版社 in 1995.

Play: *Duihua yu fanjie* 對話與反詰 [Dialogue and rebuttal], a Chinese-French bilingual edition was published in France by Waiguo zuojian chubanshe 外國作家出版社 in 1993.

Play: *Zhoumo sichongzou* 周末四重奏 [Weekend quartet] appeared in French with the title *Quatre quatuors pour un week-end*. It was published by Carnières-Morlanwelz (Belgium): Lansman in 1993. The Chinese version was published in Hong Kong by Xinshiji chubanshe 新世紀出版社 in 1996.

Essay: "Meiyou zhuyi" 沒有主義 [Without isms] was written in November 1993 and presented at a conference on "Chinese Literature over the Past Forty Years" held in Taiwan in 1993.

Essay: "Geren de shengyin" 個人的聲音 [The voice of the individual] was presented in a conference on "Nation, Society and the Individual" at Stockholm University in 1993.

Essay: "Guojia shenhua yu geren diankuang" 國家神話與個人癲狂 [Myth of the nation and insanity of the individual] was published in *Mingbao yuekan* 明報月刊 [Ming Pao monthly] (Hong Kong), August, 1993.

Essay: "Tan wo de hua" 談我的畫 [On my paintings] was published in *Mingbao yuekan* 明報月刊 [Ming Pao monthly] (Hong Kong), November, 1993.

Performance: *Shengsijie* 生死界 [Between life and death] was performed at the Centre for Performance at the University of Sydney in Australia, 1993. Directed by Gao Xingjian and translated by Jo Riley.

Performance: *Shengsijie* 生死界 [Between life and death] was performed at Théâtre Renaud-Barrault le Rond-Point in Paris, France, 1993. Directed by Alain Timárd.

Performance: *Shengsijie* 生死界 [Between life and death] was performed at the Festival de Théâtre d'Avignon in France, 1993. Directed by Alain Timárd.

Radio broadcast: *Shengsijie* 生死界 [Between life and death] was broadcast on Radio France Culture in France, 1993.

Exhibition (solo): Maison de la Culture de Bourges organized Gao's painting exhibition in Bourges, France, 1993.

Exhibition (solo): Galerie d'Art de la Tour des Cardinaux in l'isle-sur-la-sorgue in France in 1993.

Exhibition (solo): Galerie Hexagon in Aachen in Germany.

Translation: *Shengsijie* 生死界 [Between life and death] was published in French as *Au bord de la vie* by Lansman in Belgium in 1993.

Translation: Gregory B. Lee translated *Taowang* 逃亡 [Fugitives] into English and included it in *Chinese Writing and Exile* published by Center for East Asian Studies of the University of Chicago, 1993.

Translation: Excerpts of the novel *Lingshan* 靈山 [Soul mountain] was translated into French by Noël Dutrait and published in *Saprighage* in July, 1993.

Translation: "Wo de xiju he wo de yaoshi" 我的戲劇和我的鑰匙 [My drama and my key] was translated by Annie Curien and published by Philippe Piquier in a collection of essays *Literature d'Extrême-Orient au XX Siècle* in 1993.

Translation: *Chezhan* 車站 [The bus-stop] was translated into German by

Anja Gleboff and included in an anthology of contemporary Chinese drama published by Henschel Theater Press in 1993.

Translation: Mieke Bourges translated into Flemish short stories "Haishang" 海上 [At sea], "Gei wo laoye mai yugan" 給我老爺買魚竿 [Buy my grandfather a fishing rod] and "Ershiwu nian hou" 二十五年後 [After twenty-five years] and published them in a Belgian journal *Kreatief*, No. 3/4, 1993.

Visited Hong Kong in October 1993 at the invitation of the Institute of Chinese Studies of The Chinese University of Hong Kong to deliver the first Sin Wai Kin Lecture on Contemporary Chinese Culture.

Revisited Hong Kong in December 1993 to attend the International Symposium on Contemporary Playwriting in the Chinese Language hosted by the Sir Run Run Shaw Hall of The Chinese University of Hong Kong.

1994
Awarded *Prix Communauté française de Belgique* for *Yeyoushen* 夜遊神 [Nocturnal wanderer].

Play: *Shanhaijing zhuan* 山海經傳 [Story of *The Classic of Mountains and Seas*] was published in Hong Kong by Tiandi tushu youxian gongsi 天地圖書有限公司 in 1994.

Essay: "Zhongguo xiju zai xifang: Lilun yu shijian" 中國戲劇在西方：理論與實踐 [Chinese drama in the West: Theory and practice] was published in *Ershiyi shiji* 二十一世紀 (Hong Kong), No. 20 (January), 1994.

Essay: "Xiju: Rouhe xifang yu Zhongguo de changshi" 戲劇：揉合西方與中國的嘗試 [Drama: An attempt of blending the West and China] was published in *Ershiyi shiji* 二十一世紀 (Hong Kong), No. 21, February, 1994.

Essay: "Dangdai xifang yishu wang hechu qu?" 當代西方藝術往何處去 [Where is contemporary Western art heading] was published in *Ershiyi shiji* 二十一世紀 (Hong Kong), No. 22, April, 1994.

Essay: *Wo shuo ciwei* 我説刺蝟 [I tell the hedgehog] was published in *Xiandai shi* 現代詩 [Modern poetry] (Taiwan), Spring, 1994.

Performance: *Shengsijie* 生死界 [Between life and death] was performed at the Dionysia Festival modial de Théàtre Contemporain in Veroli in Italy, 1994. Directed by Gao Xingjian.

Performance: *Taowang* 逃亡 [Fugitives] was performed by RA Theatre Company in France, 1994. Directed by Madelaine Gautiche.

Novel reading: *Lingshan* 靈山 [Soul mountain] was read at Université d'Angers in France, 1994.

Novel reading: *Lingshan* 靈山 [Soul mountain] was read at Frankfurt in 1994.

Play reading: *Duihua yu fanjie* 對話與反詰 [Dialogue and rebuttal] was read at the House of Foreign Dramatists in Saint-Anbroct in 1994.

Play reading: *Shengsijie* 生死界 [Between life and death] was read at Musenturm in Frankfurt, Germany, 1994.

Performance: *Taowang* 逃亡 [Fugitives] was performed at Teatr polski in Poznam in Poland in November, 1994. Directed by Edward Wojtaszek.

Exhibition (solo): Espace d'art contemporain le cercle bleu in Metz in France in 1994.

Translation: Gao wrote his own play *Dialogue and Rebuttal* in French entitling it *Dialoguer/Interloquer*. A Chinese-French bilingual edition by Annie Curien was published in Paris by M.E.E.T. in 1994.

Translation: *Duihua yu fanjie* 對話與反詰 [Dialogue and rebuttal] was translated into German by Alexandra Hartmann and published by Brockmeyer in 1994.

Translation: *Dubai* 獨白 [Monologue] was translated into Swedish by Göran Malmqvist and published by Dramatens Forlag in 1994.

Translation: *Bi'an* 彼岸 [The other shore] was translated into Swedish by Göran Malmqvist and published by Kungliga Dramatiska Teatern in 1994.

Translation: Göran Malmqvist published in Swedish ten of Gao's plays in a collection in 1994.

1995
Essay: "Meiyou zhuyi" 沒有主義 [Without isms] was published in Chinese in *Wenyibao banyuekan* 文藝報半月刊, No. 1, 1995.

Play: *Yeyoushen* 夜遊神 [Nocturnal wanderer], which was completed in 1993, was published in French under the title *Le Somnambule*. It was published by Carnières-Morlanwelz (Belgium): Editions Lansman in 1995.

Collection of plays: *Gao Xingjian xiju liuzhong* 高行健戲劇六種 [Six volumes of plays by Gao Xingjian] was published by Dijiao chubanshe 帝教出版社 in Taipei in 1995. Plays included are:

Volume 1: *Bi'an* 彼岸 [The other shore]; and *Shengshengman bianzou* 聲聲慢變奏 [Variations on the tune: Shengshengman];

Volume 2: *Mingcheng* 冥城 [Nether city];

Volume 3: *Shanhaijing zhuan* 山海經傳 [Story of *The Classic of Mountains and Seas*];

Volume 4: *Taowang* 逃亡 [Fugitives];

Volume 5: *Shengsijie* 生死界 [Between life and death]; and *Yeyoushen* 夜遊神 [Nocturnal wanderer].

Volume 6: *Duihua yu fanjie* 對話與反詰 [Dialogue and rebuttal].

Exhibition: *Ink Paintings by Gao Xingjian*, an exhibition held at Taipei Fine Arts Museum in 1995.

Performance: *Bi'an* 彼岸 [The other shore] was performed at the Hong Kong Academy for Performing Arts in Hong Kong, 1995. Directed by Gao Xingjian.

Performance: *Duihua yu fanjie* 對話與反詰 [Dialogue and rebuttal] was performed at Théâtre Molière in Paris, France, 1995. Directed by Gao Xingjian.

Translation: Lena Aspfors and Torbjörn Lodén translated into English his essay "Geren de shengyin" 個人的聲音 [The voice of the individual] which appeared in *The Stockholm Journal of East Asian Studies*, No. 6, 1995.

Translation: Winnie Lau, Deborah Sauviat and Martin Williams translated his essay "Meiyou zhuyi" 沒有主義 [Without isms] into English in *Journal of Oriental Society of Australia* (Sydney), Nos. 27–28, 1995–96.

Translation: Noël and Liliane Dutrait's French translation of *Lingshan* 靈山 [Soul mountain], entitled *La Montagne de l'âme*, was published in 1995 and it was well received in France.

1996

Collection of essays on literature and art: *Meiyou zhuyi* 沒有主義 [Without isms] was published in Hong Kong by Tiandi tushu youxian gongsi 天地圖書有限公司 in 1996.

Included in the book are the following twenty-two essays:

"Meiyou zhuyi" 沒有主義 [Without isms];

"Wo zhuzhang yizhong leng de wenxue" 我主張一種冷的文學 [I advocate a cold literature];

"Bali suibi" 巴黎隨筆 [Jottings from Paris];

"Lun wenxue xiezuo" 論文學寫作 [On literary creation];

"Geren de shengyin" 個人的聲音 [The voice of the individual];

"Chidao de xiandaizhuyi yu dangjin Zhongguo wenxue" 遲到的現代主義與當今中國文學 [Belated modernism and Chinese literature today];

"Zhongguo liuwang wenxue de kunjing" 中國流亡文學的困境 [The predicament of Chinese exile literature];

"Liuwang shi women huode shenme?" 流亡使我們獲得甚麼？ [What have we got from being in exile?]

"Geri huanghua" 隔日黃花 [Stale chrysanthemums];

"Wenxue yu xuanxue: Guanyu *Lingshan*" 文學與玄學・關於《靈山》 [Literature and metaphysics: On *Soul Mountain*];

"Guanyu *Taowang*" 關於《逃亡》 [On *Fugitives*];

"Ling yizhong xiju" 另一種戲劇 [Another kind of drama];

"*Duihua yu fanjie* dao biao yan tan" 《對話與反詰》導表演談 [Conversation between the director and an actor of *Dialogue and Rebuttal*];

"*Shengsijie* yanchu shouji" 《生死界》演出手記 [Notes on the production of *Between Life and Death*];

"*Bi'an* daoyan houji" 《彼岸》導演後記 [Postscript to directing *The Other Shore*];

"Yao shenme yang de juzuo" 要甚麼樣的劇作 [What sort of drama do we need];

"Wo de xiju he wo de yaoshi" 我的戲劇和我的鑰匙 [My drama and my key];

"Jüzuofa yu zhongxing yanyuan" 劇作法與中性演員 [The art of playwriting and the neutral actor];

"Wu sheng de jiaoxiang — Ping Zhao Wuji de hua" 無聲的交響 —— 評趙無極的畫 [Silence in a symphony: On the paintings by Zhao Wuji];

"Ping Faguo guanyu dangdai yishu de lunzhan" 評法國關於當代藝術的論戰 [The debate on contemporary art in France];

"Tan wo de hua" 談我的畫 [On my paintings];

"Dui huihua de sikao" 對繪畫的思考 [My thoughts on painting].

Collection of plays: *Zhoumo sichongzou* 周末四重奏 [Weekend quartet] was published in Hong Kong by Xinshiji chubanshe 新世紀出版社 in 1996. Plays included are:

Zhoumo sichongzou 周末四重奏 [Weekend quartet];

Shunjian 瞬間 [An instant];

Shengshengman bianzou 聲聲慢變奏 [Variations on the tune: Shengshengman];

Wo shuo ciwei 我説刺蝟 [I tell the hedgehog].

Essay: *Goût de l'encre* was published in Paris by Editions voix Richard Meir in 1996.

Performance: *Shengsijie* 生死界 [Between life and death] was performed at Teater Miejski Gdynia in Poland, 1996.

Performance: *Shengsijie* 生死界 [Between life and death] was performed in the US. Directed by Gao Xingjian.

Translation: Winnie Lau, Deborah Sauviat and Martin Williams translated into English the essay "Meiyou zhuyi" 沒有主義 [Without isms] and published it in *The Journal of Oriental Society of Australia*, Nos. 27 & 28, 1995–1996.

1997

Awarded *Prix du Nouvel An chinois* for the novel *Lingshan* 靈山 [Soul mountain].

Essay: "Weishenme xiezuo" 為甚麼寫作 [Why do I write] appeared in Wanzhi's 萬之 edited book *Goutong: Miandui shijie de Zhongguo wenxue* 溝通：面對世界的中國文學 [Communication: Chinese literature before the world] which was published in Stockholm by Olof Palme International Center in 1997.

Unpublished typescript: *Bayue xue* 八月雪 [Snow in August] was a Zen drama written in the style of Peking opera.

Performance: *Taowang* 逃亡 [Fugitives] was performed by the Ryunokai Gekidan in Osaka, Kobe and Tokyo in Japan, 1997.

Performance: *Shengsijie* 生死界 [Between life and death] was performed at the Theater of New York City in New York, USA, 1997. Directed by Gao Xingjian.

Exhibition: He accepted an invitation to hold an exhibition of his paintings in Hong Kong, 1997.

Exhibition: He held a painting exhibition in New York, 1997.

Radio broadcast: His play *Shengsijie* 生死界 [Between life and death] was broadcast on Radio Free Asia in USA, 1997.

Radio broadcast: *Duihua yu fanjie* 對話與反詰 [Dialogue and rebuttal] was broadcast on Radio France Culture in Paris, France, 1997.

Radio broadcast: *Taowang* 逃亡 [Fugitives] was broadcast on Radio France Culture in Paris, France, 1997.

Publication of recorded conversations: The recorded conversations on literature between Gao Xingjian and Denis Bourgeois were published in book form. The title is *Au plus près du réel: Dialogues sur l'écriture (1994–1997)*, with Denis Bourgois as co-author. It was published in Paris by Éditions de l'Aube, 1997.

Translation: Jo Riley translated into English the play *Bi'an* 彼岸 and entitled it *The Other Side: A Contemporary Drama Without Acts*, which was included in Martha P. Y. Cheung and Jane C. C. Lai, eds. *An Oxford Anthology of Contemporary Chinese Drama* published in Hong Kong by Oxford University Press in 1997.

Translation: Noël Dutrait translated into French *Gei wo laoye mai yugan* 給我老爺買魚竿 [Buy my grandfather a fishing rod] and entitled it *Une canne à péche pour mon grand-père*. The French edition was published by Éditions de l'Aube in 1997.

1998

Second novel: *Yige ren de shengjing* 一個人的聖經 [One man's bible], which Gao started writing in Paris in 1996, was completed. It was subsequently published in Chinese in Taipei in 1999 and in Hong Kong in 2000.

Essay: "Xiandai hanyu yu wenxue xiezuo" 現代漢語與文學寫作 [Modern Chinese language and literary writing] was published in *Xianggang xiju xuekan* 香港戲劇學刊 (Hong Kong) in October, 1998.

Collection of essays: *L'Encre et la lumière* was published in Paris by Editions voix Richard Meir in 1998.

Performance: *Chezhan* 車站 [The bus-stop] was performed at the Theater of Cluj in Romania, 1998.

Performance: *Taowang* 逃亡 [Fugitives] was performed at Atelier Nomande, Benin, Ivory Coast, 1998.

Performance: *Taowang* 逃亡 [Fugitives] was performed by the Haiyuza Gekidan in Tokyo in Japan, 1998.

Translation: Kimberley Besio translated into English the play *Chezhan* 車站 [The bus-stop] and entitled it *Bus Stop: A Lyrical Comedy on Life in One Act*. It was included in Haiping Yan, ed. *Theatre and Society: An Anthology of Contemporary Chinese Drama*. Armonk, New York and London: M. E. Sharpe, 1998.

1999

Novel: *Yige ren de shengjing* 一個人的聖經 [One man's bible] was published in Taipei by Lianjing chuban shiye gongsi 聯經出版事業公司 in 1999.

Performance: *Yeyoushen* 夜遊神 [Nocturnal wanderer] was performed at the Theatre des Halles in Avignon in France, 1999.

Translation: Gilbert C. F. Fong translated into English the following plays, which were published in the book, *The Other Shore: Plays by Gao Xingjian* by The Chinese University Press in 1999:
    Bi'an 彼岸 [The other shore];
    Shengsijie 生死界 [Between life and death];
    Duihua yu fanjie 對話與反詰 [Dialogue and rebuttal];
    Yeyoushen 夜遊神 [Nocturnal wanderer];
    Zhoumo sichongzou 周末四重奏 [Weekend quartet];

Translation: *Yige ren de shengjing* 一個人的聖經 [One man's bible] appeared in French under the title *Le livre d'un homme seul* and published by Éditions de l'Aube in 1999.

2000

Novel: *Yige ren de shengjing* 一個人的聖經 [One man's bible] was published in Hong Kong by Tiandi tushu youxian gongsi 天地圖書有限公司 in 2000.

Play: *Ba yue xue* 八月雪 [Snow in August] was published in Taipei by Lianjing chuban shiye gongsi 聯經出版事業公司 in 2000.

Collection of essays: *Une Autre esthéque* was published in Paris by Editions Cercle d'art in 2000.

Translation: Mabel Lee translated *Lingshan* 靈山 [Soul mountain] into English and it was published by HarperCollins in Sydney in June, 2000.

The Swedish Academy announced the award of Nobel Prize for Literature to Gao Xingjian on 12 October, 2000.

Delivered his Nobel Lecture "Wenxue de liyou" 文學的理由 [The case for literature] in Chinese on 7 December, 2000.

REFERENCES

Fong, Gilbert C. F. (1999a). "Appendix A: Plays Written by Gao Xingjian." In Fong, trans. (1999c), p. 25.

—— (1999b). "Appendix C: Major Productions of Gao Xingjian's Plays." In Fong, trans. (1999c), pp. 267–269.

——, trans. (1999c). *The Other Shore: Plays by Gao Xingjian*. Hong Kong: The Chinese University Press.

Gao Xingjian 高行健 (1993a). "Gao Xingjian zhuyao zuopin nianbiao" 高行健主要作品年表 [A chronology of Gao Xingjian's major publications]. In Gao (1993b), pp. 108–110.

—— (1993b). *Shanhaijing zhuan* 山海經傳 [Story of *The Classic of Mountains and Seas*]. Hong Kong: Tiandi tushu youxian gongsi 天地圖書有限公司.

—— (1995a). "Chronology." In Lee, ed. (1995), pp. 82–84.

—— (1995b). "Gao Xingjian chuangzuo nianbiao" 高行健創作年表 [A chronology of Gao Xingjian's creative works]. In Gao (1995c), pp. 86–106.

—— (1995c). *Gao Xingjian xiju liuzhong* 高行健戲劇六種 [Six volumes of plays by Gao Xingjian]. Taipei: Dijiao chubanshe 帝教出版社.

—— (1996a). "Gao Xingjian juzuo de zhuyao yanchu" 高行健劇作的主要演出 [Major performances of Gao Xingjian's works]. In Gao (1996d), pp. 103–104.

—— (1996b). "Gao Xingjian wenxue xiju zhuyao zuopin" 高行健文學戲劇主要作品 [Major plays by Gao Xingjian]. In Gao (1996d), pp. 101–102.

—— (1996c). *Meiyou zhuyi* 沒有主義 [Without isms]. Hong Kong: Tiandi tushu youxian gongsi 天地圖書有限公司.

—— (1996d). *Zhoumo sichongzou* 周末四重奏 [Weekend quartet]. Hong Kong: Xinshiji chubanshe 新世紀出版社.

—— (2000). *Soul Mountain*. Trans. Mabel Lee. Sydney: HarperCollins.

Jiang Qing 江青 (2000). "Yu Gao Xingjian gong wu" 與高行健共舞 [Dance with

Gao Xingjian]. *Mingbao yuekan* 明報月刊 [Ming Pao monthly], November, pp. 51–54.

Lee, Mabel (1997). "Gao Xingjian's *Lingshan/Soul Mountain*: Modernism and the Chinese Writer." *Heat*, No. 4, pp. 128–157.

—— (2000). "Appendix: Major Publications by Gao Xingjian." In Gao (2000), pp. 507–510.

Lee Yulin, ed. (1995). *Gao Xingjian shuimo zuopin zhan* 高行健水墨作品展 [Ink paintings by Gao Xingjian]. Taipei: Taipei Art Museum.

Lodén, Torbjörn (1993). "Appendix: A Bibliography of Gao Xingjian's Published Writings in Chinese 1980–1992" (in "World Literature with Chinese Characterisitcs: On a Novel by Gao Xingjian"). *The Stockholm Journal of East Asian Studies*, Vol. 4, pp. 17–39.

Quah Sy Ren (1999). "The Theatre of Gao Xingjian: Experimentation within the Chinese Context and Towards New Modes of Representation." Ph.D. thesis, University of Cambridge.

Xu Guorong 許國榮 (1989a). "Fulu: Gao Xingjian zhuzuo ji yanjiu Gao Xingjian wenzhang mulu" 附錄：高行健著作及研究高行健文章目錄 [Appendix: A bibliography of works by Gao Xingjian and studies on Gao Xingjian]. In Xu (1989b), pp. 265–272.

—— (1989b). *Gao Xingjian xiju yanjiu* 高行健戲劇研究 [Studies on Gao Xingjian's drama]. Beijing: Zhongguo xiju chubanshe 中國戲劇出版社.

Yeung, Jessica W. Y. (1996). "From China to Nowhere: The Writings of Gao Xingjian in the 1980s and Early 90s." M. Phil. thesis, University of Hong Kong.

Yisha 依沙 (2000a). "Fulu: Gao Xingjian geren dang'an" 附錄：高行健個人檔案 [Appendix: Gao Xingjian's personal file]. In Yisha, ed. (2000b), pp. 89–92.

—— (2000b). *Gao Xingjian pingshuo* 高行健評說 [Studies and critiques on Gao Xingjian]. Hong Kong: Mirror Books 明鏡出版社.

Notes on Contributors

Xiaomei CHEN received her Ph.D. in Comparative Literature at Indiana University. She is Associate Professor at Ohio State University, where she teaches contemporary Chinese literature, comparative literature, drama and literary theory. Her recent research focuses on contemporary Chinese drama. Among her publications are many articles that have appeared in *Comparative Literature Studies, Paideuma, Canadian Review of Comparative Literature* and *Critical Inquiry*, as well as a book, *Occidentalism: A Theory of Counter-discourse in Post-Mao China* (New York: Oxford University Press, 1995). She is currently preparing an anthology of contemporary Chinese drama in English translation.

Gilbert C. F. FONG received his Ph.D. from the University of Toronto. He then taught at the University of Toronto and York University in Canada. He has written many articles on modern and contemporary Chinese literature and literary translation. Presently he is Professor in the Department of Translation, The Chinese University of Hong Kong and is heading a research project on the history of Hong Kong drama. His is also editor of the books, *Plays from Hong Kong* (co-edited, Beijing: Wenhua yishu chubanshe, 1994), *Hong Kong Drama Interviews* (Hong Kong: Hong Kong Drama Programme, 1999), *Chinese Drama in the New Millennium* (Hong Kong: Hong Kong Federation of Drama Societies and Hong Kong Drama Programme, 2000) and the journal *Hong Kong Drama Review*. He is translator of *The Other Shore: Plays by Gao Xingjian* (Hong Kong: The Chinese University Press, 1999).

Michael GISSENWEHRER gained a Ph.D. in Theatre Studies at the University of Vienna and continued his studies at the Central Academy of Drama, Beijing before lecturing on theatre at the University of Bayreuth and University of Mainz, Germany. He is now Professor of Theatre Studies at the University of Munich.

Amy T. Y. LAI received her B.A. and M.Phil. in English at The Chinese University of Hong Kong. She is now completing her Ph.D. in English Literature at Cambridge, on an award from Cambridge Overseas Trust and the Le Bas Research Studentship. Her publications include an article on Ding Ling and Zhang Jie in *Comparative Literature and Culture* (1999) and English translation of Singapore Chinese fiction. She also writes poetry and has published in UK magazines, such as *Breathe, The Rue Bella, Fire* and *Voyage.*

Mabel LEE was a member of the academic staff in Chinese Studies at the University of Sydney (1966–2000) where she retains an appointment as Honorary Associate Professor. She is co-editor of two University of Sydney Series: the *East Asian Series* and the *World Literature Series,* and was for many years, until recently, assistant editor of the *JOSA: the Journal of the Oriental Society of Australia.* Her research publications concern twentieth-century Chinese intellectual history and literature and focuses on changes in notions of the self and literature and the historical contexts producing such changes. Writers such as Zhang Taiyan, Lu Xun, Yang Lian, Liu Zaifu and Gao Xingjian have provided the material for her studies. After a brief meeting with Gao Xingjian in 1991, she has published several research papers on various aspects of Gao Xingjian's work, some of which are included in this volume. She is translator of Gao Xingjian's novel *Lingshan* [Soul mountain] (Sydney: HarperCollins, 2000) and his Nobel Lecture "Wenxue de liyou" [The case for literature] (Stockholm: Swedish Academy, 2000). Her most recent publication is "Nobel Laureate 2000 Gao Xingjian and His Novel *Soul Mountain*," *CLC: Comparative Literature and Culture: a WWWeb Journal,* 2.3 (2000) (http://www.clcwebjournal.lib.purdue.edu/clcweb00-3/lee00.html).

Torbjörn LODÉN is Professor of Chinese language and culture and Director of the Center for Pacific Asia Studies, Stockholm University. A specialist in Chinese intellectual history, Lodén has written on twentieth-century literary thought, aspects of Confucian thought, and on post-Mao intellectual trends. His most recent book, written in Swedish, is *Från Mao till Mammon: idéer och politik i det moderna Kina* [From Mao to Mammon: ideas and politics in modern China].

MA Sen received his Ph.D. from the University of British Columbia. He has held appointments at various universities, including National Taiwan Normal University, l'Institute des recherches linguistiques de Paris, El Colegio de Mexico, University of Alberta, University of Victoria, University of London and National Chengkung University. Currently he is teaching at Foguang University, Taiwan. He is a prolific writer and scholar. His novels, plays, essays and critical writings can be found in more than forty volumes (by various publishers in Taiwan, 1958–2000). Among them are the well-known works, *Yeyou* [Wandering in the night] (novel, revised, Taipei: Jiuge, 2000), *Gujue* [Isolation] (collection of short stories, revised, Taipei: Maitian, 2000), *Flower and Sword* (play, Oxford University Press, 1997), *The Twice Western Tides in Modern Chinese Drama* (historical studies, Taipei: Wenhua shenghuo xinzhi edition,1997), *Zhongguo xiandai xiaoshuo de zhuchao* [Main currents of modern Chinese fiction, collection of critical essays] (Taipei: Unitas Edition, 1997), and *Dongfang xiju xifang xiju* [Eastern drama and western drama] (collection of critical essays, Taipei: Wenhua shenghuo xinzhi edition, 1992).

QUAH Sy Ren received his Ph.D. at the University of Cambridge with a thesis on Gao Xingjian's theatre. He is currently Assistant Professor in the Division of Chinese Language and Culture at Nanyang Technological University, Singapore. His articles have appeared in the journal *Asian Culture* and in books on Chinese theatre.

Jo RILEY graduated in English Literature from the University of Cambridge. She gained a diploma in Chinese at Ealing College, London and studied *xiqu* at the Central Academy of Drama, Beijing before gaining a Ph.D. at the University of East Anglia. Her publications include *Chinese Theatre and the Actor in Performance* (Cambridge: Cambridge University Press, 1997) and English translation of Gao Xingjian's play *The Other Side* in Martha P. Y. Cheung and Jane C. C. Lai, eds., *An Oxford Anthology of Contemporary Chinese Drama* (Hong Kong: Oxford University Press, 1997).

Kwok-kan TAM received his Ph.D. in Comparative Literature at the University of Illinois at Urbana-Champaign. He has been fellow of the East-West Center, Honolulu and is currently Professor in the Department of English at The Chinese University of Hong Kong. He has been editor of *CUHK Journal of Humanities* and *Comparative Literature and Culture*. His publications include *New Chinese Cinema* (co-authored, Hong Kong: Oxford University Press, 1998), two anthologies, *A Place of One's Own: Stories of Self in China, Taiwan, Hong Kong and Singapore* (co-edited, Hong Kong: Oxford University Press, 1999) and *Voice of Hong Kong: Drama 1997* (Hong Kong: International Association of Theatre Critics, 1999), and a new book, *The Politics of Subject Construction in Modern Chinese Literature* (Hong Kong: Oxford University Press, 2000). He has three forthcoming books, *Ibsen in China 1908–1997: A Critical-Annotated Bibliography of Criticism, Translation and Performance* (Hong Kong: The Chinese University Press, 2001), *Sights of Contestation: Localism, Globalism and Cultural Production in Asia and the Pacific* (co-edited, Hong Kong: The Chinese University Press, 2001) and *Shakespeare Global/Local: The Hong Kong Imaginary in Transcultural Production* (co-edited, Hamburg: Peter Lang, 2001).

William TAY received his Ph.D. in Comparative Literature at the University of California, San Diego. He has taught at The Chinese University of Hong Kong and the University of California, San Diego. Currently he is Professor of Humanities at the Hong Kong University of Science and Technology. He has been editor-in-chief of the Taiwan journal *Unitas: A Literary Monthly* and member of the editorial and advisory boards of some twenty academic journals in Taiwan, Hong Kong and the United States, including *The CUHK Journal of Humanities* and *Modern Chinese Literature.* He has published extensively on Chinese literature, comparative literature, and literary and cultural theories. Among his numerous publications are the recent books on modern Hong Kong literature that he has co-authored and co-edited with Lo Wai-luen and Wong Kai-chee: *In Search of Hong Kong Literature* (Hong Kong: Oxford University Press, 1998), *An Anthology of Early Hong Kong Vernacular Literature (1927–1941)* (Hong Kong: Cosmos Books, 1998), *An Anthology of Background Materials on Early Hong Kong Vernacular Literature (1927–1941)* (Hong Kong: Cosmos Books, 1998), *An Anthology of Creative Writings by Local Hong Kong and Mainland Émigré Writers During the Chinese Civil War Period* (Hong Kong: Cosmos Books, 1999), *An Anthology of Background Materials on Hong Kong Literature During the Chinese Civil War Period* (Hong Kong: Cosmos Books, 1999), *A Chronology of Hong Kong Vernacular Literature (1950–1969)* (Hong Kong: Cosmos Books, 2000). In addition to research publications, he is also a prolific translator of English and European literature.

Terry Siu-han YIP received her Ph.D. in Comparative Literature at the University of Illinois at Urbana-Champaign. She has been professional associate at the East-West Center, Honolulu and is currently Professor and Head of the Department of English Language and Literature at Hong Kong Baptist University. She has published extensively on Chinese-Western comparative literature, Germany literature in China, gender in contemporary Chinese and European literature, and identity politics. Her publications include many articles and an anthology, *A Place of One's Own: Stories of Self in China, Taiwan, Hong Kong and Singapore* (co-edited, Hong Kong: Oxford University Press, 1999). Her two forthcoming books are *Sights of Contestation: Localism, Globalism and Cultural Production in Asia and the Pacific* (co-edited, Hong Kong: The Chinese University Press, 2001) and *Shakespeare Global/Local: The Hong Kong Imaginary in Transcultural Production* (co-edited, Hamburg: Peter Lang, 2001).